THE WRITING & CRITIQUE GROUP

SURVIVAL GUIDE

BECKY LEVINE

HOW TO GIVE AND RECEIVE FEEDBACK, SELF-EDIT, AND MAKE REVISIONS

WRITER'S DIGEST BOOKS
Cincinnati, Ohio
www.writersdigest.com

For more resources for writers, visit www.writersdigest.com/books.

To receive a free weekly e-mail newsletter delivering tips and updates about writing and about Writer's Digest products, register directly at http://newsletters.fwpublications.com.

14 13 12 11 10   5 4 3 2 1

Distributed in Canada by Fraser Direct
100 Armstrong Avenue
Georgetown, Ontario, Canada L7G 5S4
Tel: (905) 877-4411

Distributed in the U.K. and Europe by David & Charles
Brunel House, Newton Abbot, Devon, TQ12 4PU, England
Tel: (+44) 1626-323200, Fax: (+44) 1626-323319
E-mail: postmaster@davidandcharles.co.uk

Distributed in Australia by Capricorn Link
P.O. Box 704, Windsor, NSW 2756 Australia
Tel: (02) 4577-3555

Library of Congress Cataloging-in-Publication Data
Levine, Becky.
  The writing & critique group survival guide : how to make revisions, self-edit, and give and receive feedback / by Becky Levine.
      p. cm.
  Includes index.
  ISBN 978-1-58297-606-8 (alk. paper)
  1. Authorship--Style manuals 2. Authorship--Handbooks, manuals, etc.
  3. Editing--Handbooks, manuals, etc. I. Title. II. Title: Writing and critique group survival guide.
  PN147.L45 2010
  808'.027--dc22   2009026964

Edited by Scott Francis
Designed by Terri Woesner
Production coordinated by Mark Griffin

Dedication

To Oakley Hall, for starting me down the path to this
book so many years ago.

To David and Ian, for giving me the time, love, and
support I needed to stay on that path.

About the Author

Becky Levine is a freelance writer and has participated in critique groups for almost fifteen years. A past columnist for *WritersTalk* (the newsletter of the California Writers Club, South Bay branch) and a past reviewer for *The Horn Book Guide*, Becky has written features for newspapers such as *The Palo Alto Weekly* and *The Santa Cruz Sentinel*. She speaks regularly at writing clubs and conferences. She is also a member of the Society of Children's Book Writer and Illustrators (SCBWI), Sisters in Crime (SINC), Romance Writers of America (RWA), and the California Writers Club (CWC). Visit her website and blog at www.beckylevine.com.

Acknowledgments

I am lucky to live in a world of writers and readers who make my life full and keep me sane. So many people helped me on the way to this book. Lee Lofland and Hallie Ephron set up the opportunities that led me to Writer's Digest Books in the first place. Jane Friedman and Kelly Nickel guided me through the proposal process, and my agent, Jessica Faust, held my hand through the contract phase. My editor, Scott Francis, has been wonderful, making everything incredibly easy and helping me make this book the best it could be.

This book would not have been written if it weren't for Beth Proudfoot and Terri Thayer, who applied their critiquing superpowers to the manuscript—helping me brainstorm structure, reviewing every page, and pushing me to get things just right. Beth, Terri, Cyndy Furze, Martha Alderson, Jackie Seymour, and Jana McBurney-Lin have been my writing and critique support for more than a decade. These are the people you never let go of. Many local and online writers let me pick their brains about critique groups and writing in general—Susan Taylor Brown, Debbi Michiko Florence, Jim Averbeck, Darcy Pattison, Matilda Butler, Cheryl Reifsnyder. If you haven't gotten yourself "out there" on the Web yet, do it: The writers I've met through blogs, Facebook, Twitter, and the Writers Market community are the best cheering section anyone could ask for.

Finally, thank you to my parents, Gaby and Ken Levine. They created a world for me, when I was growing up, in which there was no such thing as too many books or too many hours spent reading. Without that magic, I wouldn't be here today, doing this writing thing I love so much.

TABLE OF CONTENTS

INTRODUCTION

I *have always* known I wanted to be a writer. I have also always known I didn't want to live in a cold, dark garret, starving for my art.

It would be too lonely.

When I was in college at UC Irvine, I found out that writing didn't have to be lonely. I took writing workshops from Oakley Hall, and in those classes I got my first taste of writing as part of a community. I learned much from those classes about my own writing and about how to make good comments and suggestions. I learned how much I would benefit from belonging to a critique group.

Every one of you who has picked up this book knows horror stories about critique groups. You've met or heard about the critiquer who trashed the author's story and sent her home in tears. You've listened to the critiquer who couldn't find anything constructive to say, and you've watched the author who couldn't hear the feedback he was being given. These stories are mythic, legendary in the writing world. Unfortunately, they're also true.

That's why I've written this book. I've been in strong critique groups and groups that weren't so great. I've seen poor communication between critiquers make for some nasty moments, and I've watched writers struggle, not knowing what to do with the feedback they are getting about their books. I've also seen the success of writers who have joined or built a great group, in which the members support each other in all the important ways—with encouragement and with detailed, thought-out critiques. I believe that most writers can learn to give respectful *and* useful critiques, and that they can also develop the strength to hear those critiques and work with them to take their manuscripts to a higher level of writing.

I also believe that writers need a set of tools to succeed at these goals. My hope is that this book will provide you with those tools.

The information in this book is broken down into several sections. The first chapters give you information and instructions about finding and joining a strong group or starting your own group. The middle section contains chapters that show you how to get started critiquing various genres of writing:

fiction, nonfiction, and books for young readers. After that, the next chapters tell you how to self-edit and revise your work, using the feedback you've gotten from your critique partners. Finally, I talk about the ways you can make a strong group for the future, building on the community you've developed to support the growing skills and successes of the group's writers.

You may want to read this book all the way through to get a sense of the big picture of critiquing and working with a critique group. Or, if you're settled in with a strong group already but are looking for specific help critiquing the kinds of work your group is doing, you can dip into the relevant chapters and get tips on how to dig in. If your group is going through some changing times, and you're worried about how you can all continue to work together, check out the last section, including the chapter about troubleshooting the dynamics of a group.

Throughout the book you'll find worksheets that you can use to organize your critique group and plan your critiques. For your convenience downloads of the worksheets are available (with extra space for your notes!) at http://writersdigest.com/article/critique-survival-guide.

Yes, finding and maintaining a strong critique group can be hard. It's a challenge. So is your writing, though, and you do everything possible to keep that at the top of your priority list. Do the same with your critique group. The magic of a good group makes all the struggles worthwhile, and strong critique partners can help you make every one of your writing dreams come true.

Without my critique partners, I would never have come as far in my own writing as I have. This book would never have been written or published. I wish for you a critique group that gives you the same support, strength, and community I have found in mine.

GETTING STARTED:
THE BASICS OF A CRITIQUE GROUP

Do you have a few chapters or a complete manuscript sitting in front of you, ready for critique and revision? Have you gotten a book proposal accepted by an agent, and now you're looking at putting real chapters onto paper? Are you playing with bits and pieces of your memoir, wondering about getting help putting them together?

You're ready to get critiqued.

Or maybe you're already in the middle of that process. You meet regularly with two or three other writers, you read each others' work, and you spend plenty of time talking about your projects. You are critiquers.

Except that sometimes the meetings don't go all that smoothly, or you leave feeling a bit worried or frustrated.

Whoever you are, this first section of the book should help you out. In these early chapters, I go over the main points of how critique groups work: how to figure out what you want, how to find or build a group, and how to handle the routine details of running a group. When you've read through these chapters, you'll have a better idea of your critique goals, the kind of group you want to be part of, and the expectations you have for the critique process.

Even if you have a perfectly wonderful group, you can use this section to help any new members you invite to join. These chapters will bring them up to speed with the way your group operates and let them merge smoothly and easily into critiquing with your existing members. At the end of the section, you'll find several worksheets you can use to get started looking for a group as well as with the critique process.

So pull up a chair and a cup of something hot and start reading. It's time to begin.

Section 1

Chapter 1

CHOOSING THE KIND OF GROUP
THAT'S RIGHT FOR YOU

You've decided you're ready to gather with other writers. You want to share your time and your creativity, and you want to get feedback about your own projects. You're ready to go.

Before you jump in, though, you should do a bit of thinking. Assess where you are with your writing and what you're looking for in critique partners. Look at where you live, how much free time you have and what time of day you get it, and whether you are more comfortable with the idea of critiquing face-to-face or long-distance. You'll also want to consider your compatibility with the other members in specific groups, but I'll discuss that in chapter two, "Joining or Setting Up a Group."

In this chapter, we'll talk about the choices you can make *before* you start the hunt for an actual group. You'll learn about the following types of group.

- An open or closed group
- A general or genre-based group
- An in-person or online group

There's one important thing I want you to remember. As you look at existing groups or talk to people about forming your own, you'll hear the phrase *writing group* used as often as *critique group*. Sometimes the terms are used interchangeably, but other times a writing group is just that—a group of people who get together to write. Spending this kind of time with other people can be incredibly helpful and productive, and I encourage you to find writers who are interested in joining you with their laptops. A group that gets together only to write, though, and never exchanges feedback about what they're writing is *not* critiquing. Right now, you're looking for a critique group, and that's what we're talking about.

CHOOSING AN OPEN OR CLOSED GROUP

What's the difference between an open group and a closed one? In an open critique group, the "doors" are literally open to any writer who wants to join. In a closed critique group, the members choose a specific set of writers who will meet and critique together. To get the best growth and productivity from a critique group, I recommend a closed group. However, both groups have pluses and minuses—keep reading to find out what they are.

Open Critique Groups

Most open critique groups are "sponsored" by somebody, either by the bookstore at which they take place or by an individual who runs critique groups out of her office or home. The groups typically meet at a regular time and place, and any given meeting may be a mix of writers who have been critiquing together for a while and new members who have just started attending.

Open groups are not the best solution to getting your work critiqued or developing your own critique skills. If you are a continuing member, you may spend a lot of time getting acquainted with new stories and bringing new writers up to speed about your own project. After you've committed time and energy to critiquing, you might have to wait for an author to make it to another meeting, or watch him decide critiquing isn't for him and just leave. If you've taken hours away from your own writing, only to find that time wasted, you will feel frustrated, even angry. Of course, these problems can come up in a closed group as well, but the structure of an open group demands a lower commitment level. This can create a drop-in/drop-out feeling about the group, which is one of the worst atmospheres for solid critiquing.

Because of their flexible nature, open groups tend to have members read their submissions at the meetings. Each writer may read a manuscript to herself, or one member may read the pages out loud to everybody else. I'll talk more about this in chapter two, but reading submissions at the meeting doesn't create the best environment in which to produce thoughtful, constructive feedback.

If you are just starting out with critiquing, however, and you're looking for early motivation and support, you may decide to try an open group. You'll be spending time with other writers, which is always a good thing, and—if the group leader is a good teacher—you can learn some important critique tools and techniques. Also, if you've tried to find a closed critique group in your area and haven't succeeded, you may step into an open group for a while. Odds are, you'll meet another writer or two who are "shopping" for critique partners, and, if you feel comfortable with them, you can leave the open group and set up your own, closed group.

Closed Critique Groups

The boundaries of a closed group let a specific set of writers develop relationships that support strong, productive critiquing. All the writers meet on a regular basis, committed to developing their writing projects *and* skills together over time. New writers can and do join these groups, but not at random. Existing members carefully choose and add writers they all agree will add to the strength of the group.

For the writer who is committed to making steady progress in her writing, and I believe that's you, a closed group is usually the best choice. This kind of group offers stability and consistency. Members get to know each other's projects, through multiple drafts, and they learn the strengths and weaknesses of their critique partners. In a closed group, writers develop a working relationship with depth as they help each other with short-term writing problems and long-term writing goals.

The challenges of a closed critique group are finding one that is a good match for you, as a writer and critiquer, and then making sure that group grows and develops in strength. Both these challenges, though, are worth the time and energy you put into them, because the group you build will become one of the most important resources of your writing life.

CHOOSING A GENERAL OR GENRE-BASED GROUP

Are you writing fiction or nonfiction? Children's books or adult romances? Short stories or epic novels? When you're looking for a new group, or deciding who you're going to invite to join your existing one, you'll want to think about how "wide" you want to spread the doors of that group. Do you want to be reading and critiquing all genres, or do you want to narrow your focus to the genre in which you are writing?

General Critique Groups

In theory, a general critique group is one in which members can submit any type of writing. In reality, these groups often put some limitations on the range of writing genres they will accept. One group might accept any genre of fiction, but no nonfiction or poetry; another group may read anything under the nonfiction umbrella, but no novels or short stories.

A general group can be very welcoming. Members are excited about all kinds of writing and interested in learning about the different specifications and styles that go with each. If your own writing and reading choices are broad, a general group can be a great fit. Or if you're just starting out with your writing, and your genre plans aren't set in concrete, a general group can be a great place to take your first steps. The group can help you explore your own writing and make choices about which paths you want to take.

A general group does present some limitations, however. Some of the members may not be familiar with the kind of writing you're doing. If you are writing a mystery novel, and the other writers don't read mysteries (other than a few Agatha Christies, of course), they won't be familiar with the structure and flow of books in that genre. Similarly, if a member of the group is trying to write chapter books for beginning readers, the other members may not be able to give constructive critiques about the vocabulary and rhythm a young child will need. If a group mixes fiction and nonfiction, it's difficult for all members to concentrate their reading on the genre their critique partners are exploring.

One of the most important things in a critique group is that the members know, deeply, the genres in which everybody is writing. This kind of knowledge, this understanding of a form, doesn't come from reading one or two example books but from immersing yourself in that genre, reading stacks and stacks of books because you love them and can't help yourself. As writers, we need to do this for our own genre; as critiquers, we need to do it for the genre we're critiquing. In a general group, this is a tough challenge to meet.

Genre-Based Critique Groups

In a genre-based group, though, the writers are already meeting this challenge for themselves, not just for their critique partners. In this kind of group, all the members are writing within a specific writing "world." One group may critique romance, while another reads only young-adult books. A nonfiction group may focus on magazine articles; the memoir writers get together on a different day.

The important thing about these groups is that the writers *know* their genre. They haven't just *read* a lot of books, they're reading more every week to keep up with the newest titles. Every genre changes and grows with time. Fantasy may have sprouted from the root of Tolkien, but magical creatures he never heard of walk through today's pages. Biographies used to be reserved for famous people; now you can write about anyone from a fisherman to a forensic scientist. And the critiquers in a genre-specific group know about these changes because they're constantly reading and sharing their knowledge with each other.

The weakness of a genre-specific group can be the same as its strength. If a writer decides to try writing in another genre, he may run into some bumps in the road. The group formed to focus on one genre; some members might be uncomfortable with or unsure about reading and critiquing something else. If everyone in a group has been writing memoirs, and one writer gets an idea for a commercial science-fiction novel, the members are looking at a big gear shift, both in their reading and in their thinking.

A good, solid group can handle this kind of change if they have worked together for a long time and are committed to supporting each other's writing paths, no matter which direction those go. Before you join or start a genre-based group, though, you should at least take a peek into your writing future and see where you *think* you're headed.

CHOOSING AN IN-PERSON OR ONLINE GROUP

When I first started critiquing, in-person groups were the only choice (yes, I'm dating myself here). The Internet, though, has opened up a whole new set of possibilities for online critiquing. Which type of group you decide is right for you depends on a wide set of variables, from where you live to your personality.

In-Person Critique Groups

The biggest advantage of an in-person group is just that—that you meet, physically, on a regular basis with your critique partners. When you deliver a critique, you can watch the writer whose pages you're talking about, and you are able to gauge his or her response. You can see whether he's nodding, as he understands your feedback, or if he has that little frown on his face that says he's confused. You know when to clarify, and you know when to keep rolling on. At the same time, if you're the writer receiving a critique, you have the chance, right when the feedback is fresh, to ask questions and make sure you understand exactly what your critiquers are telling you.

An in-person group also gives you a reason to get out of the house. If you are writing at home, by yourself, you can start to feel isolated and even trapped by your writing. A meeting at the coffeehouse every two weeks gets you up out of your chair and away from your computer, forcing you to join up with other writers in a cheerful, social environment that can give you just the boost you need to go back and write some more.

Many writers like the more intimate setting and atmosphere that an in-person group provides. They want to develop a local community, a circle for themselves and their writing. For other writers, though, this intimacy isn't a draw; in fact, it can be a negative. These writers may find their friendships elsewhere and see the social, emotional aspects of an in-person group more restrictive than expansive.

Even if you would like to join an in-person group, the time restrictions may create more of a problem than you are willing to take on. If you are working outside the house, or if you have young children at home, the hours you can schedule a regular meeting are probably limited. Even if you are willing to add two to four more hours of committed time to your monthly calendar, finding a group that meets within your available "free" time is going to be tricky. Finally, you may live in a small town or a rural area (or in a different country!), and "nearby" critique groups may be few and far between. An in-person group may just not work with your current lifestyle.

Online Critique Groups

Luckily, those writers who either can't find an in-person group or who feel those groups don't fit their personalities or their schedules now have options. Great options. With the Internet, online groups have blossomed into the hundreds, probably even thousands. Any problem you might face finding a local group, whether you live in a small town or a large city, disappears when you go online. Whatever choices you made in the earlier sections of this chapter—whether you decided on an open or closed group, general or genre-based—you will be able to find that kind of group online.

Many online groups do require a certain number of submitted pages per month, and most put a limit on how long you can take to return a critique. In general, though, these groups provide a freedom from schedules that can be a huge relief to someone already struggling to fit her writing into her busy life. For writers who already have a big enough social life and are looking for less intimacy in their critique group, an online group can provide a happy solution.

Writers confident in their ability to give and receive critiques may find that an online group serves them well. If, on the other hand, a writer is still feeling his way, uncertain about how to express his own feedback or interpret that of other writers, the anonymous aspects of an online group can be a problem. Because you can't see the author to whom you're sending a critique, you may hesitate to give thorough, detailed feedback. Similarly, you may find yourself with hurt feelings when you are critiqued, because you only have your critique partner's words in front of you, not his reassuring smile and voice.

Also, while the looser schedule of an online group may suit some writers, others may find that it takes away the slight nudge they need to actually write. An in-person group that meets every two weeks can be a great motivator to get a rough scene or chapter on the page and into e-mail. If you don't get those pages done, you're still going to the meeting and facing, in real time, the other writers you've committed to. The distance of an online group, even with submission requirements, can make it easier to ignore "deadlines" and push your writing aside.

Some writers who have been unable to find a local group worry that an online group won't give them the connection, the creative relationship they are looking for. I have seen in-person groups where the members remain formal or shy with each other, and I know members of online groups who have annual retreats and chat online with friendships as strong as any other in their lives. A group is defined by its members, and you can help build the kind of group you want, whether you're meeting near home or across a computer network.

Finding the right critique group for you is a journey—an adventure or a trial, depending on your attitude and your luck. One of the biggest factors in finding the best fit are the people in the group, and this isn't something you can make decisions about ahead of time. The choices I've talked about in this chapter will help you examine your own critique goals and requirements and give you a starting point for your search. Be flexible and stay open to various possibilities, and you will find a group that looks interesting and exciting. Invite yourself to test the waters. You'll be happy you did.

Chapter 2

JOINING OR SETTING UP A GROUP

One of the biggest challenges, if not *the* biggest, of the critique process is finding the right group. Is there a group meeting nearby? Is there a group on the Internet that has an available space? Where do you start looking? Will the existing members *want* you, and—more importantly—will you want *them*?

You may decide, for various reasons, not to join any of the existing groups you come across. Instead you'll set out to build your own group. Okay, how do you start? Where do you find your critique partners, and how do you tell if they'll all be compatible?

In this chapter, I'll go over the process of getting started, of working through all these questions and taking the first steps with your group. In general, whichever path you take, you'll address the same questions and situations. You'll be doing the following tasks.

- "Deciding" whether to join or start a group
- Locating a group or critique partner
- Submitting or reading a writing sample
- Catching up with projects
- Evaluating your compatibility with the group or critique partner
- Making a "final" decision about the group or critique partner
- Adding new members

"DECIDING" WHETHER TO JOIN OR START A GROUP

I've got *deciding* in quotation marks for a very good reason. Depending on where you live, this decision may not actually be up to you. If you are looking to critique locally and you live in a small town or in a rural area, it's very possible you don't live within driving distance of a single group. The Internet can take away this problem, but if you're focused on critiquing with people you can see, you'll need to start hunting for other writers—ones who are still doing the solo thing—and invite them to join the group you're building.

If you live in or near a big city, or if you're already happy friends with the Internet, you have lots of ways to find a group to join. The decision you need to make is whether you're most comfortable stepping into an established group—one where the members have known and worked with each other for months or years—or whether you want to be more in control, setting your own guidelines and directing the way the group is run.

Either way works. I've taken both routes myself, with success. The first group I joined had already been together for five years, and I happily stepped into their circle and stayed there for almost a decade until a shift in my own writing took me onto a different road. I've also started my own group, one that was genre-specific, by finding other mystery writers who were ready to critique together. You, too, can become part of a compatible, productive group, no matter which choice you start with.

For now, take a few seconds to ask yourself which path sounds better, and keep your initial answer in mind as you read through this chapter.

LOCATING A GROUP OR A CRITIQUE PARTNER

You'll notice that the word *partner* above is singular. I believe strongly that if you are starting your own critique group, you should—unless you know several writers *very* well—start that group with one other writer. Throwing too many ingredients into the critique pot all at once, without having specific guidelines and critique patterns, is a recipe for disaster. You and one other compatible writer can work together to get the core of the group established and then gradually invite other writers to join. Two people *is* a group—a small one that supports healthy growth.

Whether you decide to begin your hunt looking for that first critique partner or for a group, you have lots of resources to help you out. In your neighborhood, you can start by checking out bookstores and libraries, by going to writing-group meetings, conferences, and classes. The Internet has dozens of online sources for finding groups and critiquers, from discussion forums to national writing organizations.

Looking at Bookstores and Libraries

Bookstores and libraries are some of the first, and easiest, places to start your hunt. Most have, at the very least, a bulletin board where people post notices about groups and events; others put out newsletters with notices of meetings and events.

Your library or bookstore may also have a Web site where you can check for information. As I write this, my local chain bookstore lists two different groups on their Web site, and the independent bookseller a few more miles down the road has a group also. (Quick note: Both of these sites list their groups as "writing," not "critique" groups. Don't rule out a group until you know for sure what the members are doing!)

If you don't see anything posted about a group, talk to a bookseller or a librarian. It's possible they've heard of a local group, even one that's looking for members. And if you're building your own group, see if you can post your own flier advertising for that first critique partner.

Finally, don't forget to check out the café. Bookstores aren't the only places that have added tables and rooms where people can snack and talk; a lot of new libraries are being built with an area for coffee and conversation. Stop in a few times. Do you see a group of people talking excitedly, waving papers and red pens at each other? Or maybe there's one lone writer staring at her laptop, fingers flying (or tearing out hair!). Step over to the table and introduce yourself. (If you're feeling shy, take a deep breath first and remind yourself how important your writing is.) You never know. The group may have just been discussing where they were going to find another member. The author may have been dreaming of finding someone to tell her if she's just written something beautiful or ... not so beautiful!

Looking Online

As in every area, the Internet is the resource with the largest number of possibilities. Many writing organizations with regional branches have information about online and in-person groups. Other Web sites have been created just to support the writing community, and you can use them to search for groups or post information about your own. Here is a starter list of online resources for you to check out.

- The Society of Children's Book Writers & Illustrators (SCBWI) www.scbwi.org

- Mystery Writers of America (MWA) www.mysterywriters.org

- Sisters in Crime www.sistersincrime.org

- Horror Writers Association (HWA) www.horror.org

- Romance Writers of America www.rwanational.org/

- The International Women's Writing Guild www.iwwg.com/

- California Writers Club www.calwriters.org

- Wisconsin Regional Writers' Association, Inc. www.wrwa.net/

- Florida Writers Association www.floridawriters.net/

- ShawGuides http://writing.shawguides.com/

- Writer's Digest Conference Scene www.writersdigest.com/
conferencescene

- Wikipedia's List of Writers' Conferences http://en.wikipedia.org/
wiki/List_of_writers'_conferences

- Writers' Conferences & Centers http://writersconf.org

- Craigslist www.craigslist.org

Looking at Writing Clubs, Conferences, and Classes

Classes, writing clubs, and conferences are great places to learn about the craft of writing and to get motivated to work on your book. They're also one of the best places to meet other writers—writers who already belong to a critique group, or writers who are wishing they did. In particular, a class that meets for several weeks or months lets you get to know these other writers and make connections with the ones who score highest on your comfort meter.

If you already know other writers, definitely ask them about any clubs or upcoming events. And get on the Internet. The list I gave you above is a great place to find out about workshops near you. Many of these sites maintain constantly updated pages showing meetings, workshops, and conferences all over the country (and world!). Find out what's happening near you and then sign up for an event and go meet some local writers in person.

Take care to make the meeting worth your time and money. Talk to people. Too often, at these events, writers give in to their nervousness, shyness, or just their uncertainty about their own writing. They go from workshop to workshop without stopping to chat with the people sitting next to them.

They eat their lunch silently, listening to, but not participating in, the table talk around them.

As always, remember: This is your writing. It's important. I'm not advocating shoving yourself into the middle of someone else's discussion or waving a red flag in the bathroom line, but put yourself out there. Find out what the people around you are writing, see how long they've been at their projects. Mention what you're working on, and let everyone know you're looking for a critique group or partner to hook up with. Don't forget to swap phone numbers and e-mail addresses!

Again, as you start your search, begin with what makes you happiest. If you've been dying for an excuse to attend the annual writing conference in your hometown, you've got it. If you're in your element browsing the Internet, go for it. However you decide to take your first step, you'll start yourself on the road to finding a great critique group.

SUBMITTING OR READING A WRITING SAMPLE

Many critique groups require a writing sample from anyone asking to join the group. While it's not always possible to get a complete, true assessment of someone's abilities from a few pages, a sample is still the group's best chance to gauge the applicant's writing level. The group isn't looking to criticize or judge but simply to find someone who is a good match with the existing members.

If you're the writer hoping to be part of this group, sending a sample can feel intimidating. Depending on how much writing you've done or how many people you've shared that writing with, the request may make you feel anxious or may even send you out to buy large amounts of chocolate.

Take a breath.

Remember your writing goal? Someday you want to be sending an entire manuscript to an agent or editor. As hard as this submission feels now, it's an important step on the way to that goal. And it's a step you should take.

Don't, however, go crazy over the submission. You're *not* sending this one out for publication, and the people on the other end know it won't be perfect. In fact, they'd be pretty suspicious if it were! Besides, the existing members aren't the only ones looking for a good fit. You want to be accepted into a critique group on the basis of your real in-process writing, not the ten pages you've spent hours polishing.

However, there are a few things you can do to show you're taking the group seriously. Before you send the chapter, you should:

- set the font to 12 point, Times New Roman
- double-space the lines
- run the spell-checker
- read through the pages one final time to check for words the spell-checker didn't catch and for any passage that's seriously confusing or makes you cringe

Now send out the sample. Then pat yourself on the back, celebrate the step, and write for the next few days with your fingers crossed.

If you're in a group that receives a writing sample, or if you're just starting to build a group and are looking at writing samples from lots of applicants, don't expect the sample to give you 100 percent understanding and insight about the author. This is your first glimpse of a person's writing, though, and you need to listen to what your gut tells you. If your group is near publication, and you can see, from the writing, that the applicant is just starting on her writing journey, she probably isn't a good fit. Similarly, if everybody in the group is overwhelmed by the high quality of the sample, if they can't find a thing they would touch in a critique, they're looking at another poor match. A good group can support a range of writing levels, especially because writing skill is not always directly tied to critiquing skill. However, setting yourself up with *too* wide a variety of abilities is likely to lead to discomfort and conflict.

If you have to turn down an applicant, do so with respect. Don't critique his sample; that's not why you asked for it. If he gets a critique along with a "no, thank you," he may not be able to see your feedback as anything other than additional rejection. In fact, don't get into talking about his writing at all. Simply tell the writer he isn't the right fit for the group and thank him for his time.

It can be a good idea for a group to decide ahead of time how they'll handle writing samples. If you are setting up your own group and looking for several additional members, you can get this sorted out at the very beginning. Simply write a basic note describing why your group asks for samples, what the writer should submit, and what a "yes" or "no" response to the sample means. You can e-mail or hand the note to any applicant, and he or she will know from the start what the process is about.

CATCHING UP WITH PROJECTS

If you're joining an existing group, you're going to be dropping yourself into the middle of several different writing projects. If you're starting a group with just you and one other writer, you'll be in the same boat, just a smaller version. This is okay. You critique from what you do know, and you do your best—as time passes—to develop a strong understanding of all the books the group members are writing.

To get started you can ask each member for a summary of his or her manuscript so far. If a book is a novel, you need a basic description of the main characters, especially the hero and the hero's goal. You should also get a brief explanation of the novel's plot so far. If the project is nonfiction, you should find out the basic subject matter and projected audience. And you'll want to fill the group in on the same information about whatever writing you'll be submitting to them.

If an established group has been static, without new members for a while, they may not have this information immediately at hand. If you are invited to join, and the other members don't automatically brief you on their projects, ask them for the information. If you're starting a group, you can write up the basics about your project and hand that out to any writers you invite to join.

EVALUATING YOUR COMPATIBILITY WITH A GROUP OR CRITIQUE PARTNER

Obviously, reading sample pages can tell you something only about an applicant's writing. The sample isn't going to tell you who the writer is or whether she is compatible with the group you belong to or the one you're trying to build. If you've met the applicant in person, at a conference, or in a class, you can get a small gut feel for her personality, but that's about it. If she's contacted you online, you may not have a single clue about what this person is like.

If you're the writer who's being invited to join a group, you probably haven't even read anything by the existing members. It's not typical for existing group members to show samples of *their* writing to applicants. This is because a group may read a lot of samples before they find someone they invite to become a member, and they don't need or want to pass out their writing to people who may not join the group. As a new member, the first chance you get to really talk with the existing group, or read any of their writing, may very well be at your first critique meeting.

The first few meetings, when you join a critique group or when you meet with your (potential) critique partner, are a testing ground. You'll want to sit in on a few meetings and participate in some critique sessions before you decide for sure that a group is for you. Similarly, if you're setting up a group, you'll want to use those first sessions to truly evaluate your compatibility with another writer.

Compatibility is impossible to quantify, and your best recourse is to listen to your gut feeling about the people you're meeting. Don't tell yourself you have to stay in a group where you aren't comfortable or where your writing isn't getting the fullest respect and support. Do, however, give yourself time to get past any initial nervousness and awkwardness so you know your feelings are true. Take a few meetings to get to know the other writers. And use those meetings to find out a few facts—facts that may help you make your decision. You can gather information about the group and participate in a few critique sessions.

Gathering Information

If you're joining or building a group with people you already know, you may already know the basics about their writing lives and experience. If, on the other hand, you're starting a group from scratch or joining a group whose members you don't know, you should ask a few questions. Knowing a bit about these writers can give you a start on figuring out whether you've found the right fit for you and your projects.

Ask the members how long they've been together. If a group has been critiquing together for a few years, and you're just starting out with the critique process, don't worry about the discrepancy too much. You're going to have a chance to learn some solid skills from experienced critiquers. And you'll bring fresh insights and thoughts to the material they've been dug into for a while. If the group is fairly new to each other, you'll fit right in, and you'll begin to develop critique skills together. Knowing the group's joint history, though, will help you read the dynamics of the group and find your way to a solid place within them.

Find out where each of the members is on their writing path—how long they've been writing and how close they are to submitting work to agents and editors. If you're just starting out, you may want to know if someone

in the group has published a dozen books. On the flip side, if you've been working steadily on your own book for a year, you should probably find out if the other members are just now writing chapter one. Writers of various abilities and stages can critique together successfully; however, you can use this information to gauge your comfort with the group's experience as compared to your own.

How many pages does the group typically critique at a meeting? You probably won't get an exact number, but the answer should let you judge whether the group is writing productively or whether they're spending a lot of meeting time on things other than critiquing. You'll want to find out what the group does when they don't have pages to critique—do they find some other productive use of the meeting, or do they just decide to skip those sessions and clean their houses instead? You're looking for a group that is serious about forward movement on their projects, and these questions will help you gauge the group's commitment to that kind of standard.

PARTICIPATING IN A FEW CRITIQUE SESSIONS

Almost every story I've heard about a critique-group problem has to do with the way a member of the group presents his critiques. In chapter twenty-three, we'll talk about ways to troubleshoot some of these problems, but the first few meetings with a new group or your first critique partner are the best time to watch out for red flags.

How many different critique styles are out there? Well, how many different *people* are on the planet?! For now, though, let's just mention a few possibilities. You'll meet critiquers who are:

- direct
- timid
- supportive
- persuasive
- bossy
- encouraging

You may be looking at that list and feeling like the "bad" and "good" qualities are obvious. Not necessarily. A thoughtful, respectful critiquer may bring any of these characteristics into play as he reads your work and gives you feedback. You may even get a surprise one day as a new trait rises up in your *own* critique of someone else's work.

A personality or critique style becomes a problem only when it is taken to an extreme—when a critiquer can't find the balance that is needed. This is what you're looking for as you participate in your first few meetings. Watch each critiquer's manner. Does someone seem overly harsh to you or—at the opposite pole—hesitant to give feedback on any of the big writing issues? When you listen to the critiques, does one person in particular make your stomach cringe or your head want to shake a big "no!"?

Make sure you participate in the critiques at these early meetings. The way in which another writer receives feedback can be just as telling as how she gives it. And while you may still be developing your own critique style, it's going to be based on who you are, here and now. If, when you give a respectful but honest critique, a writer gets angry or intimidated, you need to pay attention. If you explain everything as carefully as you can, but the author can't understand your points—again, recognize that problem.

Don't let instant judgments carry you away, but pay attention to the other people's behavior and personalities. And pay attention to your own reactions to the group and its members. If you continue to feel uncomfortable after several meetings, you need to recognize and respect that feeling.

MAKING A "FINAL" DECISION ABOUT THE GROUP OR CRITIQUE PARTNER

Obviously, no decision is final. Life is about change and transitions; we don't stop growing, and we often don't grow in the direction we would predict. The same will be true for every member of whichever critique group you choose to join or build. Once you've done your best job at assessing a group or critique partner, and evaluating your own compatibility with them, you make the best choice you can at the moment. You are not sticking your feet into wet cement; you can pull free any time you need to.

If you basically feel comfortable with the group, or with the person you're inviting to set up a group, go for it. You'll get to know each other better and better the longer you critique together—and you'll have some wrinkles to smooth out—but trust yourself. If you're happy and excited about this opportunity and you're not hiding from any bad feelings, say "yes." Submit, critique, and grow your writing.

If, on the other hand, you're not feeling so great about this group or the other writer, stop. Examine your worries honestly, and, if you're fairly sure they're not just nerves, listen to them. It can be uncomfortable to tell a group you won't be staying or to tell another writer she isn't what you're looking for, but you can't shy away from this step. If you continue to critique in an environment that makes you tense or unhappy, the experience will—sooner, rather than later—hurt your writing. Be polite, be brief, and say goodbye. Then start looking for that group or writer that *is* the right one for you.

ADDING NEW MEMBERS

Even if you join an established group with three other committed writers, you will find yourself—at some time in the future—considering adding one or more new members. And if you're starting out to set up your own group, you and that initial critique partner need to actively hunt out and invite new members to build your group to a productive size.

Don't rush this process. As we'll talk about in the next chapter, there is no perfect size for a critique group. The most important thing is to build a solid core of members who really know each other's writing and who are skilled at helping each other grow and progress with their projects. If you try to add too many members at once, or don't give a new member enough time to merge with the existing group, you'll be setting up problems that threaten that core.

Add one member at a time. Gather information about that writer, just as we talked about in the earlier section of this chapter. Make sure the writer knows that the first few meetings will serve as a "trial" period, both for the existing group to evaluate the new member and for that writer to assess whether the group is what he needs. Give yourself an exit route. Explain that the group is not judging anybody's writing or critiquing ability but is looking for a writer who is the best fit for the existing group. Even if that group is only you and your one other critique partner, any new member must work well with both of you.

My rule of thumb is if the current group is strong and productive, a new member must make *everyone* happy. If even one member feels uncomfortable or unhappy with an applicant, the group needs to respect that opinion. The existing *dynamic* is what's helping the group's members write and grow, and anything that affects one member negatively also threatens that dynamic.

I'm not trying to scare you. Really! Frankly, though, it's hard to make either of these changes—to leave or to ask someone to leave. The more prepared you are, the easier the process will be for everyone involved.

Chapter 3

RUNNING A GROUP

In this chapter, I'm going to explain the basics of running a critique group, from delivering a critique submission to sitting quietly and listening when it's your turn to be critiqued. If you're just starting a group, you may have some ideas of your own about how to run it, or you may be starting a group completely from scratch. Either way, I'll help you sort out the day-to-day operations.

If you're joining an existing group or have been part of a critique group for a while, the group may already have guidelines similar to the ones I'll be talking about. Even so, this chapter may give you some ideas about how to improve the structure of your group or to resolve a problem that's been nagging at the members. Most of the material in the next pages applies to both in-person and online groups, and I'll talk about specific considerations for each as those come up.

In this chapter, we'll look at the following:

- committing time and energy
- scheduling meetings
- deciding how to use meeting time
- delivering pages for critique
- reading a submission
- writing a critique
- presenting a critique
- receiving a critique

COMMITTING TIME AND ENERGY

Most of this chapter focuses on organization and procedures that will help your group run smoothly and productively. Before I get into those sections, though, I want to give you a pep talk. Or, if you prefer, a major nag.

The most important contribution you can make to a critique group is to take it seriously. You value your writing. If you want others to give your work the respect and attention it deserves, you'll need to return the favor.

Committing to a critique group means agreeing to a date and time that will work consistently with your schedule and showing up to every meeting you possibly can. It means allotting time to read and critique submissions from the other group members and making your critiques supportive *and* detailed so they are truly helpful. It also means listening respectfully to the critiques of your own writing and actually working with this feedback when you revise.

Of course, real-life crises happen, and they do get in the way. These conflicts can be accepted and dealt with. Problems arise, though, when writers make excuses to avoid writing and critiquing. And we've all been guilty of doing this at one time or another.

These excuses run the gamut, from social obligations to our own fears about our writing and our ability to critique. Maybe your parents are cleaning out their garage, and—because you're not sure you've done a good job critiquing a submission—you decide Mom and Dad really need your help. Or you haven't written a word in three weeks, so you figure it's better not to show up at the meeting than to show up empty-handed. When you're in an online group, it's pretty easy to just stay away from that part of the Internet. If you don't actually *send* any e-mails, you don't have to fret about never attaching a chapter file.

I'm sorry. Those excuses, as tempting as they are, just aren't good enough.

We all struggle to put our work (yes, it's work, even when you're not yet being paid) at the top of our priority list. Of course family comes first, and friends run a nearby parallel path. Lots of things, though—dishes, laundry, getting the dog's toenails trimmed—can wait. Step one to recognizing and respecting your craft is reminding yourself of this fact.

Schedule your critique time (and your writing time!). If someone asks you to do him a favor or to come out and play, and the activity is a conflict, try very hard to change the *other* thing. Run the kids through the fast-food drive-in for one special dinner so you've got time to write or read. If your fears about your writing or critiquing are looming, face them. Take them with you to the meeting and share them with the group. Be respectful to yourself and the other members, and you'll all work it out together.

Really.

SCHEDULING MEETINGS

It is important to set a regular, consistent time and place for meetings. Even in an online group, you should set a schedule for checking in with each other on a regular basis. As writers, we need to save our energy for writing and critiquing, not for trying to remember where and when we're supposed to show up this week.

When you're ready to schedule regular meetings, you'll do the following organizational tasks:

- deciding where to meet
- deciding what time to meet
- deciding how often to meet
- deciding how long to make the meetings

Where to Meet

If you're in an online group, the "where" is the Internet. You have a virtual community you can access from your home, a library, or your vacation penthouse in London. You may hook into that community at an online forum, through an instant messenger, or across e-mail, but your physical base is your own.

For in-person groups, though, you will need to find an actual spot to gather. Coffeehouses are often prime meeting places. These days, many people occupy a table or two for a couple of hours to chat, to work, to catch up on their e-mail. Writers, with or without laptops, blend well into this scene. Bookstores also work for this, as long as the owner or management is okay with your group taking up a few chairs for the length of your meeting.

You can also meet at the home of one of your members or rotate through everybody's houses. If you choose to keep your meetings "residential," make sure hosting doesn't become a strain. Spending the morning cleaning and cooking (something chocolate, of course) instead of writing doesn't add pages to anybody's manuscript. Also, make sure that the driving distance to the chosen home isn't too far. One of the advantages to meeting in a bookstore or café is that, often, the location is central to all the members.

Wherever you meet, remember that you're getting together to critique, not just to chat. Sometimes the private, cozy environment of someone's familiar house makes it easier to spend the time catching up on each other's lives, rather than helping each other move forward on writing projects. If your host just got a new couch or big-screen TV, compliment him or her nicely and then get down to business. If your online group "meets" in a live chat or through IM, make sure the major percentage of your "chatting" is about the critiques.

What Time to Meet

In an online critique group, the time of day you "meet" can be scheduled or flexible. If you're connecting with each other "live" at a specific time, you'll need to treat this time the same way in-person groups treat their meeting schedule. Pick a time that works for everyone in the group and stick to it. On the other hand, if you're presenting your critiques by posting them to an online forum or sending them by e-mail, you have huge flexibility. You can "critique" at ten in the morning with your second cup of coffee; eight at night after the kids are in bed; or three in the morning when insomnia hits—it's your choice. This freedom is one of the big benefits of an online group.

If you're part of an in-person group, you'll obviously need to pick a time of day when everyone can show up for real, not just in virtual time. If everybody in your group works a full-time day job, you'll need to find a compatible evening or get together over the weekend. If a lot of the members have small children, you may find yourself meeting during preschool hours or on the one day a week when Grandma and Grandpa are playing nanny.

How Often to Meet

How often should your group meet? Obviously, like the time of day you'll get together, the frequency of your meetings can vary, depending on the members' lives and schedules. Some groups get together every week, and others stretch the time between meetings to a month. In many online groups, the members simply use the Internet to send files and comments back and forth but don't schedule any common online time at all.

My recommendation for an in-person group is that it meets twice a month. Two weeks is a good amount of time to let members balance reading submissions, do their own writing, and, oh ... having a life.

If you and the other members want to see each other more than twice a month, get together with your laptops and write. However, if your group meets more than twice a month to critique, these meetings may cut into your writing time. You'll end up frustrated, even angry, because you're putting more time into other people's manuscripts than your own. Even if you're a serious speed reader and don't feel this way, the odds are that someone in your group will.

On the other hand, a critique group that meets less often than twice a month is going to suffer, too. Meeting too infrequently can weaken a writer's motivation to get words on the page and pages out the door. If you're writing a novel, and you set yourself a goal of delivering a chapter at every meeting, a two-week deadline can put just the right amount of pressure on you to get that chapter written. Three weeks, or four, between meetings leaves you too much time to put that chapter away for a few days. This is the best way to lose your focus on the project.

For an online group, even if it doesn't have official critique times, I recommend setting some kind of schedule. You can decide that submissions are to be sent out the first and third week of the month and critiques to be delivered during the other two weeks. You can pick two days a month that everybody is required to send an e-mail or post to the group—with some kind of status report about their progress or even just to say "hello." If you can hook up in a chat group and spend time together discussing and brainstorming over a critique, this will go a long way toward developing the personal connections that make a group strong.

How Long to Make the Meetings

Two hours is a standard length of time for in-person group meetings, and that time frame usually allows two to three critiques to be presented. There are solid reasons to go with this number. A good, thorough critique can easily last thirty to forty-five minutes. Because, typically, not every writer is submitting at the same time, two hours usually gives critiquers time to present and explain their feedback and lets each author process and ask questions about the comments.

If the writers in a group all hit a productivity roll at the same time, you may find yourself pressed to give everybody a fair hearing. I don't recommend stretching out the meeting. Our brains only work so well for so long, and our nervous systems can handle only so much caffeine at one sitting. If everybody's writing and everybody's critiquing, this may be the time to schedule an extra session or two. The strongest critique groups are flexible, with all the members doing reality checks to make sure everybody feels supported and nobody feels overwhelmed.

With online groups, as in so many other areas, you're dealing with a different reality. The bottom line is that everything is faster on the Internet, including critiques. In an in-person group, people wander in, get coffee or tea, unload

their papers and pens, and compliment each other on new haircuts. It's often
five or ten minutes before a group settles down to true critiquing. If you choose
to critique together online, the ramping up to work can take as little as a single
minute. The actual critiquing will take less time than in an in-person group as
well. Still, try to set aside a solid hour to "meet" online. If you find, over time,
that you really need less or more time, you can adjust the schedule.

DECIDING HOW TO USE MEETING TIME

A critique group is for critiquing, right? Yes—whenever possible. However, as
much as we wish otherwise, every writer has lulls in his or her productivity.
There will be times when all the members in your group hit this point together.
You'll have a meeting set on the calendar, and you'll realize that nobody has
submitted pages for a critique. Or, if you're in an online group, you'll see that
nobody has submitted for the upcoming month.

Don't skip the meeting. And don't let your Internet connection stay silent.

The routine and rhythm of a critique group are great motivators for writers to keep words flowing. If you know you don't have to show up for a meeting or connect with other members online, it's that much easier to let your
writing slide. Make sure your group has a plan for the noncritique periods.
Discuss a writing book, for instance, and apply the ideas in it to your current
manuscripts. Share information about writing workshops, online classes, or
conferences. If you live near each other, see if there's an event coming up to
which you can carpool. Write together. Bring your laptops to your meeting
place and spend the hours putting words on a page. In an online group, com-
mit to writing virtually for an hour or two, with "status report" e-mails every
fifteen or twenty minutes.

DELIVERING PAGES FOR CRITIQUE

When I first started participating in critique groups, there were basically two
ways to get my submissions to the other members. If I really had my act together,
I would bring several copies of my submission to a meeting and ask for it to be
critiqued the next time we got together. If I was a couple days behind, I had to
stuff those copies into envelopes, write three or four addresses on the envelopes,
and go to the post office for stamps. After a while, I had the postage memorized,
could put the stamps on at home, and got to skip actually standing in line.

Today, it's so much easier. When I have a submission ready, I just open an e-mail window, type a quick note, and send off an attachment for the members of my group to read. No stamps, no gasoline, no lines. This works for many online groups, as well as in-person groups, although some online groups simply have you upload a file to a site where the other members can access it. Even easier.

Of course, convenience often creates a whole new set of questions. Here are some considerations for how to deliver submissions:

- deciding when to deliver a submission
- communicating about submissions
- describing the feedback you're looking for

When to Deliver a Submission

If you're in an in-person group and you want your writing critiqued at an upcoming meeting, when should you give those pages to the other group members? It's extremely important, I think, to send the pages ahead of time.

I know that, in many groups, writers bring their submissions to the meeting at which those submissions will be critiqued. This structure creates more problems than it solves. The choices here are for everybody to read the pages to themselves or for one member to read the submission out loud while the other members listen.

If everybody reads to themselves, someone inevitably finishes first and has to wait, while the other members feel rushed. "Rushed" is not a good state of mind to be thinking about a submission or preparing a critique. And the reader who is already done has nothing to do but stare at the walls.

In the other scenario, one member reads out loud. I've tried groups where this is done, and it has never worked for me. I do not absorb material well if it's being read to me, and I'm certainly not the only learner out there with this kind of brain. On top of this, every group member is being taken out of his or her comfortable, familiar reading style—the one where we hold the book in our hands and look at the printed words. Having the pages read to us distances us from the words we need to focus on. Also, if there's someone in your group who's a great reader, who puts just the right expression and emotion into the words, it's easy to get caught up and think the writing is further along than it truly is.

In either of these cases, what is the author supposed to do while everybody else reads and writes up their feedback? Chew her fingernails? Reading at the meeting sets up the author to be nervous and tense, which once again is not the best emotion in which to get handed a pile of changes and suggestions for her writing.

Finally, reading submissions at the meeting takes up time. This time could be used more productively discussing the critiques or helping the author brainstorm new ideas.

I recommend delivering pages ahead of each meeting, giving the group members time to read the material at home and prepare a thought-out, helpful critique.

How far ahead? A week is a good standard to set. Seven days gives your critique partners time to look ahead and fit that critique into a good spot on the calendar. A weekend falls somewhere onto that timeline, and, for people with full-time jobs or otherwise busy lives, Saturday and Sunday are often good times to critique. Try not to push it to less than four days, if at all possible.

Online groups typically have more flexibility about delivery and response. Still, be considerate. If everybody is required to submit a chapter or two every month, don't wait until the twenty-eighth of February to send your submission along. You've just piled that critique onto everybody's plate for March, along with all the pages they'll be reading in the next thirty days. Your group may need to set a midmonth date for submissions, along with an end-of-month date for returning the critiques.

Whichever timeline you decide on will vary for each group, though. Some readers are faster than others; different people have calmer or busier lives. Find the due date that works best for all the members in your group. Obviously, you can't set a schedule that's perfect for everybody, but try to accommodate the reader who needs a little more time and the writer who doesn't want to send out his submission quite so early.

Communicating About Submissions

Is your submission deadline set in stone? Of course not. The point of a critique group is to get our writing out there, get feedback on it, and keep going. We want to make continual progress on our writing projects. A deadline that can't be shifted can be as bad for a group as no deadline at all.

If you don't have something ready by the scheduled time, but you know you can get it out within a few more days, make some phone calls or send a group e-mail. Let your critique partners know what you have coming and check on their schedules for the week. If one of the other members contacts you, asking for a few more days, do your best to give her the time. You're a group. Talk to each other and make things work.

You'll also want to let your critique partners know how many pages you're sending out. Many groups, especially for beginning writers, have a system of submitting a chapter or two at a time. Even in a group with this kind of routine, though, there will be times when the pattern breaks. Somebody gets on a huge roll and has five or six chapters ready to go at once.

If you find yourself ready to send out more pages than usual, check in with your group. Find out if anybody else is submitting for that meeting and check whether your partners can take on the extra reading and critique time. If they're feeling pressed, you may want to save your submission for the next meeting or give them two-meetings' worth of time to prepare their critiques.

If you're on the receiving end of this kind of request, try to make it work. Look honestly at your schedule for the next week or so and see if you do have the time to read the extra pages and get your feedback ready. In a critique group, our job is not only to help our partners with the pages they've written but also to help them write as many pages as they can, to keep moving steadily forward. This is the kind of stretching of the rules that can build a strong, powerful group.

Describing the Feedback You're Looking For

When you're starting out as a writer, you may not know exactly what kind of feedback you want. In a new critique group, as well, members are often feeling their way, testing the depth of the critique their partners are comfortable with. As you get deeper into the critique process, you'll realize that, at different stages of your manuscript, you'll be looking for different types of feedback. And, naturally, the same will be true about the feedback the other members want from you.

When you're writing your first draft, for example, your goal is to get words on the page. During this stage, you may want to hear feedback that relates only to the big elements of writing—where your plot seems to be heading, how much more you need to develop your main characters. You probably don't want your critique partners to spend a lot of time on sentence-level problems or word choices.

On the other hand, as you revise (and revise!), you'll need to hear how your writing voice is coming across, and you'll appreciate any comments that help you smooth out transitions between scenes. You'll want your critique partners to flag any paragraphs or pages that jar them out of the information, and you'll thank them for the help you get with dialogue.

The thing is, you can't just expect the other members of your group to read your mind and always know what you want them to dig into. You'll need to tell them.

When you send out your pages, add a note. You can stick this in the e-mail itself or at the top of page one of the submission. Keep it brief; don't go into so much detail that you make the other members feel like you're writing their critiques for them. Just set out the basics of what you're trying to do at this point in your manuscript and what you'd like your partners to keep an eye open for as they read.

Your critique partners want to help you the best they can. Give them the information they need to do just that. And don't forget the flip side. When you get a submission from one of your partners, ask her if she's looking for something specific from your critique. Maybe she forgot to tell you; maybe she was nervous about asking. It never hurts to check.

READING A SUBMISSION

Critiquing is not just about telling an author your ideas about her work. First, you have to *read* that work and do some hard thinking about what those ideas might be. This is the skill that can be the hardest to develop and is the most important part of the whole critique process. In the body of this book, we'll go into detailed information about *how* to critique. Now, we'll talk about the basic steps of reading through submitted pages. Specifically:

- setting aside a quiet time
- slowing down and listening to your reactions
- thinking about what is and isn't working

Setting Aside a Quiet Time

I don't know about you, but when I was young, I used to do my math homework in front of the television. Needless to say, while I can add and subtract, many of those "higher," more complex math functions never made their way into my brain.

I'm actually okay with that.

What I'm not okay with is a writer treating his critique partner's work the same way. When it's time to critique, critiquing is what you should be doing.

Don't read with the TV on, and don't read while you're cooking dinner, with the kids complaining about *their* homework three feet away. Schedule a time to read when there aren't other people around, or at least when they're all as occupied with their business as you are with yours. Find a comfortable place to sit with the pages, and make yourself a cup of tea or coffee—you're going to be there a while. Keep a pencil or pen and a notebook nearby to jot down the thoughts that come to you while you read.

Then turn to page one.

Slowing Down and Listening to Your Reactions

Up to this point, I've been talking as though you're about to curl up with a good book, maybe with the cat on your lap and a fire in the fireplace. Well, yes, you can have all this when you critique. But, in reality, reading for a critique is not the same as reading for pleasure. When we read for the fun of it, we let ourselves skim, and even skip, sections that don't catch us 100 percent. We may race through settings to see what's happening with the exciting plot. We ignore a character who irritates us.

You can't do this when you read for a critique.

When you read your critique partner's writing, your job is to pay close attention to all your reactions and where they occur. These passages are the ones the authors will want to look at to see what works and what they want to revise and rewrite. They need you to point out the weak and strong spots in their stories.

Sometimes asking this focus of yourself can be tricky, even hard. If you haven't been critiquing long, you may not automatically trust your own responses, especially if the person who's work you're reading is more experienced. You may tell yourself you aren't qualified to judge strong and weak writing. If you've had a bad experience with a critique partner, in which he reacted poorly to your feedback, it may be even harder for you to dig in.

Push yourself. You owe it to the other members of your group, and you owe it to yourself. One of the most important reasons to critique is to learn more about writing in general and—by extension—about your own writing.

So, when you read, slow down. Listen for when your head or your gut tell you something isn't right. Then pay attention.

Thinking About What Isn't (and Is) Working

What do you do with these reactions? When you get a gut feeling that a passage or a scene isn't working, how do you figure out what the problem is? We're going to go into detail about this process in sections II, III, and IV, but for now, here are some ideas that will get you started.

If you're reading a passage or scene and something, anything, jars you out of the flow, stop. Reread the paragraphs or pages leading up to the place where you stalled and try to isolate the problem.

Take some time and analyze what isn't working. (Again, you'll have more help with this when you get into the next section of the book.) For now consider whether it's a problem with one of the big writing elements—plot, character, structure, voice. Then make a note about the problem so you'll remember to include it in your written critique. At the very least, mark the spot on the page where you got pulled out of the story and make a note to discuss this problem in your critique.

WRITING A CRITIQUE

Whether you're working with an in-person group or communicating online, the process of preparing a critique is the same, and it's one of the most important things for you to learn. Figuring out what's not working in someone else's story can be a big challenge. Writing it out into organized, coherent thoughts can be a *bigger* challenge. Sharing feedback with a critique partner isn't always an easy task.

In later sections of this book, you'll see examples of critiques. For now, here are some basics to get you started preparing a critique:

- starting with the good things
- critiquing—not copyediting
- explaining big, overall issues
- noting smaller problems
- offering suggestions
- ending with encouragement

Starting With the Good Things

Some of you bought this book because the only experience you've had with a critique group was a bad one. You shared your writing only to have somebody slam all the problems, ignore all the work you did, and make you wonder if you should even keep going with your book.

If this happened to you, let me say how sorry I am. Nobody should go through this experience, but—as I talk to other writers—I know it happens, and all too often. Hopefully, the information in this book will reduce the odds of a repeat performance.

Step one: Begin your critique with something nice.

Maybe you're thinking to yourself, *What if I can't think of anything good to say?*

Here's my answer: Think again.

I don't believe a page of writing exists that doesn't have something of value on it. First, there is the author's accomplishment in even getting those words out. (We all know how hard that can be.) Second, there is always the seed of what she's trying to do, even if she hasn't yet gotten close. And there's often a great line of dialogue, a beautiful detail in a setting, or a glimpse of that tight voice we all want to achieve.

Find the good thing. Write it down and remember to tell the author why you like it.

Critiquing—Not Copyediting

A comma is a good thing. Knowing where to place one in a sentence is, in my opinion, a serious life skill. However, it's not always the right tool to use when you write a critique.

A critique is not a copyedit. It's a carefully thought out set of feedback about bigger issues than grammar—issues like characterization, clarity, scene structure, and voice. If we, as writers, are doing things right, our first drafts are just that—first passes at words and phrases that are going to change ... and change again. And if we, as critiquers, are doing *our* jobs, we're not going to get out that red pencil and mark every misplaced apostrophe or backward quotation mark. Not when we know those sentences may not even make it to the next draft.

Believe me, I know how tough this can be. I did freelance editing for years, so these little problems jump out at me and demand to be noted. Okay, so note them. When you have to. But don't go overboard, and don't expect the author to pay too much attention to those marks. And if you can, save them for that last pass before he submits the manuscript, when he'll really need and appreciate your talent.

Explaining Big, Overall Issues

When you critique fiction, you're looking at things like plot, character, and dialogue. Nonfiction has its own big elements—clarity, voice, and pacing. Books for children often need a rhythm, and the vocabulary an author uses can be critical. Obviously, many of these issues overlap across genres, so the more you can learn about all of them, the more you'll be able to point out any problems to your critique partners.

When you hit a weak spot, describe the basic problem as you see it. Try to put the problem into the context of the whole project, or at least as much of that project as you know. For example, if the peace-activist character suddenly starts waving around a switchblade, explain why you don't think it fits with his patient, serene demeanor in earlier scenes. Or if you get bogged down in the family descriptions in a memoir, talk about the fact that the author may want to pick a few less details.

If you're finding a problem that shows up throughout the book, point out one or two examples in the manuscript that demonstrate the point you're making. If the hero isn't active enough, find the passages that show her reacting passively to an experience or event. If the writer repeats an explanation too often, note the places you think she could trim.

Always be as clear as you can and take the time to provide a thorough, constructive explanation. Reread your critique and make sure you are getting your thoughts across in an understandable, *respectful* way.

Noting Smaller Problems

In every piece of writing, while the big things keep the reader turning pages, it can be the small stuff that makes him stop and, basically, say, "Huh?" A chunk of dialogue falls flat or the author uses a description to explain a scene rather than by showing it in action. In a nonfiction book, the writer may have written a set of instructions in a confusing way or changed voice from supportive to bossy.

For a critiquer, these passages are often easier to see and less difficult to analyze than the bigger issues. And they're just as important for the author to deal with.

In some ways, though, these smaller problems are like the grammar errors. Over the course of a revision, many of the words will be replaced by better ones. So, when you're critiquing early drafts, tread lightly (and gently) with your pen.

On the other hand, every writer is good (and bad) at different things. One writer can think up an exciting plot twist for every scene but struggles with bringing her character's personality to the front of the page. Another writer writes edgy, sharp dialogue but isn't so great with setting.

One of your jobs as a critiquer is to help the other members of your group recognize their strengths and weaknesses. When you note one of these smaller problems, especially if you're seeing a pattern in which the writer often makes the same kind of mistake, you're helping your critique partners develop their writing skills. Not only will you help them improve their writing, you'll be "training" them to recognize the patterns themselves.

Offering Suggestions

Remember, back in school, when a teacher would write *awkward* on your essay? Or she'd circle a paragraph and tell you to "rewrite" it? How frustrating was that, having no idea what *didn't* work or what to do to make things better? Don't leave your critique partner hanging like this. Make suggestions about how he can improve a passage or a scene, how he can make his plot more exciting or help a reader understand an important concept.

When you do this, don't worry about finding the perfect solution. That's not your job—it's the author's. What you're doing when you make suggestions is finding another way to be clear about your critique. Explaining a writing problem is hard; showing an example of a *possible* fix gives the author another way to come at that problem, to understand what you're telling her.

Just in case, though, do be careful about how you present your ideas. Don't press full-speed ahead, as though you hold the winning golden ticket to publishing this author's book. Don't deliver your thoughts as though you're trying to force your plot point or sidebar idea down her throat. Do put your suggestions out there; if you don't, you're doing your critique partner a disservice. Make sure you phrase them as just that—suggestions.

Ending With Encouragement

This last part is right up there with starting your critique by mentioning something you like about the submission. That first step can help reduce nervousness and fears in the author before the critique starts; this last step takes away some of the sting or shock she may have experienced *during* the critique. No matter how positive and supportive you make your suggestions, you are—in effect—telling the author how much she needs to change in her project.

Don't make a big deal about waving pom-poms or handing out trophies. Just take a minute to remind the author how far she's come, how much she's accomplished, and how much confidence you have that she's going to turn this book into something wonderful. Depending on her state of mind, she may or may not actually *believe* you. That's okay. She'll still feel better and more able to get back to work.

PRESENTING A CRITIQUE

The act of presenting a critique is probably the point at which an in-person group and an online group have the widest gap. In this section, I'll go over the basics of presenting a critique in person, many pieces of which will apply to online groups as well. Then I'll talk a bit more about the differences in delivering a critique online.

When it's your turn to critique, your job will be to do the following:

- remember your manners
- read the overall, big comment
- go through the page-by-page comments
- discuss the author's questions

Remembering Your Manners

Be polite. Think about what you're saying when you critique and how you want to present those words. How do *you* want to be critiqued? With respect and support and encouragement? Keep those same qualities in mind as you deliver your own critiques.

Always be conscious of the fact that this is not your book. You are not the author, you do not have final say on any changes to be made, and you are not there to change the story your critique partner is writing. Years ago, I took writing workshops from Oakley Hall, a novelist, teacher, and cofounder of the Community of Writers at Squaw Valley. In these classes, Oakley Hall defined a critiquer's job as helping another writer make *the writer's* book better. I completely agree with this definition.

Reading the Overall, Big Comments

The first priority during a critique goes to the overall comments you and the other critiquers have made. These are your ideas about how the plot is moving, how you're delivering the important information, whether the author's voice is showing up on the page. Each critiquer should take turn reading these comments out loud.

When it is your turn to read, don't just recite what you have written. Think back to when you were doing the actual critique; refocus yourself on the reactions you had at the time. As you read, listen to yourself and see if a new idea pops up that expands or further explains what you have written. This is one of the big advantages of an in-person critique group. Delivering a live critique gets the juices flowing, and you find yourself discovering something totally new—maybe even brilliant—to throw into the pot.

While you critique, remember the writer whose work you're talking about—keep an eye on him and watch his reactions. This is another advantage of meeting with your critique partners in person; you get a chance to see how well an author is receiving your suggestions. If he looks confused or as though he isn't following you, slow down and back up a little. Think of a new way to explain what you've gone over and watch for the lightbulb turning on above his head.

Don't interrupt the critique to ask if the writer has questions. If you think she's still not clear about your comments, offer to talk more about it when everyone else has had their turn. Another member of the group may have hit the same snag in the story you did and be ready to offer a solution. If not, the group can discuss it after everybody has had a chance to present their critiques.

Going Through the Page-by-Page Comments

After everybody has read their big ideas and suggestions, the group can decide whether to go through the smaller comments and notes everybody has written on individual pages. Whether you go through this part of the critique depends on a few things.

If you are running short of time, skip this step. It's not essential to point out a joke that wasn't funny enough or a place where the author accidentally changed a sports car to a pickup truck. You wrote these comments (neatly!) on the pages; the writer can easily read through the notes when she's ready to revise. If she has questions, she can e-mail you or pick up the phone and give you a call.

If you do decide to go through these smaller points, be careful not to get bogged down. You do *not* have to read every comment you wrote on every page. In fact, if you try, I guarantee you'll see the writer's eyes glaze over within seconds. Instead, focus on the most important notes, the ones you think may need some clarification or the ones that point to examples of a pattern you're seeing in the story. Use this time, just like the rest of the meeting, for helping the writer make progress—to get her on the right path toward revision.

Discussing the Author's Questions

If the writer has questions about someone's critique, take time to go over them. Letting someone leave confused or worried goes against the whole purpose of the critique group, which is to educate and support.

This is not always an easy part of the critique process. We're writers, which says we're good with words but not always *so* good when we don't have a pen or a keyboard to "speak" for us. Be patient with the writer while he tries to verbalize what he's confused about. Don't get defensive if he isn't dancing with joy about a suggestion you've made. A critique group is about give and take, about tossing ideas back and forth to give each writer new, constructive material. Listen to your partner's questions and do your best to clear things up and help him move forward in his story.

Presenting a Critique Online

For many online groups, the step is nothing more than sending a file across e-mail or uploading that file to a group site. For many writers, this is ideal. They feel they get to spend more time on their writing, and they don't have any problem sorting through the written critiques, understanding the comments, and making revision changes from the suggestions.

If, though, you are in an online group, or thinking about joining one, and you would like more of the personal connection to be found in an in-person group, there are steps you can take to get there. Make use of instant messaging or a chat room so you can actually discuss the critiques.

If your group prefers not to schedule regular critiquing time, you can still use these tools to "talk" about a critique the author found confusing or to do some brainstorming if somebody gets stuck. Keep in touch with each other between submissions and critiques as well. It's easy to send an e-mail to check on somebody's writing progress or to shout out when you've finished a tricky scene. Most of us spend *lots* of time online communicating with our other friends, and there's no reason not to support each other's writing journey the same way.

RECEIVING A CRITIQUE

Let's flip the coin now. When you're on the receiving end of a critique, you have your own responsibilities. Again, this step varies widely between an in-person and an online group. I'll start with the in-person process, but—just like in the previous section—read through it even if you're in an online group. You'll be able to apply a lot of the information to your own online experience.

When you receive a critique, you'll do the following tasks:

- remember *your* manners
- refrain from interrupting, explaining, or defending
- take notes

Remember Your Manners

The members of your group have just paid your writing the respect of spending time with it, giving serious thought to its strengths and weaknesses, and writing a critique they truly hope will prove helpful to you and your story. It's now your turn to return that respect and let them pass their comments and ideas on to you.

Really listen to what the members of the group are telling you. Yes, it's your story, but you don't know everything about it, and your critique partners are coming at your story as readers. They're closer to the people who will be buying (and *selling*) your book than you are. Give their suggestions the weight and value they deserve.

No Interrupting, Explaining, or Defending

If you hang around enough critiquers, you'll start to hear this rule. As the writer, you're supposed to stay absolutely silent until all the other group members have presented their critiques. You don't cut off a critiquer to ask questions, and you don't get to explain or defend your manuscript.

Bring out the duct tape.

Okay, not quite. But almost.

Stay silent as much as possible. Interruptions can throw off your critique partners, make them lose track of what they're saying, and make them uncomfortable about giving you their feedback. And if you have to explain your writing, that writing needs some work.

Again, these rules aren't set in stone. If you really don't understand what someone's saying, so much so that you are getting distracted from his critique or losing track of his suggestions, ask a quick question for clarification. Don't just jump in—raise a hand and wait until he's clearly finished the thought. Double-check the point you're confused about and then sit back, close your mouth, and let him continue his critique.

Taking Notes

Some people have great memories. Nobody's perfect, though, and when you're hearing a critique, you're processing as well as listening. Bring a notebook and pen to every meeting, and be ready to write down anything you really want to remember.

This isn't English class. You aren't going to be tested on the material, but you want to be able to absorb the feedback, take it home, and—at some later time—work it into your revision process. If one of your partners gets a new idea that wasn't in his original critique, write it down. If you get a spark, a thought that is taking you in a new direction, get it into the notebook. If you do ask for clarification, scribble down the words that will make the idea clear again when you go back to look at the original critique.

And when you get home, take time to rewrite or type those scribbles into a legible form. You may not revise for weeks, even months. If you can't remember the feedback or read your notes, all those ideas aren't going to do you a lot of good.

Receiving a Critique Online

If, in your online group, you've organized some kind of chat setup in which you and the other members can critique "together," everything you've read above applies to you. If you're using an instant messenger, don't cut into someone else's critique by throwing your thought into the middle of her post. If you disagree or have a question, wait your turn, just as if you were sitting around a physical table. Too often we forget that typing doesn't excuse rudeness. Take the same sensitve approach you'd use in person to send your critique across the Internet.

Take time to read thoroughly the other members' comments. "Listen" to what they're saying as carefully as you would if you could hear their voices and see their faces. Take notes and think about your questions before you present them—make sure you didn't miss something they've already said. Don't switch back and forth from your chat window to check a social networking site or see if you've received any new e-mail. It can be tempting, when you're online, to rush through a discussion, to get back to work. Well, a critique *is* work, important work, and doing it online doesn't change that fact.

Section I
Worksheet 1: Choosing the Right Type of Group

Use the questions on this worksheet as a guide to your own wants and needs. As you answer each question, you'll learn more about which kind of group you're looking for and which type feels most comfortable and most suited to your personality, location, and schedule.

🌻

Are you writing with a goal of someday reaching publication?

_____

_____

- If you answered *yes*, you will want to find a group whose members are also working to be published.

- If you answered *no*, you should look for a group whose members are comfortable just sharing their writing with each other and friends or family.

Do you live in a large city with access to in-person writing resources, or do you live in a rural area or small town with few local resources?

_____

_____

- If you answered *city*, you can choose to look for or start an in-person group, or you can decide to explore online options.

- If you answered *rural area* or *small town*, you may need to look for or start an online group.

Are you comfortable with the Internet? Are you familiar with e-mail, online discussion groups, and Internet forums, or if not, are you excited about taking on something new? Or maybe the Internet is something new you don't want to step into yet?

_____

_____

- If you answered that you *like or are interested in the Internet,* you should explore all the online opportunities for finding or starting a critique group.

- If you answered that you *aren't comfortable with the Internet,* you will probably want to spend your energy and time looking for or building a local group.

Are you focused on working in a specific genre, or are you exploring different kinds of writing?

_____

_____

- If you answered *genre,* you may want to find a group of writers also working in that genre to increase your knowledge and receive feedback from critique partners who read in that genre.

- If you answered different kinds, you can look for a group whose members are writing and reading in many genres.

Section I
Worksheet 2: Asking for a Writing Sample

If your group is going to request samples from applicants, it's a good idea to have a simple form to hand out. You can use this form as is or modify it to fit the needs of your group.

🔖

Thank you for your interest in joining our critique group. We ask all applicants to the group to submit a short writing sample. We have found that reading a few pages of an applicant's project is the best way for us to assess the compatibility of an author's writing with the work our members are doing.

We will not critique your submission. If we decide not to accept you into the group, it is not a judgment of your writing but only our attempt to find new members who are the best fit with our existing group.

Please submit a sample that meets the following guidelines:

- For fiction, choose a scene or chapter from your book or a complete short story.

- For nonfiction, choose a section or chapter from your book or a complete article.

- Format the submission to 12 point, Times New Roman, double-spaced, with page numbers. Place your name and e-mail address in the header.

- E-mail the submission to _____

We will get back to you as soon as possible. Thank you for considering our group.

Section I
Worksheet 3: Evaluating a Group to Join or a Critique Partner to Add

Use the questions on this worksheet to assess your level of comfort with a potential critique group or partner. Answer the questions truthfully, and let your answers guide your decision about staying with a group or inviting a critiquer to join the group you're in.

🔻

1. How long have the writer/writers been critiquing?

   _____

   _____

2. Where is/are the writer/writers on the publication path?

   _____

   _____

3. Do I feel relaxed with the other writer/writers? Yes/No

   _____

4. Does/do the other writer/writers seem interested in my critiques? Yes/No _____

5. Do I feel that my critiques make a contribution to the group/ writer? Yes/No _____

6. When I receive a critique, do I see new, helpful ways to approach my writing project? Yes/No _____

7. Do/does the writer/writers use the critique time productively, or do I feel like I'm wasting my time at the meeting?

   _____

   _____

8. Is/are the writer/writers submitting work steadily and consistently? Does the amount of critique work seem reasonable, or do I feel overloaded?

_____

_____

9. Do the other writers get along with each other, or is there tension between them?

_____

_____

10. When I leave the meeting, do I feel energized about writing, or do I feel tired and drained?

_____

_____

Section I
Worksheet 4: Project Summary

When you find a critique partner or add a new member to an existing group, it's a good idea to summarize the project each existing member is working on. You should also ask the new member to give you the same summary of her current work. You can use the form below to collect the important information.

🌱

Fiction Summary

1. My project is in this genre:

_____

_____

2. My hero, _____ wants:

_____

_____

3. The other main characters in my story are:

Character: _____ Role: _____

Character: _____ Role: _____

Character: _____ Role: _____

Character: _____ Role: _____

Character: _____ Role: _____

Character: _____ Role: _____

Character: _____ Role: _____

Character: _____ Role: _____

4. The big plot points in my project so far are:

_____

_____

5. The theme/premise of my project is:

_____

_____

Nonfiction Summary

1. My project is in this genre:

_____

_____

2. The subject matter of my project is:

_____

_____

3. Readers need this book/article because:

_____

_____

4. The main topics I have covered in my project so far are:

_____

_____

5. The theme/premise of my project is:

_____

_____

Section I
Worksheet 5: New-Applicant Form

It's a good idea, when you are ready to add a new member to your group, to get some basic information about your applicant. This form has some basic questions you can ask the applicant to answer; feel free to delete any or add some of your own.

🖋

1. Which genre are you writing in?

   _____

   _____

2. What are your writing goals?

   _____

   _____

3. Please describe the current project you're working on.

   _____

   _____

4. What stage are you at with your current project? (First draft—how many chapters? Revision?)

   _____

   _____

5. Have you been in a critique group before? Yes/No _____

   _____

6. What happened to that group? If you left the group, can you tell us why?

_____

_____

7. What do you hope to get out of a critique group?

_____

_____

TELLING THE STORY:
HOW TO CRITIQUE FICTION
(FOR ADULT, YOUNG-ADULT, AND
MIDDLE-GRADE READERS)

A work of fiction, long or short, is made up of many inter-woven elements. At any gathering of writers, you'll hear talk about which element is the most important. Does plot or characterization drive the story? Do readers want beautiful setting or active dialogue? Should an author focus on point of view or dialogue?

The answer to all of the above is yes. A writer's job is to pay attention to all of the pieces and use them to create a balanced, well-paced, layered story. A critiquer's job is to help the writer do that.

In this section, I'll talk to you about how to critique each of these elements: plot, character, point of view, dia-logue, setting, scene structure, and voice. For simplicity's sake, I'll be talking about each piece in a different chapter, as though it exists as a distinct, separate part of a story.

You, of course, will know that that isn't really how it works.

When you do a critique, when you sit down to read a critique partner's pages and write out your thoughts and suggestions, you'll merge everything you learn in this book. You'll read not just for the separate parts but for the balance between them. You'll watch for the places where plot wipes out character or setting takes over from action.

For now, as you read the chapters in this section, concentrate on the specifics. Focus on what's important about plot, character, and all the rest. When you do a real, full critique, all the pieces will come together.

I promise.

This section is set up to make it easy for you to learn how to critique fiction. Each chapter gives you a basic explanation of common writing problems and then teaches you how to search for the reasons behind the problems. You'll look at passages from real books to see examples of strong writing. You'll also read excerpts from a sample, made-up piece of fiction that's included at the end of this introduction. Throughout the chapters, you'll use that sample to practice what you're learning, and, at the end of each chapter, you'll read through an example critique. Finally, you can use the worksheet at the end of the chapter to do your own critique of the sample or to get started on the critiques you do for your writing group.

CRITIQUING FICTION—WRITING SAMPLE

Read through the sample now and then refer back to it whenever you want to refresh your memory.

Chapter X

I turned the corner after Maguire and found myself in a dark, smelly alley that ran between the shops.

The concrete was shaded from the buildings. The wall on my left was made of bricks. It was tall, maybe two stories. The wall on my right was shingles, blue ones. Some paint had flaked off some of the shingles. There were two windows in this wall, and one in the brick wall. I touched the brick wall, and it was cold. Someone moved inside the window opposite me, and I heard people talking. A cat turned into the alley, walked past Maguire, and then passed me.

Maguire must have heard my footsteps, because he stopped, then turned.

"What are you doing, Collins?" he asked me. "I told you I didn't want to talk to you."

"You did," I answered.

"And I got nothing to say, anyway."

I looked at him and leaned against the wall. The brick was cold, shaded by the tall building across the alley. I tucked a stray curl of hair into the band holding the rest off my face.

A car backfired in the street outside the alley. I listened as the engine grew quieter, as the car drove farther away. The curl fell out of the band again, and I ignored it.

"Leave me alone," Maguire said. He was taller than me, with brown hair cut short. He wore a sweatshirt and jeans, and his sneakers were white, with a hole in the toe of the left one. He folded his arms across his belly and glared at me.

"I've got nothing else to do today," I told him.

Maguire stared at me, then checked his watch. He tapped it a couple of times. Maybe the battery had died.

I let myself slip down the wall until I was sitting on the cement. I stretched my legs out in front of me and tilted my head back against the wall.

Maguire shuffled from foot to foot, then checked his watch again. Finally, he said, "I'm out of here," and he took off down the alley.

I watched him go. I could have caught him if I'd tried. It wouldn't have even taken a sprint. But I was tired. Tired of asking questions, tired of seeing his fear. I stayed where I was, against the wall.

...

The bar was a sports bar. A mirror lined the wall behind the back of the bar, and tall, solitary bar stools lined the front. Three men occupied the stools, looking a lot like Goldilocks' three bears. One was big, with a thick Afro and a padded blue jacket. The middle-sized one was a redhead with glasses and a pipe, and the little one wore the loudest Hawaiian shirt I'd ever seen.

Just as I came in, a tall, skinny woman with gray and purple hair stuck a quarter in the jukebox, and Elvis greeted my entrance with "Jailhouse Rock." The woman swung away from the machine and jitterbugged her way back across the room, stopping to talk to an elderly couple that looked like they'd been in those chairs since the turn of the century. The last century. She shook their hands between steps, then danced all the way to her table, spinning a circle around her chair before she sat down.

The room was filled with tables, filled with people. All colors of the rainbow, both in skin and clothes, including two waitresses. The lamps over the tables had panels of fake stained glass—ugly reds and blues and yellows. There were big-screen TVs in all four corners. The same picture of the same newscaster was up on all of them. The floor was dirty, with peanut shells and various liquids spilled onto it.

The martini was dry. Too dry, but it wasn't worth the effort it would take to call the bartender back over. I sipped it and made a face, watching myself in the mirror behind the bar and thinking it was obvious why I'd scared Maguire away. Ugly. Bone ugly. I took another sip. Still too dry.

The waitress stopped and checked out the glass, ready to offer a refill, but saw I didn't need topping off. Before she could move away, I held up a hand, then lifted the glass and drained it.

"Another one, please," I said.

She smiled and took the glass. I frowned. I knew her. My eyes squinted back at me in the bar as I thought, then remembered. She was Maguire's girl. I'd seen them on Monday at the Italian restaurant around the corner, giggling over cheap red wine and bread sticks. That was the day after the cops found the body.

She brought me another martini. I nodded and thanked her, then watched as she moved away between the tables. Two guys behind me were arguing over who would buy the next round of beers. A dog came out of a corner and barked three times, then ran to the bar and dipped his head into a bowl of water waiting on the floor for him.

Murder. It really stunk.

By the time I was finished drinking, just about everybody else had split or fallen asleep. I stepped around the bodies and the puddles of beer and made my way outside, where the air was cooler and fresher but still felt like it was trying to choke me.

I pulled up the hood on my jacket, shoved my hands in my pockets, and headed around the corner.

Where Maguire's girlfriend waited for me.

"Maguire told me to give this to you." She held out a manila envelope, thick enough to hold a big stack of papers or photos. Or money.

I took it. "Okay," I said.

"He wants you to meet him," she went on. "He's holed up at the Nite Inn, down Fifty-Seventh Street." Slinging her purse over her shoulder, she said, "It's only a few blocks. I'll show you."

I took some steps. She walked quickly and checked back every few seconds to make sure I was following.

I was.

Twenty minutes later, she was knocking on the last door of a sad, paint-peeling building. Maguire opened the door and jerked his head at me. "Come on in," he said. "Let's talk."

...

I looked at the inside of the apartment. I saw that there was no kitchen. I smelled things like cat pee, sweat, and moldy vegetables. I walked around, noticing that Maguire had a lot of empty fast-food bags and soda cans. They lay on the floor. The room was square. It had two doorways. One was open, and I could see that there was a bathroom behind it. The other doorway didn't have a door on it. The closet had a pile of dirty clothes on the floor. There was a TV next to the closet.

I was tired. I looked at Maguire. He was dirty, too, like the room. He was smoking a cigarette, and he looked pretty happy. He had invited me here, and now I was waiting for him to tell me why. I felt a mix of anger and impatience, but I knew I had to stick around and hear him out.

Maguire saw me looking at the mess. He grinned around the cigarette hanging from his mouth, pulled his stained sweatshirt over his head, and tossed it onto the heap.

"Better?" he asked.

I shrugged. He could talk, or he could play games. He'd brought me here. I could wait all night if he had the time.

"Stohl," he said. "You want to know where he is."

Did I? Another wave of fatigue hit me. Despite the smell, the wall I was leaning against felt pretty good. The idea of my bed at home, the mattress thick and soft, sounded even better. "Sure," I said. "Whatever."

Maguire scowled. "It'll cost you five hundred."

I pushed myself off the wall. "You got a pen and paper?" I asked, yanking open a drawer in the tiny desk next to me. "Draw me a map."

Maguire stepped closer to me, then took the cigarette out of his mouth and flicked the ashes off the end. They landed on my shirt.

I rustled around in the desk, shoving aside piles of paper clips, candy wrappers, and two guns. "How far from here is Stohl?" I asked.

"Hey," Maguire called to the girl. "You got a pen?"

The girl checked her fingernails, then pulled a file out of her purse. She buffed the nail on one index finger and put the file away.

"Hey!" Maguire shouted. "A pen?!"

I slammed the drawer shut so hard it popped out again and fell onto the floor, spilling its contents. I reached down, grabbed the gun that had landed at my feet, and whipped it up against Maguire's temple.

"Don't talk to her like that," I told him.

He grinned. "It's not loaded."

I grinned back. "So?" I lifted my arm and, in one quick slash, brought the gun down on the back of his head. He dropped to the floor, sending paper clips skidding under the couch and into the mess of fast-food bags.

"That fingernail okay now?" I asked the girl.

...

"That's it," Maguire said. "You're on your own." He slid back out the door and into the alley. He was gone.

"Come in, please," Stohl said.

I sat in the other chair, his desk between us. "Thanks for seeing me," I told him.

"You're welcome." He rubbed his chin. He hadn't shaved today. Or maybe he just should have shaved again.

Stohl leaned forward. "You hungry?" he asked. "Want some coffee?"

"No, thanks." I yawned. "I want to sleep tonight."

He nodded. "Good of Maguire to bring you by so late."

"Good, ha. It cost me four hundred to get to you. And I still owe him another hundred."

"Four hundred dollars. You must really have wanted to see me." His voice went quiet. "Why?"

This was it. I took a breath and started talking. "On Wednesday, I was talking to a butcher on First Street. He wanted to hire me to find his wife. Whatever. When I left, this kid Sully followed me. He told me about his problem, which is that he found some CDs in the alley behind the butcher shop and took them home. He copied them onto his MP3 player. A couple of days after that, he was chased when he left work. There were three men and a big dog. He lost them in a video arcade. Sully says the dog is yours. He wants me to talk to you and tell you he'll give the CDs back. Sully's afraid of you."

"Sully's got nothing to fear from me," Stohl said.

"Really?" I asked.

"Of course not. He can bring those CDs to me anytime. Say, next week."

"I can pass your answer on to him," I told him.

"You do that."

I pushed my chair back and got up.

Stohl stood, then walked around to the front of his desk. He stopped and leaned against it, looking at me for a moment. "So," he said. "You're a detective."

I shrugged. "Most of the time."

"You like the work?" he asked.

Like? "Nobody invited me to be a gourmet chef," I said.

A short laugh got past his lips.

"I got a nephew," he said. "He's talking about starting his own agency. I tell him there's a lot of late hours." He pushed himself off the desk and walked me to the door. "Have a good one, then."

"Sure," I said and went to tell Sully the good news.

...

I'd told Sully I'd wait for him at the park the next morning, to give him whatever news I had. I'd finally gotten a few hours sleep, and I'd managed to find clean underwear to put on, so I was feeling pretty good. I sat in the last intact swing on the swing set and pushed with my feet until I was gliding back and forth. In the sandbox a few feet away, two toddlers pushed trucks back and forth, and their older brother buried dinosaurs and dug them back up. Every now and then a dinosaur got a ride in a truck.

The sun was shining, and a robin sat in the tree above me, singing. As if in answer, I heard the ice cream van jingling down a street somewhere, probably only a few blocks away. I decided that, if the van was around when Sully showed up, I'd buy us both some ice cream. It was never too early for Rocky Road.

I might even let him push me down the slide.

Two mothers walked by with their strollers, talking. The babies were talking, too; at least, they were waving their hands back and forth at each other and making gentle squawking noises, kind of like chickens pecking around in a big scattering of grain. I waved a finger at them all, but nobody noticed. I guess their conversations were all too fascinating.

The babies chattered away, playing with the toys on the stroller bar and digging for the rattles beneath their blankets. The wind picked up and tousled what little hair they had, and dust swirled up around the stroller wheels. Mary smiled at Liza, glad to be out in the early spring sunshine, then reached down and tucked the blanket more snugly around her daughter.

Sully turned the corner at the end of the street. I waved—my arm this time—until he saw me. He wasn't happy. He'd expected me to bring Stohl or one of Stohl's goons with me so he could hand off the CDs in public—with me for protection. Now he was mad that he'd come to the park for nothing.

He came up to the swing and looked at me.

"Step back," I said. Then I took a couple of big swings and, at the peak of the arc, jumped off and landed in the dirt. On my feet. Yes!

"Nice," Sully said.

He didn't mean it.

Chapter 4

CRITIQUING FOR PLOT

Plot is so many things. On the most basic level, it is the actions and events that take place in a story. On a larger scale, plot is the interwoven web that causes the main character to grow and change over the course of that story. And somewhere in the middle of those definitions, plot is cause and effect, what-if, and all the conflict that makes a reader turn pages fast to see what will happen next.

Many writing groups work by critiquing a single chapter at each meeting. If your group uses this structure, you see only a small chunk of the plot at a time. Critiquing pieces of plot can be tricky, but the longer you stay with a group, the more of every book you'll see. You'll get a better understanding of the basics of each plot and the direction in which the writers are taking their stories. You'll be able to remember what's come before and imagine what may be coming next.

RECOGNIZING THE WEAK SPOTS

In this chapter, we'll talk about how to look for the different plot elements in individual scenes and chapters. And we'll discuss the best way to do one aspect of your critique job—to help your critique partners produce the strongest, most tightly drawn plot they can.

The following list shows some possible reactions you may have to a story or a scene:

- The story moves too slowly.
- You don't feel any tension.
- The events in the story feel disconnected.
- The story feels too light or shallow.
- You find yourself confused by the story action.
- You forget about the hero.
- You're bored or frustrated.

If you are reading for a critique, and you feel one or more of these responses, you may very well have found a plot weakness.

ANALYZING THE WEAKNESSES

Once you've identified a plot weakness—once you recognize a passage or a scene that is making you uncomfortable with the story—it's time to do some thinking. You want to be able to tell your critique partner why the plot isn't working, and you want to be able to offer suggestions for improving it.

The following list shows some of the common plot problems you'll see when you critique:

- The hero doesn't pursue a goal.
- The plot doesn't present the hero with enough obstacles.
- Actions and events happen without a story reason.
- Subplots are missing or disconnected from the main plot.

The Hero Doesn't Pursue a Goal

Perhaps the most important piece of an irresistible plot is the hero's goal. To catch and keep the reader's interest, we must give our hero a story goal. A goal can be anything, really. Maybe the hero wants to find true love, or climb to the top of a corporate ladder, or find the perfect pet (which is probably just a variation on the true-love theme). Whatever the goal, however, the hero has to really, *really* want it.

How does a writer show that the hero wants his goal? We make that hero work for it. We write scene after scene in which our hero reaches for that goal, takes a step toward it, and doesn't give up when the first (or second or third or tenth) attempt fails.

S.J. Rozan, a brilliant mystery writer, has created one of the most active, goal-oriented heroes—Lydia Chin—ever to stride across a page. Lydia's focus and determination leap out of her stories. If Lydia has to wait for something to happen *to* her, she talks or paces or takes a martial-arts class. The minute Lydia can do something, anything, she does.

In *Reflecting the Sky*, a child is kidnapped, and Lydia and her partner, Bill, are trying to find him. The father has been sent to the temple to wait for instructions.

> I glanced at my watch ... "We have a little time. Let's do what we can."

> Bill took off his jacket and tie and bought a cheap Adidas knock-off bag to stuff them into. He slipped on his sunglasses and bought a new black baseball cap that said HONG KONG in bright colors. In the next stall he picked up a disposable camera. That was about all we could do for him. I bought a big straw hat and a loose blue flowered shirt …
>
> I pointed to another row of stalls, permanent ones with the same metal roll-down doors merchants use to guard against evildoers in New York. At this busy time of day, almost all the doors were up, the fortune-tellers open for business. "You stay here and wait for him. Try to look just like another pushy rude American tourist. Think you can do that?"
>
> "In my sleep," Bill said. "Where are you going?"
>
> "To get my fortune told."

Everything Lydia does in this scene is directed at learning something that will help her find the child. She goes to the temple against the father's request. She buys new clothes to hide the ones he saw her and Bill wearing earlier. She finds places for herself and Bill to merge into the crowd so the kidnapper won't notice them. A page or two later, she pays a fortune-teller three times his going rate to let her take up space at his stall.

Writing an active hero is not an easy job. An author can get so caught up in creating the other parts of a scene—the setting, the characters, the voice—that she forgets to keep her hero pushing forward. How many of us have set our hero down at a coffeehouse, or a kitchen table, then written a scene where that hero does nothing but sip tea and think or maybe talk with another character about everything that's *already* happened? As a critiquer, your job is to help the other writers in your group keep their heroes focused and active.

Remember the sample chapter you read at the beginning of this section? Let's take a closer look at a piece of it.

> The waitress stopped and checked out the glass, ready to offer a refill, but saw I didn't need topping off. Before she could move away, I held up a hand and then lifted the glass and drained it.
>
> "Another one, please," I said.
>
> She smiled and took the glass. I frowned. I knew her. My eyes squinted back at me in the bar as I thought and then remembered. She was Maguire's girl. I'd seen them on Monday at the Italian restaurant around the corner, giggling over cheap

red wine and bread sticks. That was the day after the cops
found the body.

She brought me another martini. I nodded and thanked
her, then watched as she moved away between the tables. Two
guys behind me were arguing over who would buy the next
round of beers. A dog came out of a corner, barked three times,
then ran to the bar and dipped his head into a bowl of water
waiting on the floor for him.

Murder. It really stunk.

Maguire's girlfriend is right there, bringing Collins another drink, but what does
Collins do? Nothing. She doesn't ask the waitress if she knows anything about
the murder, and she doesn't try to get Maguire's address out of her. She lets the
waitress walk away, then turns back to her drink and watches the random hap-
penings in the bar around her.

Here are a few comments that you, as a critiquer, might make about
this scene:

- Collins seems a little passive in this scene. Could Collins stop the
  waitress and ask her some questions?

- Does the waitress need to be Maguire's girlfriend? If she doesn't
  have information for Collins, maybe she should just be a waitress.

- Is this the right scene for the girlfriend to show up in? It's confusing
  to watch Collins recognize her and then ignore her. Is there a better
  scene where you could introduce this character?

The Plot Doesn't Present the Hero With Enough Obstacles

In the earlier section, we talked about a writer needing to create a hero that
readers will care about. One way for a writer to make this happen is, as we said,
to show the hero going after a goal. The other way for the writer to do this is
to make it very hard for the hero to reach that goal. The writer needs to throw
obstacles at his hero—lots and lots of them.

When a reader picks up a book, he may be escaping from his own too-
complicated world. Does this mean he wants a calm, peaceful story? No. He
wants to see someone else battling with life. He wants problems and tension
and conflict.

Do the math: Goal + Obstacles = Conflict.

Obstacles aren't always sad or scary or violent. They can be funny, too. Bertie Wooster, P. G. Wodehouse's most famous hero, wants nothing but a life of ease and bachelorhood. In "Without the Option," Bertie visits a family in which the aunt (mistakenly) thinks he tortures cats, and the niece has her eye on him as the perfect fiancé. His goal is to find some peace and quiet in the summerhouse. First the aunt shows up and then the niece.

> I had just got … [the cat] in my arms and was scratching it under
> the ear when there was a loud shriek from above, and there was
> Aunt Jane half out the window. Dashed disturbing.
>
> …
>
> I dropped the cat … and … worked round till I got to the
> summer-house. And, believe me, I had hardly got my first ciga-
> rette nicely under way when a shadow fell on my book and there
> was young Sticketh-Closer-Than-a-Brother in person.
>
> …
>
> "You're always smoking," she said, a lot too much like a
> lovingly chiding young bride for my comfort.

Bertie's lifelong goal is to enjoy life and remain single. Luckily for us, Wodehouse is equally as determined to get in the way of that goal. In this scene, Bertie, who truly likes cats, barely has time for a quick pat before the aunt's scream breaks up his peaceful interlude with the animal. His brief escape into the summer-house is just as quickly interrupted by a young woman who is everything Bertie fears—ready, willing, and able to mold him into a "better" man.

For a writer, the job of creating obstacles isn't always an easy one. Like the reader, we are rooting for our own hero, and we can sometimes get so caught up in moving that hero toward a goal that we forget to make his journey difficult. As a critiquer, you can point out the places where the hero has it too easy. And you can come up with helpful ideas about how the writer can make her hero really work.

Let's check back with Collins, the PI from our sample chapter.

> By the time I was finished drinking, just about everybody else
> had split or fallen asleep. I stepped around the bodies and the

puddles of beer and made my way outside, where the air was cooler and fresher but still felt like it was trying to choke me.

I pulled up the hood on my jacket, shoved my hands in my pockets, and headed around the corner.

Where Maguire's girlfriend waited for me.

"Maguire told me to give this to you." She held out a manila envelope, thick enough to hold a big stack of papers or photos. Or money.

I took it. "Okay," I said.

"He wants you to meet him," she went on. "He's holed up at the Nite Inn, down Fifty-Seventh Street." Slinging her purse over her shoulder, she said, "It's only a few blocks. I'll show you."

I took some steps. She walked quickly and checked back every few seconds to make sure I was following.

I was.

Twenty minutes later, she was knocking on the last door of a sad, paint pooling building. Maguire opened the door and jerked his head at me. "Come on in," he said. "Let's talk."

We've already seen Collins let Maguire run away and avoid conversation with the waitress. In this passage, it's as though Maguire and his girlfriend are tired of waiting for the PI to do anything for herself. The waitress lets Collins drink as long as she wants, waits patiently for her to leave the bar, and then practically holds her hand to get her to Maguire. Maguire starts talking before Collins even opens her mouth, ready to tell her anything she might need to know. In this scene, Collins doesn't work to reach her goal—she doesn't have to.

If you were critiquing this scene, the following comments might show up in your critique:

- You may be making it too easy for Collins. It seems as though Maguire and his girlfriend are doing all the work. I'm not seeing Collins deal with any obstacles here, so I'm having problems believing she'll solve this murder.

- I think you need to add some problems to Collins' life in this scene. What if Collins asks the waitress to take her to Maguire's motel, and the waitress refuses because she's too scared to get involved? Or what if Collins tries to follow the waitress, then gets lost because she doesn't know the city?

- Do you want us to know what's in the envelope? What if it *is* money? Or even drugs? The contents could create a problem that Collins has to deal with before she goes to see Maguire.

Action and Events Happen Without a Story Reason

What is a story reason? As we said earlier, a plot is a sequence of actions and events. These actions and events—called plot points—come one after another from the start of a story to the end. However, these plot points cannot be random. Every major plot point has to have its roots at another moment in the story. That other moment, that root, is the plot point's story reason.

Let's say you're reading a book about a man searching for his family history. He was born in California and finds out that his grandparents came there years ago from Paris. He goes to a travel agency and books a flight for France. Then, in the next scene, he's sitting on a horse, watching ostriches run across the land in Australia. The story has given you no reason for the man to have fled Down Under.

The story reason doesn't always have to come first. You might read three more pages in this book and find out that the man's plane was hijacked, or that he made an impulse decision at the airport to head south. A writer who holds back the reason can add suspense and tension to a scene. Somewhere, though, within the story, the reader must be able to find a reason for this action.

Another way to explain story reason is to say that events or actions have to be connected by cause and effect. One action is the cause; another is the effect. If the hero in the above example had gotten on that plane to Paris, the reader would know the man made the trip *because* he learned the city was his grandparents' home. The reader would see the clear cause-and-effect connection.

In Joshilyn Jackson's novel, *Between, Georgia*, the story reasons behind the characters' actions go back years, even decades. Jackson does a brilliant job of tying every plot point into something that has come before or will come after.

At the beginning of the book, Nonny returns home to Between. Just before she steps into the house, she does a quick check.

> I didn't know if Bernese was inside or still down at the jail, but I took a moment to dig down to the bottom of my purse and make sure I had my empty bottle. It was an amber plastic cylinder, safety-capped in white. If Bernese was home, I might need it.

At this point in the story, we have no idea what that cylinder is, or why Nonny might need it. By this time, though, Jackson has our trust, and we're willing to wait. Some chapters later, Bernese starts in on Nonny about the divorce, accusing her of giving up on her marriage and family.

> ... I went and got my purse anyway. I dug around in it until I found the empty amber bottle I had carried with me for a year now. I set it on the coffee table with an audible click, and then I sat back down by Mama and gave her my hands again.
>
> "What's that?" Bernese said.
>
> "That's why I'm getting divorced," I said. I sounded very matter-of-fact, almost abrupt, but looking at it, this innocuous cylinder of brownish-gold plastic, safety-capped to protect the babies I didn't have, almost undid me.
>
> ... She picked it up off the table and read the label. "Penicillin? What has penicillin got to—" The nurse in her kicked in then, and I saw her put it together in her head.
>
> ... I felt myself flushing. "I don't see a way back from going to your doctor's office and being told that no, actually, you don't have a urinary tract infection from all the sex you've been having, trying to conceive. You have syphilis."

Jackson gives us the pill vial in one scene, and then later—at just the right moment—she delivers the story reason. Nonny knows she'll need to prove to Bernese that she knows what she's doing, that she does have an excellent reason for divorcing her husband. She keeps the vial in her purse so she'll be ready for the confrontation.

Let's take another look at our own writing sample.

> I let myself slip down the wall until I was sitting on the cement. I stretched my legs out in front of me and tilted my head back against the wall.
>
> Maguire shuffled from foot to foot, then checked his watch again. Finally, he said, "I'm out of here," and he took off down the alley.
>
> I watched him go. I could have caught him if I'd tried. It wouldn't have even taken a sprint. But I was tired. Tired of asking questions, tired of seeing his fear. I stayed where I was, against the wall.

...

> The bar was a sports bar. A mirror lined the wall behind
> the back of the bar, and tall, solitary bar stools lined the front.
> Three men occupied the stools, looking a lot like Goldilocks'
> three bears. One was big, with a thick Afro and a padded blue
> jacket. The middle-sized one was a red-head with glasses and
> a pipe, and the little one wore the loudest Hawaiian shirt I'd
> ever seen.

What did you feel when you read through this passage? You probably got a bit confused about where you were and how you (and Collins) got there. You may have gotten distracted, looking for the story reason, even going back to the whole sample to reread the first paragraphs. You might have skipped ahead, hoping to find an explanation.

You didn't find it. One moment, Collins is slumped down in the alley; the next, she's in a sports bar inhabited by fairy-tale characters. And you, as a reader, don't know why she moved from one place to the other. Within the pages that we have in our sample, the writer has provided no story reason for Collins to be sitting on that bar stool.

At this point, you may be saying, "But wait. Look at Collins. She's obviously the type to go get a stiff drink after a disappointment, a failure." And you may be right. That, however, is a character reason. Character reasons are important, and we'll be talking about them in chapter five, "Critiquing for Character." What you need to know now is that a character reason is not enough. The fact that a hero *might* take an action is not an explanation of why, within the context of the story you're reading, she *does* take that action.

Let's look at some comments you, as a critiquer, might want to make about this passage.

- Why is Collins at the bar? Did she make a decision in the alley to go get a drink? Maybe you could show her making that decision in the earlier scene?

- Is this a bar that Maguire goes to a lot? Does Collins know this? When she decides to let him get away in the earlier scene, you may want to give us a hint that she knows where to find him.

- I got a bit confused when I started reading the scene at the bar. I thought we'd left Collins in the alley, so it took me a while before

I realized the "I" on the bar stool *was* Collins. You might want to make clear that we're still with the PI.

Subplots Are Missing or Disconnected From the Main Plot

Do you want the bad news or the good news first? The bad news is that one plot isn't enough. The good news, though, makes up for it—well-written subplots add an almost magical fullness to fiction. They build in layers of action and reaction and create a story with the depth a reader wants.

A subplot is any story line that plays (sometimes just barely) second fiddle to the primary story. A subplot has the same basic elements we've been talking about for plot—a character has a goal and must deal with lots of obstacles.

A subplot doesn't have to be attached to a secondary character. The hero can have a plot and a subplot. A mystery detective, like our Collins, has to solve a crime, but she may have a family problem to work out as well. A romance hero may be struggling to find true love at the same time that she is worried about getting a promotion at work.

The most important thing to remember about a subplot is that it does not and cannot exist in a vacuum. Every subplot in a story has to connect in some way to the main plot.

In a historical novel, even a major event can become a subplot. In Rosemary Wells' YA novel, *Red Moon at Sharpsburg*, India Moody's goal has her pushing against the limits of what a woman can do. She wants to study science and to research bacteria. The Civil War, looming huge and destructive on almost every page, becomes a subplot to India's story. It kills her father and sends her mother into illness, but it also opens possibilities for India's future. Emory Trimble, who teaches India chemistry, asks her to work as his laboratory assistant after the war.

> "When? When will the war be over?" I ask him. I avoid asking just exactly how this is going to be accomplished.
>
> "Soon," he says. "Not too long. We will lose, of course. The North has as many soldiers as ants in an anthill ... We are going to lose. A quarter of our young men will be dead and another maimed. And the old men will talk of honor. It is all such a lie."
>
> I pout my lip but don't argue.
>
> "There will be a new day," says Emory. "The war will be the end of more than slavery. Women are going to do all kinds of

things they were never allowed to do. Right now there are women in the North demanding the right to vote. There'll be more and more of them parading and writing after the war. They'll get the vote. They'll pry it out of the men's hands. Women will go to college, own property, everything. You wait and see."

I try and think of this new day. "Do you really want me to be with you?" I whisper. "Because, Emory, I have the money. I have the money to study at Oberlin."

"How can you have that money?"

"I just found it on the battlefield at Sharpsburg."

He doesn't ask how.

In truth, India took the money off a dead soldier while she was searching for her father. The subplot of the war's violence and death connects with her main plot—the money she gives her mother means India doesn't have to stay and take care of her. The money gives India the freedom to leave. On top of that, the war's subplot impacts India's main goal—to go to college and study science—by creating new possibilities for her as a woman.

Let's have a final look at the plot in our writing sample.

Maguire must have heard my footsteps because he stopped, then turned.

"What are you doing, Collins?" he asked me. "I told you I didn't want to talk to you."

"You did," I answered.

"And I got nothing to say, anyway."

I looked at him and leaned against the wall. The brick was cold, shaded by the tall building across the alley. I tucked a stray curl of hair into the band holding the rest off my face.

A car backfired in the street outside the alley. I listened as the engine grew quieter, as the car drove farther away. The curl fell out of the band again, and I ignored it.

"Leave me alone," Maguire said. He was taller than me, with brown hair cut short. He wore a sweatshirt and jeans, and his sneakers were white, with a hole in the toe of the left one. He folded his arms across his belly and glared at me.

"I've got nothing else to do today," I told him.

Maguire stared at me, then checked his watch. He tapped it a couple of times. Maybe the battery had died.

> I let myself slip down the wall until I was sitting on the ce-
> ment. I stretched my legs out in front of me and tilted my head
> back against the wall.
>
> Maguire shuffled from foot to foot, then checked his watch
> again. Finally, he said, "I'm out of here," and he took off down
> the alley.

In our short sample, we see Maguire twice—in this scene and again, later, when his girlfriend brings Collins to the motel. He's most likely a major secondary character; he needs a subplot.

In this scene, Maguire talks and fidgets. He's clearly tense about being with Collins, but the writer has given us no information about why he's nervous. As a reader, you could guess—maybe he's afraid of the killer—but a reader shouldn't have to guess. Maguire's dialogue doesn't show us where he would rather be or why. Maguire needs a goal, the goal needs obstacles, and the writer needs to show these on the page.

If you were reading this scene for someone in your writing group, here are a few critique comments you might make:

- Who is Maguire? What is his connection to the murder?

- Maguire looks at his watch a lot. This makes me feel as though he is late for an appointment or has somewhere else he wants to be. Could you use the dialogue between Collins and Maguire to give us some information about that?

- What is Maguire's subplot goal? When Collins chases him into this alley, is this an obstacle to that goal? How? What can Maguire say or do that gives us an idea about that goal or shows him trying to get past this obstacle? Could Collins do something that makes the problem worse for Maguire?

Chapter 5

CRITIQUING FOR CHARACTER

How many times have you been told to create characters your readers *care* about? A hundred? A thousand? However often you've heard or read it, you can never be reminded too often. Characters are the glue that hold your book together, the pieces of your story that give it depth and multiple layers. Readers buy series books because they fall in love with the heroes, and they return to their favorite stand-alone authors because of those writers' ability to bring characters alive on the page.

When you're critiquing for character, you face some of the same challenges that you deal with in critiquing plot. You can find both characterization strengths and weaknesses in single passages and scenes, but you'll also need to watch how a character develops over the length of the whole story. In this chapter, we'll talk about some of the character elements you want to be watching for when you critique part or all of a manuscript and, of course, whenever you write.

RECOGNIZING THE WEAK SPOTS

Because the characters are so critical to your engagement as a reader, you'll have some strong reactions as you critique when you come to passages where the characters fall flat. Also, because characters build across story, your reactions to poor characterization will feel worse the more pages you turn. The following list shows some of the possible responses you'll have as you read about the people in a story:

- You get bored with what the characters are saying and doing.
- You lose track of which character you're reading about.
- You get angry at a character.

- You feel frustrated.
- You find it easy to put the book down.

If you are reading for a critique, and you feel one or more of these responses, you may very well have found a character weakness.

ANALYZING THE WEAKNESSES

Here are some of the common problems that can cause a character weakness:

- A character isn't complex enough.
- Characters don't show enough reaction.
- A character behaves inconsistently.
- A character doesn't grow.

In the following sections, we'll take a closer look at each of these problems, and you'll learn how to recognize some causes behind those characterization weaknesses you're sensing.

A Character Isn't Complex Enough

A character isn't a real person, but every character needs to come off the page as if he or she *were* real. In fact, readers often require characters to be more real than anyone they might actually meet on the street. If you talk to somebody for fifteen minutes, odds are you won't get much of a glimpse into his personality. By the time a reader has been into a book for fifteen minutes, though, she *must* have a sense that the main characters, at least, are complicated, with many pieces. Otherwise she's probably going to put that book down and walk away from it.

As a writer, you need to make sure your hero isn't all good and your villains aren't all bad. Even your secondary characters must have conflict within them to keep your reader hooked.

As a critiquer, it's your job to help your partners develop all the depth their characters need.

The people in Joshilyn Jackson's book, *Between, Georgia*, are wonderful examples of layered, complex characters. She has developed each personality to its fullest so that readers see all the layers these characters bring to the story. Nonny's aunt, Genny, is a fragile, fearful woman, emotionally dependent on Nonny's blind and deaf mother, Eustacia. Underneath all Genny's anxiety and terror, though, is an iron rod of strength that keeps her character from being too simple or flat. She refuses to let anyone hide things from her sister. Nonny describes a typical confrontation between Genny and Nonny's other aunt, Bernese:

> ... I couldn't lie to [Mama]. That was Genny's rule. If it happened in Mama's presence, if it happened in the room with her, Genny insisted that we never hide it. Bernese still refused to get that, and 80 percent of our ugliest family fights began with Bernese saying, "Don't say this to Eustacia, but ..." While she was saying it, Genny would be simultaneously signing, *Don't say this to Eustacia, but ...* into Mama's hand.

Genny goes beyond declaring and arguing. She actively prevents Bernese from breaking her rule. Contrasted with the Genny who flutters her way through life, who is so anxious she picks and tears at her own skin, this strength shows a Genny who is made up of real, true opposites.

If we go back to our sample scene, we'll get a look at a character who's not nearly as developed. In chapter four, we talked about the fact that Collins doesn't do enough to go after her goal. She lets opportunities (and people) escape. Look at this passage:

> Maguire saw me looking at the mess. He grinned around the cigarette hanging from his mouth, pulled his stained sweatshirt over his head, and tossed it onto the heap.
>
> "Better?" he asked.
>
> I shrugged. He could talk, or he could play games. He'd brought me here. I could wait all night if he had the time.
>
> "Stohl," he said. "You want to know where he is."
>
> Did I? Another wave of fatigue hit me. Despite the smell, the wall I was leaning against felt pretty good. The idea of my bed at home, the mattress thick and soft, sounded even better. "Sure," I said. "Whatever."

By this point, Collins' character is getting a bit boring. She's too passive, and she stays that way for too long, without any other aspect of personality showing through. Even after Maguire has sent for her, even after his girlfriend drags Collins to his apartment, the detective doesn't act. She's becoming too flat, and she's probably losing the reader's interest.

As you critique this scene, here are some comments you could make:

- Collins is starting to feel somewhat apathetic, and I don't think this is what you want for her. Is there another aspect of her personality you could show us here?

- Could Collins do something different in this scene, something that comes from deeper inside her? Maybe she's a neat freak, and Maguire's mess sends her into action. Or she could get a second wind, when she hears Stohl's name, and show us what she's like when her quarry's in sight.

- Is Collins really this patient? Is there perhaps another part of her that's starting to bubble with impatience at how Maguire has jerked her around tonight? I'd like to see that layer of her character.

Characters Don't Show Enough Reaction

As we move through life, life moves around us. And we, as real people, are constantly responding to nature, events, sounds, other people. Sometimes our reaction is visible or auditory—we point or we shout. Other times, only we know what the stimulus does to us—our stomach tightens, or our head starts pounding.

For writers, it can be tricky to remember that our characters have reactions, too. As we put a scene on a page, we can get caught up in writing the action and the dialogue, even the setting. We forget how much our reader wants to identify with and connect to the characters. If the story moves along, and the characters fail to respond to events within that story world, the reader is going to get very frustrated.

When you are critiquing, you need to help the other members in your group make sure the hero not only acts but *reacts*.

In Angie Fox's paranormal romance *The Accidental Demon Slayer*, the hero, Lizzie, falls into a pit. Her self-proclaimed protector, a sexy, shape-shifting griffin named Dimitri, stands at the edge, looking down at her.

> "Don't move, Lizzie."
>
> Yeah, right. I didn't have the luxury of slowing down. I tested my ankle. It hurt like heck, but I had to keep moving.
>
> "Listen to me," he said, serious as death. "Look to your right. Turn slowly."

> I didn't like that tone. I turned. The fissure ended about
> six or seven feet to my right, the rock forming a vee. And
> in that vee ... Oh no. I saw movement. I squinted, my heart
> slamming in my throat. A big, black snake coiled in a nest
> of fallen leaves.
>
> "Yaak!" I jerked back and it hissed, its white mouth il-
> luminated in the moonlight. Cripes.

Not only does Lizzie react to the snake, she reacts to what Dimitri is saying and *how* he says it. Even Dimitri, in his one line of dialogue, changes
his tone so that Lizzie will take him seriously. The back-and-forth between
the two characters shows that, even though Lizzie's *in* the pit and Dimitri's
lucky enough to be at the top of it, they're in the same scene, responding to
everything in that moment, on the page.

Let's look back at Collins again and see how well she reacts.

> Maguire scowled. "It'll cost you five hundred."
>
> I pushed myself off the wall. "You got a pen and paper?"
> I asked, yanking open a drawer in the tiny desk next to me.
> "Draw me a map."
>
> Maguire stepped closer to me, then took the cigarette
> out of his mouth and flicked the ashes off the end. They
> landed on my shirt.
>
> I rustled around in the desk, shoving aside piles of paper
> clips, candy wrappers, and two guns. "How far from here is
> Stohl?" I asked.
>
> "Hey," Maguire called to the girl. "You got a pen?"
>
> The girl checked her fingernails, then pulled a file out of
> her purse. She buffed the nail on one index finger and put
> the file away.

It's possible, of course, that Collins is choosing not to show Maguire her
reactions to his demand for money and his rudeness with the cigarette. However, the passage *reads* as though she doesn't notice what he says or does.
She doesn't acknowledge him, not even with a hidden physical response or a
short internal thought. Similarly, Maguire doesn't react to Collins, and his
girl friend totally ignores her. The characters in this scene behave as though
they're in a bubble, isolated from the people around them.

If you were critiquing this passage for character, you might make these comments:

- Is Collins planning to give Maguire the money? Or is she stalling for time because she doesn't have it? Could you show, in her reaction, what she thinks of his demand?

- I'm having trouble knowing whether Maguire's girlfriend is ignoring him or just doesn't hear him. Should she answer his question about the pen?

- Why does Maguire flick the ashes on Collins? Is it in response to her silence about the money?

A Character Behaves Inconsistently

Earlier in the chapter, we talked about a character having layers—distinctive, even contradictory aspects of his or her personality. These various shades, though, have to fit what the reader knows about that character. One of the most frustrating things for a reader is when a character he's been following through a story acts, well ... out of character. Unless there's a strong motivation, a shy teenager can't suddenly shout for attention, and a usually ultraorganized mother shouldn't spend an entire scene looking for the credit card she lost.

As we write, we learn more about who our characters are. Because of this, it's easy to drop in a trait that doesn't fit what you've written so far or forget and have a character behave in a way you've "decided" he wouldn't. When you critique, you can keep an eye out for these slips, point them out to your partners, and make suggestions about how to merge all the pieces of a character into one consistent whole.

In the YA novel *The Adoration of Jenna Fox*, Mary Pearson has created a character who starts the story with little, if any, memory of who she is. Jenna's need to know what happened to herself and her friends, to define who she is, is one of the forces that drives the story. In an early scene, we see this need established.

> I sit in my bed, in the dark, listening to the midnight creaks
> of our house, trying to conjure more than their faces, trying
> to push them into rooms, desks, and voices that will trigger

> more. But only their faces, close, eye to eye, are revealed.
> They linger before me like they have found my scent.
> *Tell me.*

In a later scene, Jenna is after a secret her parents have hidden in their bedroom closet.

> I take the stairs two at a time, my clumsy feet stumbling
> twice, my hand gripping the railing to keep me from a free fall.
> I tumble to the floor at the last stair, scrambling on all fours
> as I right myself. I run down the hall and grab the crowbar
> just outside Lily's door that she left as promised, and then I
> burst into Mother and Father's room, letting the door bang
> into the wall. My fingers shake as I try to maneuver the key
> into the closet lock.
>
> ...
>
> "God, let it fit!" I cry, shaking and twisting the key. It slides
> in. I sob and turn the lock, and the door swings open.

In both scenes, the strength of Jenna's determination comes through clearly. The early scene, showing the power of her wish sets the context for the later scene in which she physically forces her way through the house and into the room where the secrets are hidden. By the time Jenna slams open her parents' door, the reader has no doubt that the action comes from deep within her true character.

Again, let's go back to our sample scene. Collins has been pretty steady in her attitude and behavior. What happens if she suddenly switches gears out of her lethargy?

> The girl checked her fingernails and then pulled a file out of
> her purse. She buffed the nail on one index finger and put
> the file away.
>
> "Hey!" Maguire shouted. "A pen?!"
>
> I slammed the drawer shut so hard it popped out again
> and fell onto the floor, spilling its contents. I reached down,
> grabbed the gun that had landed at my feet, and whipped it
> up against Maguire's temple.
>
> "Don't talk to her like that," I told him.
>
> He grinned. "It's not loaded."

I grinned back. "So?" I lifted my arm and, in one quick slash, brought the gun down on the back of his head. He dropped to the floor, sending paper clips skidding under the couch and into the mess of fast-food bags.

"That fingernail okay now?" I asked the girl.

As much as we may be rooting for Collins to take on Maguire, this behavior is out of character for our hero. The earlier scenes haven't set us up for Collins' explosion, and this passage provides no new information that makes her actions understandable or believable.

If you were critiquing this scene, here are some comments you might want to make:

- I love that Collins *does* something here, but I don't understand why she does it. What makes her finally take charge?

- Collins' actions come as a surprise. Is there something you could weave into the story earlier that would give us a context for her behavior here?

- Is this the kind of thing Collins does when she reaches the last straw? If that's what you're going for, we probably need to know this about her before this scene.

A Character Doesn't Grow

While a character does need to stay true to his personality, he cannot go through the whole story without change. Change over time is growth, and every main character—especially the hero—must grow. It's an unhappy reader who closes a book in which the hero is exactly the same at the end as she was at the beginning. In fact, the reader may not even finish the story if she gets halfway through and is still reading about a static character.

When you're critiquing, you can help the author make sure his characters develop fully across the length of his manuscripts.

Take another look at the excerpts from *The Adoration of Jenna Fox* that I showed you in the last section. In the first passage, Jenna's need is shown through the strength of her wishing, even as she sits quietly in her bed. In the second scene, Jenna is active, forceful, racing through the house like a whirlwind. Over the pages of the story, Jenna gains physical strength and coordination as her health returns, and she digs deeper and deeper into the secrets her parents are hiding. All these steps lead Jenna (and the reader) to the increased power she brings to her quest at the end of the book.

To show that Collins goes through her story without changing, we'd have to get rid of the scene where she attacks Maguire. Let's leave it there for now, but pretend you didn't read it. What if, instead, this was the passage you saw?

> Maguire shoved up to me. "Five hundred dollars, I said. Now." He slammed the drawer shut, almost catching my pinkie finger inside.
>
> I sighed and dug into my back pocket. "I've got four hundred," I told him. "Get me to Stohl tonight, and I'll go to the bank for more tomorrow." I held out a stack of twenties and tens with a few ones mixed in, waiting to see if he'd take it.
>
> He did.

In this alternate passage, showing Collins easily handing over all the money she has, we're back to the Collins who is the same throughout the story. The things that happen to her don't affect her behavior or her feelings. Our PI doesn't have enough character arc, so the reader won't be curious about where this hero will take us, and herself, next. We see the same behavior on every page, we know she isn't growing, and we struggle to care about her story.

As a critiquer of this scene, here are some comments you could make:

- I like the way the plot is advancing, but I'm a little worried about Collins. She seems to stay very much the same, even as actions and events happen around her.

- Do you want to think about ways Collins could start to change? By the end of the story, she'll need to be in a better (or worse) place than she is at the start, and I don't see her moving in either direction yet.

- What is Collins' character arc? What personal problem is she facing at the start of the story? You can think about how she'll solve that problem by the end and what changes she'll need to go through first.

Chapter 6

CRITIQUING FOR
POINT OF VIEW AND VOICE

A lot of times, when writers discuss point of view, we talk about the mechanics—first person with an "I," third person with a "he," "she," or "they." We discuss close third person, where you get into a character's thoughts, and distant third person, where you don't. We explain that omniscient point of view, which we rarely use anymore, gives us sort of a mind-reading, bird's-eye view, with a narrator who knows (and shows) what everybody is thinking.

Point of view is much more than these facts, though, and—in its larger concept—it's inextricably linked with voice. From a reader's perspective, voice is the way we "hear" the story, but from the writer's perspective, voice is the way we, or rather the narrator, tells that story. The narrator can tell a story only from his or her personal point of view. The way the narrator sees the world, sees events unfolding, is limited by his knowledge, his experience, his personality. And so, frankly, is the way the narrator "speaks."

For writers, one of the hardest things to do is stay within the narrator's perspective and voice. As critiquers, we can point out the places where the author struggles with these elements, and we should help him or her hone in on the solid point of view and voice the story needs.

As you read and critique, here are some of the reactions you may have to a voice and point of view that aren't clearly or strongly written:

- You get confused about who's telling the story.
- You feel like you're listening to the author, not a narrator.
- You feel distant from the story.
- You aren't interested in the hero.
- You have trouble digging into a scene.
- You're not having an emotional response to the story.
- You feel like you're being lectured.

ANALYZING THE WEAKNESSES

When you're reading a scene or manuscript, make sure to pay attention to how the narrator speaks and what he or she actually says. It's easy, when critiquing, to assume that the point-of-view character is always in the right—it's her story, and she knows how to tell it. It's also easy to assume that the narrative *has* a voice; we get so caught up in looking for plot and character problems, we just accept how the story is told as the only way we could hear it.

Push yourself to really examine the point of view and voice. "Listen" to the narration and make sure it belongs to someone distinct and separate from the author. Take the time to catch places where the writer has slipped out of the correct point of view or dropped the strong voice from a scene or passage. Make notes for your critique partner and offer suggestions about how to fix these flaws.

The following sections highlight these common problems that can weaken point of view and voice:

- The point-of-view character knows more than he or she possibly can.
- The narrator's voice isn't distinct enough.
- The transition between multiple points of view is unclear or rough.
- The narrator drops out of voice.

The Point-of-View Character Knows More Than He or She Possibly Can

Technically, the point-of-view character is limited in exactly what, or how much, information he can know. If you're writing in first person, for example, your narrator cannot know what another character is thinking unless he is told, and he can't show an action or event unless he's seen it. The same rules apply for close third-person point of view. Only an omniscient narrator can know (and reveal) everything about everybody.

Those are the basics, and sometimes they feel like straightforward, if aggravating, rules. Beyond these rules, though, the *limits* that point of view places on writing are a tool for creating a tight story line; developing a strong, distinct character; and creating suspense. In *The Adoration of Jenna Fox*, Jenna's amnesia creates an incredibly narrow point of view, which adds to the mystery and tension the reader experiences. Because of Jenna's surgery, she doesn't eat or drink regular food but just drinks a daily dietary supplement; she also can't taste things. When she has a flash of memory about drinking, and liking, hot chocolate, she is elated and runs to make herself a mugful. As she takes a sip, she is hit simultaneously with the complete lack of flavor and the noise of her mother, Claire, screaming at her to stop. Later, we get this look at Jenna's perspective on the scene:

> I'm certain it is Claire's fault. Everything. Why does she whimper and cower so? Is she guilty? She cried when I dropped the mug. I wanted to hit her. *It's mine, dammit. Mine.* But it must be hers, too, with the way she takes it on. It is like she owns every shortcoming I have. Maybe she just plain owns me. She tried to explain it away. *It's temporary. Your taste will return. You shouldn't have food anyway.* I spent the next hour locked in my bathroom, staring at my tongue. It's normal. Rough and pink and fleshy. What's wrong is somewhere else inside. Something that is disconnected within me.

Jenna has no idea why her mother freaked out at the sight of her drinking something real. Neither does she understand why she can't taste anything or eat solid foods. Jenna knows, at this point, only what she has been told, and that data amounts to almost nothing.

Because of this lack of information, Jenna's point of view is incredibly tight. The boundaries of what Jenna knows force that same limitation onto the reader, actively pulling him or her into the mystery that Jenna must solve. The reader experiences the same frustration as Jenna and turns the pages with the same drive that pushes Jenna.

Let's look at a passage in our writing sample, in which Sully shows up at the park to meet Collins.

> Sully turned the corner at the end of the street. I waved—my arm this time—until he saw me. He wasn't happy. He'd expected me to bring Stohl or one of Stohl's goons with me so he could hand off the CDs in public—with me for protection. Now he was mad that he'd come to the park for nothing.
>
> He came up to the swing and looked at me.
>
> "Step back," I said. Then I took a couple of big swings and, at the peak of the arc, jumped off and landed in the dirt. On my feet. Yes!

"Nice," Sully said.

He didn't mean it.

First, this passage breaks the rules of first-person point of view. Collins, seeing Sully at a distance, magically shares just what he's thinking and feeling. She can't see his face, and he isn't yelling at her; she cannot *know* that he's mad. This is not information Collins can, at this point, give the reader.

Beyond this, Collins takes away the reader's chance to experience suspense, to worry about what Sully will do with the news Collins is bringing him. She doesn't show us his expression or body language, doesn't give us details that would help us understand what mood he's in. She gives us no clues to play with, to guess at what's coming, what scene we'll see when Sully gets to the swing. By allowing Collins to step outside her point of view, the writer has taken away the scene's tension.

The Narrator's Voice Isn't Distinct Enough

The best explanation I can think of that "shows" what voice and point of view can do is this: When I read a book where those elements are strong, I come away certain that, if I met the story narrator on the street, I would recognize him or her. And it wouldn't be the color of her hair and eyes that would look familiar, it would be her personality. If I stood and talked to her for a few minutes, I would be able to state the book where I'd "met" her before. When I experience this feeling, I know that the author has created a truly distinctive voice.

Obviously, not every book achieves this goal, and stories can be written beautifully around fascinating characters and an exciting plot. A powerful voice, though, and skillfully crafted point of view can push any book into brilliance, into a story that a reader will not, cannot forget. As a critiquer, you can encourage the other members of your group to push their narration, to reach for a voice that creates its own solidly real character.

The narrator and hero of Sue Stauffacher's *Donuthead* is Franklin Delano Donuthead, a fifth grader who moves through the world in a state of serious worry and anxiety—on the alert for any possibility of illness, injury, or crime. Life is acceptably safe until his mother and Sarah, a girl from school, decide to teach him baseball. Despite his fears, Franklin has determination. Here's the first pitch:

> I willed myself to lean forward and concentrate. Really this
> was very simple if I just broke it down into a physics problem.

This was all about velocity. My bat would repel this sphere at high velocity.

My mother wound up. Despite my mental preparations, I froze in position as the ball sailed past, dangerously close to my nose. But I didn't step back or drop the bat, which was, I believe, a minor victory worth celebrating.

Sarah tossed the ball back to my mother. We repeated this exercise several times. Everyone seemed to understand that a person with my delicate constitution required a great deal of warming up.

Nobody but Franklin would describe this moment in just these words. Sure, there are people who come at baseball scientifically, but they don't use physics to push away their fear of being clobbered by the ball. Franklin's vocabulary shows us how smart he is, but it also shows us that he uses big words and high-level thinking to rationalize his anxieties.

Franklin's voice is extreme, and Stauffacher keeps it this way throughout the book. This voice creates a character we *know*, whose actions and reactions all make sense because they come from this person who sees and shares his world so uniquely. Franklin is different, but if you met him on the street, you would know immediately who he was.

Let's look at the voice used in our writing sample. We'll go back to the sports bar for a moment.

The martini was dry. Too dry, but it wasn't worth the effort it would take to call the bartender back over. I sipped it and made a face, watching myself in the mirror behind the bar and thinking it was obvious why I'd scared Maguire away. Ugly. Bone ugly. I took another sip. Still too dry.

The waitress stopped and checked out the glass, ready to offer a refill, but saw I didn't need topping off. Before she could move away, I held up a hand and then lifted the glass and drained it.

"Another one, please," I said.

She smiled and took the glass. I frowned. I knew her. My eyes squinted back at me in the bar as I thought, then remembered. She was Maguire's girl. I'd seen them on Monday at the Italian restaurant around the corner, giggling over cheap

red wine and bread sticks. That was the day after the cops
found the body.

Collins' narration does have a voice. As you read the scene, you can see the tough, cold PI who spends too much time sitting in bars and not enough time leaving them. You get short, terse sentences and dark self-judgments that make it clear Collins is not happy—with this case or her life.

The problem is we've seen this voice too often. Hard-boiled-mystery writers Dashiell Hammett and Raymond Chandler did it best, and lots of writers have been doing it well, with their own variations, ever since. While this voice may be fun to read, it's not presenting the reader with anything new or different. Collins' voice is not unique, which means that she—as the hero—isn't either.

If you were critiquing this particular scene, here are some comments you might make:

- I like the basic voice you use for Collins, but I'd love to see you make her more of an individual. At this point, I'm kind of picturing her in a trench coat and fedora, looking a lot like a female Humphrey Bogart. Is there something about Collins that is different from other PIs, something that could show up in the way she sees the world?

- You may want to think some more about Collins' likes and dislikes, or—even better—her obsessions and her hatreds. When she narrates a scene, how can you use those feelings, those truly distinc-tive personality quirks, to affect the way she tells us her story?

- Collins' voice may go almost too well with the scene she's showing us. That voice is so much the sound of a dark, noisy bar that we feel anybody in the room could be narrating what's going on. Should you push Collins' voice in the other direction? Okay, she's probably not going to be chirpy or cheerful, but is there a voice that would be in *contrast* with the life she leads, to really show us the individual who's moving through this world?

The Transition Between Multiple Points of View is Unclear or Rough

Multiple points of view present their own sets of challenges, but using this technique can add extra layers to a story. An author can build a full picture of the story world, layering in the separate, conflicting, and often fascinating perspectives of different characters. As a writer, keeping the points of view (and voices) individualized is critical to moving the story along smoothly.

When you critique a story with multiple points of view, your job is to help the author keep the different views distinct. You can also watch the places where the point of view changes and check that the author has made the transition smoothly.

In *Run*, Ann Patchett writes in third-person point of view, giving us glimpses into several characters' perspectives. She doesn't separate the different points of view by chapter, either, but mingles them within every chapter, smoothly establishing each change without pushing the reader out of the story.

Kenya, a young girl whose mother is hit by a car early in the story, loves—no, she needs—to run. Running is who she is. Because of the accident, and because that accident turns her life upside down, many chapters and many hours go by in which she gets no chance to run. Finally, her brother Tip, who—until the day before—didn't know Kenya even existed, takes her to the Harvard University track.

> ... She was picking up her pace now on the track, but not to where she would take it. She could have run this fast in the snow. She let herself float forward, every step a leap, her legs stretching out like scissors opened wide. She was a swimmer, a gymnastics star, she was a superhuman force that sat outside the fundamental law of nature. Gravity did not apply to her. "Meditation in motion," her coach would say. She heard his voice in her head as she lapped the talking girls, as she swept past the one who was there to run.
>
> ...
>
> Tip had never seen anything like it. Not just the speed but the utter effortlessness of it all, the way the toes of her shoes barely touched down before she set off again. She was a sprinter, clearly she was a sprinter, and yet she just kept going until he started to change his mind and wonder if

she wasn't going to knock out a half marathon on the track
while he sat there waiting.

Yes, Patchett does place Tip's name firmly in the first sentence of his point of view, but even if she hadn't, it would be clear that we'd left Kenya's perspective. The first passage is an amazing piece of action seen from inside; we almost feel more what it is like to be in Kenya's thoughts than on the track. In the second passage, we are clearly seeing Kenya from the point of view of an outsider, someone who can watch in awe but only guess as to what she is truly doing, what she will do next.

Let's go back to our writing sample, to Collins as she watches the people at the park.

> Two mothers walked by with their strollers, talking. The babies were talking, too; at least, they were waving their hands back and forth at each other and making gentle squawking noises, kind of like chickens pecking around in a big scattering of grain. I waved a finger at them all, but nobody noticed. I guess their conversations were all too fascinating.
>
> The babies chattered away, playing with the toys on the stroller bar and digging for the rattles beneath their blankets. The wind picked up and tousled what little hair they had, and dust swirled up around the stroller wheels. Mary smiled at Liza, glad to be out in the early spring sunshine, then reached down and tucked the blanket more snugly around her daughter.

In this passage the point of view changes from Collins to Mary without a reason (the switch doesn't add to the story). Unfortunately, the change is also confusing. We don't know, even after going back and rereading the passage, *when* Mary's point of view took over from Collins'. We're sure of the change in the last sentence because only Mary, not Collins, can know how she feels about being at the park. But who was watching the babies chatter? Who noticed the wind get stronger? The reader comes to Mary's point of view like a bump in the story and has to fumble around to get his footing back. This kind of point-of-view transition is awkward and pulls the reader out of the book.

If you were critiquing this passage, here are some comments you might want to make:

- I felt taken out of the story here when Mary's point of view took over. Seeing her name jarred me, and shifting into her maternal view of the park and the babies confused me about what was happening in the scene.

- I lost track here of whose point of view we were in. I know, at some point, we switch from Collins to Mary, but I didn't realize it until I saw her name.

- At this point, both Collins' and Mary's points of view sound and feel pretty much the same. I'd like to see a clear difference in how they think and how they see what's going on at the park.

The Narrator Drops Out of Voice

Even a writer who captures the exact voice he's looking for in his book, who creates a voice that pulls his reader deep into the story, can slip. As a writer puts words on the page, he juggles all the big elements of fiction we've been talking about. Sometimes the strong voice we've developed simply slips away; sometimes we replace it with the equally strong, but misplaced, voice of a secondary character. One of the most common problems is when the author's own voice takes over the story, either to inform, educate, or—the worst—to moralize.

In *The Brief Wondrous Life of Oscar Wao*, Junot Díaz stays tightly within whichever narrative voice he's using at the moment. Because history and legend have as big a role in the book as the main, current-day characters, Díaz has a lot of information to pass on to us. He weaves these details beautifully into the story as he tells it.

> But the fukú ain't just ancient history, a ghost story from the past with no power to scare. In my parents' day the fukú was real as shit, something your everyday person could believe in. Everybody knew somebody who'd been eaten by a fukú, just like everybody knew somebody who'd worked up in the Palacio. It was in the air, you could say, though, like all the most important things on the Island, not something folks really talked about. But in those elder days, fukú had it good; it even had a hypeman of sorts, a high priest, you could say. Our then dictator-for-life Rafael Leónidas Trujillo Molina.

If Díaz slipped out of voice in this passage, or in any of the many other background scenes he gives us, he would lose the reader. The voice he uses is so strong, so unique, we would instantly feel jarred and frustrated. If he, as the author, took over for his narrator, we'd feel as though the teacher had stepped up to the chalkboard and started the lecture. And we'd, at the very least, skip this passage looking for a return to voice or, at the worst, put the book down and walk away.

Look again at the first paragraph of our park scene, this time reading for voice.

> I'd told Sully I'd wait for him at the park the next morning to give him whatever news I had. I'd finally gotten a few hours sleep, and I'd managed to find clean underwear to put on, so I was feeling pretty good. I sat in the last intact swing on the swing set and pushed with my feet until I was gliding back and forth. In the sandbox a few feet away, two toddlers pushed trucks back and forth, and their older brother buried dinosaurs and dug them back up. Every now and then a dinosaur got a ride in a truck.
>
> The sun was shining, and a robin sat in the tree above me, singing. As if in answer, I heard the ice cream van jingling down a street somewhere, probably only a few blocks away. I decided that, if the van was around when Sully showed up, I'd buy us both some ice cream. It was never too early for Rocky Road.

Okay, it's great for Collins that she got a good night's rest. Lots of sleep, though, is not a good enough reason for her to lose the tough voice she's used throughout the rest of the story. In this passage, she's cheerful, active, and welcoming in her observations. She uses long sentences instead of the tight, clipped phrasing in the earlier passages. Her humor is silly and upbeat instead of dark and sarcastic.

We don't know if this is the author's voice that has taken over for Collins. It could be another character the author is trying to develop, who slipped into the author's subconscious, or it could be a character in a book the author is reading, not writing. Or it could simply be that the writer got caught up working out what was going to happen next in the story, what conflict she should be producing, and forgot to tell the story in Collins' voice. Either way, however it happened, Collins needs to come back.

If you were critiquing this excerpt, you might make these comments:

- I think you lost Collins' voice here. I can believe she feels better, but I don't believe that her take on this park would really be this bubbly and cheerful.

- You may want to rewrite this section, put the observations about the park back into Collins' voice. What happened to the dark things she sees and says?

- Oops! Collins must have had a *really* good night! But I think she needs a bit of her old doom and gloom back. Watch the voice!

Chapter 7

CRITIQUING FOR DIALOGUE

Dialogue is more than people talking. Dialogue done well can, and should, be the life of the party that is a book. Good dialogue is active, full of energy and a strong voice, and pulls the reader along with the characters and the story line. In real life, people often speak the first things that pop into their heads. We don't always take time to think about the sentences, emotions, or attitudes about to come pouring from our mouths. As writers, on the other hand, we have to consider every word our characters speak.

When you're critiquing another writer's work, pay close attention to her dialogue. What are the characters saying, and how are they saying it? If you're pulled out of the story by a passage of dialogue, try reading it out loud. How does it sound? Take the time to play with your critique partner's words and help her make her dialogue strong enough to pull the reader into the characters' lives as well as into their conversations.

RECOGNIZING THE WEAK SPOTS

For critiquers, skimming (and ignoring) a section of work is always a danger, but it seems to happen often with weak dialogue. We pass over a conversation to get back to the story or the characters. Don't give in to the temptation. Stop, reread, and make sure the dialogue is *contributing* to the story, to the characters in the scene. When you read a book, you expect an author's writing, including the dialogue, to command your full attention. Help the writers in your group make sure they're achieving that goal.

Here is a quick list of signals that you've hit a spot of dialogue that needs some work:

- You don't care what the characters are saying.
- You can't picture the conversation in your mind.

- You feel as if you're watching two talking heads, with no emotion or action.
- You're irritated at what the characters are (or aren't) saying.
- You lose track of the story while you read the dialogue.
- You get confused about who's speaking.

ANALYZING THE WEAKNESSES

Again, as with all your critiques, you'll want to give the writer as much help as you can when you make notes about his dialogue. Take the time to really study the dialogue and see if you can figure out *why* it isn't working for you. Think about suggestions you can offer to make the dialogue better; even play with the words a bit to show the author some other possibilities.

The next sections will go into detail about common problems that cause dialogue weaknesses.

- The dialogue doesn't contribute to another story element.
- The dialogue dumps information on the reader.
- The dialogue beats are absent or weak.
- The dialogue doesn't show conflict or tension.

The Dialogue Doesn't Contribute to Another Story Element

In many ways, dialogue is like the multitool of fiction. You know, those huge more-than-pocketknives that have everything in them—screwdrivers, bottle openers, nail files, *and* the kitchen sink? Well, when you look closely at dialogue, you'll find tools for character, plot, setting, voice, you name it.

Here's the thing. We have to make our dialogue do the jobs of all those tools. Dialogue needs to always be doing at least one other function besides showing the characters talking. It needs to advance the plot or reveal character or show setting.

Jim Butcher's Harry Dresden books are tight, fast, and funny. His books race along too quickly to give time or space to narrative summaries or long descriptions, so he uses his dialogue to give readers all the information they need. Take a look at this piece of dialogue from early in the fourth book in the series, *Summer Knight*. Harry is meeting his friend Billy at a park in Chicago.

"Billy," I responded. ... "How's the werewolf biz?"

"Getting interesting," he said. "We've run into a lot of odd things lately when we've been out patrolling. Like this." He gestured at the park. Another toad fell from the sky several feet away. "That's why we called the wizard."

Patrolling. Holy vigilantes, Batman. "Any of the normals been here?"

"No, except for some meteorological guys from the university. They said that they were having tornadoes in Louisiana or something, that the storms must have thrown the toads here."

I snorted. "You'd think 'it's magic' would be easier to swallow than that."

Every author must create a setting, but a fantasy or science fiction writer has to build an entire world. He or she has to establish the where and the who so the reader knows the game rules. Butcher does his world building right here in these few lines of dialogue.

We know immediately that we're going to be dealing with wizards *and* werewolves. We also know that these magical beings exist within the "normal" world, where most people don't believe in magic, even when it's flying (or falling) in their faces. Butcher could have told us about the magic by describing Billy the werewolf or by giving us some detailed character history about Dresden. Instead he uses the dialogue, the *funny* dialogue, to reveal both the characters and the whole world they move in. Along the way, Butcher also sets up the first problem of the plot—the fact that Chicago seems to be raining toads.

Let's look at some of the dialogue in our sample scene.

"That's it," Maguire said. "You're on your own." He slid back out the door and into the alley. He was gone.

"Come in, please," Stohl said.

I sat in the other chair, his desk between us. "Thanks for seeing me," I told him.

"You're welcome." He rubbed his chin. He hadn't shaved today. Or maybe he just should have shaved again.

Stohl leaned forward. "You hungry?" he asked. "Want some coffee?"

"No, thanks." I yawned. "I want to sleep tonight."

He nodded. "Good of Maguire to bring you by so late."

"Good, ha. It cost me four hundred to get to you. And I still owe him another hundred."

Okay, so Collins finally got to one of her goals; she's meeting with Stohl. And they're talking. Unfortunately, they're not saying anything. They're being polite and chitchatting, and they're going over information we already know—that Maguire brought Collins here and that she's tired. The dialogue doesn't advance the plot, tell us what Stohl's place looks like (any room can have a desk and two chairs), or teach us something new about either character. The words the pair speak could be doing much, much more.

If you were critiquing this section of dialogue, here are some comments you could make:

- Is this how Stohl and Collins would talk at this meeting? Wouldn't Collins have some specific, case-related questions to ask Stohl? And wouldn't he want to know why she's there?

- What does Stohl's office look like? You might have the characters' dialogue show us some interesting details of the setting.

- Have Stohl and Collins met before? Do they have an established relationship that would affect the way they talk to each other? Are they tense, angry, worried? Can you use the dialogue to show some of their feelings toward each other?

The Dialogue Dumps Information on the Reader

The flip side of dialogue not doing enough is dialogue that tries to do *too much*. Although many writers know better than to deliver big chunks of character background or long plot summaries in narrative, we often slip up and forget that the same rule applies to dialogue. We look at the quotation marks we're putting around the text, and we go ahead and have a character tell the readers everything *we* want them to know. We forget to think about whether the words are what the story needs the character to say.

In Adam Rex's middle-grade novel *The True Meaning of Smekday*, Gratuity Tucci's Earth has been taken over by Boov aliens. All humans are being relocated to Florida, and she decides to drive there herself, with just her cat, Pig, for company. Then she meets her first Boov, who offers to fix her car and come with her on the journey.

When Gratuity comes outside to check on the car, she finds it totally transformed, with tubes and hoses connecting parts she's never seen before.

> "This seems like an awful lot of trouble for one flat tire," I said.
>
> The Boov stuck out his head.
>
> "Flat tire?"
>
> I stared blankly for a second, then walked around to the other side. The tire was still flat.
>
> "The car, it should to hover much better now!" he called happily.
>
> "Hover?" I answered. "Hover *better*? It didn't hover at *all* before!"
>
> "Hm," the Boov said, looking down. "So *this* is why the wheels are so dirty."
>
> "Probably."
>
> "Sooo, it did to roll?"
>
> "Yes," I said crisply. "It rolled. On the ground."
>
> The Boov thought about this for a long few seconds.
>
> "But ... how did it to roll with this flat tire?"

In this passage, we're given several pieces of information. As a straight fact, we learn that Boov vehicles travel through the air. We find out that this Boov, at least, is still grappling with the English language and that he doesn't have a complete grasp of the way this world operates. Finally, the dialogue sets up the often confusing, sometimes frustrating, always hilarious relationship that Gratuity and the alien will have through the rest of the story.

Rex could have stopped the fast, interactive dialogue after Gratuity's first statement and simply had the Boov narrate an explanation of what he's doing and how the "new" car works. Instead he wove the information in with characterization, action, and humor in a way that makes that information go down just like Mary Poppins' medicine—easily and sweetly.

Let's see how Collins' dialogue with Stohl is going.

> "Four hundred dollars. You must really have wanted to see me." His voice went quiet. "Why?"
>
> This was it. I took a breath and started talking. "On Wednesday, I was talking to a butcher on First Street. He wanted to hire me to find his wife. Whatever. When I left, this kid Sully followed me. He told me about his problem, which

is that he found some CDs in the alley behind the butcher shop and took them home. He copied them onto his MP3 player. A couple of days after that, he was chased when he left work. There were three men and a big dog. He lost them in a video arcade. Sully says the dog is yours. He wants me to talk to you and tell you he'll give the CDs back. Sully's afraid of you."

Putting Collins' explanation into a piece of dialogue doesn't make it feel any less like plain information. She simply recites the details, most likely a summary of something that's already happened in an earlier scene. We don't see the interaction between Stohl and Collins as she talks, so we can't guess how he's receiving the information or what he might be going to do. The dialogue is too flat, without Collins' usual attitude or personality mixed in, so we can't see how she's feeling as she presents her case.

If you were a critiquer with this passage in front of you, here are some comments you could make:

- You may want to edit Collins' dialogue down so that it feels like Collins is telling Stohl the whole story, without the reader being fed the information a second time.

- This dialogue seems too distant from the way Collins would be talking to Stohl. The words feel more like the author's than the characters', as though the author needs to present this information to the reader.

- Collins talks for a long time here in one piece of dialogue. Can you break up her report with some action on her part or interaction with Stohl? Doing this would make the passage feel more like a real conversation.

The Dialogue Beats Are Absent or Weak

Dialogue beats are the words and phrases surrounding a character's spoken words. Just as an example, in the sentence, "'That's *my* chocolate bunny,' Mary said, grabbing the rabbit from her little brother," *grabbing the rabbit from her little brother* is the dialogue beat.

Dialogue beats add extra layers to the things our characters say. They give us insight into a character's feelings and attitudes, and they show the full meaning behind the spoken words. Often, as we write, we get caught up in the actual dialogue and either forget completely about the dialogue beats or fail to use them as much as we should. As a critiquer, you can watch for places where the author has skipped beats or hasn't played with them quite enough.

In Dana Stabenow's *Breakup,* Kate Shugak's friend Mandy has begged Kate to take care of her rich, snobby parents for a day. Kate agrees, then ends up dragging Mom and Dad through a day of rampaging bears, dead bodies, and family shoot-outs. They end up at a friend's house just in time to shock and anger Mandy.

> "... And then, on top of everything else, you have the gall to take them out to Bernie's and get them stinking drunk?"
>
> "She didn't get us drunk," Mrs. Baker said, sitting up straight in her chair, suddenly very dignified.
>
> "Nah," Mr. Baker said with an expansive wave of his hand, unfortunately the one that held his coffee cup, and launched a spray of hot black liquid across the kitchen floor. "We wanted the trough. She just drink us to the led."

You get a hint that Mandy's parents have been drinking, in Mr. Baker's last sentence, but Stabenow uses the dialogue beats to deliver the true sense of *how* drunk they are. Mrs. Baker's extra care sets things up, and Mr. Baker's uncharacteristic drama and clumsiness tie it together. We don't just know Mandy's parents are drunk, we get to see just how these two individuals *do* drunk.

Here's another passage of dialogue from Collins' story, this time without any beats.

> "Sully's got nothing to fear from me," Stohl said.
>
> "Really?" I asked.
>
> "Of course not. He can bring those CDs to me anytime. Say, next week."
>
> "I can pass your answer on to him," I told him.
>
> "You do that."

There's nothing wrong with the things Collins and Stohl are saying here. The problem is that, because there are no dialogue beats, we can't see *how* the two characters are talking. We don't know what they actually mean. We're pretty sure Stohl is some kind of gangster, so is he being honest when he says Sully will be safe? Collins knows even more about Stohl than we do; does she believe his assurances, or is she skeptical? Dialogue beats would let the reader see all the nuances of the conversation; they would make clear the *feeling* of the dialogue instead of just the words.

If you were critiquing this piece of dialogue, you might want to make these comments:

- I'm not clear whether I should accept what Stohl is saying, or if I'm supposed to find a hidden meaning in his words. Could you use dialogue beats to show us his movements, his facial expressions? That might give us a better idea of what's going on.

- Does Collins trust Stohl? Is she really planning to tell Sully he can safely bring the CDs back? I don't think that's what you want to show here, but without dialogue beats, I can't know for sure.

- What are Stohl and Collins doing while they talk? Are they just sitting still, or are they using body language to convey important subtext? You could put some of that action into dialogue beats to show us more of what's going on.

The Dialogue Doesn't Show Conflict or Tension

Conflict and tension move a story forward. Somebody wants to achieve a goal and something (or another somebody) gets in the way of that goal. One of the things dialogue can do is add tension to a scene. Obviously, not every inch of dialogue has to be about conflict; a character can ask for a cup of coffee and get one, or she can tell her dog he's a "good boy" without getting bitten. Still, the more we use dialogue to *show* the story's tension, the stronger that dialogue, and that story, will be.

As a critiquer, take the time to look (and listen) closely to the dialogue the writer has created. Help him amp up the tension, put speakers at odds with each other, and use his words to create story conflict that pulls the reader along.

Junot Díaz's *The Brief Wondrous Life of Oscar Wao* is *about* conflict. The Cabral family is either cursed or extremely unlucky. The various members of the family feel angry, sad, and hurt—by the world and by each other. The narrative *and* the dialogue are heavy with tension throughout the story. As a young girl, Oscar's mother, Beli, is beaten nearly to death by men who work for the wife of the dictator Trujillo. She is found at the side of the road by a group of musicians.

Down the band peered, rubbing their lips and running nervous hands through thinning hair.

What do you think happened?

I think she was attacked.

By a lion, offered the driver.

Maybe she fell out of a car.

It looks like she fell *under* a car.

Trujillo, she whispered.

Aghast, the band looked at one another.

We should leave her.

The guitarrista agreed. She must be a subversive. If they
find her with us the police will kill us too.

Put her back on the road, begged the driver. Let the
lion finish her.

Silence, and then the lead singer lit a match and held
it in the air and in that splinter of light was revealed a blunt-
featured woman with the golden eyes of a chabine. We're not
leaving her, the lead singer said in a curious cibaeña accent,
and only then did Beli understand that she was saved.

With very few words, Díaz sets up a major conflict. Before the musicians
even know that Trujillo is behind Beli's beating, they debate what could have
happened to her. The different opinions, while not presented in anger, have
the effect of showing us how badly Beli is hurt—nobody can agree on what
could have caused such horrible injuries. Then, as soon as Beli drops Trujillo's
name into the mix, the words become an argument—more tense for being
whispered, as though Trujillo himself may overhear them. Until the last sentence, the musicians, Beli, and the reader are held in suspense as to whether
she will be rescued or left to die.

Let's look back at the dialogue between Collins and Maguire's girlfriend,
just after Collins leaves the sports bar.

"Maguire told me to give this to you." She held out a manila
envelope, thick enough to hold a big stack of papers or photos. Or money.

I took it. "Okay," I said.

"He wants you to meet him," she went on. "He's holed
up at the Nite Inn, down Fifty-Seventh Street." Slinging her

purse over her shoulder, she said, "It's only a few blocks.
I'll show you."

I took some steps. She walked quickly and checked
back every few seconds to make sure I was following.

Collins simply accepts the girlfriend's directions here, so the dialogue creates
no tension. There is no conflict in the two women's words—the girlfriend tells
Collins to follow her, and Collins agrees. Yes, the dialogue moves Collins
toward her meeting with Maguire, but it fails to create suspense or worry in
the reader about whether Collins will get there. Because the dialogue sets up
no tension about what is going to happen, the reader has nothing to hope
for, no reason to root for Collins.

As a critiquer, if you were reading this dialogue, you might make these
comments:

- Why does Collins go with the girlfriend so easily? Wouldn't she
  suspect a trap? Maybe she could argue with the other woman
  about who should take the lead or demand to know where
  they're going.

- I think this dialogue is too relaxed for the scene. I'd like to see
  the two speakers express some tension about what they're doing—
  maybe anger that Maguire has thrown them together or fear that
  one of them will hurt the other.

- These two speakers are too similar here. Their goals are identi-
  cal, and I think you could almost switch their words without
  it making too much difference. Can you put their goals into
  conflict? Can you use their dialogue to show them more at odds
  with each other?

Chapter 8

CRITIQUING FOR DESCRIPTION

You hear a lot today about the importance of filling your pages with fast action and snappy dialogue. As wonderful as Victorian novels might be, the days of books with long descriptions of people and places (setting) are gone. This does not mean, however, that description isn't important. It is.

As writers, we must make sure our descriptions move as quickly as everything else. We need to drop in the bits and pieces that flesh out our characters and settings without asking our readers to step out of the story they're immersed in. When you're critiquing, you will help the author weave descriptions seamlessly through his or her scenes, with just the right balance of detail and information.

RECOGNIZING THE WEAK SPOTS

When we're reading a manuscript, it's easy to get caught up in the beauty and imagery of a setting or physical description. Because of this, we often forget to check whether the prose is *just* lovely or whether it also adds to the story or characterization—its true purpose. As you critique for setting, here are some of the reactions you may have to a passage that isn't doing its job:

- You get distracted.
- You get lost in all the words.
- You get bored.
- You forget what's happening in the story.
- You feel disconnected from the narrator.
- You feel like the story has slowed down too much.

ANALYZING THE WEAKNESSES

Description can be one of the trickier parts of a story to critique. The words can be so beautiful you hesitate to ask the writer to pull those words apart.

Be careful, though, not to ignore your feeling that a setting or the character description could be stronger. As usual, you owe it to your critique partners to give their work the closest examination you can.

In the chapter, we'll look at the following common problems that can create weak description:

- The description has too many details.
- The description doesn't evoke an image or feeling.
- A setting isn't active.
- A character description lacks personality.

The Description Has Too Many Details

We all know the advice about picking your battles. Well, in writing a setting or other description, the key is to pick the details. Rather than including every fact about a place or a person, we need to include just the pieces of information that convey a *sense* of that setting or character. As a critiquer, your job is to help the writer know when she's crossed the line into detail overload and to help her figure out which details are the right ones.

In Larry McMurtry's book *Telegraph Days*, Nellie Courtright moves to Rita Blanca, a tiny town somewhere in No Man's Land, and takes the job of telegraph operator. After dinner her first night in town, she goes to look at the office.

> Since there was a little light left in the summer sky I left the two of them to their pipes and strolled down the street to my new place of business, the telegraph office. It wasn't locked, but it was snaky. I had taken the precaution to borrow a spade from Mrs. Karoo, and I used it to ease two bull snakes and a small copperhead out the door. Of course, bull snakes won't tolerate rattlers, so there was none of that breed to be seen, though I did have to mash a bunch of black widow spiders and one sizable tarantula. There was the dust of the ages on the windowpanes, but the most important thing of all, the telegraph key, seemed to work fine. Zeke Ryan had been thoughtful enough to cover it with a snug leather cloth.

McMurtry doesn't spend a lot of time describing the physical appearance of the building that houses Nellie's office, either outside or inside. Instead he focuses on the details that give us a feel for how abandoned the office has been, as well as the bits of description that let us see Nellie's own experience and the attitude she brings to her new job and life.

Let's take a look at the full description of the sports bar where Collins meets up with Maguire's girlfriend. She walks inside and sees this scene.

> The bar was a sports bar. A mirror lined the wall behind the back of the bar, and tall, solitary bar stools lined the front. Three men occupied the stools, looking a lot like Goldilocks' three bears. One was big, with a thick Afro and a padded blue jacket. The middle-sized one was a red-head with glasses and a pipe, and the little one wore the loudest Hawaiian shirt I'd ever seen.
>
> Just as I came in, a tall, skinny woman with gray and purple hair stuck a quarter in the jukebox, and Elvis greeted my entrance with "Jailhouse Rock." The woman swung away from the machine and jitterbugged her way back across the room, stopping to talk to an elderly couple that looked like they'd been in those chairs since the turn of the century. The last century. She shook their hands between steps, then danced all the way to her table, spinning a circle around her chair before she sat down.

As nice as some of this description is, we really don't need it all. First of all, as we discussed back in chapter four, the reader doesn't yet know why Collins has come to this bar, and this much setting makes that question hang around too long.

The details about all the other people in the room are distracting. They pull the reader away from Collins, from her character and her actions. This long stretch of words, entertaining or not, takes over the story instead of contributing to it as a whole.

If you were critiquing this setting, here are some comments you could make:

- Do you need all these details? I think you could cut some of them and still give us a feel for the place Collins has walked into.

- Will we find out later that some of these people are connected to Collins' investigation? If not, maybe you could clear some of them out or replace them with someone who will have a role in the story.

- Is there some way you could use one of these people, or the TV games or the jukebox, to highlight a character trait of Collins'? We do get to "see" the room through her voice, which is good, but could she interact with something or someone in the scene? Maybe she could bump into the jitterbugging woman and refuse an offer to join in the dance.

The Description Doesn't Evoke an Image or Feeling

Description isn't easy to write. We look at a place or a person, with everything that makes it interesting to us, and—as writers—we try to present the whole image in a few words. It's not enough to describe the color of our character's hair or the smell of the coffee brewing. We have to handle the description in a way that brings the whole picture into the reader's mind, makes him feel as though he's *in* the scene, not just reading about it.

As a critiquer, you can help the author draw the beauty they see in their minds strongly onto the pages of their book.

In Olive Ann Burns' *Cold Sassy Tree*, the narrator, Will Tweedy, gets himself up on a train trestle and can't get off before the train reaches him. At the last second, he drops down between the rails.

> The engine's roar pierced my eardrums anyway, making awful pain. I was so scared I could hardly breathe, and there was a strong smell of heated creosote. Hot cinders spit on me from the firebox. ...
>
> I found myself counting boxcars, by the sound of them, which was a long sight different in this position, with my eyes shut tight against the dust and cinders, from being in Cold Sassy waiting for the train to get by so I could cross from South Main to North Main. The train had to end. Trains always do. It seemed like this one never would, but brakes were screeching and the clickey clacks on the rail were slowing. ...

First, Burns gets in four out of the five senses and, if you count nearly suffocating from fear as a kind of taste, she manages all five. Obviously, not every description requires that every sense is represented. However, a scene where the only visual reporting is the darkness of closed eyes requires the author to think beyond sight, and Burns weaves all the sensations beautifully into this passage. We are *there* with Will, on the trestle, inundated as he is by the sounds and smells and feel of the roaring train. In fact, we are so immersed in the moment we barely have time to recognize, until after we've finished reading the scene, that Burns has delivered the picture into our brains, as well as the feelings.

Let's look at some more description in Collins' world. Here we are back at the alley into which she originally chased Maguire.

> I turned the corner after Maguire and found myself in a dark, smelly alley that ran between the shops.
>
> The concrete was shaded from the buildings. The wall on my left was made of bricks. It was tall, maybe two stories. The wall on my right was shingles, blue ones. Some paint had flaked off some of the shingles. There were two windows in this wall, and one in the brick wall. I touched the brick wall, and it was cold. Someone moved inside the window opposite me, and I heard people talking. A cat turned into the alley, walked past Maguire, and then passed me.

Yes, you can probably see the alley. You know what the building walls are made of, as well as the path between them. You have a few details that add a little more information to the picture. The image you get, though, is pretty dry and factual. This alley could be any alley, in any city, in any story. It needs something distinctive to really create a picture for the reader.

In addition, the description of the alley evokes no sensations in the reader. We don't have a feeling that we're part of the scene, standing in the alley with Collins. In fact, it could be anybody describing the alley, because the description steps out of Collins' usual voice. The bland details, basically listed out on the page, only push us further away from the story.

If you were critiquing the alley setting, these are a few comments you might make:

- How does Collins react to ending up in the alley? What do the tall buildings and the shadows make her feel? Can you add some of her emotion to the description so we feel the setting the way *she* feels it?

- Can you use Collins' senses (smell? sound?) to evoke the full experience of being in the alley? Can you add those details to what she sees?

- Is there any way to push this description more toward the extreme, make this alley unusual or unique? I'd like to feel that I'm in the *specific* alley Collins is standing in.

A Setting Isn't Active

These days, omniscient narration is a pretty rare thing. Instead description is almost always written through the eyes (or brain) of a character, usually the hero. If the action is rolling along, as it should be, the narrator isn't standing still staring at whatever it is she's seeing. The character is moving, along with everyone and everything else on the page.

Descriptions need to be active, not static. Readers need to see a setting as the characters move through it, and they need to learn about characters by their interactions with their setting and each other. As a critiquer, you can help the other members in your group make sure they write descriptions with movement, settings that—as much as any plot point—pull the reader along the page and through the scene.

In S. J. Rozan's *Reflecting the Sky*, the book opens by dropping the reader right into the middle of Hong Kong.

> Damp, soupy heat washed over me as I pushed out through the revolving door. The bright morning glare was already hazed up by the shimmering exhaust of a river of cars, buses, and trucks. I looked left, looked right, got my bearings, and headed briskly down the sidewalk.
>
> ... Jostling, rushing pedestrians, many of them yelling into their cell phones, hurried past in both directions, making me feel like I had to work to keep my footing or I'd be tossed on their tide and swept away. Bill caught up to me as I stopped at the first corner, waiting with a crowd eight deep for the light to change.

As always, Lydia moves and moves quickly, but in this scene even she can't stay ahead of the energy that is Hong Kong. Everything is active in this description, from the heat washing over Lydia to the glare "hazed up" and the tide of people that threatens to sweep her away. Opening a book with setting can be dangerous because it runs the risk of losing the reader who is eagerly waiting to jump into the story. Rozan's setting is so active she bypasses that risk altogether, barely giving us a second to breathe, let alone wonder about whether or not to keep reading.

Here's a bit more description of the sports-bar setting in Collins' story.

> The room was filled with tables, filled with people. All colors of the rainbow, both in skin and clothes, including two waitresses. The lamps over the tables had panels of fake stained glass—ugly reds and blues and yellows. There were big-screen TVs in all four corners. The same picture of the same newscaster was up on all of them. The floor was dirty, with peanut shells and various liquids spilled onto it.

The earlier passage with the woman dancing through the room was active. This part of the setting, though, loses movement. We assume that Collins is somewhere in the room, but we don't see her, and, as far as we know, she could be standing in one place. We aren't shown any movement—everything in the passage is described statically. This effectively drops Collins out of the scene as a narrator, and, as a result, the reader drops out as a participant.

If you were critiquing this passage, here are few comments you might want to make:

- Where is Collins in this scene? Is she moving into the room from the door? Talking to or interacting with any of the other clients? Looking for somebody? You probably want to weave her movements into the setting.

- Is anyone watching the TVs? Are the people at the tables talking or moving? Are the waitresses taking orders or bringing drinks? Could you show us more of the action in this scene? Let us see the people are doing things.

- This setting is very static. The objects and people in the room are described, but it's as though they're in a painting. This distances us from Collins' perspective, making the scene feel as though she's not part of it. Show the setting as Collins sees it.

A Character Description Lacks Personality

Other than very minor, walk-on characters, most characters in a story will show up more than once, often several times before the action reaches the climax. Readers don't want to be reintroduced to a character every time he or she appears on the page. They want to quickly identify and recognize that character and move on with the story.

It's our job as writers to provide descriptions that make our characters memorable. This can be hard to do without resorting over and over to obvious details like huge tarantula tattoos or an all-pink wardrobe. When you're critiquing, you'll note the times a writer remembers, or forgets, a character, and you'll help your critique partners find a seamless way to weave character personality into the description.

In Butcher's *Summer Knight*, Butcher places wizards, fairies, and various paranormal creatures in his story and gives the reader the ability to keep them all straight. Early in the story, the hero, Harry Dresden, follows three changelings—part human, part something else. The changelings wait for him outside a funeral home, and Meryl, the biggest changeling, jumps him to protect her friends. Here's Butcher's first description of Meryl.

> The third was the brawny, homely young woman with the muddy green hair and heavy brow. She had on a pair of jeans tight enough to show the muscles in her thigh and a khaki blouse. ... She just turned, her arm sweeping out as she did, and fetched me a blow to my cheek with the back of one shovel-sized hand.

We get to know Meryl more throughout the story, and each time Butcher reminds us, briefly, of her size and strength. He also makes continual, subtle notes about her kindness. Here is Meryl's last appearance in the story.

> The troll was huge, and green, and hideous, and strong. It wielded an axe in one hand like a plastic picnic knife and was covered in swelling welts, poisoned wounds, and its own dark-green blood. It had a horrible wound in its side, ichor flowing openly from it. It was dragging itself along despite the wounds, but it was dying.
> And it was Meryl. She'd chosen.

Meryl's green hair in the first description returns in the color of the troll's skin and blood. The strength with which she knocks Harry into the air the first time they meet is what keeps her moving in the battle, despite all her wounds. Most important, the care she took of the other changelings in the earlier scene comes back at the end as she races to rescue her best friend, Lily, from a deranged and dangerous faerie queen. Harry has no problem recognizing (or worrying about) Meryl. Neither does the reader.

What does Maguire look like, when we first see him in the alley?

> "Leave me alone," Maguire said. He was taller than me, with brown hair cut short. He wore a sweatshirt and jeans, and his sneakers were white, with a hole in the toe of the left one. He folded his arms across his belly and glared at me.

He looks like any one of a thousand guys the author could have peopled this story with. We don't know how tall Collins is, so her comparison of Maguire to herself doesn't give us real information. *How* short is his hair cut? He wears nondescript clothing with nothing to make it stand out, other than a hole in the toe of one shoe. If, every time a reader sees Maguire, she has to look at his feet to recognize him, that reader is going to get pretty irritated.

Nothing about this description shows us who Maguire is. We don't know if he's tense or relaxed, irritated or amused. We guess he's a crook, but we have no idea what kind. We need a stronger sense of Maguire's personality.

If you were critiquing this description, you might make these comments:

- Can you give us more details about Maguire's appearance? Does the sweatshirt have a picture or a saying on the front? Is his hair long or buzz-cut almost all the way off? Are his jeans new, or are they faded and torn, almost falling off him?

- What kind of person is Maguire? Is there something you could weave into this description that would reveal some of his character to us? Maybe he rubs his toe back and forth over the ground, which is *why* the shoe has a hole in it. Is he clean or dirty? Does he look like he's at the top or the bottom of the crime food chain?

- I'm afraid that next time I see Maguire I won't remember who he is. Is he going to be important to the story? If so, I think we should learn more about him in this description so we'll recognize him next time he shows up.

Chapter 9

CRITIQUING FOR SCENE STRUCTURE

Readers fall in love with characters, are fascinated by theme, and get caught up in finding out how a plot will end. One thing, though, keeps those readers actively turning pages, and that is a tight, well-written scene.

No matter how much you've developed your hero or woven a fascinating theme into your tale, if a scene isn't structured tightly, with the right amount of what-if tension, the reader will put that book down. And if a party or a movie or another book comes along, she may not remember to pick it up again. The scene is the author's best tool for making sure that doesn't happen, for making it seriously hard for the reader to walk away from the story.

RECOGNIZING THE WEAK SPOTS

As a critiquer, your job is to make sure you are pulled along through each and every scene you read. You can help your critique partners by pointing out places you think the structure is weak and by offering suggestions about how to tighten it up.

As you read and critique, here are some of the reactions you may have to a weak scene:

- You get bored by the events in the scene.
- You don't care about the characters or the things that are happening to them.
- You get distracted from the overall story line.
- You feel like the characters are just killing time.
- You start wondering what's for dinner.

ANALYZING THE WEAKNESSES

When you're reading a story for critique, you may find yourself rushing through the current scene. There can be two reasons for this quick reading. One—the good reason—is that the scene has grabbed you and won't let you go. Two—the not-so-good reason—is that the scene has lost you, and you're trying to speed ahead to the next, hopefully better, scene.

Your job as a critiquer is to slow down, stop the rush. The scenes you want to skim past are exactly the scenes from which you need to take a step back. Look closely at what isn't working, at why you're so willing to leave these pages behind and flip ahead to what you hope is waiting for you.

The following sections discuss these common scene problems:

- The scene doesn't advance the overall plot.
- Tension doesn't increase across the scene.
- The author has written summary, not scene.
- The scene starts or ends in the wrong place.

The Scene Doesn't Advance the Overall Plot

Every individual scene is a microcosm, a distinct story showing a specific problem in a specific moment in time. At the same time, though, every scene must be part of a book's overall plot. Sometimes a scene moves a story forward; often it takes the characters a step or two back. Either way, the scene *must* affect the main story line. As a critiquer, you can help your critique partners make sure their scenes are parts of a whole, that the big plot weaves through every one of their smaller stories.

In Adam Rex's *The True Meaning of Smekday*, Gratuity's overall story line takes her through a huge chunk of the country, with the initial purpose of reuniting with her mother. On the way, Gratuity, Pig the cat, and J.Lo (the Boov traveling with her) get stuck driving in the middle of a hurricane and are surrounded by water.

> Then something happened. I don't know why Pig did it. I think she was afraid of the water and the wind, and there was a lot more of that outside the car than inside. But a thousand generations of weird cat biology goaded her on, and she pounced from the headrest and straight through the window. … Pig and a vintage Polaroid dropped into the floodwaters below.

> I drew a sharp breath, but before I could shout or scream,
> J.Lo had forced the window all the way down and dived in
> after her.
>
> I was suddenly alone and useless inside the car. The rain
> battered the roof like a drumroll. I could think of nothing to
> do. Not one thing. And then J.Lo shot out of the water like a
> salmon in a nature film and dumped Pig through the window.
> She was fine.

A few minutes pass, in which Gratuity and J.Lo pull themselves together and calm down. Then Gratuity, on impulse, gives J.Lo a huge hug.

Until the moment Pig jumps out the window, Gratuity and J.Lo have existed in an uneasy truce, bound by the practical need each has for the other. After this scene, Gratuity and J.Lo add a second goal to their story lines. They're going to find Gratuity's mother, and they're going to rid the planet of the Gorg, the other aliens who have invaded and now threaten both humans and Boovs.

When J.Lo rescues Pig, and Gratuity hugs him, they become actual friends and a team. Their relationship arc reaches a new point, one they had to achieve before they could unite against the Gorg. The scene, while a wonderful capsule in itself, also moves the overall plot forward.

Let's look at the alley scene in our writing sample one more time, with the first meeting between Collins and Maguire.

> Maguire stared at me, then checked his watch. He tapped it
> a couple of times. Maybe the battery had died.
>
> I let myself slip down the wall until I was sitting on the
> cement. I stretched my legs out in front of me and tilted my
> head back against the wall.
>
> Maguire shuffled from foot to foot, then checked his
> watch again. Finally, he said, "I'm out of here," and he took
> off down the alley.
>
> I watched him go. I could have caught him if I'd tried. It
> wouldn't have even taken a sprint. But I was tired. Tired of
> asking questions, tired of seeing his fear. I stayed where I
> was, against the wall.

We've seen this passage before, when we talked about Collins being too passive a hero. The bigger problem here, however, and through the entire conversation in the alley, is that the scene isn't connected to the larger story. Here, Maguire runs away, but at the end of the bar scene, he has sent his girlfriend to bring Collins to him. The alley scene shows a moment of interaction between Collins and Maguire, but if we deleted the entire scene, the change would make no difference to the overall plot. The story could continue without any of these words on those pages.

If you were a critiquer reading this passage for scene structure, here are a few comments you could make:

- Why is Collins in the alley with Maguire? What does this scene have to do with Collins' story goal of solving a crime?

- How does this scene tie into the big picture of the whole book? I don't see this scene impacting where the story goes after this point. Can you find a way to make their presence in the alley impact the big plotline?

- Later in the story, Collins meets up with Maguire. Is there something you could make happen in this scene that would tie into that future meeting? Could Collins threaten Maguire if he doesn't talk to her, so that—after thinking about it—he sends his girlfriend to hook them up?

Tension Doesn't Increase Across the Scene

What *does* keep a reader turning pages? Tension. No, this doesn't mean an author has to write, every time, the kind of scene that has knives and guns flying and blood dripping from everybody. What tension means is that a scene creates a feeling in the reader of "What's going to happen next?", a thread of what-if running through his response to the story. Tension can be a fear, yes, but it can also be a wondering, a curiosity.

Whatever it is, every scene must have some kind of tension, and this tension has to increase as the scene progresses. The writer has to make the reader feel that *something* is coming, that the more pages she turns, the closer she is to finding out what that something is.

In *Cold Sassy Tree*, Will's well-loved grandmother dies, and, three weeks later, his grandfather marries a much younger woman who has been making and selling hats out of his store. His daughters suffer both from embarrassment and from fear that he will leave all his money to this woman. The night after Will's near death on the trestle, Will's grandfather brings his new bride to the house, where half the town has gathered. He calls his daughters to come greet their new stepmother.

> What else could a daughter do? Mama walked over and pecked Miss Love on the cheek. Loma stalked into the room, her face beet-red, and did the same. But they nor the bride said a word. Everybody else was quiet, too. Watching. All you could hear was the clock ticking and Mr. French's fork tapping his dessert plate.

After this, Will and his grandfather go into the kitchen to talk until his grandfather remembers he has left his new wife in a room where nobody wants her to be.

> We got back to the parlor just in time to hear my daddy, in a strained and formal voice, making polite conversation by telling Mrs. Love Simpson Blakeslee what was coming along in our garden in the way of vegetables.

Finally, when everybody, including the bride, is more than ready for her to make her escape, the grandfather decides the whole company should join him in prayer.

> "Lord above, afore this gatherin' assembled, I ast You to bless the memory of Miss Mattie Lou."
>
> Everybody gasped. Nobody expected him to bring *her* up.
>
> ... "And now I ast yore blessin' on this here girl I married today." Miss Love raised her head and stared up at Grandpa, mouth agape. I do think his were the only eyes in the room still shut.

The longer Will's grandfather and step-grandmother stay at the house, the more tense the scene gets. Not just because the grandfather is pushing the social boundaries of his world, embarrassing both his new wife and daughters, but because the reader wonders more and more what will happen *because* of his actions. The reader is turning pages to see whether anyone will tell him to stop, whether one of his daughters will blow a fuse, and whether his new bride will break and run to escape the situation.

With every page, things get worse and worse for the characters and—you got it—better and better for the reader.

So, if we go back to Collins' story, what happens to the tension when she and Stohl talk?

> Stohl stood, then walked around to the front of his desk. He stopped and leaned against it, looking at me for a moment. "So," he said. "You're a detective."
>
> I shrugged. "Most of the time."
>
> "You like the work?" he asked.
>
> Like? "Nobody invited me to be a gourmet chef," I said.
>
> A short laugh got past his lips.
>
> "I got a nephew," he said. "He's talking about starting his own agency. I tell him there's a lot of late hours." He pushed himself off the desk and walked me to the door. "Have a good one, then."
>
> "Sure," I said and went to tell Sully the good news.

First, Stohl greets Collins cheerfully and with all good manners. Then he listens to her client's problem and easily reassures her that she, and her client, can stop worrying. They're in no danger from him.

If anything, the tension drops at the end of this scene. There's a brief second when the reader can wonder why Stohl is asking Collins about the job, but that disappears into a disappointing back-and-forth about career paths. With the lack of conflict—of what's-going-to-happen-now moments—the reader doesn't have a reason to turn the page and has too much of a reason to drop the book and pick up something else.

If you were critiquing this scene, you might make these comments:

- One of these characters is a crook, and the other's a PI. I think they should at least be threatening each other, arguing, if not breaking into a real fight. Is there something they can disagree about?

- I don't feel like there's enough tension or conflict in this scene. What is Collins' goal for this scene? Is there an opposing goal you can give to Stohl so we'll see the two of them at odds?

- I'd like to see things in this scene start out badly, as soon as Collins walks into Stohl's office, and then watch them get increasingly worse. At this point, I don't think the reader is wondering about what will happen to Collins, and he *needs* to be worrying.

The Author Has Written Summary, Not Scene

Show, don't tell. Every writer has heard this, but we still struggle to write strong, active scenes that show what's happening, rather than passively narrated descriptions that summarize character actions and emotions. We work to produce scenes that *show*, move more quickly, and involve the reader more strongly in the characters' lives and feelings. Summary has its place in small bits, but too much of it slows the pace and distances the reader from the characters.

In Fox's *The Accidental Demon Slayer*, we learn early on that Lizzie is adopted, and, a little further along, we find out that her birth mother disappeared right after giving Lizzie up for adoption. As Lizzie heads into her final, and most dangerous, battle, we get this passage.

> "Lizzie, no!"
>
> Terror seized me as I watched my hands disintegrate. There was no pain, only a horrible numbness. Blood poured from my wrists. It too faded, along with my forearms, my elbows, my—oh my god!
>
> "Elizabeth Gertrude Brown! Stop that immediately!"
>
> The spell blew away on the breeze. Bit by bit, like a macabre puzzle, my hands came together again. I swallowed hard and flexed my fingers, trying to get a grip on what had happened.
>
> I stood there for a long moment, stunned.
>
> "I'm sorry I yelled, but you should be immune to those spells. I don't know what's gotten into you," she scolded.
>
> It couldn't be. "Mom?" I asked shakily, forcing myself to tear my eyes away from my arms and hands. How else would she know my middle name?

In this scene, Fox *shows* us everything. Her vivid description of what the spell is doing to Lizzie has physical detail and emotional reaction. We see the spell disappear, despite Lizzie's own ability to fight it, because of the shock she experiences at hearing her full name. And we watch her pull back, not from the fear, but from that shock—the sudden, stunning knowledge that she is seeing her mother for the first time in her memory. Fox gives us all this without summarizing, or *telling*, a single drop of action or emotion.

Let's check out another moment from our sample. Here's the narrative when Collins first walks into Maguire's place.

> I looked at the inside of the apartment. I saw that there was no kitchen. I smelled things like cat pee, sweat, and moldy vegetables. I walked around, noticing that Maguire had a lot of empty fast-food bags and soda cans. They lay on the floor. The room was square. It had two doorways. One was open, and I could see that there was a bathroom behind it. The other doorway didn't have a door on it. The closet had a pile of dirty clothes on the floor. There was a TV next to the closet.
>
> I was tired. I looked at Maguire. He was dirty, too, like the room. He was smoking a cigarette, and he looked pretty happy. He had invited me here, and now I was waiting for him to tell me why. I felt a mix of anger and impatience, but I knew I had to stick around and hear him out.

In this passage, Collins *tells* us about what she's seeing, thinking, and feeling. Actually, the *author* does the telling. We're too far away from the character and her reactions to feel like the description is coming from her. We're given the bare surface of any details, rather than hard, tangible sensations the reader could grab on to. The passage uses vague words like *tired* and *dirty*, instead of showing us the actions that would make us feel we're following Collins through the apartment.

The summary pushes the reader away from the story instead of pulling him into it. If you were critiquing this scene, you could write these comments:

- What does Collins feel about this room? *Tired* isn't enough, I don't think, to give us the detailed reactions she must be having. Can you bring us closer into the scene and show us some of her responses?

- This passage is very "telling," as though the author is standing outside the room and describing the basic facts she wants us to know about it. I'd like to be in the room with Collins, feeling the dirt and smelling the stench.

- Can you get more specific with your details? I'd like to know where the fast-food bags are from and how littered they make the room feel. I'd like to experience Collins' tiredness, watch her eyes itch and her body need support. What does frustration feel like? Like a tightening forehead or a sour stomach? Clenching fists? Can you show us more of these images?

The Scene Starts or Ends in the Wrong Place

We've all heard that the first five pages of a book are critical for catching a reader, for catching an agent or editor. If you watch someone in a bookstore, he takes a book off a shelf, skims the first page, and then either puts the book back or carries it up to the cash register. At the opposite end of the spectrum, every reader wants to know how a story will end; it's one of the big reasons we keep turning the pages of a book. Well, the beginning of a scene is just as important for keeping a reader hooked, and a weak scene ending can be just as disappointing and frustrating for that reader as an unsatisfactory ending to a whole novel.

One of the biggest changes in fiction over the past decade is the speed with which a writer must pull a reader into the scene. We have less room for "warm-up" pages that orient the reader slowly in time and space. At the same time, the reader doesn't want us summarizing and explaining at the end of the scene; she wants a snappy ending or a cliff-hanger, something that leaves her no choice but to keep reading. As a critiquer, you can help the other members of your group write tight scenes that start and end at just the right places to make their readers happy.

In *Telegraph Days*, Larry McMurtry has his scene beginnings and endings down. He leaves the reader wanting more as each scene closes and pulls him instantly into the next scene.

Shortly after Nellie and her brother Jackson move to Rita Blanca, a local gang—the six Yazee brothers—ride into town ready to shoot it up. Jackson, a new deputy who has never shot a pistol, wanders out half asleep, without his shoes, and manages to shoot all six Yazees dead. After a moment of silence, Jackson stirs himself.

> "I need to get my boots on," Jackson said. "I'm apt to get bit by a stinging lizard, or else step on a grass burr. I hate those mean little stinging lizards."

> Then, with the whole town watching, Jackson strolled
> back into the jail and finished his nap.

After the intensity and excitement of the Yazees thundering down the street
on their horses, and Nellie being a few seconds away from death by stampede
or bullet, Jackson's response comes as the biggest shock of all. The towns-
people cannot believe, first, that only the bad guys are dead, or, second, that
Jackson isn't more affected. The scene ends like the eye of the hurricane, and
the reader has to turn the pages to see what the second half of the storm
will be like.

And McMurtry gives us the following passage.

> The first person to recover from the shock of the big fight that
> wiped out the Yazee gang was Beau Wheless—for maybe ten
> minutes, Beau was as stunned as the rest of us, but then his
> business instincts kicked in and kicked hard. A capacity for
> rapid response to commercial possibility probably explains
> why Beau Wheless was the richest man in Rita Blanca.
>
> "Come on, Billy, help me line up these Yazees," he said to
> his son. "Let's pile up their guns and valuables—and search
> close. I think we've got the makings of a fine little museum
> here."

Another writer might have taken the time to describe those "ten minutes"
of shock. The scene opening would have described the street and its occu-
pants—both dead and alive. Nellie, the narrator, would have produced some
paragraphs about her own feelings. McMurtry knows better. We start, not at
the shock, but at Beau Wheless' recovery from it. Within two sentences, Beau
is moving and planning, turning a near disaster into a marketing dream. Rita
Blanca has no time for mourning dead outlaws or discussing near what-ifs.
McMurtry knows better than to ask the reader to spare that time either.

How do Collins' scenes begin and end? Here is a scene ending from the
sample, followed by the start of the next scene:

> A short laugh got past his lips. "I got a nephew," he said.
> "He's talking about starting his own agency. I tell him there's a
> lot of late hours." He pushed himself off the desk and walked
> me to the door. "Have a good one, then."
>
> "Sure," I said and went to tell Sully the good news.

...

I'd told Sully I'd wait for him at the park the next morning to give him whatever news I had. I'd finally gotten a few hours sleep, and I'd managed to find clean underwear to put on, so I was feeling pretty good. I sat in the last intact swing on the swing set and pushed with my feet until I was gliding back and forth. In the sandbox a few feet away, two toddlers pushed trucks back and forth, and their older brother buried dinosaurs and dug them back up. Every now and then a dinosaur got a ride in a truck.

The sun was shining, and a robin sat in the tree above me, singing. As if in answer, I heard the ice cream van jingling down a street somewhere, probably only a few blocks away. I decided that, if the van was around when Sully showed up, I'd buy us both some ice cream. It was never too early for Rocky Road.

I might even let him push me down the slide.

Two mothers walked by with their strollers, talking. The babies were talking, too; at least, they were waving their hands back and forth at each other and making gentle squawking noises, kind of like chickens pecking around in a big scattering of grain. I waved a finger at them all, but nobody noticed. I guess their conversations were all too fascinating.

We already talked about how the ending of the scene with Stohl has no tension. That lack of conflict is one reason the reader may not care to keep reading. The other reason is that the scene ends with no open question, no setup to inspire the reader to wonder what will happen in the next scene. We know what will happen—we know the good news Sully is going to hear, and we aren't very excited to see him get it.

The opening of the next scene fails to catch the reader quickly. It may be a beautiful day in the neighborhood, but the reader doesn't want to spend this much time reading about it. She's starting the scene, hoping that something interesting will happen when Collins and Sully meet up. She wants to *see* that meeting, and she wants to see it quickly—a lot more quickly than she's getting it. Four paragraphs may not seem like all that much to read through, but even that little space, if it isn't used to suck your reader in, is long enough to lose her.

If you were critiquing these scene endings and beginnings, you could make these comments:

- Can you add a line or two to the end of the first scene to make us more interested in reading on? Is there a hint that Collins' job isn't going to be as easy as she, and the reader, think? Or does she end the scene with a bit of internal thought, showing that she's skeptical about Stohl's response and that she's really thinking about the plan she and Sully will have to make?

- Can the second scene move more quickly? If you need Collins to describe the day, can you use her thoughts and attitude to pull us into what's going on? Is she on high alert because she didn't believe Stohl, and she's watching for trouble? Or maybe she's worried that Sully won't believe her, and she's working out a plan to keep him from tagging along behind like a lost puppy.

- Is there a reason both Collins and Sully can't be there right at the beginning of the scene? Can you drop us into action and dialogue and then weave in the setting and Collins' mellow feelings around those? I'd like to see this scene really take off.

Section II
Worksheet 1: Critiquing Fiction

This worksheet is organized around the fiction categories we talked about critiquing in this section. Within each category, you'll see questions you can ask yourself that will help you recognize and comment on any weaknesses you find while you are critiquing. If you have trouble finding the answers to these questions, first push yourself to look more deeply, and then, if you still aren't clear, make sure to note this difficulty in your feedback to the author.

For practice, use this worksheet to do your own critique of our sample scene. Or you can use it to start the critique process on actual projects submitted by the writers in your group.

♀

Plot

- Can you identify the hero's overall goal? Describe it here or note that you aren't seeing it clearly. What steps is the hero taking to achieve that goal?

  _____

  _____

- What are the cause-and-effect story reasons behind the characters' actions?

  _____

  _____

- What are the subplots in the story? What connections has the author made between these subplots and the hero's main plot?

  _____

  _____

- What other plot comments and suggestions can you give the author?

_____

_____

Character

- How do the hero and other characters react to the world around them? How do they respond to each others' dialogue and to the actions and events taking place?

_____

_____

- How has the author portrayed her characters as real, layered people? What complex and contradictory traits do the characters possess? How do they show those traits with the actions and their dialogue?

_____

_____

- What happens to the hero that affects him strongly? What events occur to add to the hero's growth over the course of the story? How does the author show that growth?

_____

_____

- How does the character behave that may be inconsistent with his personality? What actions do you see that don't match the character development the author has created in the story so far? What story reasons, if any, does the author give for these shifts?

_____

_____

- What other character comments and suggestions can you give the author?

_____

_____

Voice and Point of View

- How would you describe the voice of the story? What kind of personality do the voice and point of view evoke? What examples can you point to that demonstrate the voice and point of view?

_____

_____

- Where do you see places that the narrator slips out of her own point of view? If the story is told in multiple points of view, track where and how the shifts are made clear and where they may be confusing.

_____

_____

- How does the point of view show the world through the hero's perspective? What has the author done to filter the actions and events of the story through the hero's way of seeing things?

_____

_____

- What other voice and point-of-view comments and suggestions can you give the author?

_____

_____

Dialogue

- What do the dialogue beats tell you about the characters? How do the beats layer in extra meaning to the characters' spoken words?

  _____

  _____

- What does the dialogue contribute to the story? How does the dialogue reveal or impact the plot? What does the dialogue tell you about the setting? How do the hero's spoken words differ from the narrative point of view?

  _____

  _____

- How is information revealed through dialogue? Can you show the author any places she may have used dialogue to dump too much information all in one chunk? How can the author trim this information, and where can she weave it through the story?

  _____

  _____

- What other dialogue comments and suggestions can you give the author?

  _____

  _____

Description

- How active are the author's settings? How does the author show characters moving through their world?

  _____

  _____

- How many details does the author use in her descriptions? Are there places the author could trim the words used to convey a character's appearance or a setting?

  _____

  _____

- How well does the author paint a picture of her characters? What kind of image do you see when you first meet a character in the story?

  _____

  _____

- What other description comments and suggestions can you give the author?

  _____

  _____

Scene Structure

- What does the author do to keep tension rising across a scene? How does the author increase the level of tension to keep the reader turning pages?

  _____

  _____

- What does the hero want in this specific scene? What does he do to get what he wants? How does the author make the goal hard for the hero to obtain?

  _____

  _____

- Where does the author start and end the scene? Would there be a better moment to drop the reader into a scene? How does the author keep the tension up at the end of the scene to keep the reader hooked?

_____

_____

- What other scene-structure comments and suggestions can you give the author?

_____

_____

FICTION CRITIQUE EXAMPLES

The following pages provide an example critique of our fiction writing sample. The first pages takes pieces of that sample and shows notes you might make as you read through the scenes. The second page shows an example of an overall critique you might present to the author.

Sample Manuscript Pages with Line Notes

"Leave me alone," Maguire said. He was taller than me, with brown hair cut short. He wore a sweatshirt and jeans, and his sneakers were white, with a hole in the toe of the left one. He folded his arms across his belly and glared at me.

> What is Collins' goal here? What does she want from Maguire? Should she be more active toward that goal, or is there a reason she is just waiting? We may need to see another layer, maybe with internal thoughts, to understand.

"I've got nothing else to do today," I told him.

Maguire stared at me, then checked his watch. He tapped it a couple of times. Maybe the battery had died.

I let myself slip down the wall until I was sitting on the cement. I stretched my legs out in front of me and tilted my head back against the wall.

Maguire shuffled from foot to foot, then checked his watch again. Finally, he said, "I'm out of here," and he took off down the alley.

I watched him go. I could have caught him if I'd tried. It wouldn't have even taken a sprint. But I was tired. Tired of asking questions, tired of seeing his fear. I stayed where I was, against the wall.

🌢

Just as I came in, a tall, skinny woman with gray and purple hair stuck a quarter in the jukebox, and Elvis greeted my entrance with "Jailhouse

Rock." The woman swung away from the machine and jitterbugged her way back across the room, stopping to talk to an elderly couple that looked like they'd been in those chairs since the turn of the century. The last century. She shook their hands between steps, then danced all the way to her table, spinning a circle around her chair before she sat down.

The room was filled with tables, filled with people. All colors of the rainbow, both in skin and clothes, including two waitresses. The lamps over the tables had panels of fake stained glass—ugly reds and blues and yellows. There were big-screen TVs in all four corners. The same picture of the same newscaster was up on all of them. The floor was dirty, with peanut shells and various liquids spilled onto it.

♣

By the time I was finished drinking, just about everybody else had split or fallen asleep. I stepped around the bodies and the puddles of beer and made my way outside, where the air was cooler and fresher but still felt like it was trying to choke me.

I pulled up the hood on my jacket, shoved my hands in my pockets, and headed around the corner.

Where Maguire's girlfriend waited for me.

"Maguire told me to give this to you." She held out a manila envelope, thick enough to hold a big stack of papers or photos. Or money.

I took it. "Okay," I said.

"He wants you to meet him," she went on. "He's holed up at the Nite Inn, down Fifty-Seventh

Sidenote (right margin, top): There are a lot of details in this setting. They're all pretty interesting, but I'm not sure you need them all—maybe pick and choose the more important ones? Also, you may want to have Collins interact more with the setting, show her moving through it, reacting to the people (or being reacted to).

Sidenote (right margin, bottom): This scene lacks tension. These women aren't friends; they actually have the potential to be antagonists, but we don't see any real emotion between them. Is the girlfriend angry that Collins is hassling Maguire? Or jealous about the meet? Is Collins worried that the girlfriend is part of a trap? Or irritated with Maguire for not coming? You could use their dialogue and dialogue beats to show more conflict.

Street." Slinging her purse over her shoulder, she said, "It's only a few blocks. I'll show you."

I took some steps. She walked quickly and checked back every few seconds to make sure I was following.

I was.

❧

Maguire stepped closer to me, then took the cigarette out of his mouth and flicked the ashes off the end. They landed on my shirt.

I rustled around in the desk, shoving aside piles of paper clips, candy wrappers, and two guns. "How far from here is Stohl?" I asked.

"Hey," Maguire called to the girl. "You got a pen?"

The girl checked her fingernails, then pulled a file out of her purse. She buffed the nail on one index finger and put the file away.

"Hey!" Maguire shouted. "A pen?!"

I slammed the drawer shut so hard it popped out again and fell onto the floor, spilling its contents. I reached down, grabbed the gun that had landed at my feet, and whipped it up against Maguire's temple.

"Don't talk to her like that," I told him.

I like that Collins takes action here, but I'm not sure her behavior is quite believable. The sudden power seems inconsistent with her usual passivity. Can you give us a strong, scene-based reason for the change or set up this aspect of her personality in an earlier scene?

❧

He nodded. "Good of Maguire to bring you by so late."

"Good, ha. It cost me four hundred to get to you. And I still owe him another hundred."

"Four hundred dollars. You must really have wanted to see me." His voice went quiet. "Why?"

There are a couple of things happening here that I think you could work on. Collins' explanation reads a bit too much like an info dump—can you break it up with action/interaction and some dialogue beats?

This was it. I took a breath and started talking. "On Wednesday, I was talking to a butcher on First Street. He wanted to hire me to find his wife. Whatever. When I left, this kid Sully followed me. He told me about his problem, which is that he found some CDs in the alley behind the butcher shop and took them home. He copied them onto his MP3 player. A couple of days after that, he was chased when he left work. There were three men and a big dog. He lost them in a video arcade. Sully says the dog is yours. He wants me to talk to you and tell you he'll give the CDs back. Sully's afraid of you."

"Sully's got nothing to fear from me," Stohl said.

Also, Stohl makes it very easy for Collins to achieve her goal (keeping Sully safe). Should he perhaps throw some obstacles in her path?

❧

The sun was shining, and a robin sat in the tree above me, singing. As if in answer, I heard the ice cream van jingling down a street somewhere, probably only a few blocks away. I decided that, if the van was around when Sully showed up, I'd buy us both some ice cream. It was never too early for Rocky Road.

Collins shifts voice here. She switches from her usual dry, dark narration to a voice that sounds upbeat. Did you mean to make the change? If so, you might want to give a reason.

I might even let him push me down the slide.

Two mothers walked by with their strollers, talking. The babies were talking, too; at least, they were waving their hands back and forth at each other and making gentle squawking noises, kind of like chickens pecking around in a big scattering of grain. I waved a finger at them all, but nobody noticed. I guess their conversations were all too fascinating.

The babies chattered away, playing with the toys on the stroller bar and digging for the rattles beneath their blankets. The wind picked up and tousled what little hair they had, and dust swirled up around the stroller wheels. Mary smiled at Liza, glad to be out in the early spring sunshine, and then reached down and tucked the blanket more snugly around her daughter.

Sully turned the corner at the end of the street. I waved—my arm this time—until he saw me. He wasn't happy. He'd expected me to bring Stohl or one of Stohl's goons with me so he could hand off the CDs in public—with me for protection. Now he was mad that he'd come to the park for nothing.

He came up to the swing and looked at me.

"Step back," I said. Then I took a couple of big swings and, at the peak of the arc, jumped off and landed in the dirt. On my feet. Yes!

"Nice," Sully said.

He didn't mean it.

Collins steps out of her close, first-person point of view. She can't know that Sully isn't happy, that he's mad, because she's not seeing or hearing anything to show that. Maybe just let Sully get a little closer so she can see his face, or let him say something to show his feelings?

SAMPLE OVERALL PLOT CRITIQUE

Jane,

You're setting the stage for a very good story. I think you have details here that can send your detective digging into her mystery, stir her curiosity, and get her closer to solving the case. You have a great voice going and I'd love to see you make it even *more* distinctive.

There are a few things I think you'll want to think about as you move forward and before you go back to revise.

You may want to work on the overall arc of the plot. Because Collins is a detective, we can assume that her goal is to solve a mystery, but we don't see her doing a lot to get *to* that goal. I think she needs to do some more actual detecting. She lets Maguire run away, she doesn't make any plans for the investigation, and she ignores Maguire's girlfriend until she has no choice. I like her dark attitude and voice, but I think we need to see her taking more action and thinking more about what she's going to do.

Also, I don't see much growth in Collins over these pages. Other than the time she loses her temper with Maguire (which actually feels *out* of character), she stays pretty static—going about her business with a low level of energy and responding slowly to what happens around her. I think, in future scenes, if not these, you'll want to do more to show Collins changing, getting affected by story events and learning from them. She needs to be at a different point, personalitywise, by the end of the book than she is here.

I'd like to see more tension in these scenes. While Collins doesn't work too hard to get what she wants, she still gets those things pretty easily. Can some of the characters create obstacles and problems that she needs to overcome? I think Stohl particularly could be a major antagonist, instead of assuring her so quickly that he's happy to see her and that her client, Sully, is safe. Some sections of dialogue—those between Collins and the girlfriend, and between Collins and Stohl—also lack tension. A few dialogue beats showing action and some of Collins' internal thoughts would go a long way toward changing that.

I think your settings go back and forth between too much and not enough detail. We get lots of description about the sports bar and the park, but I think we could do with a bit less there. I'd like to see just a few pieces of information about both places, with a sense that those pieces are important to Collins. I'd like to see her interact with those details and move through the settings, rather than just describe them. In the office scene with Stohl, I think we need *more* details. These, too, would need to be important to the scene, to the conversation, and the actions that are happening.

I'm not getting a strong sense of what your characters look like. I would love some kind of description of Collins—at least a couple of things about her that would help me picture her. What kind of clothing does she wear? Is she thin and lean, or has all that alcohol damaged her body? Is her hair short and businesslike or long so she can hide behind it? And then just a bit more on each of the other main characters, enough to give us a basic sense of who they are, but not so much that we get lost in the descriptions and forget about the story.

GETTING THE FACTS RIGHT ...
AND INTERESTING:
HOW TO CRITIQUE NONFICTION

Nonfiction contains an incredible range of genres, from memoir to how-to. A writer of nonfiction has something important to say, just as important as the words coming from a novelist, and his job is to get that something on the page in a way that will intrigue, captivate, and help his readers. Knowing the facts or the technology is not enough, a nonfiction writer must clarify these details into information the reader not only can take in, but that she'll happily digest and learn from. When you're critiquing nonfiction, you'll need to work hard to help writers achieve this clarity, to give them suggestions and comments about writing strong prose that will make their readers keep turning pages.

In this section, I talk about how to critique various types of nonfiction. I've dedicated a separate chapter to critiquing each of these forms.

- Magazine articles
- Nonfiction book proposals
- How-to and self-help books
- Memoir
- Travel books and articles

Each of these types of books makes different demands on the writer and on the critiquer reading the writer's manuscripts. If you're reviewing a manuscript for one of your critique partners, you can read through the chapter that talks about working on his genre. The information and tips will help you dig in and start developing the kind of feedback he needs.

At the same time, all nonfiction shares important elements for the writer and critiquer to think about. Organization and the "right" level of detail are challenges all nonfiction

Section III

writers face and all nonfiction critiquers can help with. If your critique group regularly writes and critiques any kind of nonfiction, the information in the following chapters will help you produce the most constructive, useful critiques you can.

CRITIQUING NONFICTION—WRITING SAMPLES

In each chapter of this section, I use bits from real books as examples of strong nonfiction writing. I also use made-up excerpts to show examples of nonfiction writing with some common weakness and to teach how to critique this kind of writing. The following pages contain these "fake" excerpts. You can read through these samples now and then refer back to them as you work through the specific chapters.

Magazine-Article Sample: "How to Relocate Easily (and Happily) to the Mountains"

Many people dream of living in the country, away from the "rat trap" of the city in which they work and play. They imagine quiet, peaceful moments, sitting inside by the fire or outside staring at the stars. Birds will tweet, coyotes will howl, an occasional bobcat will saunter by. These people can give up the crowded streets of an urban neighborhood and get away from the shouts and screams of angry households. They can even brew their own coffee and stop dealing with lines out the door of the local coffeehouse. Their children will run free on the hills, build birdhouses, and weave macramé. Every evening will find the family gathered together, with Mom or Dad reading aloud from a favorite novel. Mornings will be a pleasure to wake up to, with sunshine streaming in the curtainless windows, and alarm clocks will become an evil tool of the past. Life will be good.

The week after we moved to the mountains, my husband spent an entire Saturday inside the water-storage tank. The bottom and sides were covered with silt and ... gunk that had settled in there from the water system (no, we weren't on public water lines) over who knew how many years. The tank is black plastic, which—even in April—heats up to a pretty nasty, suffocating temperature, especially when you're stuck inside it. Scrubbing. Yes, he climbed out for lunch, and, yes, I—the helpful wife—came out to call an occasional echoey hello down to him. I also kept him company while he, after finishing the job, waited for the tank to refill so he could take a shower. And I didn't put a clothespin on my nose.

Then there was the day he decided to test the fireplace. It's a big fireplace—takes up one entire wall of the living room—and it's covered with a facing of rocks. Impressive is the right word for it. Until you try to use it.

I missed the excitement, but came home to hear the story about how the flue didn't "draw." (Until that day, I'd thought draw was something you did with a pencil.) I also got the details of how, if you didn't notice right away that the flu didn't draw, you came into the house to find the entire living room filled with smoke, so much so that to see (and breathe), you had to drop to your hands and knees and crawl across the floor. Then reach up to open every door and window in the house to let the air in.

Because you'd already had your suffocation experience in the water tank the day before.

...

If you're smart, you're going to clear your roof of debris by the end of autumn, before the California rains start, and you're shoveling mulch instead of leaves. If you forget, however—if livetrapping and transporting the local raccoon family has kept you busy through the holiday season—don't worry. When you see the puddle on your floor that means "roof leak," you'll know it's time to get up there now. It's relatively easy to do the job, rainstorm or not.

Pull the ladder out of your garage and lean it up against the side of your house. Take a minute to see that the feet are securely planted on level ground and somewhere they won't slip. Then stick your shovel and rake under your arm and climb on up. It's probably a good idea to wear a raincoat with pockets so that when your bifocals get fogged up, you've got a safe place to tuck them away. Then work your way across the roof, digging the soggy leaves from the gutters (and anywhere else they've piled) and toss them off the roof. (You can deal with that mess later!) Do watch for slippery spots; even California winters can be cold enough to create surprise icy patches.

Nonfiction Book-Proposal Sample: *Raising a Reader*

The Market: Most families in the United States have at least one child. Research shows that a child who reads has a better chance for success in school, college, and their professional career. Parents who have young children will pick up *Raising a Reader* for ideas about how to start their infant with board books, and grandparents will come to it looking for advice about birthday presents. Teachers may find the book a good resource to supplement the materials they receive at continuing-education workshops.

The Competition: *Teach Your Toddler to Read* takes parents through the basics of phonics before they drop their child off at kindergarten. Essays and instructions written by professional teachers help parents give their toddlers a step into academics by setting up school at home. Each lesson takes the family through another piece of the big picture. *Raising a Reader* does not contain reading lessons.

The Author: Carly Sussman is the mother of one son who is an avid reader. She began reading to him when he was an infant, progressing through picture books and beginning readers, until they were diving together into full-length novels. They still share a love of books, swapping stories back and forth and recommending new authors to each other. Carly is the neighborhood go-to resource for other parents looking for new titles for their own kids, and she has a close relationship with her local librarians.

Excerpt from Sample Chapter—"At the Bookstore"

At the bookstore, it's important to study the child's habits. Observe whether they walk back and forth between shelves, or whether they seat themselves on the floor and resist further movement. A notebook can be an optimal tool at this time. A journal of the child's behavior, over time, can demonstrate their book-purchasing patterns. As you progress with developing the child's interest in reading, the notes you record will increase chances for success.

How-To Book Sample: *How to Share Your Home (and Life) With a Pet*

Table of Contents

Introduction

Unless someone in your family has a bad allergy, there will come a time in your life that you start to seriously consider adding a pet to the household. This may happen when you graduate college and get your own first apartment, when you get married or buy a house, or when your children are old enough to start begging. You may be completely enthusiastic about the idea, or be determined that no creature with fleas will enter your household. However you started out, you've picked up this book because a pet is imminent.

An animal is another warm body, one that makes unique demands on and brings unique benefits to a family. As much as they would like to, they don't eat your food, and they—except for a few rare exceptions—don't know how to flush a toilet. They can't run the vacuum or dust the bookshelves.

They can, and do, appreciate a good snuggle, and they typically greet you at the front door with love in their eyes (especially if you left their food bowl full in the morning). They're always up for a good game and don't know how to be a "poor sport."

Pets are furry and winged, scaled and feathered. They run, swim, fly, and slither, and they are sure—however they move—to weave their way into your life, like the threads of your most comfortable blanket.

Self-Help Book Sample: *Overcoming Your Writing Fears*

Chapter 3. Baby Steps or Giant Steps?

Once you've decided to face your fears and anxieties about putting your own words on the page, how should you start? Should you dip a single toe into the water or hold your nose and jump in with a cannonball splash?

Go for it. Dive right in; the water's fine. If you tiptoe along, creeping around corners flashlight-first, you're going to get nowhere fast. Stretch your writing muscles and sit down at that computer. Get the thickest binder you can find, because you're going to need it to store the pages that will come pouring out of your fingers and printer. Sure, you'll feel nervous—your stomach will twitch, and your head will ache, but it's time to push aside all those reactions holding you back.

Believe me, I know how you feel. "Been there, done that." My brain has a whole list of tricks it has thrown at me to keep me from writing, and I've stepped around every trap it's laid. I write, despite the stress or tension it creates in me, and I produce.

...

Where will those giant steps take you? You'll have chapters piling up on your desk, words you've written, stories you've created. Those printouts will smile up at you and make you satisfied and proud, sure of your abilities.

Yes? Of course, yes! Now turn the page to the next chapter and get ready for your pep talk on revision!

Memoir Sample: *Growing Up With Grandparents*

For a few years, my maternal grandmother lived in our hometown, just a few blocks from my parents' veterinary clinic. We would visit her at times, just the three girls, and I remember some of the things she used to entertain us with. She had a trunk of yarn, and she would teach us how to knit, if we wished. In the middle of some those skeins, she had hidden a prize that we could "win" when we finished knitting up the skein. She made us sandwiches of butter and sugar, and she sent us outside into her garden to walk the rows. In one area, she grew chives, and we were allowed to snap off the tops and eat them.

...

We climbed down the steps the hotel had installed for the tourists—easy access from Grandma and Grandpa's room to the sands and ocean of Pismo Beach. We found an open space to drop our towels and buckets, then stripped off our sweatshirts and pants, even though we shivered in the fog. We lined up, the three young girls and the tall, skinny grandfather.

"Ready ... " Grandma called. "Set ... Go!"

And we ran.

Grandfather gave us all a head start, but we didn't go slowly. We pounded down the hard sand near the water, kicking up little chunks of dirt and leaping over seaweed and broken shells. We raced as hard as our legs and hearts would let us.

It didn't matter. He was too fast.

He beat us every time, coming up on us from behind, passing us one at a time, but always passing us. He called himself a greyhound, but he didn't run with grace. Instead, he seemed all bones and joints—elbows high and out, skinny knees pumping high.

We ran, if possible, even faster, our breath coming short, and our skin heated against the cold air. It was no use, though. We couldn't catch up, not until we reached the end of the course, where he waited for us. And we threw ourselves on him, hugging and laughing, happy to be with him and to have been beaten again.

...

I stood outside the door of the hospital room and looked in. The cold I had was keeping me in the hallway, because—after having a pacemaker placed next to his heart—the last thing Grandpa needed was a case of the sniffles. So I waved, and I looked, relieved in the doctor's report that the procedure had gone smoothly and my grandfather would be fine. He lay against the pillows, his thin white hair combed back from his bald spot, somehow looking so much older than he had last month. But he talked to my parents and grandmother, and I knew he'd be home soon, out of the cold metal and sterile white of the hospital bed.

...

When my grandfather died, he was eighty-seven years old, and he'd spent the last few years moving from a cane to a walker to a wheelchair. He'd had a series of little strokes that had not only hit his legs and back and arms, but also attacked his throat muscles so that he had serious problems getting words out. They were there, in his mind—he knew what he wanted to tell us. He just couldn't ... always.

My grandmother had help taking care of him, but she still—in her own eighties—did as much as she physically could. She'd get him situated in the living room, then do her own stuff around him—tidying, cooking a little, reading the newspaper—and coming back and forth whenever he needed her or she thought he did. They'd been married sixty years; he didn't always have to talk for her to know what he was thinking or wanting.

When we came to visit, we'd sit on the couch opposite Grandpa's wheelchair. We'd talk with Grandma, tell her about our days, our work, our own children. We'd include Grandpa by turning to face him, by waiting to see if he would manage to force out a comment. Then we'd go on with Grandma, having a cookie or two from the plate she'd brought from the kitchen. We'd listen to a few of her worries or anxieties. She never shared many, though, even when the problems and sadness were set out so clearly right there in front of us.

Sample Header: Travel-Writing Sample:
Walking the Lake District

On day four of my trip, I find myself at the edge of Lake Buttermere. It's the midpoint on my travels, and I feel acclimated to the area—not quite a native, but something past a tourist. My new coat fits better, and the first-day blisters from the boots have calloused over. I've learned that a good wind can come up at any time, and so my hair is braided tightly against my head, and my knit hat is in an accessible pocket. I buy a packet of "crisps" at the teahouse for an extra lunch treat, and I head out.

...

As I stare up at the green and orange hills rising in front of me, I can't help but go back to my bedroom as a child, curled up with another of Arthur Ransome's books. I see the Swallows and Amazons puffing up through the heather, sweating with the weight of their packs. Nancy is in front, of course, waving at the others to keep up, and Roger is bouncing around like a rabbit, unable to keep a straight course, even with the hard climb.

I can almost smell the pages of the book, my mother's copy, spine cracked from all the reading, pages dog-leafed from the many places we've all had to stop reading for homework or dinner. The sunshine breaking through the clouds around me is bright, but in my mind I am in my cool, dark room, supposedly "sleeping in" on a Saturday morning, but really just lying there grabbing more hours of reading. If I get up, if I show my face, there will be breakfast and chores and errands. If I don't open the door, I can stay tucked away in here for hours, climbing the hills with my favorite British kids.

...

I'm ready to take my first steps. First, though, I have to get through, or over, the intricate contraption built into the fence to keep sheep in. Or maybe out. The mechanism looks like a mix between a turnstile at a subway entrance and the entrance gates to Disneyland. It's got a set of crossbars that don't quite intersect with each other but that have no form or pattern I can identify. I can imagine that this obstacle would deter a sheep; it intimidates me. I shift my pack higher onto my back, make sure my water bottles aren't coming loose, and grip the top bar. I place one booted foot firmly on the lowest bar and my other on the next one up. Moving slowly, keeping my pack in balance, I climb up and up. At the top, I look down, impressed and amazed that I have made it this far without getting tangled inside the contraption. Then I make my way down, watching for loose shoelaces. At the bottom rung, inside the gate, I make a triumphant leap the last few inches, landing with both feet planted firmly on a clump of heather. Done. I am smarter and more coordinated than a sheep.

...

As I slide down the hill, skidding between the rocks on the trail, I meet a family making their way up. The father waves, and the mother tells me, "Hello," her accent announcing them as British. They stop at a curve in the path. I nod as I go by, eyes intent on my boots, mind focused on not tripping and rolling the rest of the way to the bottom. The lake glistens blue beneath me, too cold I'm sure, but still throwing up the tempting idea of a cool swim in the hot sunlight. The sheep dotting the hills look like white cotton balls with noses, and I feel as though I could jump off the hill and land safely on one of their cushiony backs.

Chapter 10

CRITIQUING A MAGAZINE ARTICLE

Magazines offer a world of freelance opportunities for writers. That world is a big one, but it's also extremely competitive. A writer needs to be able to produce tight, well-written pieces that target a specific audience and hook that audience from word one. When you're writing for magazines, you must balance delivering your information with writing in a voice that keeps the reader engaged.

If your critique group works on magazines articles, you'll need to be familiar with the parts of a good article. Your job will be to recognize a weak hook and help the writer strengthen it. You'll be checking whether the author has picked interesting details to share, and whether he or she keeps the focus of the article flowing from beginning to end. As critique partners, you can help each other increase your chances of getting articles into print.

RECOGNIZING THE WEAK SPOTS

Critiquing a magazine article is a very different experience from critiquing a book. As readers, we may immerse ourselves thoroughly in a few magazines, but more often, we skim through them quickly. They're in our doctors' offices, on the coffee tables at our friends' houses, and at the beauty parlor or barbershop. We pick up the magazine for a few minutes and skip around, dipping into an article here or there.

When you critique, you have to push yourself past this light level of reading. You have to break the habit of hurrying through and slow yourself down to really look at all the components of the piece. The author wants this article to be the one that *keeps* a reader's attention, and your careful critique will help her achieve that goal.

As you read and come across weak spots in a magazine article, here are some reactions you may have:

- You lose interest in the topic.
- You get confused about what the article is saying.
- You get irritated with the author.
- You wonder about the purpose of the piece.
- You feel overwhelmed by information.

ANALYZING THE WEAKNESSES

When you critique a magazine article, you'll be watching for how quickly you get pulled into the story and for how strongly you want to keep reading after that. You'll want to note whether you find the information interesting or useful and whether the author's focus is clear and strong.

In this chapter, we'll look at the following common problems you may come across while you critique magazine articles:

- The article has a weak hook.
- There is a poor balance between anecdotes and information.
- The piece isn't targeted at the magazine's audience.
- The article's organization makes information hard to find.

The Article Has a Weak Hook

If a book reader reads a page or two and then decides whether to keep going, a magazine reader reads one or two *paragraphs*. This means the opening of the article—the hook—is of utmost importance. The hook has to pull in the reader and convince him to keep reading. And, before that, the hook has to catch the *editor* and make her think seriously about buying the article.

As a critiquer, you can help the author write a tight hook with a strong voice. You can talk about the small, right piece of information he can use to intrigue or excite the reader. You can help him produce the strongest hook possible.

In her article, "Kitties on the Couch" (*Cat Fancy*, January 2009), Katie Costello leads off with this first sentence.

> Behavior problems are the No. 1 reason for feline relinquish-
> ment and euthanasia.

Whew. Costello doesn't pull any punches. She sets out, immediately, the incredibly high risk—the possibility of death—for cats who aren't trained out of poor behavior. The reader is caught. Even if the reader isn't planning on abandoning a cat because it fights with the other pets, Costello has just used the dramatic opener to up the stakes for all animals. She shows the reader that this problem is bigger than he may have realized. He's going to read further to see how big this problem is and what he, specifically, should be doing to prevent it in his own home.

Here's the opening paragraph from our sample article, "How to Relocate Easily (and Happily) to the Mountains."

> Many people dream of living in the country, away from the "rat trap" of the city in which they work and play. They imagine quiet, peaceful moments, sitting inside by the fire or outside staring at the stars. Birds will tweet, coyotes will howl, an occasional bobcat will saunter by. These people can give up the crowded streets of an urban neighborhood and get away from the shouts and screams of angry households. They can even brew their own coffee and stop dealing with lines out the door of the local coffeehouse. Their children will run free on the hills, build birdhouses, and weave macramé. Every evening will find the family gathered together, with Mom or Dad reading aloud from a favorite novel. Mornings will be a pleasure to wake up to, with sunshine streaming in the curtainless windows, and alarm clocks will become an evil tool of the past. Life will be good.

The prose in this first paragraph is nice. It evokes an image of just the sort of rural paradise many people probably do fantasize about. However, while this may seem like a good tone to set, it's actually too *much* like that image—the author hasn't brought anything new to the paragraph. She hasn't dropped in that different, interesting detail that will make the reader say, "*This* is an article I want to read." The paragraph doesn't have a dramatic statement, or a twist, or a bite of humor about this idyll. The truth is, this paragraph doesn't have a hook.

If you were critiquing this opening for a writer, you could make one or more of the following comments:

- I think you need something more in this paragraph to really catch your audience. They probably already know the things you're telling them; in fact, they may have turned to the article because they *are* dreaming about a life just like this. What can you add that they *haven't* thought of?

- Most readers will probably know that this "dream" isn't realistic. Can you flip some of the information in this paragraph to show some of the other side of rural life—maybe a skunk or no electricity with which to make coffee? Can you do this humorously so they'll laugh and get interested?

- What will your article offer readers—other than this description of the nice side of country life? Are you going to tell them how to deal with the reality of living in the mountains so they can at least have some of the fantasy? Are you going to educate them so they'll believe they might be able to make this move? Can you include that angle in the hook paragraph?

The Article Has a Poor Balance Between Anecdotes and Information

People read articles and subscribe to magazines because of specific interests—cats, cooking, the news. Those readers want to know an article is written by someone who knows the topic well. They want to be able to identify with that author. What the reader doesn't want is to be buried in personal stories and revelations.

If we're writing for magazines, we need to juggle how much of ourselves (i.e., our own experiences) to share with the reader and how much to leave out. We will be playing with the right balance as we write, and chances are we're not going to get it right the first time.

When you're critiquing an article, you can help the author by looking for this balance. You can note specific places where the balance between anecdotes and information isn't working and offer suggestions about how to shift the focus one way or the other.

In the article "Beyond the Burn" (*Runner's World*, February 2009), Ed Eyestone discusses new discoveries about lactic acid. He starts us off with a small story from his youth, when he "would endure long massages, believing that it would flush the evil brew out of my muscles ... "

After the brief trip back in time, Eyestone quickly drops us into the body of the article, focusing on the more current perspective and information about lactic acid. One short paragraph later, he's giving us a definition.

> Lactic acid is a byproduct that's created when we burn gly-
> cogen without oxygen as we run. The higher the intensity of
> the run, the more lactic acid we create.

Eyestone is writing an informational article, not an autobiographical piece. He has a limited number of words with which to deliver as many helpful details as possible to his audience, and he doesn't use up those words on long, personal stories. He gives his readers just a taste of his own experience to establish his credibility as the author of this article, then he moves into tightly written explanations and tips.

Let's compare the anecdotal information in our article to that in Eyestone's piece.

> The week after we moved to the mountains, my husband
> spent an entire Saturday *inside* the water-storage tank. The
> bottom and sides were covered with silt and ... *gunk* that
> had settled in there from the water system (no, we weren't
> on public water lines) over who knew how many years. The
> tank is black plastic, which—even in April—heats up to a
> pretty nasty, suffocating temperature, especially when you're
> stuck inside it.
>
> ...
>
> Then there was the day he decided to test the fireplace.
> It's a big fireplace—takes up one entire wall of the living
> room—and it's covered with a facing of rocks. *Impressive* is
> the right word for it. Until you try to use it.

These two paragraphs following the lead are stories. They do demonstrate a contrast with the perfect world shown in the lead, but the writer doesn't bother to point out the irony. Instead they leave the reader wondering why the stories are here. On top of that, the reader is now three paragraphs into an article and hasn't yet been given any concrete information. This opening might be okay if the writer were writing an autobiographical piece, but this is a how-to article. The author is not fulfilling his promise to instruct.

If one of the writers in your group shared this section, you might make these critiques:

- I laughed out loud in the paragraph about the fireplace. It's a great story. I think, though, that the personal accounts in this piece go on for too long. Can you pick just one of the anecdotes? You may even want to trim down that one a bit.

- You're writing a how-to article, but I'm not seeing any solid information yet. I'm afraid the reader will get frustrated from the lack of specific instructions.

- Maybe you could break the article out into sets of instructions and use your stories as examples of how those instructions can be helpful. In other words, if you're telling the reader to check out the water system, you could use the tank story as a reason to do this *before* buying a house.

The Article Isn't Targeted at the Magazine's Audience

One of the most important factors in writing for magazines is research—finding out as much as you can about the magazine you're querying and the people reading it. It isn't enough to decide to write a piece about knitting and then send letters or articles off to ten craft magazines. As writers we need to understand the level of knowledge the audience has and the kind of information they're looking for. And we need to give that to them.

When we're writing articles, we often get so caught up in the material we forget to watch out for the audience. We know what we want to talk about, and it's easy to lose focus on the readers for whom we're writing. Our job, when we write for magazines, is to make sure we adjust that focus and write specifically for our reader.

If you're critiquing a magazine piece, you can watch for how well the author manages this task. If you're not familiar with the specific magazine, talk to the writer about it. Get an understanding of the audience and critique with that audience in mind. You can help the writer produce an article that will truly address that magazine's readership.

In Brad Kollus' article "What's in It for Them?" (*Cat Fancy*, January 2009), he starts off like this.

> It might seem obvious that cats benefit from a relationship with humans, but new studies show a more complex picture. Some cats benefit from that human-feline bond more than others. And the extent of which cats benefit has a lot to do with the owner.

Kollus targets exactly the kind of information his audience is looking for—research that proves that how they interact with their cats is important. *Cat Fancy* readers are, obviously, very attached to their pets. They know very well how happy their cats make them, and they are highly motivated to return the favor. Kollus promises, right up front, that he's going to help them do just that.

Kollus backs up his lead with evidence from studies that show specifically what an owner can do to improve her cat's life. Kollus provides his reader with data to think about and jobs she can do. The scientific angle to the article gives weight to Kollus' story. Even without the research he cites, however, Kollus' understanding of his audience shows up clearly in that first paragraph. His story focus hits the audience right on target.

Here's the first bit of instructional detail from our how-to excerpt.

> Pull the ladder out of your garage and lean it up against the side of your house. Take a minute to see that the feet are securely planted on level ground and somewhere they won't slip. Then stick your shovel and rake under your arm and climb on up. It's probably a good idea to wear a raincoat with pockets so that when your bifocals get fogged up, you've got a safe place to tuck them away. Then work your way across the roof, digging the soggy leaves from the gutters (and anywhere else they've piled) and toss them off the roof. (You can deal with *that* mess later!) Do watch for slippery spots; even California winters can be cold enough to create surprise icy patches.

Let's talk about the audience for this material. Who is this magazine written for? This is probably acceptable information for some young, active homeowners, but what if the author is submitting this piece to a magazine called *South Carolina Senior Citizen Safety*? I don't think so. Okay, I've pushed this for humor's sake, but also to make a point. Research is critical for magazine writing, and a good critiquer can help a writer do some reality checks—not just about *what* he's writing but *who* he's writing it for.

If you were critiquing this piece, you could include these comments and questions:

- Who is your audience for this article? Are the readers do-it-yourself types or more wealthy people used to paying others to do this kind of work? If they're the latter, wouldn't they find some information about how to *find* those workers more helpful here?

- You said you were writing this article for a senior citizens' magazine. The information you're giving them feels pretty casual, maybe even unsafe. I think you'll want to either rethink the instructions you've picked or the magazine you're going to query for this article.

- Do you think a lot of people from South Carolina will be thinking about moving to the mountains in *California*? Could you do more research about rural life in the South so you can target that readership specifically?

The Article's Organization Makes Information Hard to Find

Some magazine articles tell a story or at least let their narrative flow from a beginning to an end. Other articles set out to give the reader immediate information or instructions on very specific topics. In the latter types of pieces, organization is critical. The reader may or may not read an entire article, but she won't read any of it if she takes a look at the page and can't quickly see what she's getting.

When we're writing this kind of article, we must be sure our material is organized into clear categories and that the article headings announce loudly and clearly what the reader will find under each one.

As a critiquer, you can test these headings and the organization by reading carefully. Can you guess what's coming? Does the information meet your expectations? If not, take the time to let the author know where he needs to do some more work.

In "Tape Yourself," (*Runner's World*, February 2009), Beth Dreher pulls the reader into the article with a quick description of the tape the athletes wore at the Beijing Olympics. She then adds a short paragraph of information about why this tape is helpful. Immediately after this lead, Dreher shifts modes into information delivery. She titles each section of the article simply, with the names of different injuries and the reason to use tape for each. Here's what jumps out at the reader when he glances at the page—in large, pink font and slightly smaller, bold, black font below.

A. ACHILLES TENDINITIS: Protect the tendon from overuse.
B. PLANTAR FASCIITIS: Support the foot while relieving pain.
C. RUNNER'S KNEE: Decrease stress on the patellar tendon.
D. SHINSPLINTS: Take the pressure off irritated shins.

Beneath each heading are a few steps for taping the specific injury, but the reader doesn't have to read them all. Imagine the poor reader who has all four injuries at once and has to figure out where to put all that tape! Dreher has made it easy for each reader to hone in on the specific help he or she needs. The athlete with plantar fasciitis can instantly get instructions for easing the pain in her foot. She'll probably store the article away, in case of future injuries, because the author's information has been useful and simple to find.

Let's take another look at the roof-cleaning passage in our sample how-to article. Here's the first paragraph that talks about the activity:

> If you're smart, you're going to clear your roof of debris by the end of autumn, before the California rains start, and you're shoveling mulch instead of leaves. If you forget, however—if livetrapping and transporting the local raccoon family has kept you busy through the holiday season—don't worry. When you see the puddle on your floor that means "roof leak," you'll know it's time to get up there now. It's relatively easy to do the job, rainstorm or not.

The author does tell the reader *when* he should think about cleaning his roof, but the information is buried inside a paragraph, and the following instructions (as we saw earlier) focus on doing the job when it's too late. The details would be much easier to find if the author pulled them out into a bulleted list or step-by-step procedure with clear headings to identify what was coming. The reader could skim those headings and find out exactly what he needed to know and *when* he needed it.

If you were critiquing this section for organization, you could make these comments and suggestions.

- What do you think about providing a calendar to go with this article so readers can see specific important tasks scheduled in their appropriate season or month?

- You mix in the tools readers will need for this job with the regular text of your paragraph. How about pulling out a list of tools they'll need to do the task so they'll know what to collect (or buy!) ahead of time?

- You're kind of hiding the how-to information in this article in the text. Have you thought about some clearly defined fun heads to guide readers to the information they need?

Chapter 11

CRITIQUING A NONFICTION-BOOK PROPOSAL

When you are trying to sell a novel, you write (and *revise*) the entire book before querying an agent or editor. With a nonfiction book, however, the first step is to write a book proposal and get that ready to submit. This proposal is your selling tool. It must convince that agent or editor she wants you to write the entire book so she can help you get it published.

A nonfiction proposal is made up of many distinct pieces, and each piece can have its own style and voice. Just as you would with the actual book, you'll bring the proposal, with all its parts, to your critique group. Your critique partners will be invaluable tools to help you get that proposal into the best shape possible.

RECOGNIZING THE WEAK SPOTS

When you sit down to critique a nonfiction-book proposal, you're reading for clarity and information. You're also reading to determine whether the proposal has the power to sell the author's project. You'll respond to weaknesses in description or style, but you'll also have reactions about passages that set out to convince the reader of the project's importance. Here are some of the responses you may have as you read a proposal:

- You may be disinterested.

- You may get bored.

- You might feel confused about the project.

- You might be unsatisfied.

- You may lose focus.

ANALYZING THE WEAKNESSES

As you read through a nonfiction-book proposal, put yourself in the seat of the agent or editor. Does the proposal convince you this is a book the market needs and that you'll be able to sell? Watch out for places you can suggest ways to strengthen the author's authority and the details he's provided.

In this chapter, we'll talk about the following common weaknesses you will see when you critique a nonfiction-book proposal:

- The proposal doesn't demonstrate the existence of a market.

- It doesn't show how this book differs from the competition.

- It doesn't establish the author as an expert with a platform.

- The sample chapter is written in the same voice as the rest of the proposal.

The Proposal Doesn't Demonstrate the Existence of a Market

When we decide to propose a nonfiction book, we know that book is an important one for us to write. We know about the readers who need this information. In a proposal, though, we have to prove this knowledge. We must convince an agent or editor that the book's market is big enough to justify its publication. We also have to show where that market is and that we can access it.

As a critiquer, you can help the author determine whether he has solidly demonstrated the existence of this market. You can check the information the writer presents in the proposal, toss out ideas for other data, and make sure he's presenting his evidence clearly and professionally. You can even nudge him to do more research when you think that will help.

In their book proposal for *More Than a Party: How to Plan Events that Create People Connections and More*, Sabrina Hill and Joni Russell describe the market for their book. Their audience is "the women who plan life's events," and they define that audience.

- 25–60 years of age, primarily married, getting married or in relationships

- Interested in lifestyle issues

- An active participant in social, academic, corporate or religious communities

- Planning or intending to plan birthday parties, baby showers, weddings, bachelorette parties, club meetings, and school events for children, families, and friends

After this general description, Hill and Russell go on to list specific groups to whom they will market the book, making sure to include the membership numbers of those groups. This information is a critical part of any nonfiction proposal. The stronger the marketing plan an author presents to an agent or editor, the more likely it is that the proposal will be accepted and the book published. The groups these authors list include the following:

- Meeting Professionals International (MPI)—membership 19,000

- Mimegasite—membership 20,000

- Hospitality Net—membership 23,000+

Not only do the authors show they have a clear understanding of their readership, they take care to provide specific facts about the size of that readership. They show that they have done their research about the book's potential market and that they are prepared to reach that market to sell the book.

Our sample proposal is for a book called *Raising a Reader*. Here's the beginning of the marketing section.

> Most families in the United States have at least one child. Research shows that a child who reads has a better chance for success in school, college, and their professional career. Parents who have young children will pick up *Raising a Reader* for ideas about how to start their infant with board books, and grandparents will come to it looking for advice about birthday presents. Teachers may find the book a good resource to supplement the materials they receive at continuing-education workshops.

In this paragraph, the author is trying to identify the market for a book about teaching kids to read and to love reading. This market, though, isn't proven in any way. The author tells us about families and readers, but she doesn't give us any data to back up the claims she's making. She projects reasons for people to buy the book, but she doesn't support those projections with facts or evidence. This section shows us what the writer *believes* about her market, not what she has researched and now *knows*.

If you were critiquing this proposal, you could make these comments:

- This market description feels a bit vague. It makes me ask questions about how many children every family *does* have and what research you've done about this "better chance for success." Can you fill in the actual facts?

- Your descriptions of the types of people who will read these books don't feel like proof of a market. They feel more like the *ideas* you have about that market. I think the agent or editor will want more concrete data.

- Do you have some numbers to include in this section? Can you talk to booksellers regarding who's buying other parenting books or regarding other books about reading and literacy? Are there any organizations on the Web focused on this issue that you could get statistics from? If you belong to any of these organizations, you should definitely mention them and that you will contact them about the book as part of your marketing plan.

The Proposal Doesn't Show How This Book Differs From the Competition

Writing a nonfiction-book proposal requires a lot of different pieces of research. One of the things we authors need to know is whether any published books are already out there discussing the same topic as our own. In the proposal, we need to identify any of these competitive books and explain how they differ from or fail at our new goal.

When you're critiquing a proposal, you can check whether the author has given a strong, concise explanation of the other books' contents. You can help the author produce a clear statement of why these books don't meet the readers' needs and show her own book to its best advantage.

In her proposal for *Make Mom Happy by Mail*, Trudy Triner lists three books that could be seen as competition for hers. Here is her description of one of those books.

Are Your Parents Driving You Crazy? Expanded Second Edition: Getting to Yes With Competent Aging Parents by

Joseph A. Ilardo: This book is a guide to solving common dilemmas faced by aging parents and their children such as driving, finances, not listening to healthcare providers, arguments among siblings regarding care for parents, etc. This book deals with the difficulties of dealing with aging parents. In contrast, *Make Mom Happy by Mail* focuses on the positive difference you can make by simply being responsive to their need for simple, ongoing communication and connection.

In this example, Triner gives a brief summary of the book that may be in competition with her proposed idea. She then states the distinction between the approach of this other book and her own, making it clear to any agent or editor that a need for her book does exist in the current market.

Let's go back to the proposal for *Raising a Reader*. Here's a description of another book that may compete with the author's.

Teach Your Toddler to Read takes parents through the basics of phonics *before* they drop their child off at kindergarten. Essays and instructions written by professional teachers help parents give their toddlers a step into academics by setting up school at home. Each lesson takes the family through another piece of the big picture. *Raising a Reader* does not contain reading lessons.

The summary of *Teach Your Toddler to Read* gives strong details about the contents of that book. The details may even be *too* strong, making the blurb sound like a marketing piece for the competition. The biggest problem, though, is the final sentence of the paragraph. In this sentence, the author makes a distinction between the two books. That distinction, however, explains only what the proposed book does *not* do, instead of letting the reader know exactly what the author's book offers that the competition does not.

If you were critiquing this proposal, you could make these comments:

- I like the description of the other book, but I think you could give us more information about your own. What will your book do that is *different* from what you tell us about the other one?

- I don't think you're quite selling your book strongly enough here. I'm not seeing, yet, why I should buy your book and not this other one.

- You may want to trim the details about the competition book. Can you shift the balance so you're giving us concrete information about your book in *contrast* to the other?

The Proposal Doesn't Establish
the Author as an Expert With a Platform

When we start writing, we may have a great idea for a nonfiction book, but—in our proposal—we aren't just selling that book, we're also selling *ourselves* as the best author of that book. I am a writer, and I have almost fifteen years experience participating in critique groups. I've also done a lot of freelance manuscript editing. These facts qualify me to write this book, to share with you the things I've learned about critiquing and revising a project. I am not, however, going to sign up to write a book about fly-fishing in Alaska.

When you're critiquing a proposal, you need to make sure the author is presenting his or her background, experience, and credentials in a way that will make an agent or editor say, "Yes! This is the right person to write this book!" Writing strongly about himself or herself isn't always easy for an author to do, but a good critique can help him shine his own light brightly on the page instead of tucking it under that dark bushel.

Here's a bit from Hill and Russell's proposal, about themselves—"The Authors."

> For the last decade and a half, we have planned events for many major companies in Silicon Valley, including Hewlett-Packard, Lucent Technologies, Silicon Graphics, Inc., AOL. ...
>
> ...
>
> We teach our event planning principles locally and have worked with San Jose State University to help them revise and revitalize their Professional Certificate Program for Event and Meeting Management. We have taught the "Universal Principles of Event Planning" and "Fundamentals of Event Management" through the San Jose State Professional Development Center.

The authors are actual event planners; in fact, they've been doing this kind of work for fifteen years for some very big clients. They've also taught college classes in event planning, showing that they don't just work well behind the scenes but can get in front of a large group and share their knowledge. They make it clear that they understand the material they'll be including in the book and that they're capable of passing that material on to their audience.

Here's a bit about the author of our sample nonfiction book proposal.

Carly Sussman is the mother of one son who is an avid reader. She began reading to him when he was an infant, progressing through picture books and beginning readers until they were diving together into full-length novels. They still share a love of books, swapping stories back and forth and recommending new authors to each other. Carly is the neighborhood go-to resource for other parents looking for new titles for their own kids, and she has a close relationship with her local librarians.

Carly clearly loves books and would love to write one about teaching reading. However, she needs to list a lot more credentials to show she is capable of doing that. This bio describes a person who may be considered an expert by her friends, but it doesn't list any actual credentials or experience. If the author has a background in education or has worked with young children, those facts should be mentioned. If the author has taken workshops on literacy or worked with any literacy organizations, that information needs to be included in this section.

This author may be a lovely person, but she is not presenting herself in a way that will convince an agent or editor she can write this book.

If you were critiquing this part of the proposal, you could make the following suggestions:

- I'm worried that you aren't listing enough qualifications here. Are there organizations you've joined or worked with that you could include in your bio, things related to reading and children?

- This reads a bit as if you're "padding" the section about yourself. I think the message you're conveying is that *you* don't consider yourself enough of an authority.

- Is there research you've done that makes you more of an expert on this subject? Can you include a brief summary?

The Sample Chapter Is Written in the Same Voice as the Rest of the Proposal

When we're developing a nonfiction-book proposal, we have two audiences to consider. We need to write the proposal for the agent or editor, but we also need to remember the other reader—the one who will be browsing the finished product at the bookstore. The sections I've discussed so far—about the market, the competition, and the author—need to be written professionally to sell that agent or editor on the book. The proposal also must include at least one sample chapter, and this chapter should be written for that other reader, the one who really needs the information you're selling.

It can be tricky to write these different sections, to switch style and voice between the two. When you're critiquing a proposal, you can let the author know if he needs to move further in one direction or the other. You can help the author make sure he's getting the appropriate information and delivery into the important places.

Here's a passage from Trudy Triner's proposal in which she is describing the audience for her book.

> The book's main audience are Baby Boomer men and women—those born between 1946 and 1964. This is a large demographic, comprising a market of 76 million people. And unlike the younger generations who are saving to buy houses and cars and struggling to raise a family, Boomers have a fat wallet of disposable income (some experts have approximated that Boomers have nearly a trillion dollars of spending power).
>
> According to research, Boomers are most interested in such topics as alternative health, entertainment, finance, health, hearth and home, hobbies, family, fitness, and travel. Additionally, this generation is going through a life stage filled with lots of tough issues, including retirement, investment planning, healthcare, and caring for aging parents. *Make Mom Happy by Mail* will be an indispensable book for this generation.

And here are the opening paragraphs of the sample chapter in Triner's proposal.

Out of breath and desperate, my son Jack and I race down
the United concourse in Denver toward gate B21. If we miss
our flight, we miss the family reunion. Twelve-year-old Jack
is close to tears. A late flight from San Francisco has made
making our connection almost impossible, but we see the
gate, and it's still open.

"Hurry Mom! Hurry!" Jack calls back to me as I struggle
with my heavier load.

The gate agent spots us and mercifully holds the door
she was about to close. We race down the jetway and onto
the plane, and then fall into our seats panting and laughing.

In the first passage, Triner writes professionally, describing the research she
has done and the information she has learned. She presents factual details
in a voice that is clearly directed at the agent and editor who wants to know
why he should read her book.

The second passage, from the sample chapter, is not an organized delivery of facts but an active scene. Triner shows herself and her son racing to
make the plane that will take them on a family vacation, the trip where she
will visit her own aging mother. The paragraphs show the reader—the agent
or editor who may accept the proposal—the strength of her family connections and the warmth and humor with which she will tell the rest of her story.
Triner's voice, in this piece, shows the voice of the author readers will be living
with for several hundred pages, the one who will help them build the same
kind of connections in their own lives.

Let's compare a couple passages from our sample nonfiction book proposal. First, here's the market description we looked at earlier.

Most families in the United States have at least one child.
Research shows that a child who reads has a better chance
for success in school, college, and their professional career.
Parents who have young children will pick up *Raising a
Reader* for ideas about how to start their infant with board
books, and grandparents will come to it looking for advice about birthday presents. Teachers may find the book
a good resource to supplement the materials they receive
at continuing-education workshops.

And here is a paragraph from a sample chapter titled "At the Bookstore."

At the bookstore, it's important to study the child's habits. Observe whether they walk back and forth between shelves or whether they seat themselves on the floor and resist further movement. A notebook can be an optimal tool at this time. A journal of the child's behavior, over time, can demonstrate their book-purchasing patterns. As you progress with developing the child's interest in reading, the notes you record will increase chances for success.

The voice in these two passages is very similar, distant from the actual parents and children that the author is discussing. This may be appropriate when the writer is presenting information to the agent or editor, when she is writing to establish her credibility as a professional. In the sample chapter, however, the author needs to recognize her other readers the parents who love and are concerned for their children—who want to hear from a writer who understands and recognizes those feelings. In this paragraph, the writer has not achieved that goal.

If you were critiquing this proposal, here are some comments you might make about the two different sections:

- You may want to take another look at your sample chapter. At this point, it feels like you're writing it for the agent or editor. I think you need to remember that your audience for *this* section is the parent who is hoping to learn from you.

- Do you want both these sections to have the same tone? You may want to loosen, or soften, the voice in the sample chapter.

- Can you picture yourself as a teacher, passing your information on to your reader in person? That may help you develop the right voice for this chapter.

Chapter 12

CRITIQUING A HOW-TO OR SELF-HELP BOOK

When you walk through a bookstore, the shelves housing how-to and self-help books take up a big percentage of the available space. Subjects vary from telling you how to grow award-winning vegetables to healing from a major life trauma. Despite this huge range, all these books have one thing in common—their job is to teach readers something new.

A writer who uses a book to teach other people faces a challenge. Not only do we need to produce a book that will get picked off one of those full bookstore shelves, we need to write that book in a way that truly supports and aids our readers through their learning journey. As a critiquer, you can help the author achieve this goal by making sure the information is useful, accessible, and encouraging.

RECOGNIZING THE WEAK SPOTS

As you're critiquing a how-to or self-help book, you'll have a lot of things to keep track of. You'll want to check whether the necessary information is on the page and is clearly explained. You'll also be "listening" to the way the author conveys that information. If the author's voice doesn't keep the reader interested and make her feel supported, the details that author has provided become irrelevant.

Here are some reactions you may have as you critique a how-to or self-help manuscript:

- You get confused.
- You become irritated or aggravated with the author.
- You feel stuck.

- You feel as though the learning task is too big.
- You don't identify with the problem the author is trying to solve.

ANALYZING THE WEAKNESSES

When you are reviewing a how-to or self-help manuscript, make sure you take time to really consider how helpful the book will be. Look at the instructions and see how clearly they're delivered. Could you do the task easily if you followed the steps given? And consider how you feel about the voice. Does the author comes across as someone you *want* to learn from, or do you feel too distanced from him as a teacher?

The following problems are common causes of weaknesses in how-to and self-help books:

- The book doesn't establish a goal for the reader.
- The author's voice doesn't connect with the reader.
- The author doesn't make the information easy to find.
- The book doesn't include practical exercises for the reader.

The Book Doesn't Establish a Goal for the Reader

When a reader buys a book to learn a new task or work through a problem, she has to make choices about which book that might be. As she flips through the first few pages, she's looking for reassurance that she'll find what she needs. A book with a general focus that just talks around a problem or a process is not going to be as useful or as appreciated as one that lets the reader know just how she'll benefit by reading it.

When you're critiquing a how-to or self-help book, you need to check whether the author has identified this benefit. You should look at where he sets his goal for the book and think about if he's done so quickly enough. If you feel the author needs to make clearer the benefit the reader will be getting from the book, make sure you let the author know.

In Michael Hauge's book, *Selling Your Story in 60 Seconds*, Hauge is very clear about his book's subject and what he is setting out to show the reader. Hauge writes the following passage.

> This book is about selling. But despite the catchy title, it's not really about selling your screenplay or novel. It's about selling someone the *opportunity* to read your story. This book

will teach you how to convince potential agents and buyers
to spend their most valuable asset—their time—in exchange
for the personal and financial riches your story will bring.

This passage starts at the bottom of the introduction's first page. It is a fairly sure bet that most readers will flip to and at least skim this page when they're checking out a book. Stating the goal this soon significantly increases Hauge's chances that the reader will buy, and be helped by, his book. Take a look, too, at how clearly Hauge says what he's setting out to do. He is *not* teaching writers how to sell their book; he's helping them learn how to get agents and editors to *read* the book. That's a very specific, distinct step in trying to get published, and Hauge's description tells you this is exactly the step he's going to help you with.

Let's look at part of the introduction from our how-to sample, *How to Share Your Home (and Life) With a Pet*. After talking about reasons people might have for getting a pet, the introduction gives some pretty general chitchat about animals.

They can, and do, appreciate a good snuggle, and they typically greet you at the front door with love in their eyes (especially if you left their food bowl full in the morning). They're always up for a good game and don't know how to be a "poor sport."

Pets are furry and winged, scaled and feathered. They run, swim, fly, and slither, and they are sure—however they move—to weave their way into your life, like the threads of your most comfortable blanket.

The reader who picks up this book and skims the introduction is going to have trouble figuring out why she should read further. The author gives some details about animals and describes the positive feelings they engender. The author does not, however, tell the reader what she'll learn from the book. There is no statement of the book's goal or of the goal on which the reader should be focused.

If you were critiquing this passage, here are some comments you could make:

- I like the cheerful voice in this introduction, but I think you'll want to give readers a bit more information. What are you going to teach them about pets in this book? What specific techniques or tools will you give them?

- When readers buy your book, what do they want from it? Do they have a goal about the things they need to learn before they buy a pet? Should you talk about that goal in this section or about your *own* goal for them?

- This introduction feels pretty vague. Can you get a bit more specific about what's coming in the main chapters of the book?

The Author's Voice Doesn't Connect With the Reader

Here's an obvious statement: Readers come to self-help and how-to books because they need ... help. Go ahead, say, "Duh." Then think a minute. When you go to a live person for help, who are you more likely to listen to—a person who greets you with sympathy and understanding, or one who gives you the cold shoulder and scorns your problem?

I thought so.

An author has to make a connection with his reader. This connection can be harder to achieve without the live interaction a teacher has with his or her students. When you're critiquing this kind of manuscript, you can help the writer convey his understanding and knowledge of the reader's problem or need—i.e., convince the reader she has come to the right place for help. You can work with the writer to make sure his voice has the right mix of empathy and authority.

In *Finding Your Own North Star*, Martha Beck talks about how to find the path through your life that will make you truly happy. She has the right credentials to teach the skills she discusses—she has spent years helping people examine and reorient their lives. However, it is her wonderful voice and complete honesty that make the reader accept her help.

Beck talks about how we all have an "Everybody" we carry around with us—that usually imaginary group of people we believe are judging (negatively) the choices we make. Beck writes the following passage.

> ... [W]e're going to give the social self exactly what it wants— Everybody's approval—while also allowing you to take directions from your essential self. This is the only way to find your North Star, but you may not like how we have to go about

> it. See, you want the Everybody you have now, the people whose influence landed you in your present life, to approve of your essential self. This will happen right after Hell becomes the official Olympic ice-dancing venue, and you may have that kind of time, but I don't. I'd rather take the quick approach by *exchanging* your present generalized other for a whole new Everybody.

Beck doesn't talk down to the reader, as though the steps she's suggesting are easy. She writes with a reassuring and encouraging voice. She also uses gentle humor, including herself in the joke, to lower the reader's tension over the challenges she is asking him or her to face.

At another place in the book, Beck describes a moment when she was a college freshman, trying to choose a major, and remembered how much she enjoyed drawing as a child.

> ... The feeling was so surprising and lovely that I burst out laughing.
>
> I cannot tell you how atypical this was. For several scared, bewildered, and lonely months, I hadn't so much as smiled for an I.D. photo. Now I felt as though I'd discovered the canary in the coal mine of my soul, still singing away under tons of bedrock. Emily Dickinson's line "Hope is the thing with feathers" popped into my mind, and for the first time, I knew what she meant.
>
> ...
>
> Of course, when this happened to me in the bookstore, I didn't listen. Within thirty seconds, my social self had launched a full frontal attack. ... A degree in art, my friends had all agreed, was worse than useless. So much for *that* idea. My body seemed to crash back into the chair and my mood into its inky funk.

In this passage, Beck further establishes herself as an authority by sharing times in her own life when she has had to practice just what she preaches. Beck's magic moment didn't solve her problem. She shows the reader that she has, at times, failed to follow the path she wanted, just as the reader has. Beck makes sure she is honest about this. Instead of using this story *just* as an example of the good feeling that comes with making the right choice, she carries it through to the end, admitting that it took her years to start truly listening to those feelings and to herself.

Here's an excerpt from chapter three of our self-help book, *Overcoming Your Writing Fears*.

> Go for it. Dive right in; the water's fine. If you tiptoe along, creeping around corners flashlight-first, you're going to get nowhere fast. Stretch your writing muscles and sit down at that computer. Get the thickest binder you can find, because you're going to need it to store the pages that will come pouring out of your fingers and printer. Sure, you'll feel nervous— your stomach will twitch, and your head will ache, but it's time to push aside all those reactions holding you back.
>
> Believe me, I know how you feel. "Been there, done that." My brain has a whole list of tricks it has thrown at me to keep me from writing, and I've stepped around every trap it's laid. I write, despite the stress or tension it creates in me, and I produce.

This author's voice is brisk and upbeat, even pushy—telling the reader what to do but forgetting to give the reader the confidence that he *can* do those things. The admonition to the reader to ignore his feelings comes across as less than reassuring, because it pretty much sounds like the author is already ignoring them.

The second paragraph does bring in the author's experience, but in a vague way that doesn't give the reader any reason to buy into the author's authority as a true expert. The author shares no specific story of his own writing fears; the words fail to set up a connection between that author and the reader.

If you were critiquing this book, you might make these comments:

- I'm not sure this is the voice you want to use for the book. Writing fears are a big deal, and the voice feels as though you're treating them too lightly.

- I think readers may need some reassurance that you, as the author, recognize what they're going through. Can you mix in, with your positive affirmation, just a bit more sympathy for what they're going through?

- Who do you want to present yourself as to readers? You're a teacher who can help them learn to problem solve their fears. I would work on getting that feel onto the page.

The Author Doesn't Make the Information Easy to Find

Organization is one of the most important elements of a how-to or self-help book. It doesn't matter how much information we, as writers, provide or how well we analyze an emotional state; if readers can't find what they want to know, they'll end up completely frustrated with the book (and with us!). Some readers do read self-help and how-to books from cover to cover, but many skip around, looking for answers to specific, immediate questions or problems. If they have to work to find those answers, they're going to quit reading.

It's easy, as we're writing, to get caught up in the details we're trying to share and forget about whether we're successfully organizing those details to make them easily accessible. As a critiquer, you can pay close attention to whether the book's structure will help the reader or get in his way.

In *How to Cheat at Cleaning*, Jeff Bredenberg sets out to make all our lives easier. He covers the spectrum of cleaning your house (inside and out), from getting rid of old junk to organizing the junk you decide to keep to dragging your entire family in on the fun.

Let's look at Bredenberg's table of contents:

Perfectionism is So Overrated
Rewriting the Rules Your Mother Taught You
Let Your Cleaning Tools Do the Work
Clutter Control Made Easy
Spouse, Kids, Friends, and Hired Professionals
Sanitation *and* Sanity: Kitchens and Bathrooms
Where You Live: Keeping It Clean in the Living Room, Dining
Room, and Bedroom
Laundry Got You Out of Sorts?
Your Desk and Work Areas: Winning the Paper Chase
The Great Outdoors: Decks, Sidewalks, Driveways, Gutters,
Siding, Windows, and Entryways
Cars: Backseat Archaeology
Babies, Toddlers, and Pets: the Things We Do for Love

If the people I hang out with are any indication, Bredenberg has a huge potential reader base. In his table of contents, he's given all those readers a great tool for finding information. His chapter titles reflect the thought Bredenberg has put into organizing his information into distinct, useful chunks his readers can dip in and out of as needed. Few, if any, of these readers have the leisure to curl up with a glass of wine and read through the book slowly. Thanks to Bredenberg, they won't have to. They can go straight to the information and instructions they need, at that minute, and save the rest of the book for another day.

Here's the table of contents for our how-to book about pets.

i. Introduction
I. Getting Started
II. Asking Around
III. Taking the First Important Steps
IV. Rearranging and Replacing
V. Meow, Ruff, Tweet, Neigh
VI. You and the Kids
VII. The Shopping Trip

At first glance, the chapter heads look like decent pointers—those "first important steps" sound good. If you have children, you probably do want some information about how to teach them about animals. Look more closely, though, and you'll see that even with those chapter titles you don't know what information the book will provide. Think about a specific question you might have: What if I want to get a dog from a rescue organization? Which of these chapters would have the best chance of answering that question?

I'm guessing you don't know.

Again, the table of contents, while a way "in" for the reader, is important for another reason—it reflects the organization and clarity that reader can expect (or not) in the rest of the book. These chapter heads show that the author has not identified the various reasons a reader would come to her book and hasn't yet organized her material into appropriate, helpful categories.

If you were reading this book for structure, here are a few comments you could include in your critique:

- I like that you're making your headings entertaining, but don't forget to use them to also define what the book will teach the reader.

- I think your headings are a bit vague. Can you focus more on specifics and make clear what each chapter of the book contains?

- A TOC needs to reflect what the reader needs, the information for which the reader will come to a book. You may need to do a bit more research to find that out.

The Book Doesn't Include Practical Exercises for the Reader

Theory is fine, and everybody needs thorough explanations to learn something new. The best way to incorporate a new concept into your own life, though, is to practice—to apply that information to a real situation. The writer who is trying to teach her readers must keep the practical in mind as she writes.

If you're critiquing a how-to or self-help book, you can help the writer think about various ways readers will use the information. You can brainstorm with her for exercises and worksheets that let those readers take the teaching beyond the book. When an author is immersed in writing out her ideas, in getting them clearly onto the page, stepping back to think about tools can be a difficult task. A good critiquer can help the author make sure her tools are truly useful.

In *The Coward's Guide to Conflict*, Tim Ursiny includes exercises and suggestions for practicing his techniques at the end of each chapter. One of Ursiny's ideas is that people avoid conflict too often, which doesn't help them solve an existing problem. In chapter three, "The Top Ten Reasons People Avoid Conflict," Ursiny discusses common reasons people back off from conflict. Here is one of the exercises he includes at the end of this chapter.

> **Self-reflection exercise: Rate your fear**
>
> On a scale of 1 to 10, rate how much you experience each of the ten fears when considering facing a conflict.
> (1 = Not at all; 5 = Somewhat; 10 = Extremely fearful):
>
> | | |
> |---|---|
> | Fear of harm | _____ |
> | Fear of rejection | _____ |
> | Fear of loss of relationship | _____ |
> | Fear of anger | _____ |
> | Fear of being seen as selfish | _____ |
> | Fear of saying the wrong thing | _____ |

Fear of failing   _____

Fear of hurting someone else   _____

Fear of getting what you want   _____

Fear of intimacy   _____

After discussing each of these fears thoroughly in the body of the chapter, Ursiny gives the reader a chance to apply his theory to the reader's own personality. By focusing on all the possible fears a person may experience about conflict, Ursiny lets the reader assess which of those fears she is actually dealing with. Recognizing your own problems is the first step toward resolving them, and Ursiny makes sure the reader can take this step. He doesn't leave the reader on her own, trying to sort through the chapter's information and apply it to her own life; instead he gives her a tool for doing just that.

Let's see what happens in our excerpt from *Overcoming Your Writing Fears*. Here are the last two paragraphs of that chapter.

> Where will those giant steps take you? You'll have chapters piling up on your desk, words you've written, stories you've created. Those print-outs will smile up at you and make you satisfied and proud, sure of your abilities.
>
> Yes? Of course, yes! Now turn the page to the next chapter and get ready for your pep talk on revision!

The author tells you what you're going to get from following the instructions, from believing the author when he tells you what you need to do. The author does not, unfortunately, give you a way to test out what you're learning. The quick summary at the end of the chapter, with the announcement of what's to come, skips past practice time.

The author could have set you up with a worksheet to assess which "giant" steps feel possible or provided instructions for a short meditation exercise to be done before writing. Either of these would have provided the reader with a chance to play with the ideas he has taken from the chapters, to apply those ideas to his individual situation.

If you were critiquing this ending, you might make these comments to the author:

- Are there any exercises you can create that would let the reader try out your ideas? Is there a worksheet that would help the reader really get what you're telling her?

- People believe in a new technique when they see it work. If you include a practice idea for the readers, one they can play with, they'll have more confidence in you as a teacher—and in themselves as writers.

- Are you sure this is the best way to end your chapter? It feels a bit abrupt. Maybe you could include a mini project for readers to do before they move on to learning about revision.

Chapter 13

CRITIQUING A MEMOIR

Memoir, as a genre, has grown incredibly in the past decades, and more and more writers are putting pieces of their own lives on paper. If your critique group works in memoir, your members can have a wide range of goals for their projects. Some may be writing for personal exploration, some to share memories with their families, and others to reach publication. In this chapter, we'll be talking about critiquing with that last goal—to bring a memoir into the best possible state to submit to an agent or editor. However, as you critique, make sure you know the specific reasons behind each writer's words and talk to her about the kind of critique she's looking for.

When you critique memoir, it is important to remember that, while you're reading about a real person, you're still looking for important elements of storytelling. A memoir writer faces a tough challenge, looking for and writing about these elements in his own life. A strong critique partner can help the author shape seemingly isolated moments into a complete story. She can encourage that author to look for the connections that tie his anecdotes together and to share those connections with his readers.

RECOGNIZING THE WEAK SPOTS

Some people have led very exciting lives or have lived through an incredible time in history. Others have experienced one particularly intense moment. All are reasons an author may decide to write a memoir. When, as a critiquer, you sit down to read a memoir manuscript, you need to make sure you're listening to your reactions about the author's *writing*, not just the experiences he's describing. To truly help the author, you need to make sure you "test" how well he tells his story, and give him the same constructive comments you would if this story were fiction.

Here are some reactions you may have while you're critiquing pages of a memoir:

- You lose track of the story.
- You're uninterested in the hero (yes, the author!).
- You feel distant from the experiences in the book.
- The story seems to drift.
- You find yourself wondering *why*?

ANALYZING THE WEAKNESSES

As with any other genre, you'll come across common problems as you critique a memoir. You should be reading both for the story the writer is telling and for your own emotional connection and response to that story. In this chapter, we'll discuss the following weaknesses:

- The writer backs away from sharing his or her feelings.
- The writer forgets about "show, don't tell."
- The memoir doesn't convey a sense of rising tension.
- The memoir doesn't seem to provide a context for the writer's personal story.

The Writer Backs Away From Sharing His or Her Feelings

When we read a novel, we need to connect with the hero of the story. We want a character we can identify and empathize with, someone we care about to pull us through the pages of the book. The same is true for a memoir, the major difference being that the hero is also the author.

As we write about ourselves, put the story of our life (or a piece of that life) onto paper, we can easily get caught up in simply detailing the events through which we lived. Just like a novelist, we're dealing with dialogue and setting and often historical moments other people will have experienced. We feel an obligation to get the facts "right" and to make sure we detail everything that happened for our readers.

When you're critiquing a memoir, you should watch for places the author may have skimmed, or even skipped, over her personal experience of the events she's relating. You can help the writer make sure she's sharing her own feelings and getting a good balance between those and the facts of the story.

In *Operating Instructions: A Journal of My Son's First Year,* Anne Lamott describes her fears before her son, Sam, was born, and the fears she still experiences as he grows through those first early days.

> I had these fears late at night when I was pregnant that I wouldn't be able to really love him, that there's something missing in me, that half the time I'd feel about him like he was a Pet Rock and half the time I'd be wishing I never had him. So there must have been some kind of a miracle.
>
> I never ever wish I hadn't had him.
>
> But I do sometimes wish I had a husband and a full-time nanny. And that I could still have a few drinks now and then. I am coming up on three and a half years clean and sober. The memories are still very clear of how lost and debauched and how secretly sad my twenties and early thirties were. ... But there are still times when these movies start to play in my head, where I see myself putting the baby down to sleep and then sitting and sipping one big, delicious Scotch on the rocks. Just sipping, just sipping one fucking drink.

Lamott could have stopped her narrative after she tells us she has no regrets. Instead she opens us up to the full reality of her personal experience with motherhood. Having a child has *not* made all her problems go away; in fact, there are many times when the tiredness and the twenty-four-seven-ness of the job make things worse. She tells you the good *and* the bad and gives the specific, concrete details that let us connect—not just with the story itself—but with the person who lived through that story.

Here's a passage from our sample memoir, *Growing Up With Grandparents:*

> My grandmother had help taking care of him, but she still—in her own eighties—did as much as she physically could. She'd get him situated in the living room and then do her own stuff around him—tidying, cooking a little, reading the newspaper—and coming back and forth whenever he needed her or she thought he did. They'd been married sixty years; he didn't always have to talk for her to know what he was thinking or wanting.
>
> When we came to visit, we'd sit on the couch opposite Grandpa's wheelchair. We'd talk with Grandma, tell her about our days, our work, our own children. We'd include Grandpa by turning to face him, by waiting to see if he would manage to

> force out a comment. Then we'd go on with Grandma, having
> a cookie or two from the plate she'd brought from the kitchen.
> We'd listen to a few of her worries or anxieties. She never shared
> many, though, even when the problems and sadness were set
> out so clearly right there in front of us.

The author creates a picture here of her grandparents' lives after the grandfather has suffered a series of strokes. The writer shows the closeness the couple still experiences and the momentum of their days.

However, the author stops just short of sharing her own part of the experience. She describes a visit, but even in those few sentences, she is distant from the emotions; in fact, the writer is simply part of an undefined "we." There is no sense of sadness or pain or stress from the author's perspective.

If you were critiquing these passages, you might make these comments:

- This description paints a sad, hard picture, but I'm not really feeling the emotion of it. How did you feel when you visited your grandparents at this time? Were you sad? Angry?

- I'm not seeing much involvement of the "hero" here: you. You probably want to weave in your reactions to the scene, not just the actions.

- This feels a bit like you're just telling us about your grandparents. I'd like to know/see more about your grandparents *and* you.

The Writer Forgets About "Show, Don't Tell"

A memoir is an exploration of one's life. When we work on one, whether it is a full-length book or a short article, we are focused on navigating through our personal, private moments and relating those to the reader. It is easy to get caught up in simply narrating the story, talking *about* the experiences and events we remember.

If you're critiquing a memoir, you can help the writer weave in some of the structure of fiction. You can watch for places where the author is telling, instead of showing, and you can help him build scenes that let the reader participate in the experience.

Brian Copeland's memoir, *Not a Genuine Black Man: My Life as an Outsider*, is the story of his childhood in San Leandro, California, during the years when the city council was actively trying to keep black families from living there. Copeland did large amounts of research about those years, and it would have been easy for him to simply talk to the reader about the facts he discovered. He doesn't do this. Instead he shares the world with that reader.

Shortly after Copeland's family moves to San Leandro, his grandmother takes him for a haircut. The barber watches them come into the shop.

> ... Then ... he smiled.
>
> "May I help you?" he said, the word "help" taking on a friendliness in the tone he used.
>
> Grandma didn't smile. She looked back at him, hard, stern.
>
> "He need to get his hair cut," she said in her no-nonsense way.
>
> "I'm sorry," the barber said, still smiling. "We don't cut his kind of hair."
>
> He pointed to a sign on the wall that read, NO NATURALS, NO RELAXERS. Why didn't the signs just say, NO BLACKS OR ART GARFUNKELS ALLOWED?
>
> "We don't know how to cut that type of hair," he said, still smiling.
>
> I could feel the stares of the other patrons boring into me, each set of eyes a pair of hot, miniature drills cutting me, searing me.

Copeland doesn't *tell* us the barber and all his customers are racist; he doesn't write a sentence saying his feelings were hurt. He *shows* the interchange between the man and his own grandmother, and he describes his own emotions so his readers recognize and understand the hurt. Copeland picks the details and the tension that build a great, active scene.

Let's look at this paragraph from our sample memoir.

> For a few years, my maternal grandmother lived in our hometown just a few blocks from my parents' veterinary clinic. We would visit her at times, just the three girls, and I remember some of the things she used to entertain us with. She had a trunk of yarn, and she would teach us how to knit, if we wished. In the middle of some those skeins, she had hidden a prize that we could "win" when we finished knitting up the skein. She made us sandwiches of butter and sugar, and she sent us outside into

> her garden to walk the rows. In one area, she grew chives, and
> we were allowed to snap off the tops and eat them.

In this passage, the author tells us about her grandmother, about the years she lived near the family. The problem is that the writer is just *telling*. She describes what she and her sisters did while at her grandmother's house, but she doesn't show us any of those activities in scenes. The narrative lacks action and the concrete details that would pull the reader into the memories.

If you were a critiquer for this manuscript, you might make these comments about this paragraph:

- I like these memories. I think any one of them would make a great scene for you to write. I'd love to see you out in the garden, feeling the dirt under your feet, actively breaking off the chives, and tasting the piece in your mouth.

- This paragraph is a nice passage, but it's a little too "telling." Can you pick a particular moment to take us back to, with the specific details you remember experiencing while you were at your grandmother's?

- Can you bring in some of the elements of a basic scene here? Some action and maybe some dialogue? These things would make the passage feel more like part of a *story*.

The Memoir Doesn't Convey a Sense of Rising Tension

In every book, the writer's goal is to keep his readers turning pages. Even if we are writing for our family, we want them to stay interested and intrigued, to feel as if they really want to find out what's going to happen next. A story arc, one that shows the hero/author having a goal and facing obstacles, as in fiction, is the best way to keep readers hooked.

In *Operating Instructions*, the question for the reader is whether, or at least how, Lamott will survive this first year of motherhood. Yes, she wrote the book, so we know she made it through, and we assume (so we can even open the book) that Sam is okay, too, by the end of the story. Lamott, though, keeps the tension up throughout the year of entries.

We learn that in the middle of the year Lamott's best friend, Pammy, is diagnosed with cancer.

April 5

Something has happened that is not possible. Pammy found a lump in her breast today.

April 6

Just like that. Boom. Can you imagine? Just like that. I feel a dread like hearing sirens late at night, like I did with my dad. I know it's bad. There's no doubt in my mind.

August 20

Pammy's very sick from the latest round of chemo. My heart is broken.

...

I feel like the exhaustion and constant fear about Pammy make me like some small little animal who lives on the ocean floor, who has an ink sack in its body, like a squid, that it's supposed to use for self-protection. But in my case, left to my own devices, I panic and end up ink-jetting myself.

Not all of Lamott's problems come from being a new parent. When her first and strongest support system is threatened, the tension of her own life increases more than tenfold. Lamott has shown us how having Pammy in her life has eased and softened the hard edges of single motherhood. As we watch Lamott deal with her friend's illness, we worry more, not less, about how this year is going to turn out for the writer and her son.

In this next passage, our sample author visits her grandfather in the hospital.

I stood outside the door of the hospital room and looked in. The cold I had was keeping me in the hallway because—after having a pacemaker placed next to his heart—the last thing Grandpa needed was a case of the sniffles. So I waved, and I looked, relieved in the doctor's report that the procedure had gone smoothly and my grandfather would be fine. He lay against the pillows, his thin white hair combed back from his bald spot, somehow looking so much older than he had last month. But he talked to my parents and grandmother, and I knew he'd be home soon, out of the cold metal and sterile white of the hospital bed.

The writer is taking us back to a time when her grandfather is stuck in the hospital. He's had a pacemaker put in, and she isn't able to get inside the room to talk with him, hug him, see for herself that he's all right. This scene has the potential to be tense, to hold the reader in suspense while the author describes the experience. Unfortunately, the writer diffuses that possible tension by letting the reader know quickly that the grandfather will be all right, that the doctor has already reassured everybody about his recovery.

If you were critiquing this scene, you could make the following comments:

- What were you feeling *before* you talked to the doctor and found out your grandfather would be all right? Were you worried? Afraid? I'd like to see these emotions in this scene and feel the tension you must have experienced.

- You tell us right away that your grandfather was all right, that the procedure was a success. I don't want you to manipulate us with fear, but you might play with telling this story in a different sequence so readers do have a what-might-happen-next feeling as they read.

- I'm not sure this scene has the power it could have. You may have distanced yourself a bit too much from the worries, the wonderings you lived through when you first saw your grandfather in the hospital. Even with the doctor's reassurances, you were seeing someone you loved in a new way. You may want to put some more of that tension onto the page.

The Memoir Doesn't Provide a Context for the Writer's Personal Story

To paraphrase Mr. Donne, no writer is an island. Even memoir writers, telling the story of their own experiences, have to fill in the details of the world around them. This can be tough to do, as we dig deep into our own past and put our personal memories into manuscript form. A good critique partner can point out where the story needs some external information and can ask the questions that help the author fill in that extra layer.

In *Not a Genuine Black Man*, Brian Copeland works hard to set the details of his own time in San Leandro into a historical context about the city itself. Copeland tells the story of his mother taking the family to a brunch at a restaurant where the waitress gives them horrible, rude service because they are black. His mother leaves a huge tip, despite the protests of his grandmother.

Copeland's mother hopes that, if another black family comes to the restaurant, the waitress might think to treat them decently. After the scene, Copeland writes the following.

> One of the most egregious cases [of racism] I've heard of in-
> volves a popular restaurant in the San Leandro/Hayward area
> that my mother took us to a few times when we were kids. For-
> mer employees have told me that it was a common practice in
> the 1960s and 1970s for the restaurant staff, at the direction of
> the management, to oversalt the food of black patrons to dis-
> courage their continued patronage. I remember thinking back
> then that the food was kind of salty, but the place was packed.
> I figured that it must have been my pedestrian palate so I never
> said a word; nor did my mother. The only blacks in the place
> were not going to tell a building full of whites that the emperor
> had no clothes. And that he was too salty.

Copeland takes care not to keep the story he tells *too* close to himself. Along with the emotional moments of his own experiences, he takes the reader outward into the larger world within which he was living. He increases the power of his scenes by showing they aren't isolated incidents and revealing what was going on all around him ... and us at the time.

In this scene, from our sample memoir, the author describes a race with her grandfather.

> We climbed down the steps the hotel had installed for the tour-
> ists—easy access from Grandma and Grandpa's room to the
> sands and ocean of Pismo Beach. We found an open space to
> drop our towels and buckets, then stripped off our sweatshirts
> and pants, even though we shivered in the fog. We lined up, the
> three young girls and the tall, skinny grandfather.
> "Ready ..." Grandma called, "set ... go!"
> And we ran.
>
> ...
>
> He beat us every time, coming up on us from behind, pass-
> ing us one at a time, but always passing us. He called himself a
> greyhound, but he didn't run with grace. Instead he seemed all

bones and joints—elbows high and out, skinny knees pumping high.

We ran, if possible, even faster, our breath coming short,
and our skin heated against the cold air. It was no use, though.
We couldn't catch up, not until we reached the end of the
course, where he waited for us. And we threw ourselves on
him, hugging and laughing, happy to be with him and to have
been beaten again.

This is a close-up scene, full of action and personality. The reader is with the
author and her grandfather, experiencing the race and the fun. There is a hint,
though, of a larger world beyond the author's steps across the sand, when the
author talks about Pismo Beach and tourists. Where is the family during this
scene? There is a city there, a place that many people visit, not just the kids. Is the
beach crowded with those tourists? Does the race have an audience, other than
the children's grandmother?

The scene has a feel of isolation to it, but we're not sure if that's a real repre-
sentation. The writer could have added a few details to give us a bit more of the
full picture, have taken us out beyond the family moment to the larger context
of the place and time.

If you were critiquing this scene, you might have the following comments
to make:

- I really like this. I can really see the race. But Pismo Beach rings a
  bell—didn't Bugs Bunny try to get there? Don't they have clams?
  You might stretch your setting a bit, outside the actual description
  of the race, to give us a better feel of place.

- Do the kids live in Pismo Beach, or are they staying at the hotel with
  their grandparents? Is the beach a usual for them or something new
  and exciting? I wouldn't mind getting a bit more feel for how the
  author's childhood was connected to this place.

- What does the beach look like? You do a great job of getting the *feel*
  of it across, but I think some visual imagery would be helpful. I'd
  like to know if it's crowded or empty, if their hotel is in an isolated,
  secluded spot, or if they're in the middle of all the tourism.

Chapter 14

CRITIQUING TRAVEL WRITING

Travel writing makes two big groups of people seriously happy—the writers and the readers. The writers not only get an excuse to journey to the countries and cities of their choices, they get to share their love of those places with an audience. Readers get to explore the world, either in preparation for their own trips or virtually by soaking up location and culture from the printed page.

In this chapter, I won't talk about travel guides. I'm going to show you how to critique travel articles for magazines and the kind of travel "adventure" book that has become so popular in recent years. When we write in these genres, we face the very big challenge of distilling a huge amount of information and experience into a book or article a reader can pick up and hold. At the same time, we must keep that distillation entertaining enough to make the reader happy.

A good critiquer can help a writer meet these challenges.

RECOGNIZING THE WEAK SPOTS

As you critique travel writing, you'll need to go through a filtering process. Because a new place or culture can, in and of itself, have an exotic, exciting feel to it, you'll need to make sure you don't bring too much of your own expectations and beliefs to your reading. Casablanca reeks of mystery and danger, even for those who have managed to get through life without seeing the movie.

When you read to critique, though, your job will be to ground yourself in the actual writing on the page, to judge whether or not the writing is conveying its own impression of a place or people. You'll be helping the author make sure her manuscript catches and keeps the reader, no matter what preconceived notions that reader might bring along for the ride.

Here are some reactions you might have to a weakness in a travel article or book:

- Your curiosity isn't satisfied.
- You're bored or uninterested.
- You feel distant or "outside" the place the author is writing about.
- You are confused about the people and culture.
- You feel frustrated.

ANALYZING THE WEAKNESSES

When you critique a travel book or article, read to see how well the author transports you to the place he's writing about. Do the details evoke a picture for you, and do the stories peak your curiosity and interest? Watch for places the writer may need your help sorting through details, and make note of ways in which he can improve his descriptions.

In the following sections, I'll talk about these common problems you may see as you critique travel writing:

- The author spends too much time on the personal.
- The author uses too many or too few details.
- The author ignores or condescends to the inhabitants of a place.
- The author doesn't have a theme or purpose to frame the story.

The Author Spends Too Much Time on the Personal

Travel writing is about a place; memoir writing is about an author's journey. Today these lines are being blurred in many books. Still, travel writers shouldn't let their own story take over from the story of the people and places they visited. A reader comes to an article or travel book to learn something new, to be caught up in another world.

As a critiquer, you can let the writer know if he's including too many anecdotes or when he's lost sight of the country or city he's moving through. You can help the author write a tight piece that has the right balance between capturing the feel of a place and weaving in the right amount of personal details.

Michael Palin's *Sahara* is a marvelous read about his travels through the countries that occupy the Sahara desert. In the introduction, he talks about his childhood—about the exotic illustrations on a box of dates his father received every year from Algeria and about falling in love with *Tales from the Arabian Nights*. Palin describes his enchantment:

> Curved swords, soft silks, tassels and see-through skirts. Mirages and genies, huge jellies and lubricious oils and unguents. The desert world seemed, apart from the odd beheading, to be a place of complete sensual fulfillment.
>
> …
>
> Almost fifty years later there came a chance to expose my childhood fantasies to the harsh glare of reality.

The memories, the nostalgia, give one of the "whys" behind Palin's journey, but he keeps those memories, for the most part, within the two pages of this introduction.

Here is a paragraph from day one of the trip.

> The Britishness of Gibraltar, which began with Admiral Rooke's invasion in 1704, is well entrenched. Contemplating my map of North Africa outside Pickwick's Pub, I order a coffee. No messing with *latte* or *machiato* here.
> "Coop or Moog?" I'm asked in a thick Geordie accent.
> I choose cup.

Palin is present throughout the book as an actor, a participant—one with insights and opinions. However, he never lets his "angle" become more important than the information he has to share with us about the Sahara's history, people, or current culture. In this scene, he describes ordering coffee, but that action is simply part of showing us that the British history of Gibraltar continues on today, all the way through to the regional accent of a very British waiter.

Let's look at a bit of our sample travel piece, "Walking the Lake District."

> As I stare up at the green and orange hills rising in front of me, I can't help but go back to my bedroom as a child, curled up with another of Arthur Ransome's books. I see the Swallows and Amazons puffing up through the heather, sweating with the weight of their packs. Nancy is in front, of course, waving at the others to keep up, and Roger is bouncing around like a rabbit, unable to keep a straight course, even with the hard climb.

> I can almost smell the pages of the book, my mother's copy, spine cracked from all the reading, pages dog-leafed from the many places we've all had to stop reading for homework or dinner. The sunshine breaking through the clouds around me is bright, but in my mind I am in my cool, dark room, supposedly "sleeping in" on a Saturday morning, but really just lying there grabbing more hours of reading. If I get up, if I show my face, there will be breakfast and chores and errands. If I don't open the door, I can stay tucked away in here for hours, climbing the hills with my favorite British kids.

The author is standing at the start of her hike, looking at the real thing—the hills she's going to climb. Instead of describing the actual scenery, though, she keeps us in the past—in the nostalgic comfort of morning reading and in the imaginary world of her book friends. The memories are nice, but this is the second paragraph, and the past is sticking around for too long. The reader wants to learn about the real thing, to go with the author as she climbs the solid hill in front of her.

If you were critiquing this passage, you could make these comments.

- I love the image of you deep in the stories of your childhood, but I think you may be spending too much time there. Can you shift the balance so there is less nostalgia and more description of the scene you're looking at?

- You're writing about a hike you took around this lake. Can you "get moving" through the scenery, show the reader the experience, and just sprinkle small bits of memory into the action? I think this would keep the reader more connected with this piece.

- What is unique about the Lake District, about this lake, separate from the storybook associations? Your primary job is to introduce your readers to this region, to help them see it in their mind's eye. I think you may be letting your personal story overwhelm that goal.

The Author Uses Too Many or Too Few Details

Travel writing is about giving your readers a sense of place, a *full* sense of place. This means that, whether you're writing a magazine article about a town or a book about a country, you need to create a picture of the entire world for your readers. Too often, writers misinterpret this goal as meaning they must get every detail of every image on the page. They may also have trouble deciding just which details are the important ones.

A good critique partner can help the author through this problem. She should be on alert for passages that go on too long or that go too *deep* into details. She can help the author sort through all the information and make choices about which bits and pieces are really important for the manuscript and its readers.

In her article "Solitary Refinement" (*Town & Country Travel*, Winter 2008), Katherine Taylor describes her vacation through Patagonia. Here's her description of the forest ranger's office at Nahuel Huapi National Park, which used to be the childhood home of her guide, also named Nahuel.

> The three-room house is turquoise, a fact that somehow endeared me both to Nahuel and to this small island full of parrots and berries and trees carved with the initials of lovers.

In this one sentence, Taylor has given us a single detail of the ranger station and three details about the whole island. They are small details—a color, a bird, a fruit, and a piece of romance. And yet, with these images, we get a sense of the place she is moving through—a place that uses its own bright colors to match or, perhaps, celebrate the natural energy of the island. Rather than getting caught up in completely describing the house or identifying the types of berries or trees, Taylor has used words lightly—just enough to prick our imaginations.

Let's switch now to a piece of our sample travel piece. Here's the description of the sheep guard from our excerpt, the gate the author has to get through to start her hike.

> The mechanism looks like a mix between a turnstile at a subway entrance and the entrance gates to Disneyland. It's got a set of crossbars that don't quite intersect with each other but that have no form or pattern I can identify. I can imagine that this obstacle would deter a sheep; it intimidates me. I shift my pack higher onto my back, make sure my water bottles aren't coming loose, and grip the top bar. I place one booted foot firmly on the lowest bar and my other on the next one up. Moving slowly, keeping my pack in balance, I climb up and

up. At the top, I look down, impressed and amazed that I have
made it this far without getting tangled inside the contraption.
Then I make my way down, watching for loose shoelaces.

Maybe the author is from the city; maybe she's never seen a sheep gate before. As fascinating as the gate is, she's given the reader a bit too much information about it in this section. A sentence or two about the basic mechanics of how the gate works, about the fact that it keeps the sheep contained, would be enough. The reader does not need to watch the author's entire climb up and over the fence; instead, the reader is ready to get on with the hike ... and the story.

If you were critiquing this description, you might make one of the following comments:

- Cool gate, but I think you're overdoing the description a bit. What details do readers really need in order to *see* the gate in their minds, to know how it relates to the Lake District, and to get how it works into your adventure? I think you need to pick and choose which information to keep.

- Can you summarize this gate a bit more quickly? My guess is your readers are ready to see the lake and hear about your climb, and this much information will make them impatient.

- Is the gate important? I know it was really there, but does it have a connection to the story you're telling about this part of your journey? This may be a detail you don't *need* to share.

The Author Ignores or Condescends to the Inhabitants of a Place

Travel can mean anything from museums to food, from wildlife to music. The one constant, however, is people. Whether you're watching native craftspeople work or mingling with locals in a bar, you're seeing and participating in culture. Conveying this aspect of a country or region is one of the most important—and sometimes the most difficult—of a writer's jobs.

Even if language isn't a barrier, the travel writer has to reach for an understanding of the way people live by spending a relatively short time with them and conveying that understanding on the page. When you're critiquing a piece of travel writing, you can help the author deliver a complete, true sense of a culture. You can help her balance the details about the people she meets with the perfect description of a wine or the set of tiles decorating a fountain.

In Niger, Palin spends a few days riding and walking through the desert with a camel train led by a man named Omar.

> I like to walk and talk with him, as it takes the mind off the monotony. We talk about the recent war between the Touareg and the government in Niamey. The Touareg, rather optimistically, demanded more funds and less interference. The north of the country virtually closed down for six years, Omar had friends killed and arrested and most of the foreign visitors were frightened away. As he was taking tourists on desert safaris for ten times the money he made from salt caravans, this seriously affected his livelihood. But he never considered giving up and doesn't expect he ever will. He likes walking with the camels. He says it gives him time to think.

Palin doesn't describe Omar, and he doesn't assess or judge him. He tells us the information he gathered from Omar, about both the country and the man, and he delivers that information in a way that lets us imagine the two of them together, walking slowly across the sand and sharing pieces of their lives. Palin has done what every storyteller must—show, not tell.

What about our Lake District hiker? Here's her first encounter with other people on the mountainside.

> As I slide down the hill, skidding between the rocks on the trail, I meet a family making their way up. The father waves, and the mother tells me, "Hello," her accent announcing them as British. They stop at a curve in the path. I nod as I go by, eyes intent on my boots, mind focused on not tripping and rolling the rest of the way to the bottom. The lake glistens blue beneath me, too cold I'm sure, but still throwing up the tempting idea of a cool swim in the hot sunlight. The sheep dotting the hills look like white cotton balls with noses, and I feel as though I could jump off the hill and land safely on one of their cushiony backs.

The Lake District is one of the most popular destinations in England. This means people go there from all over the country (and the world), and each of these people has his or her own reason for making the trip—his or her own story. Perhaps the writer didn't speak with this family, but the article could still include some details about them—their clothing, their interactions, whether they looked like they were having fun. Are they obviously tourists, or do they seem to be locals out for the day? *All* the hikers on this hill, not just the author, are part of this world, and by not including a bit more about them the author has failed to show that world in its entirety.

If you were critiquing this passage, you could make these suggestions:

- Whoa! Wait! Who was that family? Why are they there? How do the kids feel about making this climb? Has anyone there read Ransome's books? This little glimpse of other people makes me ask a lot of questions—are there any answers that would tie in with the story you're telling?

- What kind of people come to the Lake District? I think the people on this hike are part of the place you're describing. I would be careful not to dismiss them as unimportant.

- Did you stop and talk with these people at all? Did you find out anything about them? I think it would really add to the story if you showed how the locals (or other tourists) interacted with the environment.

The Author Doesn't Have a Theme or Purpose to Frame the Story

Travel books are incredibly popular these days, and many authors are interested in writing travel articles. We do research, collect background information, and then take our notebooks along on a trip to get caught up on what's actually happening in the place about which we want to write. We piece all that data into several pages of writing with detailed facts, interesting conversations, and beautiful descriptions.

Too often, though, we find ourselves with an article that is a series of passages, not yet connected into a story. We lack the theme of the article, the purpose for writing (and reading) those words. As authors, our job is to push ourselves to the next level to find the thread that will pull the article together into a cohesive whole.

When you are critiquing a piece of travel writing, you are looking for that thread. If you don't find it, you need to let the author know and work with him to bring it out.

In "Italy, Rediscovered" (*Town and Country Travel*, Winter 2008), Meg Nolan shares with the reader her travels through Italy and the reason behind this piece.

> Second- or fourth- or eighth-time visitors want to be immersed in the Italian lifestyle, which means lounging in a courtyard surrounded by family or sipping a *limoncello* with nothing but the Bay of Naples in front of them.

Nolan is writing her article for the travelers who have seen all the important, beautiful sights of Italy. She promises the reader, and structures her article around, places closer to the heart of the Italian life, far removed from the typical tourist spots. She has a specific theme for her story, which is to show travelers the quiet, peaceful corners of the country.

In our sample, what is our author trying to convey about the Lake District? What is she trying to show her readers about that part of England? Here's the opening of our excerpt section.

> On day four of my trip, I find myself at the edge of Lake Buttermere. It's the midpoint on my travels, and I feel acclimated to the area—not quite a native, but something past a tourist. My new coat fits better, and the first-day blisters from the boots have calloused over. I've learned that a good wind can come up at any time, and so my hair is braided tightly against my head, and my knit hat is in an accessible pocket. I buy a packet of "crisps" at the teahouse for an extra lunch treat, and I head out.

The author delivers a good sense of her feelings as she starts out on this day. The reader sees her settled into a routine, used to the pattern of the trip. The author doesn't, though, give a reason for being there in the first place. The reader could, from the passages about the Ransome books, assume or guess that the writer is on some kind of footsteps-following trip, walking the same paths a favorite author took years ago. The reader doesn't *know*, though, and an author shouldn't leave her readers guessing.

If you were reading this section for a critique, here are some possible comments you might make:

- Why did you go on this hike? Why did you decide to include the story of it in your manuscript? I think you need to give a brief statement of your reasons here to let your readers know what they are.

- Does this stop at Buttermere fit into a larger picture of your vacation? Should you give the reader a brief reminder of this picture as we get started on this leg of the journey? Your reader might appreciate the refocus.

- Why might your reader be curious about/interested in this lake and your day there? Can you use the audience focus to weave a thread through the story?

Section III
Worksheet 1: Critiquing Nonfiction

This worksheet is organized around the nonfiction categories we talked about critiquing in this section. Within each category, you'll see questions you can ask yourself that will help you recognize and comment on any weaknesses you find while you are critiquing. If you have trouble finding the answers to these questions, first push yourself to look more deeply, and then, if you still aren't clear, make sure to note this difficulty in your feedback to the author.

For practice, use this worksheet to do your own critique of our sample scene. Or you can use it to start the critique process on actual projects submitted by the writers in your group.

❧

Organization and Structure

- Can you identify a consistent pattern in each chapter and a logical path through the manuscript? Are there places the author should tighten or rethink this organization?

  _____

  _____

- How does the author bring important information to the front? Would to-do lists or a bulleted structure be helpful?

  _____

  _____

- If the author is writing a memoir, what elements of story does she use to engage the reader? Are there ways the author could strengthen the plot or characterization of the project?

  _____

  _____

- Other organization and structure comments and suggestions can you give the author?

_____

_____

Voice

- How does the author use voice to convey expertise? Are there ways better project a sense of authority?

_____

_____

- How does the author hook the reader? How can the author improve the voice to connect more strongly with the reader?

_____

_____

- What other voice comments and suggestions can you give the author?

_____

_____

Level of Information/Details

- Consider the author's balance of personal stories and useful information about the project's topic. What can he do to shift that balance in a way that would most help the reader?

_____

_____

- Where could the author trim, add, or highlight details that would improve the manuscript?

_____

_____

- Additional comments and suggestions for using details:

_____

_____

Understanding of/Focus on Audience

- How does the author show that she understands her audience? Describe any areas you see for improvement.

_____

_____

- Can you identify the specific perspective the author brings to this project? What new information does she provide?

_____

_____

- How does the author share the project's purpose or theme?

_____

_____

- Other comments and suggestions concerning audience:

_____

_____

Opening of Article/Book

- Are there ways to strengthen the project's hook?

_____

_____

- Is there a place at the opening where the writer could "show" a scene, rather than "tell" or describe an event or process?

_____

_____

- Are there ways the author tighten the opening and pick up the pace so the reader doesn't lose interest?

  _____

  _____

- Additional comments and suggestions for openings:

  _____

  _____

Tools for Readers

- What tools and exercises does the author provide?

  _____

  _____

- What could the author do to make the exercises clear and simple to follow?

  _____

  _____

- Are there ways to restructure information as sidebars or step-by-step procedures that could make it more accessible and helpful to the reader?

  _____

  _____

- Other comments and suggestions about tools for readers:

  _____

  _____

NONFICTION CRITIQUE EXAMPLES

The following pages provide an example critique of one of our non-fiction writing samples. The first page takes pieces of that sample and shows notes you might make as you read through the scenes. The second page shows an example of an overall critique you might present to the author.

Sample Manuscript Pages With Line Notes

Table of Contents

I like the sound of these headings, but they are a bit vague. Can you carefully think about what each chapter contains, then show this to readers in a specific heading? Just clarify a bit more what readers will get when they turn to a section of the book.

Introduction

Unless someone in your family has a bad allergy, there will come a time in your life that you start to seriously consider adding a pet to the household. This may happen when you graduate college and get your own first apartment, when you get married or buy a house, or when your children are old

I like this opening, in terms of the scenarios it sets out. I think, though, that your readers are also going to be looking for a reason to buy your book—a goal you have for how, specifically, you will help them. You may want to spell out this reason here.

enough to start begging. You may be completely enthusiastic about the idea, or be determined that no creature with fleas will enter your household. However you started out, you've picked up this book because a pet is imminent.

An animal is another warm body, one that makes unique demands on and brings unique benefits to a family. As much as they would like to, they don't eat your food, and they—except for a few rare exceptions—don't know how to flush a toilet. They can't run the vacuum or dust the bookshelves.

They can, and do, appreciate a good snuggle, and they typically greet you at the front door with love in their eyes (especially if you left their food bowl full in the morning). They're always up for a good game and don't know how to be a "poor sport."

> You're drifting away from your topic of pet buyers to focusing on the pets. This may be confusing.

Pets are furry and winged, scaled and feathered. They run, swim, fly, and slither, and they are sure—however they move—to weave their way into your life, like the threads of your most comfortable blanket.

> How about using this section to tell readers about the book—what's in it and how they can find the information they want? I think they're going to get bored with all this general description.

SAMPLE OVERALL NONFICTION CRITIQUE

Martin,

I love the idea of a book for people getting ready to buy a pet. So many people just fall in love with the idea of a dog or cat and then—when it's too late—wake up to all the things they should have figured out before bringing the animal home. It's clear, too, from your writing, how much you care about animals and want people to make the best choices about their pets.

There are a few things I think you could work on to make the table of contents stronger and to improve the opening of the book. I'll go over them here, and I've marked places in the manuscript that I think could use some tweaking.

I can see you've worked to make your table of contents grab the ear of the reader. I like that. However, I think you may have sacrificed come clarity for catchiness. When I look at the headings, I'm not really sure what each chapter is going to contain. For example, what would I read "Asking Around" to learn about? Where to find a pet? Which kind of animal would be right for my household? Or whether someone had a pet he was giving away? Similarly, while I think using the animal sounds for a chapter title is funny, I don't know whether I'm going to get a comparison of different animals and breeds or whether that chapter will tell me how to take care of every animal I might possibly own. I think you should play around some more with these headings. Get a real sense, for yourself, of what's in each chapter and then make sure each chapter title shares that sense with the reader.

In terms of the introduction, I think you need to get more quickly to the gist of what your book is about. This is the first, and maybe the only, page that a reader will turn to in the bookstore, to decide if she wants to buy your book or someone else's. The reader is looking at these paragraphs to find out what your book is going to teach her and what benefits she'll get from reading it. This is where you have to hook her.

Are you going to break down your book into big steps for all animals—deciding on a pet, buying a pet, introducing a pet to the home? Things like that? Or are you going to use each chapter to talk about a different animal, the pros and cons of having this kind of pet, why someone would pick this animal over another? This is the kind of information readers will be looking for here—a solid statement of how you are going to help them. You can also expand on the TOC a bit here and describe the way readers can use the book's organization to suit their specific reading needs.

You may also want to give readers a tiny bit of background about yourself, just enough to show them that you know what you're talking about—that you are an authority on this topic.

It's going to be a great book! You just need to bring forward the important things you want to say and strengthen their delivery at these important first sections.

MORE THAN A FORMULA:
HOW TO CRITIQUE BOOKS FOR YOUNGER CHILDREN

For many people, one of their greatest pleasures is seeing a young child curled up with a book, oblivious to the world going on around them. Writers for young children fall in love with the idea of writing a book—one that will take a young reader away from everything else. Books for young children must—like every book—entertain, inform, and tell a good story. Children's books, though, also have their own specific set of writing—and critiquing—criteria. For that reason, I have set the chapters about how to critique for young children into their own separate section.

Each chapter in this section talks about how to critique a specific type of book for young children. In these chapters, you'll learn about critiquing these genres:

- picture books
- beginning-reader books
- chapter books

Each of these genres has special considerations for writers and critiquers. If you're reviewing a picture-book manuscript, you can read through that chapter to get instructions and tips for the kinds of problems you'll be seeing. Similarly, if a writer in your group has written a beginning-reader book or a chapter book, the specific chapters for those books will help you get started with the appropriate kinds of questions and suggestions for the writer.

At the same time, if you regularly critique any kinds of books for young readers, you will probably want to read all three chapters in this section. All young children, at various stages of reading development, struggle with the same kinds of problems—vocabulary or sentence structure that is too hard, stories that don't engage them, and information they can't understand. We'll talk about how to critique for all these weaknesses, along with many others common to these three genres, throughout this section.

Critiquing Books for Younger Children—Writing Samples

As in the other sections of this book, I teach how to critique books for young children by using excerpts from published books and samples that show common mistakes writers make. Read through the following writing samples for picture books, beginning readers, and chapter books, and refer back to them as you work through the specific chapters.

Fiction Picture-Book Sample: *At the Circus*

Kirby sits.
He wants to see the trapeze artists
swing and play
over the net.
The wooden bench where he waits is hard.
The tent smells like peanuts, cotton candy, and dirt.
Animals, too—elephants and lions and little dogs
    with ruffles.
Kirby wrinkles his nose.
The ringmaster walks
to the center of the circle.
He wears a tuxedo and a tall black hat,
and he stands on an upside-down box,
Painted red with blue and yellow stars.
He cracks his long, black whip
LOUD,
and three white horses with pink feathers on their
    saddles and heads
race in circles
around him.
Kirby waves.

Nonfiction Picture-Book Sample: *Cookies of the World*

Take a bite of *mandelbrot*, and what happens?
The little loaf of "almond bread" will break between
   your teeth,
with a snap and crumble onto your tongue.
What will you taste?
The almonds! Some vanilla, too, and just a bit of yum-
   my toastiness from the oven.

Russian tea cakes
explode in puffs of powdered sugar when you take
   a bite.
The cookie dissolves in your mouth
and leaves a delightful flavor of walnuts and butter
and, yes! More vanilla!

Fiction Beginning-Reader Sample: *The Sink Stinks*

Cups and plates
stack up
in giant, horrendous heaps.

The sink stinks.

Mom is at her job.
Dad is sick.
My brother Sam is doing his science homework.

The sink stinks.

I get a stool.
I climb up.
The water is cold.
I make it hot.

The sink stinks.

I scrub.
I rinse.
I stack.

I dry.

The sink doesn't stink.

Nonfiction Beginning-Reader Sample: *What's in a Book?*

Open the book.
What do you find?
A page with lots of words, words that fill up that page.

Turn the page.
What do you get?
A page with words and pictures, color and shapes to
    cover that page.

Read the exciting words.
What do you learn?
An entertaining story. A new fact.

Look at the pictures.
What do you see?
A pretty painting. An inspiring photograph.

Open the book.
What do you find?
A gift just for you.

Fiction Chapter-Book Sample: *Me and Suzie McFee*

I climb up the bus stairs. The bus is crowded. I see a few
empty spaces. Should I sit next to my once best friend, Suzie
McFee? Or should I take the place next to Robert Jefferson?
He has his whole face in a *Star Wars* book. He'll read until
we get to the museum.

He'll read *at* the museum.

Then I see it. Miss Calypso is our bus driver. There is a
seat behind her. This seat is empty. I sit down. I spread out,
sort of, so it looks like there isn't any more room. Except
then Mrs. Schneider gets in. She tells me to move over. Miss
Calypso starts the engine.

Cough. Sputter. Black smoke comes out of the engine. Mrs. Schneider leans forward. She steps on my foot, and I say, "Ow," but she ignores me.

"Is there a problem?" she asks.

Miss Calypso waves a hand. "Nah," she says. "There's always smoke. It's just the carburetor or fan belt."

"Eep?!" Mrs. Schneider says. "Should we fix something?"

"Too late now," Miss Calypso says. "Unless you want to be late."

Mrs. Schneider sits up straight. She bumps my shoulder this time.

I say, "Ow," again, louder, but she still ignores me.

"We must get to the museum by 9:00," Mrs. Schneider says.

"Yep," Miss Calypso answers. "We'll be there."

More black smoke comes from the window.

...

Suzie grabs hold of Angelina's arm. She pulls her toward the butter churn. I take two steps after them. I will be able to make better butter than Angelina. You have to be strong to make butter. Angelina is little, like a mouse or something. I helped my father carry all the heavy boxes when we moved.

All of a sudden, Mrs. Schneider stands in front of me. She's holding a dress. It's one of those old-fashioned ones from the dress-up station. It's "historic," the museum lady told us.

"Put this on, Bonita," she tells me. "Pretend you're a visitor from another farm."

Visitors didn't churn butter, I'm pretty sure.

I take hold of one sleeve. It's rough. And the dress is ugly. It's brown with icky yellow lace and about a hundred buttons. I can tell I will trip in it if I walk. Which I think visitors do.

Just then Robert Jefferson bursts into the house. He has his plastic light saber, and he's waving it around. "Mrs.

Schneider!" he shouts. "The bus is on fire! The Empire has attacked!"

"Call the fire department!" Mrs. Schneider screams, and she runs toward the door.

She's still holding the dress.

So am I.

Riiiip!

Nonfiction Chapter-Book Sample: *All About Your Veterinarian*

When your veterinarian was in college, he or she took lots of classes. In college, many classes are very big, with hundreds of students in every room. Your veterinarian had to study science, like anatomy, and she learned about math, too. Her school books were really big and *heavy*. She also had notebooks she wrote in so she could remember what the teachers told her.

Your veterinarian also had to take tests. She took tests in every class, and she had to do well on those tests. If she did badly on too many tests, she might not have finished school and might not be a veterinarian today.

...

Your veterinarian probably keeps information about his animal patients inside a computer. When he examines an animal, he may write notes about that animal on a piece of paper or type them directly into the computer. His computer has special software on it, called a database, that stores information about the animal into separate sections, called *fields*. For example, the database has a field for the pet owner's name, the pet's name, and what kind of animal it is. All the information your veterinarian types into the computer is saved there. The veterinarian can see it on the computer monitor whenever he needs to, and he can print out a paper copy as well. Also, if another veterinarian wants to see the information, your veterinarian can easily send an electronic version of the database file.

Chapter 15

CRITIQUING PICTURE BOOKS

Everybody has the picture book they remember most from their childhood or from reading to their own children. *Green Eggs and Ham. Goodnight Moon. Miss Spider's Tea Party.* I could go on. You could make your own list. The genre is one of the most popular to read and, of course, one of the most popular to write.

Any writer who has worked on a picture book knows that shorter does *not* mean easier. Picture books can be some of the most difficult fiction or nonfiction to create, with challenges from getting every word on every page just right, to leaving "space" in the story for the illustrator's contribution. A good critique group can help the writer develop a picture book that young children (and their parents) will love.

RECOGNIZING THE WEAK SPOTS

Critiquing a picture book is very different from critiquing any other kind of fiction or nonfiction. If you're in a critique group in which someone is writing picture books, and you're not familiar with the genre, I highly recommend making a trip to your library and coming home with a stack of recommendations from the librarian. It wouldn't hurt to read a book about writing picture books as well. You can best help the picture-book writer in your group by educating yourself about what makes a strong picture book and applying what you learn to your critiques. And as you read, you'll need to pay attention to the responses your brain gets from your eyes *and* your ears.

Here are some of the reactions you may have when you hit a weak spot in a picture book:

- You get bored.
- You feel like falling asleep. (This is good only if you're reading a bedtime story!)

- You feel impatient.
- You can't follow the story.
- You don't sense any rhythm to the words.

ANALYZING THE WEAKNESSES

When you sit down to critique a picture book, you are doing a very different kind of reading. You need to remember that you're working with only part of the book—the illustrations are still to come. You need to think about the fact that the book will probably be read out loud and that the child it's being read to may be receiving the words on the page through her ears instead of her eyes. In this section, we'll talk about some of the common problems you may run into, the problems that cause your not-so-good reactions to the manuscript.

- The words create too much of the imagery.
- The language doesn't have the rhythm to be read out loud.
- The child hero isn't actively involved in the story.
- The author forgets he or she has a dual audience.

The Words Create Too Much of the Imagery

The writer is only one of the people working to create a picture book. The other artist involved is the illustrator, the person whose drawings or paintings or computer art complement the author's story. In many cases, the writer and illustrator never meet or talk to each other. Still, the picture-book author must keep in mind that somewhere—at the other end of his manuscript—is a person waiting to contribute her part to the project.

In most fiction and much nonfiction, the writer is responsible for all the imagery in a story. We need to use concrete, specific details to paint a picture of the characters, setting, and action in our readers' minds. For a picture book, though, the writer shares this job and must be careful not to take over too much of the imagery the reader gets from the page.

A good critique group can help the writer achieve the right balance of details. They can discuss whether the author is leaving enough to the imagination or whether he's painting a picture that's too narrow for the illustrator to add to.

In Bonny Becker's *A Visitor for Bear*, Bear turns away a mouse who wants to visit. After he sends the mouse away, Bear returns to his morning routine.

He closed the door and went back to the business of
making his breakfast.

He set out one cup and one spoon.

But when he opened the cupboard to get one bowl...

There was the mouse! Small and gray and bright-eyed.

Becker doesn't use up her word count with information about Bear's kitchen. She leaves those pieces of the story for the illustrator (and the child's imagination) to fill in. Instead she picks the details that tell us something important about the characters. She repeats the "one" quality of all the dishes Bear is getting out for himself. She lists three physical aspects of the mouse, but the last one—the most unusual—carries the most weight. When the child listening to or reading the book puts it away (for the time being), she will carry with her the fact that this mouse is "bright-eyed."

Here's a section from our picture-book sample, *At the Circus*.

The ringmaster walks

to the center of the circle.

He wears a tuxedo and a tall black hat,

and he stands on an upside-down box,

Painted red with blue and yellow stars.

He cracks his long, black whip

LOUD,

and three white horses with pink feathers on their

saddles and heads

race in circles

around him.

Let's look at the specific details in this passage. We know what the ringmaster is wearing, and we know just what the box he's standing on looks like. Not only do we see the feathers on the horses, we know the feathers are pink, and the horses are white. The writing doesn't leave enough room for the illustrator's imagination to play. In essence, this means the writer isn't leaving room for the child's imagination either.

If you were critiquing this manuscript, you could make these comments:

- You've got some great details here. I think, though, you may want to let some of them go. You're filling in every piece of what Kirby sees, which doesn't leave much to the child's imagination.

- Are you sure you want to show us exactly what the ringmaster and horses look like? I think you're supposed to leave some of that up to the illustrator.

- Can you pick one really specific and different fact about the ring-master and one about the horses? I'd love to see something really cool that gets my brain playing.

The Language Doesn't Have the Rhythm to Be Read Out Loud

Picture books often become treasured parts of a child's library, read over and over as he gets older. The first few times, though, that he sits with a picture book, he's typically listening to that book being read. Some picture books are written as poetry, with a clear rhyme, but many are not. Every picture book, however, must have a pattern in the words, a rhythm to their sound that will work with the story to hook the young listener.

Getting this rhythm onto the page may be the hardest thing a writer can set out to do. Even when we have the story and characterization down, we'll spend many revisions playing with the words that tell that story and show those characters; we'll move pieces around, shorten and lengthen lines, test word after word for the same sentence.

A good critiquer can help the author get the balance right, can read the text out loud and listen to the sound. She can make suggestions for shifting the rhythm, for making different word choices, and, if the picture book rhymes, for revising the poetry.

Melanie Walsh's *10 Things I Can Do to Help My World* talks to kids about the things they can do to keep Earth clean and healthy. Walsh creates a child narrator (immediately putting a child into the hero's seat!).

> I always ...
> throw my trash away.
> I will ...
> feed the birds in winter.

Each line break I've shown here is a place for the reader (or listener) to turn the page of the book. The pattern of the sentences gives a short teaser about that child hero, followed by the longer, active description of what the child does to help the planet. The page break gives an added bit of suspense for the listener as he waits for his mom and dad to turn the page and tell him what the hero does this time. Every set of two pages follows this set rhythm, which helps the child listener feel the repeated pattern of anticipation and resolution. This pattern ensures that *10 Things I Can Do to Help My World* will be a book the child starts to "read," saying the words he's memorized after only a couple of passes.

For this section, let's use a bit from our nonfiction picture-book sample, *Cookies of the World.*

> Take a bite of *mandelbrot*, and what happens?
> The little loaf of "almond bread" will break between
> your teeth,
> with a snap and crumble onto your tongue.
> What will you taste?
> The almonds! Some vanilla, too, and just a bit of yum-
> my toastiness from the oven.

Do you see or hear any rhythm in these lines? The author has played with using questions, but they are mixed in with the other sentences without any particular focus on line length or breaks. Try reading this passage out loud—do you feel as though there's a natural rise and fall of words that your voice wants to follow? Probably not. As a reader, you would find yourself starting at the beginning of a line or a sentence and just going along to the end.

If you were critiquing this passage, you might make these comments:

- I think you'll want to play with the words more here. I like the imagery you create, but I'm not sure you have the "sound" of the sentences right yet.

- Is there a different, distinct sentence and line structure that would give your words more rhythm? Can you work with a re-petitive pattern—maybe something that starts every major line with a strong verb or a vivid noun?

- I think the child is going to have difficulty following these lines as they're written. If you can set up a pattern, she will learn it quickly and be able to ride along with the reading, based on her understanding of what's coming next.

The Hero Isn't Actively Involved in the Story

One of the most important, and most difficult, tasks for a writer of children's books is to make sure the hero is an active participant in the story. It's not always realistic, or even possible, for a child character, or the animal the author puts in the hero role, to solve its own problem without the help of an adult. However, that hero must impact the resolution, must play a very strong role in moving that problem along through the story.

A good critique partner can help a writer strengthen his hero. She can make suggestions for giving the main character a stronger role, for creating obstacles and problems that have to be battled. She can help the writer bring his hero to the front of the story and keep her there.

In *A Visitor for Bear*, Bear doesn't do a very good job keeping the mouse away. He tries, though.

> This time, before he went back to the business of making his breakfast, Bear shut the door very, VERY, VERY firmly, locked it, boarded the windows shut, stopped up the chimney, and even plugged the drain in the bathtub.

Like any child, Bear is a hero who does not have complete control over his life. It is not always possible for him to get what he wants. The important thing for the young reader, though, is that Bear *tries*. He acts, and his actions have a strong impact on the story. Because it is so important for him (he thinks) to be alone, he works incredibly hard to achieve that goal. His efforts raise the tension of the story so the child listening will be completely caught up in wondering whether Bear will be successful and, if he isn't, what he will do next.

Let's take another look at our circus story.

> Kirby sits.
> He wants to see the trapeze artists
> swing and play
> over the net.
> The wooden bench where he waits is hard.
> The tent smells like peanuts, cotton candy, and dirt.
> Animals, too—elephants and lions and little dogs with
>   ruffles.
> Kirby wrinkles his nose.

Kirby does have a goal—to watch the trapeze artists—but he's very passive about it. He sits, and he wrinkles his nose at the smell around him. Later we see him wave at the horses. Kirby's main activity is to wait—this is not a strong character trait. Even if the child listening to the story believes in Kirby's patience, she's not going to identify with it or be hooked into the story. Also, if you look at the whole sample, you'll see words that would—in a picture book—be broken up over three or four pages. This means that, in all likelihood, there will be a page or two where Kirby doesn't even show up; that's too long for the hero to be missing from his own story.

If you were critiquing this passage, you might make these comments.

- Kirby doesn't seem very involved in his story. Can he do something other than watch and react?

- Should Kirby be doing something to go after his goal of seeing the trapeze artists? I can imagine lots of funny (to the children!) ways a young boy could disrupt the circus in his attempts to move things along.

- Are there enough problems here for Kirby to be dealing with? Increasing the obstacles might make him more of a participant.

The Author Forgets He or She Has a Dual Audience

As we discussed earlier, most picture books have two "readers"—the child who is listening to and looking at the story, and the adult who is doing the actual reading. While we write for the child, we should also remember who's buying the book and who has, perhaps, the higher boredom factor. I'm sure there's a special shelf in many houses where a parent has hidden a few picture books in desperate hopes that the child will forget they exist.

The picture books that succeed the most are those that entertain or interest *both* the child and the adult. If you're critiquing a picture book, you can help the author by both imagining yourself as the child being read to and the grown-up reading the book out loud. You can suggest ways to balance the needs of the two audiences and help the writer produce a book that will more than satisfy both.

In *10 Things I Can Do to Help My World*, Walsh writes in two layers. She uses the simple, basic sentences we saw in the excerpt above. On a few of the pages, however, she adds an extra detail, an interesting fact for the parent.

I try ...
to turn off the tap when I brush my teeth.

Every time you do this, you save eighteen glasses
of water.

That last line, the detail about the eighteen glasses, is one that will make the adult reader respond. He may think, "Huh! That many?" or "I knew that. I'm pretty good!" In some way, though, the line will give him something to read that goes beyond the basics of the other sentence. The extra bit also gives him something to use as a stepping stone for a conversation with his child about how much water is really *in* eighteen glasses. By remembering all her readers, Walsh has created a book about the environment that parents will be *happy* to share with their children.

Let's go back to the sample from our book about international cookies. Here's the second passage.

> Russian tea cakes
> explode in puffs of powdered sugar when you take
>   a bite.
> The cookie dissolves in your mouth
> and leaves a delightful flavor of walnuts and butter
> and, yes! More vanilla!

The exploding sugar may catch the kids, but the overall vocabulary—words like *dissolves* and *delightful*—is directed more to the adult who's reading the book out loud. Even those phrases, though, don't have anything new for that adult. The author is walking a middle ground between the child listener and the grown-up reader rather than reaching out for more extreme points and really entertaining everybody.

If you were critiquing this passage, you might say some of these things:

- I think you want to find a more fun or exciting "in" for the child you're writing for. Kids love cookies, yes, but they want to *eat* them. If you want them to love *reading* about them, you'll need to think more about what will intrigue them.

- Have you thought about including easy forms of the recipes for these cookies? You could keep the text light and fun for the kids and then give the parents some extra details in the recipes. They could help the kids make the cookies, too.

- I would work either on the sentence patterns of your prose or on the details you're picking to highlight for the kids. I know rhyming is incredibly hard—but have you thought about a short poem for each cookie? You could give a little bit of history about each cookie in a sidebar, which would keep the grown-ups interested, too.

Chapter 16

CRITIQUING BEGINNING-READER BOOKS

When a child starts down the path of learning to read, he has a huge challenge in front of him. In the same way, any writer who sets out to write a book for this child has an equally big task—and responsibility. As the new reader starts to work out words and sentences, she faces potential success *and* potential frustration. An author can help increase the success factor by writing a book that is simple and easy but also entertaining enough to keep the child going.

Even though beginning-reader books are made up of very few words, the choice of those words and the mix are critical. When you're critiquing this genre, you can help the writer work within that limited space to get a story or some interesting facts onto the page. You can read to see whether he's doing this in a way that will captivate his young reader—that will encourage that child to keep going on her learning curve. You can help the writer through the revisions it will take to get this balance just right.

RECOGNIZING THE WEAK SPOTS

Beginning-reader books are not written for grown-ups. Yes, this seems an obvious statement, but it is a fact that makes this genre one of the toughest to critique. These are not books most adults would sit down to read for pleasure; however, it is adults who are choosing and buying them in large quantities. Those adults are judging whether this book will interest their child, whether it will help their child with his or her reading.

These judges set the standard high for beginning-reader books and make the genre very competitive. If you're in a critique group in which someone is writing a beginning-reader book, you'll have to pay close attention to every word and every sentence. You need to give the same help with plot and character and voice as you would with a full-length novel or self-help book.

Here are some responses you may have if you read a weak part of a beginning-reader book:

- You feel like you're reading a wide range of vocabulary.
- You can't find a story line to follow.
- You're not caught by the hero.
- You don't care about what the author is telling you.
- You don't want to turn the page.

ANALYZING THE WEAKNESSES

In this chapter, we'll talk about some of the common problems that are behind weaknesses in books for beginning readers. Here are some of the weaknesses you may come across as you critique:

- The vocabulary is too high-level.
- The author uses too many words without beginning sounds.
- The sentence structure is too long or complex.
- The story doesn't entertain.

The Vocabulary Is Too High-Level

As we discussed earlier, the most important thing a beginning-reader book can do is make the child reader feel successful. So, no matter how cool or intriguing a word may be, if it demands too high a vocabulary from that child, it doesn't belong in the book. If you ask a new reader to get through too many syllables, or work with too many words that don't "sound out" according to phonetic rules, you're asking that reader for too much.

If we were all Dr. Seuss, writing a book with a few simple words would be easy. Because we're not, every writer of a beginning-reader book needs to work at getting rid of the words in the manuscript that are too long or complex and replacing them with words that are short and simple but still interesting to a child. A good critiquer can support the author in her group who is striving toward this goal by pointing out the words that still need to go and suggesting new alternatives.

In *Fishy Tales*, a DK Readers book, the author is giving kids a few fun tidbits about what they might see in the ocean.

> Here is a coral reef.
> What do you see?

The longest word in this passage is *coral*—two syllables. That word is high-lighted at the bottom of the page as a new vocabulary word, a signal for a parent that she may need to help the child with it. The other words are all words a new reader can sound out, or words that children are taught to rec-ognize early—like *here* and *you*. The author has written two short lines of text, one a sentence and one a question, to help the reader practice what those end punctuation marks mean. With a little work, the child can read through this text and turn the page—always an accomplishment.

Let's look at a few lines from our sample nonfiction beginning-reader book *What's in a Book?*

> Read the exciting words.
> What do you learn?
> An entertaining story. A new fact.
>
> Look at the pictures.
> What do you see?
> A pretty painting. An inspiring photograph.

The author has a bit of work to do on the word choices in these lines. Many young children understand words they are not ready to read. They may have heard, and seen, some of these words in a picture book that their parent read to them. However, even if a child does know the meaning of *exciting* or *inspiring*, a beginning-reader book is not the place for those words. By the time the young reader has sounded out all three syllables, she will have lost her connection to the word, the sentence, and the book. Nothing is more discouraging to a child trying to be successful at reading than having to ask for help several times on one page.

If you were critiquing these pages, you might make these comments:

- Remember how young your readers are and how much you want them to succeed with your book. I think they're going to be struggling to get through this page.

- Picture a new reader sounding out some of those longer words. You probably want to play with your vocabulary level—bring it down a bit.

- Do you think your audience is going to know what *entertaining* means? Can you use a simple word there? Something like *fun* or *cool*?

The Author Uses Too Many Words Without Beginning Sounds

Some children seem to start reading without any coaching; one day a child is listening to you, the next day he's taking the book from your hands and showing you what he can do by himself. Other children read with instruction, sometimes from a parent or older sibling, sometimes from a teacher once they start school. Those children follow a definite learning structure, starting with basic "beginning" sounds like short and long vowels and building from there. An author who is writing for a reader at this stage needs to be aware of those early sounds and use them in her writing.

If you're in a critique group in which someone is writing a beginning-reader book, you can help watch for words that go too far beyond the readers' abilities, that may discourage that reader and make him put down the book. You can suggest alternative words for the author to play with as well.

In *Drip, Drop*, Sarah Weeks tells the story of Pip Squeak, a mouse dealing with a leaky home in the middle of a storm. He tries to catch all the rain but can't keep up.

> It filled the pot.
> It filled the pan.
> It filled the cup.
> It filled the can.

Short-vowel sounds, like the *a* in *cat*, are some of the first sounds children are taught to read. In this passage, every word except *the* (which is taught as a word to be recognized) uses short-vowel sounds. The four new words at the end of each sentence are some of the easiest for new readers to sound out. By having the rest of the words repeat each other, Weeks has given these readers just a bit of work to do as they read, ensuring they'll turn the page with pride. At the same time, she even manages to put in a bit of rising tension, as more and more of Pip Squeak's appliances fill up with water.

Let's look at our fiction beginning-reader sample, *The Sink Stinks*. Here are the first two pages.

> Cups and plates
> stack up
> in giant, horrendous heaps.
> The sink stinks.
> Mom is at her job.

Dad is sick.

My brother Sam is doing his science homework.

The sink stinks.

Because of the title, we know this is a book for children who are progressing onto simple words with more than short-vowel sounds. The author has used both long-vowel words, like *plates*, and short-vowel words, like *up*, in the book, as well as words like *sink* that don't fit into either category. He has also, however, slipped in a few words with two vowels in a row, like the *ie* in *science* and the *ou* in *horrendous*. Depending on the child's reading level, she may or may not be able to successfully read these words.

If you were critiquing these pages, you might want to make the following comments:

- You're using a lot of great beginning words. Do you know if your reader is ready to sound out words like *heaps*, with the two vowels together creating the long *e* sound?

- The *o* sound in *brother* is one of those odd vowel sounds. What do you think about getting rid of the name "Sam" and changing *brother* to *sis*, which uses a straightforward short *i* sound (and is a lot shorter, too!)?

- Do you want to use words that require children have to sound out two vowels after another, like *giant* and *science*? They may be fine, but I thought I'd point them out, in case you want to verify the reading level of your audience.

The Sentence Structure Is Too Long or Complex

Vocabulary and word choice are important parts of a beginning-reader book. Just as important, though, is the length of the sentences those words make up. A child who is sounding out words as she reads needs to see that end-of-the-sentence punctuation quickly so she doesn't get discouraged or just plain tired out! Sentences with more than a few words are harder for a new reader to get through. Sentences with too complex a structure are also tough, so a writer of beginning-reader books needs to make sure he's writing sentences with a clear subject and without too many commas or conjunctions.

When you're critiquing a beginning-reader book, you can help the author pull back, as needed, from long or complex sentences. You can point out places she could simplify her writing and suggest ways to trim the wording.

Here's another page from *Fishy Tales*.

> Here comes a shark.
> It looks for food.

The author has given the reader two short sentences to make his way through. The two-page spread with this information also labels a few of the shark's body parts, which gives the child one or two other words to read and learn. He may have a new sound or two to work out—the *sh* in *shark* and the double-*o* in *looks* and *food* set a nice challenge. The most important thing, though, is that by reading eight words, the child will have completed *two* sentences, which, for a beginning reader, feels wonderful. Each sentence, each page, is another mark of the progress she sees herself making.

Here are some more pages from *What's in a Book?*

> Open the book.
> What do you find?
> A page with lots of words, words that fill up that page.
>
> Turn the page.
> What do you get?
> A page with words and pictures, color and shapes to
>   cover that page.

Look at the difference between the first two sentences on each page and the third. The first two have three to four words each. When the young reader starts on the third line, though, he faces a dozen words before he reaches the period. Both of the third lines are fragments, rather than complete sentences. The child has to get through most of the line before he even sees a verb, or "action word."

If you were critiquing these pages, you might make these comments:

- I think the third and sixth sentences are too long. What if you just dropped the second half of each and put periods where the commas are now?

- Those two long sentences aren't really sentences. They're fragments. Can you rewrite so each starts with a simple, but strong, subject and verb? I think the child reader will more easily follow that structure.

- If you keep these two long lines, I think you'll want to look at the second half of each. The subject gets a little confusing. For example, the first long line starts with *A page* as the subject, but after the comma, the first noun is *words*. I think this structure may be a bit tough for new readers.

The Story Doesn't Entertain

So far, we've been talking about the more technical aspects of writing a book with which a young child can make progress and feel good about her growing skills. There's another factor, however, that every writer working in this genre needs to remember. Even with all the rules and guidelines, we must write a book that a child loves, has fun with and is excited about. Whether it's fiction or nonfiction, that book still needs to tell a story, and it has to be one that makes the child *want* to keep reading.

One of your most important jobs, when you're critiquing a beginning-reader book, is to help the writer look for the elements of story in his manuscript and point out where they may be missing. You can help the author juggle the tasks of helping a child learn and writing a book that will make that learning happen in a fun way.

Let's look at the ending of *Drip, Drop*. The storm has ended, and the leaks have stopped.

> "Come jump in the puddles,"
> his friends all said.
> But Pip Squeak ran
> and jumped in ...
> ... bed.

Pip Squeak's friends, who have slept and risen to a sunny day, are ready to play. Pip Squeak, on the other hand, has been up all night and has had enough water. The child reader will laugh at the funny little twist that Weeks writes at the end, in which the only place Pip Squeak wants to jump is somewhere that *doesn't* splash. Weeks even manages a cliff-hanger by breaking the last sentence so that the child has to turn yet one more page to find out what Pip Squeak is going to do. With a few words and sentences, Weeks has written a simple but entertaining story that young readers will smile and laugh at *and* to which they'll come back for more fun practice.

Here are the ending pages of *The Sink Stinks*.

> I get a stool.
> I climb up.

The water is cold.
I make it hot.

The sink stinks.

I scrub.
I rinse.
I stack.
I dry.

The sink doesn't stink.

The hero in this book is pretty active, taking on the chore of getting the dishes washed. And the author is using short, easy words and sentences in these last pages. The story, though, does not have much fun or energy to it. The author has not indulged the readers with any twists or surprises, and the hero's actions are as simple as the words, with no humor or exaggeration to hook the young reader. There is not a lot of story tension in *scrub ... rinse ... stack ... dry.*

If you were critiquing this passage, you might make some of the following comments:

- You're definitely using words the kids will be able to read. You may, however, want to tweak a few of those words to make things more interesting or exciting. For example, think about replacing *stack* with something that creates a stronger image—maybe *splash*? And you could try *grab* or *drag* instead of *get.*

- You've got the basic story down nicely. Is there any revising you can do to make that story more fun, more entertaining? What about fiddling with the ending a bit—maybe adding one more sentence that says *I do!* Kids might really like the humor.

- This child is very active, which is great. Even in a very simple story line like this, though, you may want to make things harder for the hero. Can you think of any obstacles—maybe he trips while he's carrying the stool, or he uses too much soap? You might even play with ending *The Sink Stinks* sentence with an exclamation point instead of a period.

Chapter 17

CRITIQUING CHAPTER BOOKS

A chapter book is a bridge. It crosses the gap (of varying length) between books for children who are just learning to read and for those who can pick up any book in the kids' section of the library and dive right in. An author writing a chapter book needs to layer in all the elements of a novel or nonfiction book for older readers. At the same time, we can't forget that the children we're writing for may still be intimidated or put off by things like too-long chapters, vocabulary they don't know, or a voice that identifies with a much older reader.

Developing a full, intensifying plotline with complex, layered characters, or delivering detailed, interesting information is tough enough; doing all this *and* keeping things simple enough for young readers is a huge challenge. A critique group can help an author achieve the right balance by reading carefully for content *and* voice, by checking the level of detail and description, and by helping the writer revise to get it all just right.

RECOGNIZING THE WEAK SPOTS

When you're critiquing a chapter book, you need to read deeply for the core story and the strong elements of character that the writer is trying to develop in his manuscript. You need to help the author bring those to the surface where the reader can find and respond to them. At the same time, you'll be watching for threads that distract from the story, and you'll be thinking about whether the voice is strong enough to keep the young reader hooked and entertained. As you read a chapter book, here are some responses you might have to weaknesses:

- You get distracted.
- You are bored.

- You feel like the author is writing for an adult, rather than for a child.
- The voice feels too heavy.
- You're trying to rush through the chapters.

ANALYZING THE WEAKNESSES

A critiquer reading a chapter book needs to gauge whether the story or information will truly engage a young reader. There are children who, at this stage, will read any and everything. On the other hand, other children will toss a book down at the first place they get bored or frustrated. When you're critiquing, you need to watch for places the author can amp up the entertainment or clarify an explanation. You can help the author fine-tune the manuscript so it will truly keep her audience hooked.

In this chapter, we'll talk about some of the common causes behind weaknesses in chapter books. You'll learn about critiquing for these problems:

- The story isn't about a child's world.
- The author fails to connect a nonfiction subject to a child's interests.
- The author's explanations are too complex.
- The chapters present too many problems.

The Story Isn't About a Child's World

Every reader should be able to identify or connect with a story. As readers get older, their experiences grow, and the way they see the world widens. When a child is just starting out with chapter books, however, her world view is still pretty narrow—it revolves around her. This doesn't mean young readers don't want fantasy books or science fiction or even a good mystery. What it means is that, wherever the setting, whether the hero is a child, an adult, or an animal, the story has to be about something the young reader cares about.

Barbara Park's Junie B. Jones series is one of the best-selling set of chapter books on the market. Junie's life is never easy, but it's always real. In *Junie B. Jones and That Meanie Jim's Birthday*, Junie gets into an argument with Jim about birthday parties. Jim yells at her.

> "... [M]y birthday is this coming Saturday! And tomorrow I'm bringing invitations to every single person in Room Nine! Only *not* to you! ..."

...

> Meanwhile, I just kept on standing and standing there.
> 'Cause something had gone a little bit wrong here, I think.

Every school child knows the dread of not being invited to a party, and every child understands the power one child can have over another by wielding the "list." Park sets up the situation beautifully, showing Junie's surprise at the sudden results of her argument with Jim. For children, consequences often seem to come out of nowhere, and readers will completely identify with Junie's confusion at how she got into this mess.

Here's an excerpt from our fiction chapter-book sample, *Me and Suzie McFee.*

> I climb up the bus stairs. The bus is crowded. I see a few empty spaces. Should I sit next to my once best friend, Suzie McFee? Or should I take the place next to Robert Jefferson? He has his whole face in a *Star Wars* book. He'll read until we get to the museum.
>
> He'll read *at* the museum.
>
> ...
>
> *Cough. Sputter.* Black smoke comes out of the engine. Mrs. Schneider leans forward. She steps on my foot, and I say, "Ow," but she ignores me.
>
> "Is there a problem?" she asks.
>
> Miss Calypso waves a hand. "Nah," she says. "There's always smoke. It's just the carburetor or fan belt."
>
> "Eep?!" Mrs. Schneider says. "Should we fix something?"
>
> "Too late now," Miss Calypso says. "Unless you want to be late."

The author starts to set up a very real situation for children—the where-to-sit-on-the-school-bus question. Unfortunately, the scene then detours into a discussion, between the two adults, about the bus engine. Bonita is *in* the scene because Mrs. Schneider steps on her foot, but that is the only connection young readers will have with the engine problem. They will be much less interested in what's happening at the front of the bus than they would have been if Bonita had made her way down the aisle and faced the dilemma of where to sit.

If you were critiquing this scene, you might make these comments:

- I understand Bonita's fear, but I think you're giving her an out here, an escape, that won't work for the readers. They'll want to see how the problem plays out for Bonita.

- I really wanted to see who Bonita sat with! Don't you think the kids reading your book will, too?

- I don't know that the problem with the bus is going to be something your readers want to see. Wouldn't they rather listen to dialogue between Bonita and the other kids than between the grown-ups?

The Author Fails to Connect a Nonfiction Subject to a Child's Interests

Once a child has mastered the basics of reading, he often finds himself hungry for new material, new information, and facts. Nonfiction authors can help feed this hunger by writing about science, animals, and famous people. If we're writing a nonfiction chapter book, we face a similar challenge to fiction authors. We need to deliver enough details and information to satisfy our young reader, without overwhelming him with so many facts that he gets tired out and stops reading.

As a critiquer, you can help the writer achieve this goal. You can ask for more details when you think the author hasn't quite supplied enough, and you can point out where he needs to simplify the text or amp up the entertainment factor.

When he wrote *Who Was Albert Einstein?* Jess Brallier faced the task of telling kids about one of the smartest men in history. Einstein, like many famous figures, didn't have a typical childhood, and he made his major contributions to science when he was an adult—years older than the elementary-school child reading this book. Early in the book, Brallier talks about how Albert spent his free hours as a young boy lying on his back and thinking big questions about space. Brallier writes the following words:

> It was as if Albert had been born to think. ... Just as some kids dream of being mechanics or veterinarians, Albert was destined to be a thinker.

Brallier does detail the complexity of Einstein's mind, even when he was young, but makes sure, immediately after, to help his readers connect with the man. He shows them that, as brilliant as Einstein was, he was the same as any child who has dreams of what she will do when she grows up. He also gives his readers a clear, distinct word—a label—for what Einstein was. Brailler equates *thinker* with two other jobs or careers kids are familiar with, helping them see Einstein within a world they understand.

Here's a section of our nonfiction chapter-book sample, *All About Your Veterinarian*, that describes what college is like:

> When your veterinarian was in college, he or she took lots of classes. In college, many classes are very big, with hundreds of students in every room. Your veterinarian had to study science, like anatomy, and she learned about math, too. Her school books were really big and *heavy*. She also had notebooks she wrote in so she could remember what the teachers told her.
>
> Your veterinarian also had to take tests. She took tests in every class, and she had to do well on those tests. If she did badly on too many tests, she might not have finished school and might not be a veterinarian today.

The author has started off with a good plan, to talk about the veterinarian's days at school—a subject with which most children will connect. The writer hasn't gone far enough, though, in actively making that connection for the young reader. He hasn't compared or contrasted college classrooms or teachers to those the child sees in his or her own daily life. In addition, the author has focused on the reading and writing part of veterinary school, rather than the time a veterinarian spends hanging out with dogs and cats and even horses—which is probably what a child picking up a book about vets really wants to read.

As a critiquer reading this passage, you might make these comments and suggestions:

- I think you may need to look for ways to make this material more fun for kids. What activities do veterinarians do in college that would really hook your young reader?

- Can you get the vet students outside with the farm animals? Or learning how to take care of dogs and cats? I think children will like this kind of information.

- You might want to trim some of the classroom descriptions. And I think you might show the kids how vet school is the same as their school in some ways and different in others. If your readers can compare college to what they're doing every day, they'll connect more strongly with what you're telling them.

The Author's Explanations Are Too Complex

Children are curious. They want to find out about the world, and they are *not* happy to be told something is too hard for them to understand. And yet the complexity of some topics, such as science or history, makes teaching these subjects to young readers a serious challenge. An author who takes up this challenge needs to find just the right words to break down complicated and advanced material into small, comprehensible pieces that her readers can absorb.

If you are critiquing a nonfiction chapter book, you can help the author by noting any place you think the language or information is too high-level. You can suggest ways to bring that language to a level where his reader can understand it, and you can help him to do so without his having to talk down to the reader.

In *Who Was Albert Einstein?* Jess Brallier tackles describing Einstein's Theory of Relativity. Here's a bit of Brallier's explanation.

> If you look up at the sky and see a plane in the distance, it doesn't appear as if it's going very fast. You stand there and watch as the plane seems to move slowly across the sky.
>
> Yet if you were standing next to it, the plane would zoom past you in a split second. BLAM! BOOM! Gone!
>
> ... The speed of a moving object depends on how it's being viewed.

Brallier takes one of Einstein's biggest contributions to science *and* history and makes it easily comprehensible to his readers. As in our other excerpt, Brallier works within the world the child already knows—the idea of an airplane looking as if it's moving slower than it really is. He makes sure he doesn't just explain Einstein's theory, but also provides a concrete example that *shows* the meaning of that theory. The young reader will walk away from this book with an understanding and an explanation she can easily repeat every time she sees an airplane. And she will!

Let's go back to *All About Your Veterinarian*. Here's a sample that explains how a veterinarian might use a computer:

> Your veterinarian probably keeps information about his animal patients inside a computer. When he examines an animal, he may write notes about that animal on a piece of paper or type them directly into the computer. His computer has special software on it, called a database, that stores information about the animal into separate sections, called *fields*. For example, the database has a field for the pet owner's name, the pet's name, and what kind of animal it is. All the information your veterinarian types into the computer is saved there. The veterinarian can see it on the computer monitor whenever he needs to, and he can print out a paper copy as well. Also, if another veterinarian wants to see the information, your veterinarian can easily send an electronic version of the database file.

Yes, there are first and second graders out there who can understand how a database works; some of them could even explain it to me. For most young readers, though, the information in this passage is too technical. The description uses too many new vocabulary words, like *database* and *field*.

Even if the young reader of this book could understand the terminology, the author has still written *more* technical detail than is appropriate for this book. A six- or seven-year-old reading about veterinarians is not looking for this much information about how a computer works. He will like finding out that a veterinarian uses a computer, and he'll think it's important that the computer has information about his pet. The detailed explanation this author provides, though, goes too far and will make the child lose interest in the book.

If you were critiquing this book, you might make these comments:

- I think you may be going into too much detail about the database software. I think your readers will want to hear more about the veterinarian and not so much about the inner workings of the computer.

- Are you pushing the range of vocabulary a bit high? Will your targeted reader comprehend phrases like *database software* and *electronic version*?

- How technical do you want to get here? Are you sure the reader needs to know more than that veterinarians use computers while they work, just like the readers' parents probably do?

The Chapters Present Too Many Problems

In an adult novel or a novel for an older child, the story often contains multiple plot threads, and many character arcs intersect back and forth within scenes. If we're writing a chapter book, we will still be thinking about subplots and character layers, but we'll need to be careful not to make the story *too* complex for our audience. If we give the hero too many problems to deal with at once, for example, we may overwhelm the reader who is trying to keep track of them all.

A critique group can help an author follow the plot threads and the character interactions and throw up a flag if they think things are getting too complicated. They can help the writer balance the need to develop a strong story with the need to keep his young reader happily reading that story.

In *Junie B. Jones and That Meanie Jim's Birthday*, Park entertains her readers but makes sure to keep her chapter structure simple. When Junie is finally invited to Jim's party, she goes to buy him a birthday present, and she finds a toy tool belt she loves. This chapter has two scenes—one at the toy store and one at Junie's house. Here is the transition between the scenes, after her mother buys the present.

> I held it on my lap all the way home in the car.
> Then I runned into the house. And I zoomed to my
> room. And I put that thing on me again.
> "Now I can do odd jobs!"

Park uses the toy tool belt itself to take Junie, and Junie's readers, from the toy store back to Junie's own room. Junie is totally focused on the belt, and the readers follow her path by joining her in that focus. Park doesn't bring in external details from the world outside Junie's car or introduce another story thread. She keeps to the main focus of the chapter, the belt Junie has picked out "for Jim"—the belt that is going to set off the next problem for our hero.

Let's see another scene from *Me and Suzie McFee*.

> Suzie grabs hold of Angelina's arm. She pulls her toward the butter churn. I take two steps after them. I will be able to make better butter than Angelina. You have to be strong to make butter. Angelina is little, like a mouse or something. I helped my father carry all the heavy boxes when we moved.
>
> All of a sudden, Mrs. Schneider stands in front of me. She's holding a dress. It's one of those old-fashioned ones from the dress-up station. It's "historic," the museum lady told us.
>
> "Put this on, Bonita," she tells me. "Pretend you're a visitor from another farm."
>
> Visitors didn't churn butter, I'm pretty sure.
>
> I take hold of one sleeve. It's rough. And the dress is ugly. It's brown with icky yellow lace and about a hundred buttons. I can tell I will trip in it if I walk. Which I think visitors do.
>
> Just then Robert Jefferson bursts into the house. He has his plastic light saber, and he's waving it around. "Mrs. Schneider!" he shouts. "The bus is on fire! The Empire has attacked!"
>
> "Call the fire department!" Mrs. Schneider screams, and she runs toward the door.
>
> She's still holding the dress.
>
> So am I.
>
> Riiiip!

A lot is happening in these paragraphs. Suzie chooses Angelina over Bonita, Mrs. Schneider tells Bonita to play dress-up instead of making butter, and the dress Bonita is holding tears. Which plot thread is Bonita supposed to deal with first? The author has set up three strong problems, all of which will need to be woven through the scene and, possibly, into the next chapter. This is too much for a young reader to follow easily. The author risks overwhelming that reader, causing her to put down this book and start hunting for another.

If you were critiquing this scene, you might consider making some of these comments:

- Wow! There's a lot of action here. Are you going to develop each of these problems fully in this chapter? That may be a little too much for your audience.

- Does Bonita have to play dress-up? What if she followed Suzie and Angelina and faced the obstacles of a threesome for most of the scene? Then you could have Robert and his bus fire come in at the end of the chapter, if you needed, and set us up for the next scene's problem.

- I think you may have to choose one, or at the most two, of these plot threads. Three big conflicts like this seem awfully heavy for a single chapter in this kind of book.

Section IV
Worksheet 1: Critiquing Books
for Young Readers

This worksheet is organized around the categories for young readers we talked about critiquing in this section. Within each category, you'll see questions you can ask yourself that will help you recognize and comment on any weaknesses you find while you are critiquing. If you have trouble finding the answers to these questions, first push yourself to look more deeply and then, if you still aren't clear, make sure to note this difficulty in your feedback to the author.

For practice, use this worksheet to do your own critique of our sample scene. Or you can use it to start the critique process on actual projects submitted by the writers in your group.

☙

Reading Level

- How well does the vocabulary fit the needs of the child reader? What changes could the author make to suit the vocabulary more to their young audience?

  _____

  _____

- How long and complex are the sentences in the book? Are there explanations that are too complicated? Should the author trim or simplify sentences or information?

  _____

  _____

- How complex is the overall story structure? How many plot threads and characters are in the book? How can the author simplify the story structure?

  _____

  _____

Audience

- Does the book reflect the world of a child? How could the author direct the project more tightly toward what a child is interested in reading or learning about? What could the author do to shift the focus?

  _____

  _____

- What sense do you have of a pattern in the book's writing. How has the author used rhythm or repetitive structure to help a child follow along and stay interested? How can the author improve her word choices and sentence flow?

  _____

  _____

- Has the author considered an adult as a secondary audience? What can the author include in the story that will help the adult reader enjoy the book, as well as the child he is reading to?

  _____

  _____

Story

- How active is the hero in solving or impacting the story problem? What actions does the hero take to try and achieve her goal? What could the author do to make the hero a stronger participant?

  _____

  _____

- How entertaining is the story? Has the author included enough tension, excitement and/or humor to keep a child's attention? What can the author add or change to improve the story?

_____

_____

- How many details has the author filled in with words? Has the author left room for an illustrator to add images from her imagination and for the child to make up its own pictures as well? Are there details the author should highlight and others they should trim?

_____

_____

BOOKS FOR YOUNGER READERS CRITIQUE EXAMPLES

The following pages offer an example critique of our picture book writing sample. The first page takes pieces of that sample and shows notes you might make as you read through the scenes. The second page shows an example of an overall critique you might present to the author.

Sample Manuscript Pages with Line Notes

Kirby sits.

He wants to see the trapeze artists

swing and play

over the net.

> This first line presents us with a pretty passive hero. The first thing we see Kirby do is "sit." This doesn't set him up to be an active participant in his own story.

The wooden bench where he waits is

hard.

The tent smells like peanuts, cotton

candy, and dirt.

Animals, too—elephants and lions and

little dogs with ruffles.

Kirby wrinkles his nose.

> You're providing a lot of details. I like how you used just a few specific smells, but when you get to the ringmaster, I think you're giving too many details. You're pretty much telling the reader (and the illustrator) exactly what everything looks like.

The ringmaster walks

to the center of the circle.

He wears a tuxedo and a tall black hat,

and he stands on an upside-down box

Painted red with blue and yellow stars.

He cracks his long, black whip

LOUD

> Could you show Kirby react to the LOUD crack of the whip? Could he do something that would affect the story, change the direction of its path?

and three white horses with pink feath-

ers on their saddles and heads

race in circles

around him.

Kirby waves.

> Again, you may want a few less details here about the horses.

> The last thing we see Kirby do is wave. At the beginning, he wanted to see the trapeze artists. They never came, but we don't see him try, somehow, to get to watch them. Also, the other acts aren't shown as a problem. Could you show Kirby facing, and dealing with, more obstacles?

SAMPLE OVERALL PICTURE BOOK CRITIQUE

Dana,

I love the idea of this little boy at the circus. I think kids will want to see the circus acts through his eyes, and they'll get excited about the animals.

I think you have some revision to do, though. The first thing I'd like to see you do is really think about what Kirby wants in this story. At the very beginning, you say that he wants to see the trapeze artists, but that goal pretty much disappears in the rest of the story. We don't see Kirby do anything that might let him see that act, and we don't see him bothered by the fact that they never appear.

Overall, I think we need to see a lot more of Kirby's reactions to and feelings about to what *is* in front of him in the tent. At this point, he's still a bit of a passive observer who relates what shows up, but doesn't get involved himself. He doesn't get happy or sad, mad or excited. The children reading this book, or having it read to them, will want to identify with Kirby; they'll need to experience his feelings about being at the circus right along with him.

Once you know what Kirby wants, I'd like to see him take action toward getting that goal. He can be clever or mischievous or just LOUD like the ringmaster's whip, but he needs to do something in the story. And what he does needs to affect the ringmaster or the animals, so that there can be another problem for Kirby to face. And ultimately, shouldn't he get to *see* the trapeze artists?

You may also want to look at the details you're putting on the page. Don't forget, you need to leave "space" in the images for the illustrator. They will want to bring their own ideas about this circus scene to the page, to *highlight* the words you've put there. Also, if you fill in every aspect of the scene, the child's imagination won't have room to put some of his own ideas and pictures into the story. I think it's important for a picture book to give children that chance.

Great start! I can't wait to see what you do to bring Kirby to the front of his story.

WHAT TO DO NEXT:
HOW TO REVISE AND SELF-EDIT FROM A CRITIQUE

Getting started on a revision can be both exciting and scary. While you've been writing, ideas have been simmering in your head—your own thoughts and suggestions you've received from your critique partners. You've been doing some self-editing as you write, applying what you know about the genre you're writing in and making big choices to guide the overall direction of the project. You've picked the basic plot or organization to follow; you've made a decision about what voice to try out. You know you're getting closer to producing a book or story or article that is complete, tightly written, and ready for submission.

At the same time, you're looking at the work you've already done and facing the task of taking it apart. When you're revising from a critique, you know you've got a lot of work to do other than just rewriting. You're going to have to sort, organize, and *think* through all the comments you've gotten. And you're going to have to do this while remembering and staying true to the vision you have of your project.

Before we dive in, I want to talk about *when* to revise. This is one of the debates that rages between writers, in person and in cyberspace. Should you revise as you write—looking back at previous pages and chapters and making changes before you move on? Or should you write straight through each draft and put off revising until you have written *The End*?

In general, I'm an advocate of moving forward with each draft. First of all, if you deliver a chapter for critique at the next meeting, and you are waiting for feedback on that chapter before you continue to write, you're losing a lot of productive time. More importantly, though, as you write, you learn more and more about the book you're creating. The book grows not only in pages, but in the ideas you have about what you want to do with it. If you spend too much time revising before these ideas come to fruition, you run a big chance of wasting those revision hours. They may be completely inapplicable to the new pages you're writing.

Does this mean you should just bring home your critiques, stick them in a pile, and ignore them until you're done with the complete draft? Definitely not. As I'll talk about in these chapters, you will want to review the feedback you've gotten, to make sure you keep in mind any big issues your critique partners have found. As you write forward, these problems will stay in your mind, and you'll start to try out solutions in the new chapters. This is part of self-editing—doing the work of applying what you're learning to your writing and your revising.

When you go back to address the critique comments, you'll have a stronger understanding of what they mean and also some ideas about how to fix them. And, of course, there will be times when you feel you have to resolve a problem that's shown up in critique before you move on, that you have to rewrite a scene or tighten a thread just so you *can* continue to write. All these reasons are good ones to do a bit of revision. Just don't get too caught up in perfecting the words that, very possibly, you'll be deleting in the next draft.

In the next few chapters, we'll walk through the steps of revising from a critique. You'll learn how to start slowly, working through the easy changes first. We'll talk about the best way to come at the big ideas you've gotten from your critique group, how to evaluate each suggestion, and how to stretch yourself to really look at your book in a new way.

When I first started critiquing and being critiqued, I spent as much time (or more) revising my first drafts as I did writing them. I would come home from a critique meeting and sit down with the comments I'd received. I'd open up the file, and I'd dive in, making the small and big changes, crafting sentences to a higher level and improving all the things like characterization, dialogue, setting, and story that were part of that scene. Then I'd sit down and start drafting the next chapter.

Because, yes, I hadn't dared to write more until I knew what was "right" or "wrong" with the chapter I'd sent out two weeks before. How could I keep going without fixing any problems I might have missed?

As you can guess, my projects were not moving along at light speed.

More recently, I've adopted the opinion that you should *not* revise during the writing process. Whichever draft you're on, I say, don't stop. If you get an idea about an earlier scene, well, that's what sticky notes are for. Write down the thought, stick it on the pages where it applies, and go back to the scene you're writing. Keep moving forward. You can't know the beginning until you get to the end. Even if you've been there before.

Realistically, as is usual with extremes, neither method is the complete answer. I do believe that we can do too much, *way* too much, revision on early chapters before we have written a complete draft. Spending time fiddling around with phrasing or descriptions when you don't even know if you're keeping a chapter (or *where* you're keeping it) can be a waste of time. On the other hand, if you get stuck, if you don't know where the next scene or chapter should be going, it may be a good time to take a long look at where you've been. You may want to play with your hero's goal or bring in an antagonist more strongly. You may need to write a new scene or two to get the plot back on path (old or new). Go for it.

As you revise—as you *learn* to revise—watch for the balance. One of the most important things about revision is being able to work with the big picture of your book. Focusing too much on the small details too early in the project can cloud that picture and consume your time and energy without much to show for it. On the other hand, writing too fast and too hard without *some* kind of direction can get you lost. Don't be afraid to go back and rework things, as long as you're reworking the *big* things.

Chapter 18

MAKING THE EASY CHANGES

You thought sitting through a critique session of your work was hard? Now take those stacks of pages home, with all the praises and notes and comments and problems. Put that stack next to your computer, open a file, and start revising.

It's not that simple. Revising with only your ideas can be tough. Doing the same task with the often conflicting thoughts of several other writers can make you feel overwhelmed really fast. In this chapter, we'll look at some good ways to ease yourself into the revision process, ways that let you make the most of the critiques you've been handed. In the following sections, we'll talk about these tasks:

- recognizing and caring for your emotions
- reading the overall comments
- entering the "yes or no" changes
- defining *awkward* and *unclear*
- translating a "wrong" comment
- using your highlighter as a security blanket

RECOGNIZING AND CARING FOR YOUR EMOTIONS

You've just had a great critique. Okay, sure, your group had suggestions, but basically they raved about your writing and story. You've got a stack of comments, and you race home and turn on the computer, ready to jump into revision mode.

Or maybe the critique wasn't so great. Everybody was encouraging, giving you pats on the back for how hard you've worked, , but it's clear they aren't hooked by the chapters they read. You have a stack of comments, and you're not very revved up about weaving them into your book. After this kind of critique, a nap can sound really good.

Who wouldn't rather get a critique full of praise and positive feedback? Here's the thing, though. Other than the mood it puts you in, one critique or another is not going to make a big difference to your revision process. Odds are, no matter how great you feel at the end of a critique meeting, you'll find something in the comments that will puzzle, worry, or stress you. The flip side is that, even if you're feeling like Chicken Little, you never know when one comment will start a whole string of ideas—good ones—flying through your brain.

No matter how you start out, your feelings during a revision will go up and down. You'll feel great; you'll feel miserable. You'll want to hug your critique partners; you'll want to ... well, let's not go there.

You need to be ready for these feelings and respect them. What you need to *not* do is let these feelings stop you from revising. You joined a critique group because you wanted not only to write, but to write something *really good*. You want to see your book, with a beautiful cover, sitting on the shelf of a bookstore or in a reader's hand.

If you look in a thesaurus, it will probably list *criticism* as a synonym for *critique*. I disagree with this. A criticism implies only negative feedback, while a strong critique will be the right balance of positive *and* negative. The reality is, however—unless you're William Shakespeare or J.K. Rowling—there will be criticism somewhere in every critique you receive. And, at times, someone will be rude or harsh, and you'll feel hurt.

Most of our bad feelings don't come from the words written on our manuscripts, though, or from the person who wrote them. Instead they come from within ourselves. They reflect our own doubts about ourselves as writers—as skilled, creative craftspeople. Even when your critique partners comment with understanding and respect, you will have moments when you feel you have failed—failed your group, your story, and yourself.

Don't try to deny these feelings. Be ready for them to come, and, when they do, recognize and acknowledge them. Then get to work. The strongest weapon against self-doubt is the confidence that comes from strengthening skills. Go get yourself a big piece of chocolate and start revising.

READING THE OVERALL COMMENTS

The first thing to do, when you sit down to revise, is to look at the big, overall critique that each of your critique partners has written up. These are the notes we talked about earlier in the book that, at a critique meeting, each critiquer reads aloud—the comments about big plot and character issues, questions about the books organization or structure.

Even though I don't want you to use these comments yet (in fact, I don't want you to use them until the next chapter), you need to take the time to read through them. It's going to take you a while to process these ideas, to translate them into your story. Get them into your brain, then let them simmer while you address the other parts of your revision. Make a few notes to yourself if you want and then put those pages aside for later.

ENTERING THE "YES OR NO" CHANGES

Your first step in revising from a critique is the easiest. You're going to deal with any comment or suggestion you can address with a clear, definite solution. These are little notes your critique partners have made on each page that you can make a quick decision about, to which you can easily say yes or no.

"Yes or no" changes are comments and questions like the following:

- Mary's shirt was red in chapter three. Did you want it to be pink here in chapter four?
- You spelled *oppositional* with three *ps*.
- The mayor doesn't *own* a gun.

It will only take you a few seconds each to make a decision about Mary's shirt, to correct your spelling, and to either give the mayor a gun or let someone else do the shooting. Make the change and check it off on the manuscript.

I've got a couple of reasons for suggesting you get these comments out of the way. First, nothing feels as good as putting a checkmark on a critique page. You'll feel productive, and productivity keeps you feeling motivated. Working on the easy changes lets you slip into the revision process gently, which brings down your fear and worry levels.

The other thing that happens as you cruise through these first comments is that, even if you're making only the really simple changes, you are reading *all* the feedback. You have to—it's the only way you can decide whether a suggestion or question is an easy one to face. As you skim through the comments, you're absorbing them. You're dropping them into your brain, along with the big overall issues you've already filed there. And everything's bubbling together.

Every time you read a comment, you think about it. The thinking is not always a conscious act, but it's happening. When you come back to this comment, when you are ready to revise around it, you'll already know it. It may not be your friend, but it won't be a shock to your system either. Familiarity reduces stress. Get acquainted with your critiques, and you'll be that much more ready to pull them into your story.

DEFINING *AWKWARD* AND *UNCLEAR*

In the chapters on how to critique I did a lot of coaching about writing clear and helpful comments. I encouraged you to work hard not just to tell a writer that something isn't working, but to explain why. If you and your critique partners follow that path, when you receive critiques there should be fewer of these vague comments for you to work with.

They won't all be gone, though.

That's because none of us, as critiquers, are perfect or consistently brilliant. Every now and then, as we read, we come across a phrase or sentence, or even a paragraph, that doesn't work for us, and we don't know why. As good critiquers, we don't want to just let it slip by without even pointing it out to the author, so we write *awkward* or *unclear* or something equally unhelpful. We write it even as we cringe.

Now, as the writer, it's your turn to address these comments.

Read the passage the critiquer has marked. Read the paragraphs or the page before it. Does the passage jar you, jump out from the rest of the scene, as it did for your critique partner? Has your voice slipped a fraction, or is your character behaving subtly off key? Think about the common problems we've talked about in other chapters and see if any of them apply to this section.

As difficult and frustrating as digging for someone else's meaning can be, these moments are one of the true benefits of the critique process. Another person, a reader with some distance from your book, has caught a bit that feels off. You, the writer, get to take that notification and look more closely at your work. You get to apply your inside knowledge, your deeper understanding of the project, to this section. This combination of perspectives, this—yes, teamwork—often gives you the perfect tools to determine what's wrong and how to fix it.

You won't find an answer to every one of these comments. Sometimes neither you (nor your critique partner) will ever know *what* is awkward; at other times you'll figure out what she meant, and you'll disagree. That's fine.

Between the two (or three or four) of you, though, you'll get further in understanding and improving your project than you will by yourself.

TRANSLATING A "WRONG" COMMENT

You've thought about your book a lot. Whether it's a novel or a memoir or a how-to book, you've developed a picture of the project in your mind. That picture may have gaps in it—you may need some help filling in the right colors—but you have a gut instinct about what will and won't work.

Which is why, sometimes in a critique, you're going to come across a comment that just feels wrong. I define *wrong* here as emotionally wrong, not necessarily factually untrue. In other words, these are the comments to which your initial response is "No way, no how, nuh-huh, not on your life."

Okay, so take a breath. Nobody's forcing you to put in every single change or suggestion made by one of your critique partners. But before you take the scissors and cut her comment out of your printed copy, take a closer look at it. Because there are some other possibilities about what's going on here.

First, the critiquer may actually be right. Really. Not every time, but *sometimes* our own resistance to a new idea is the best clue that we should think more deeply about that idea. If you've been stuck with your plot or squirming uncomfortably at your balance of description and action, you may actually need someone else to point out a new direction. A suggestion that feels off in your first read may—just may—turn out to be the feedback that lets you make your project shine again.

Another reason is similar to the problem we talked about earlier when a critiquer can't explain why she doesn't like a sentence or a passage. In the same way, a critiquer can take a stab at explaining her negative response and totally miss the mark. This does not mean, though, that the section can't be improved. If more than one of your critique partners have marked the same place, this is a big clue that something isn't working.

While you may very well decide, as the responsible author, to disagree with and ignore a suggestion, you should still—also as the responsible author—reread the passage. Tell yourself that, for some reason, the words jarred your reader, brought him out of the chapter. Look at it with fresh eyes without focusing on the specific comment. You'll be surprised at how often you'll find the "right" change, the one you *do* need to make.

USING YOUR HIGHLIGHTER AS
A SECURITY BLANKET

Happiness is not always a warm puppy. Sometimes it's a brand-new, shiny high-lighter. My preference is purple, but go ahead and use orange, if you must.

When you first start revising after a critique, one of the most impor-tant things is, as I said earlier, to move quickly through the changes that take little thought. You want to get on a roll, to get the minor problems (or nonproblems) out of the way and get yourself going with a strong feeling of accomplishment.

Any question that you have to think about can slow down this process. The first "I don't know" that slips into your brain during this early stage can become a worry, a problem—a much bigger deal than it needs to be. We all know the inner editor—the mean, bossy voice in our head that fusses over our writing, that tells us what's on the page isn't good enough and keeps us from rolling strongly and confidently through our first drafts. Well, this creep comes back during revision, especially when you're looking at a critique comment to which you don't have an instant solution.

Here's how you deal with this editor in the early stages of revision. Take that highlighter, uncap it, and cover that note in purple. There. Now move on. Use that highlighter to push away the worry, to let you rest secure in the knowledge that you're not ignoring the comment, that you won't forget about it. You'll come back to it later when you're dealing with the big-picture issues—when you're in serious *thinking* mode. For now, paint it with your highlighter and keep going. And know that, when you've gone through these revision steps with the small changes, you'll be that much more ready to move onto the bigger, more intensive revisions to come.

Chapter 19

TACKLING THE BIG STUFF

So you've gotten the small things out of the way. Now it gets fun!

Yes, of course, it gets hard. A lot of the freedom you felt during your first draft goes away now, and you're faced with shaping the output of that freedom into something more cohesive and coherent.

There is a magic to the revision process, though, that is different from anything you'll find in straight writing. Yes, you'll struggle with thinking of new ways to write a passage you thought was fine, and you'll spend a lot of time working out plot points and narrative voice. You will also, however, see the truth of your project, be it fiction or nonfiction, rise up out of the murkiness that was your early draft. You'll learn more about how to develop and tighten a structure, and you'll add to your abilities to self-edit your chapters as you write and revise. Your story will take form, you'll make connections you never thought of—you will have epiphanies about your writing.

Revision is a bumpy roller coaster, but there are plenty of *"whees"* to balance out the screams of terror. And while no formula can solve all the ups and downs, we're going to talk about some of the steps that can make the ride more manageable:

- looking at the big picture
- assessing comments
- fitting the pieces into that big picture
- rewriting instead of revising

So, hands inside the cart, safety restraints on, and ... let's go.

LOOKING AT THE BIG PICTURE

When you wrote your first draft, you may have written totally free-form, with the words just pouring onto the page, or you may have followed some sort of outline. Either way, unless your brain is a *lot* more capable than mine, you went off on tangents, you dropped structure and organization, you wrote some paragraphs using the wrong voice. Mistakes like these in an early draft are okay; in fact, they're a sign that you're allowing yourself the freedom of thought you need to write that draft.

When you revise, it's time to pull everything together, to fill in holes and tie things into a neat package with a pretty bow on top. To do this, you need to take a step back and remind yourself of the big picture for your project.

The best way I've found to do this is to get away from my computer and away from my manuscript. I make a mug of tea (I give you permission to substitute coffee, Diet Coke, or Ovaltine), get a notebook and pen, and sit in a nonwriting chair. Get yourself settled, then close your eyes and visualize. Ask yourself some of the following questions.

For fiction:

- What is your hero's main goal or quest?
- What is the theme of your story?
- Who (and it's *not* you) is telling the story?
- What are the big plot points that occur in the beginning, middle, and end?
- Who are the most important secondary characters, and what do they do to help/hinder the hero?

For nonfiction:

- Who is your reader?
- What is the overarching structure of your project?
- What is the connecting theme or purpose of your book?
- What voice are you using to deliver your information?
- What are the key points you *must* pass on to your reader?

Use your notebook and pen. As the answers to these questions come to you, take notes. Make them legible because you're going to want to look at them again as you work through the next few drafts. If you've got a good place, tape the answers up near your writing space and read them each day as you sit down to work. The more you can keep these ideas in mind as you revise, the more self-editing and addressing your critique feedback you can do, and the more smoothly the process will go.

ASSESSING COMMENTS

When you revise by yourself, you only have to worry about whether *you* know what you're doing. When you're part of a critique group, and you sit down to revise a project, you face the challenge of judging comments and suggestions from several other people who may not always agree with each other or with you. Revision is also the stage in which you'll really understand that this challenge is worth the struggle—the variety and diversity of the critiques will keep you thinking, keep you creating, and keep you amazed at the new ideas and connections you come up with.

You've already got out of the way the comments that didn't take a great deal of thought. Now, as you work through your stacks of feedback and critiques, you'll be making choices—some small and some big—about the remaining comments and suggestions. You're going to need to decide if, and how, the comments fit into that big picture you just reacquainted yourself with. Here are some questions that can help you evaluate what changes you should make.

- How (and how much) would this comment change your project?
- How does the comment *feel*?
- Who made the comment?

How (and How Much) Would This Comment Change Your Project?

Remember your big picture? There will be many times when one of your critique partners makes a suggestion that has the potential to change that picture. Some of the horror stories you hear about critique groups are based on negative versions of this kind of comment—ones that totally ignore the author's own vision for his or her story and push the critiquer's idea as a replacement.

A new direction is not always a bad idea, especially when the critiquer has really been thinking about the book *you* are writing. Depending on what stage of revision you're at, you'll look at these comments in a different way. If you've already revised the book six times and are close to finishing the project and submitting it to an agent or editor, you may very well pass on a suggestion that would require a major change of plans. If, however, you're working on an early revision, you should take a serious look at the critiquer's suggestion.

Weigh the difficulty of making the change against the advantages to your project.

Possible advantages for fiction:

- The change will considerably increase the tension of your story.
- The change will make your hero more interesting, exciting, appealing (you fill in the rest!) to your reader.
- The change will significantly tighten the connections between your scenes.
- The change will create a strong, active voice for the story.
- The change will layer a solid, important theme throughout your story.
- The change might solve a story problem you're currently struggling with.

Possible advantages for nonfiction:

- The change will make your information much more accessible to your reader.
- The change will create a voice that makes your reader feel comfortable trusting you as an expert.
- The change will allow you to trim a lot of extraneous material.
- The change will produce a thread that connects all the information you're delivering.
- The change will show the reader why he or she needs your information.

If a critiquer's comment, mixed with some serious thought and work of your own, will improve your project in any of these ways, you need to implement it. It won't be easy, and you'll have some headaches and probably a lot of muttering out loud to go through, but it will be worth it. These are the changes that help the hard work of revision turn a book into something magical.

How Does the Comment *Feel*?

We face choices every day of our lives. We've all, at some time or other, guessed a number between one and ten to decide on a movie or flipped a coin to choose between the brownie and the chocolate-chip cookie.

And you all know this feeling: The coin lands heads—brownie. And your gut says, "Oh, darn." Two minutes ago you were positive you couldn't decide. Now you know—you want the cookie.

This is the gut test.

When you sit down with your critiques and read through them, you're giving each comment this test, whether you know it or not. One suggestion makes you smile, and another leaves a sour taste in your mouth. Give yourself permission to pretty much go with your happy thoughts, open the file, and make those changes. I don't recommend, however, skipping the comments that make you react less positively. Instead I'd like you to look more closely at these, to dig for a meaning or solution you might not see at first.

I preach getting to specifics—nouns, verbs, adjectives in all forms of writing, and the theory holds true for revising from a critique. Examine your feelings and try to figure out *specifically* what they're telling you. Are you:

- dissatisfied about what the suggestion will do to your project?
- unclear about what changes the comment will require?
- frustrated that the critiquer didn't understand what you were trying to say?
- afraid that you aren't capable of making the necessary changes?

If you can clearly see that responding to a comment will take your book somewhere you don't want it to go, you can choose to put that comment aside. You may come back to it later (with an aha!), but if it truly does not fit at this time, don't try to force it.

None of the other emotions, however, are good reasons for bypassing a critique suggestion. Instead they are reasons for taking the suggestion very seriously. If writing were easy, everybody would do it. If it were easy to do all by ourselves, we wouldn't need feedback along the way. When you find yourself resisting a comment because you don't know what to do with it—or because you're afraid you won't be able to figure that out—it's time to get to work. When you think a critique partner hasn't understood a passage or a chapter, you'd better take a look at how well you got across what you were trying to say. If your critique partner doesn't get it, how will a reader (possibly an agent or editor!) react to it? And if *three* critiquers don't get it—red light! Take another look.

Who Made the Comment?

There's a big reason this book is about being part of a critique *group*. Many people critique with one other person, and this process can be very valuable. I believe, however, that the variety of opinions and perspectives we get from a group are the things that push us into new, exciting ideas of our own.

As your group develops, as you spend more time critiquing together, you will develop a full sense of who each critiquer is. You'll learn the strengths (and weaknesses) of each of your partners, and you'll learn how much weight you need to give each part of their critiques. One of your critiquers may be brilliant with dialogue—able to tell in a split second which part isn't working and why. Another may catch the gaps in your instruction sets—the spot where your reader is going to get lost. On the other hand, your dialogue wizard may be weaker with things like keeping your hero active, and your step-by-step guy may not be much help on keeping your voice strong.

Using this knowledge is not ignoring the work your critique partners put into your project. In fact, you need to be careful at times not to go into autopilot and assume you can skip a certain type of comment by a particular critiquer. Everybody in your group is learning as they go, and you don't want to miss the first time one of your partners makes the transition from plot wiz to developing great character insight.

Here are some questions you can ask yourself as you evaluate the critique's source:

- Is the critiquer seeing *my* project accurately?
- Is the critiquer missing the cause of the problem?
- Do my other critique partners agree or disagree with the comment?
- Does the critiquer's comment spark *any* ideas for my revision?

Give every comment a fair hearing. Also let yourself recognize that a comment may have been made out of one person's critique weakness instead of from her strength.

FITTING THE PIECES INTO THAT BIG PICTURE

Revising from a critique can look like a huge, overwhelming task, but—when you break it down—it becomes a repetitive, familiar process. You evaluate each comment, as we've talked about, and then you take the comments you want to work with and find a way to make the necessary changes. This last step is the one that tends to intimidate and frighten us.

Go back again to that big picture you have of your project. Look for the best way to weave each comment—each small piece—into that big picture. You need to find out how *and* where the change fits in your book and be ready to extrapolate from the specific suggestions to bigger revisions through the whole project.

Here are some steps that can help you implement actual changes:

- Deciding on the immediate change.
- Carrying the change through the rest of the book.
- Implementing the overall comments.

Deciding on the Immediate Change

The easiest way to tackle a critique revision is to go page by page. This doesn't mean that, at various stages, you won't find yourself hopping around within your project, fixing all the places the dog is the wrong breed or clarifying some basic information that shows up in three different chapters. In general, though, you'll read through the critiques you get from beginning to end, making changes as you go. You'll address each comment on the page it occurs.

If you can fix the problem by changing a few words or by quickly rewriting a larger piece of text (maybe a chunk of dialogue or a set of instructions), go for it. Reread the old material, take another look at the critiquer's suggestions, and type away.

Many critique comments, however, are bigger than this and take more energy. If you're lucky, the comment has set off a big, neon-pink lightbulb in your brain, you are filled with inspiration, and you can open the necessary file and have the new material flow directly onto the page.

If the lightbulb doesn't flare, don't panic. It may just be time to step away from your computer. It is very hard to *think* about your project when the cursor is flashing on the page and your fingers are poised over the keyboard ready to type. At this point, your brain is telling you to write before you are ready. Tell your brain to hold on.

Here are some things you can do to think out your revision:

- With the comment in mind, reread the entire scene or chapter.

- Take notes. Write down your own thoughts about this change, about what you need your characters to do, or how you need to describe this particular setting.

- Play with different brainstorming techniques. Some people use index cards or sticky notes that let them easily rearrange a book's structure. Others scribble single words on a page, inside big circles, and connect them with lots of lines and arrows.

- Read the section out loud. It's amazing how *hearing* a passage instead of reading it can make a problem, and a solution, suddenly clear.

- Rewrite a little bit of the chapter to see if you can get a new voice going or a different direction for the action.

- Call or e-mail one of your critique partners. This can be the critiquer who made the comment, if you want to ask her some questions or hear more about what she was thinking. It can also be a different critiquer, someone who is good at getting past stumbling blocks and helping you sort and organize your thoughts.

- Don't worry about perfection. So many times I hear writers worry about whether they've made the *right* choice or implemented the *right* change. The important thing is to change something. As you keep working, as your critique group reads more of the book, you'll get closer and closer to knowing what "right" means for this project.

If you are really stuck, bring out your highlighter again. Revision is not an all-or-nothing process. As much as we'd all love to write a first draft and then revise everything once, simply and cleanly, this rarely happens. Revision takes time and thought; it's a whittling away of things that don't work and a testing of things that might work. Keep track of the critique problems you haven't solved and be ready to come back at them during a later pass.

Sometimes, by the time you do face these problems again, you've done so much rewriting that the original material no longer has a place in your project. The more work you do on your writing, the more clearly you see what fits and what doesn't. This is the joy of revision—especially revision with a critique group.

Carrying the Change Through the Rest of the Book

In a full critique, you'll receive many different comments on many different pages. Sometimes a critiquer will have seen a single thing that needs changing, but more often, he'll have realized at a particular spot in the project that something isn't working, and he's marked it on that page. This doesn't mean that page is the only place the problem occurs, just that this was where his understanding dawned. An experienced critiquer may mark other places through the book where he sees the problem repeating, but you can't, and shouldn't, ever assume the critiquer has caught every occurrence.

If you're critiquing a project chapter by chapter and revising as you go, you can start by tracking each comment through the chapter in which the critiquer made her note. At some point, though, you will be revising your entire manuscript based on critiques you've gotten back about the whole thing. You're going to be the one responsible for making sure you revise with that big picture in mind.

As you critique, you'll need to think not just about the chapter in which you're reading the comment but about any other places in the project you'll need to revise. If you're writing a full-length book, this can mean anywhere between one hundred fifty and three hundred–plus pages to consider. Even if you're writing a short story or an article, you need to make the necessary changes to each scene.

You can use these methods to break apart your project and identify the parts affected by a comment.

For fiction:

- Identify the beginning, middle, and end of the story. Every important plot and character thread needs to be represented in each of these sections. Make sure you address the problem in all three places and check where and how you need to revise for consistency and continuity.

- If you are revising an action or event, locate each place where this plot point has consequences in the story. Make sure the consequences work with the new change, and if they don't, keep revising.

- If you change a character trait, read every appearance of that character. Make sure the character's behavior throughout the story stays consistent and believable with the change you've made.

- If you shift point of view, getting closer to or more distant from the narrator, you'll need to revise the voice throughout your story to reflect that change.

- If you delete anything—from a secondary character to a setting to a conversation—you'll need to revise any connected material from the story. This may mean giving an action or emotion to a different character, writing a new setting description, or finding a new way to deliver information that was in the dialogue you took out.

For nonfiction:

- If you change the style you use to deliver a set of instructions, you will need to revise every place that you step your reader through a task.

- If you come to a new realization of the theme in your memoir or travel article, you'll need to read each story and event in the project to make sure they reflect the new connecting thread.

- If you shift voice to more casual or more formal, you'll need to change the tone of the whole book, making sure your reader has a consistent delivery style of information to process.

- If you change the structure of your creative nonfiction story, moving actions in a memoir or locations in a travel journey, read through the project to make sure events are organized clearly, without confusion.

You're probably saying, "Whoa!" Yes, revision is a lot of work—a lot of reading and rereading and looking at the same pages many times for different reasons. Don't panic, though. Even if you're like me—getting older and watching your memory fade—you will be surprised at how quickly and completely you get to know your project. Work with the revision process for just a little while and you'll build a kind of map of that book inside your head.

You'll find a change to make in chapter two, and you'll remember the three scenes—two in the middle and one at the end—that are affected by this revision. You'll rewrite an early set of instructions about running a software utility, and you'll "see" the six other chunks of information that talk about that utility. Increase how much you talk about the influence of an old friend on your life, and you'll know just where else she needs to show up in your memoir. The longer you revise, the less labor intensive and the more intuitive the process becomes.

Also, remember that you don't have to make all the changes at once. In early drafts you don't want to get too far ahead of yourself, because your project has more changes to come than you've yet imagined. You can print out your whole first draft and, as you change something early in the book, simply write notes and stick them to the other chapters you think may need more revision. Then keep working through the comments on the current chapter.

As you get closer to finishing the project, you will find yourself working through all the pages at once. Revising at this point is a matter of making important and final connections. You'll make one last revision to a plot thread in chapter two and know exactly how to take that change through chapters ten, sixteen, and twenty. You'll tweak some information in the introduction to your self-help book and then jump right to the ending to rewrite the concluding wrap-up and tie the whole project together. By this time, however, you won't be reading page after page to make your changes, you'll be opening the exact file and scrolling quickly through to the point of revision.

Revising is making changes, but revising is also getting to completely, truly know your project inside and out.

Implementing the Overall Comments

Not every change is marked on a particular page, or on a selection of pages. Remember, in chapter three, we talked about how to write a critique. One of the big steps was explaining the big overall comments that you had about a writer's submission. You saw examples of that kind of write-up in the various sections about how to critique.

During revision, these comments can be the most challenging, and the most important, to incorporate into your project. This process is a bit different than the steps you used to put in the smaller changes. Revising around big comments takes a lot more thinking time, time you may actually want to spend away from your computer, or—if you revise by hand—away from the red pen.

The first step in revising from an overall critique is to make sure you understand the feedback. A critique partner may have told you that they didn't think the hero in your novel was "strong" enough. Does this mean that the hero isn't taking active enough steps toward her goal? Or does it mean that the critiquer can't see, in his mind, what the hero looks like? Maybe the critiquer means that the hero's narrative voice isn't edgy, or funny, or colorful enough.

If you're writing a nonfiction project, the feedback may tell you that your manuscript needs a tighter focus. Should you clarify the specific audience for the book? Do you want to take another look at the goal you've stated for the project? Or does the critiquer want you trim some of your anecdotal stories.

If you aren't clear on what a comment means, find out. If your critique partner has pointed to examples where she sees a problem occurring in your project, take a look at those. You may understand, in a flash, what the critiquer means. Read through a single scene or chapter, with the comment in mind. Once someone has pointed out a weakness, you may find it staring right at you from the pages. If there's something you can't figure out, though—if you can't determine what the critiquer means—talk to them. Send an e-mail or make a phone call, and talk it out. A verbal explanation, or a little impromptu brainstorming, should make everything clear.

Once you understand the comments, sit back and "look" at them. Like I said, it's often best to do this away from the computer. Try a different chair, or even a different room. I head to my rocking chair with clean pages from my project and a blank notebook page at hand, to scribble down ideas as they come to me.

Let's take one of the examples I listed above. What *if*, in your novel, the hero isn't being active enough in going after his goal? Start by reading a few pages in a scene or two. Remind yourself what the hero's goal is in those scenes. Check out what he's doing, and how he does it. Maybe he's following another character's lead instead of stepping out in front for the battle. He could be taking some steps toward his goal, but they're too small, or he's moving too slowly, cautiously even. Maybe you've let him get distracted and go off on a few tangents. Or he might be just reacting to events, instead of proactively making strong choices.

How about your nonfiction problem—your critique partner requested a tighter focus. You figure out that you haven't been clear enough about how your book will help readers. So you start looking for places where that might be true. Just as with the novel, you pick a few chapters and scan for places where you should be highlighting those benefits. And you see that, while *you* know what's great about your project, you have not laid it out for the reader. You haven't given that reader any goals that the book will help them achieve, and you haven't explained to the reader *why* they should do the exercises you've provided.

So you've identified the problem, and you see how it's playing out in your book. Time to think about solutions. Here's where you get into that deep revision and self-editing that will really bring your whole book together.

While the individual changes you make at this point may be small—in word count—they will be huge in terms of importance.

Let's go back to your hero's goal. You're going to make him more assertive, force him to move into the lead and to take some serious risks. When you do this kind of revision, you're making the following kinds of changes:

- You'll change the choices your hero makes.
- You'll change the actions the hero takes.
- You'll change the hero's personality to mesh with his new behavior.
- You'll change the dialogue that shows the hero interacting with other characters.
- You may change the settings to accommodate the hero's new choices and actions.
- You'll try playing with the narrative voice to reflect this more active hero.

In other words, the changes you make in this revision will affect and tie together every layer of your story.

Let's think about that nonfiction critique. You need to make it clear to the reader why they should read and use your book. As you revise, you'll make these kinds of changes:

- You'll add some text to the book's introduction.
- You'll weave reminders into the main chapters.
- You'll connect the exercises and examples to the book's purpose.
- You'll play with the voice to make the reader feel supported by the book's goal.

Again, you'll carry these big revision changes through every part of your manuscript. The most important thing you can do as you revise and self-edit from your critique feedback is to move forward with an open mind. While you work on these changes, remember that you *know* your book. That sounds trite, but it's important. You have written every word on every page, and you are responsible for the connections you've already made, early and unclear though they may be.

The trick to this stage of revising is to immerse yourself in your project and, at the same time, look at it from the outside. You need to keep all the layers of your story or all the information and structure of your nonfiction project present in your mind as you work.

Different writers use different techniques to achieve this kind of split vision. Here are a few you can try:

- Spend a few minutes before each revision session just "sitting" with your project. You can call this meditation, or visualization, or just quiet time. With fiction, think about your hero's personality, picture an important setting in the book, or "talk" to yourself in the narrative voice. For nonfiction, remind yourself of your purpose in writing the book, imagine a reader working with one of the exercises, or retell yourself one of the stories you've used to illustrate an important point.

- Make a collage for your project. Cut out pictures from magazines or print images from the Internet, then glue them all to a big piece of construction paper or butcher board. Prop up the collage, or hang it on a wall, somewhere you can glance at it whenever you need to get a full sense of the world you're creating or discussing in your book.

- If you do better with structure, create some kind of chart to keep close by. This can be an illustration of the main plot arc in your novel, or a diagram that shows the purpose of your nonfiction book at the center, with lines radiating out to the reason behind each chapter.

- To keep it simple, write the single-sentence premise of your novel or the reason you took on this nonfiction project on a single piece of paper. Tape it to your computer monitor. Use it to show you the core idea for your book, whenever you feel the need for a quick reminder.

The point of all these techniques is the same. They help you push the external world away and bring back the world you're creating.

Revision is hard work. Even the writers who love revision will tell you this. Revision is also, though, the stage where you make new connections—where you bring together the disparate pieces of your manuscript into a coherent, linked whole. It is the time in which you will make discoveries you never expected—when a minor character takes on the role of primary antagonist, when you realize that a couple of paragraphs perfectly evoke that person from your past you've been trying to bring onto the page.

Stay open as you revise, and be ready for the surprises that will come. The more time you spend revising—on individual projects and over the course of your writing life—the more skills you'll grow. You'll move forward with confidence, and you'll keep those two parts of your brain—the one looking at details and the one holding onto the big vision—in synch and working together.

And you'll see the magic.

REWRITING INSTEAD OF REVISING

Sometimes when you revise you'll need to make a brain shift out of your usual pattern of work. On a typical day of revision, you're tackling bits and pieces of your book, however spread out they are in the book. You're changing existing text, playing with wording, tightening up passages already on the page.

Sometimes this process is not enough. A good critique partner doesn't just skim the surface of your writing; she digs deep into the meat of the entire book. You'll get comments from your critique group that make you refocus the theme of your story or reorganize the entire structure of a few chapters. Sometimes, when you're looking at this kind of critique, the best thing you can do is to completely let go of the work you have already done. Step away from the words on the existing pages, open a brand-new file, and start writing—*rewriting*—all over again.

This stage of revision can be frightening and potentially discouraging. You've worked hard to get your project to this point, and now you're going to trash big chunks of what you wrote. Writing all new text can feel like a step back, especially if you're a few drafts into the book when you decide it's necessary. How can anything you write fresh, as its own first draft, be anywhere as good as what you're deleting?

Actually, it can. When you *rewrite*, you're doing so with a much better understanding of your book than you had the first time through (and very possibly the second and third times, too). In fiction, you know much more strongly where your hero is going, what he needs to do to get there, and how each scene has to be structured to help him out. In nonfiction, you've got down the organization and voice, and the pattern into which all your chapters need to fit.

How do you know when it's time to step back from the existing words and come back at your project with a whole new set? Here are some questions you can ask yourself to help make that decision:

- Are you getting the same comments from your critique group about a chapter, no matter how many times you revise it?

- Have you revised a chapter several times but are still frustrated by it?

- When you sit down to revise, are you caught up in playing with very small pieces of the chapter?

- Do you feel unhappy when you revise a chapter, even if you're successfully at following the critique comments?

- Are you finding excuses to skip revising a chapter—anything from refusing to rewrite the story beginning for the hundredth time to deciding it's time to iron your pillowcases?

Any of these "symptoms" may be a clue that the words are not the problem with this part of your revision. When you can't fix the words, you are probably at the point where you need to dig deeper, even throw away those words completely.

When you "start over" with a rewrite, you are actually doing no such thing. You're taking everything you've learned along the revision road and writing a scene or chapter to fit tightly into a more cohesive, coherent whole. The new writing may need a bit of copyediting and polishing, but it will most likely be a piece of the puzzle that fits much more tightly and delivers much more force and energy to your manuscript.

IN YEARS TO COME:
HOW TO MAINTAIN AN
EVOLVING GROUP

A lot of us join critique groups at the beginning of our writing careers. The structure of regular meetings provides a solid schedule that keeps us motivated, encouraged, and on a regular writing schedule. The longer we write, however, the more experience and skills we develop. If publication is our goal, we'll start learning more about the business, and we'll get closer and closer to the real possibility of seeing our work on a bookstore shelf.

As you make your way further along this path, your critique needs may very well change. A good critique group will evolve with its members and stay flexible about the type of critiques they give as well as the timing of those critiques.

The chapters in this section discuss the changes likely to come to your members and the ways in which your group can and should adapt to those changes. We'll talk in detail about how to run a brainstorming session and how to troubleshoot problems that arise in the group. We'll go into detail about the kind of critiquing you and your partners will do as you each get closer to finalizing your books and sending them out. And we'll go over a few more tasks you can take on, if you choose, to help each other network and promote your published books.

I have worked with many of my critique partners for more than a decade, and the connections and relationships I've built with them are some of the most important in my life. We are more than writers and critiquers; we are friends who have supported each other through good and very bad times in our personal lives. And that is important to me.

Section
VI

The most important thing, though, is the support we've given each other—and the support you and your critique partners can give to each other—on our writing paths. It is no coincidence that, after years of working together, some of us are published, and others are submitting completed manuscripts to agents and editors. The feedback we've shared with each other, the education we've all gained, is a big part of the success we've had. Without it we'd be writers, yes, but writers on our own and—I'm willing to bet—further away from our goals.

This is the kind of critique group I wish for you, one that gives you the support and experience you need, and one you can stay with for many years on your own writing path. With patience and persistence, I believe you can build this kind of group, and I believe you will see it seriously add to your writing abilities and your success.

Chapter 20

BRAINSTORMING

One of the most important things a critique group can do for its members is to include brainstorming as part of the group's agenda. You'll do little bits of this all the time as you critique—it's the back-and-forth discussion that comes up after all the critiques have been read or when an author has questions. As your group develops and the members dig deeper into their books you'll want to treat brainstorming as a separate, distinct task.

If you get stuck with your project, if you can't see where to go next, it's time to schedule a brainstorming session. Simply let your group know that, instead of submitting pages for critique, you want to use a time slot for thinking up some new ideas. If you're working in an online group, and the members don't have a standard "meeting" time, you can ask everybody to participate in an exchange of ideas, either in a chat room or just across e-mail. If you're meeting in person, everybody should bring their pens and notepads and come ready for thinking.

In this chapter we'll talk about some of the elements of brainstorming and the ways you can use this tool most effectively. You'll learn about the following parts of brainstorming with your critique group:

- submitting for a brainstorming session
- creating a supportive brainstorming environment
- asking open questions
- accepting ideas from others
- summarizing the brainstorming session

SUBMITTING FOR A BRAINSTORMING SESSION

Just as you submit pages for a critique session, you should deliver a submission for your brainstorming time. This may seem silly, since the problem is that you *don't* know what you're doing. You do know more than your critique partners, though! Give it your best shot. Type up a small blurb or list to give your brainstorming partners some insight into why and where you're stuck. Here's some basic information you should try to include.

For fiction:

- the big plot points, so far, of your story
- your hero's goal, as you understand it for now
- what you were writing about when you got stuck
- any questions you've been wrestling with
- any possible paths you've been considering for the story

For nonfiction:

- The overall premise or purpose of your book
- The audience for the book
- The level/focus of information you're trying to deliver
- What you were writing about when you got stuck
- Any questions you've been wrestling with

It can be a good idea to send along the current chapter you're working on. At this point, don't worry about whether you're submitting garbage or not; you're asking for help, and the other group members are there to provide it. Let them know you're definitely *not* looking for a critique at this point but that the submission is just to provide a starting point for the brainstorming.

If you really feel overwhelmed, and even coming up with some basic information about your project seems impossible, still schedule the brainstorming session. Don't underestimate the abilities of your critique partners to help you get started. You may think you're coming to the meeting completely empty-handed. Believe me, you won't leave that way.

CREATING A SUPPORTIVE BRAINSTORMING ENVIRONMENT

We've talked about the ways in which delivering or receiving a critique can be tricky and can make both the author and the critiquers nervous. Well, a brainstorming session has its own stresses. With a critique, the author has spent some time on the writing she submits, and the critiquers have been able to prepare and think about their critiques before the meeting. At a brainstorming session, everybody is coming to the discussion fresh. They're

expected to think on their feet (or from the couch), to come up with helpful, even brilliant, ideas on the spur of the moment. The author is opening
herself up by sharing a very rough version of her writing and by admitting
she doesn't know what to do next.

For a brainstorming session to be truly successful, every participant has
to feel supported and safe. Everyone has to *know* they can ask questions
and share ideas without being judged or criticized. This is the magic part of
brainstorming—no suggestion is right or wrong, no comment gets a yes or
no response. Every idea is a possibility.

If you are the author, *listen*. Take notes on everything your critique partners talk about. You're in the middle of—if not a storm—a strong breeze of
creativity. You can't listen, sort, and make decisions all at the same time. If
you're lucky, somebody will toss out a thought that turns on the light switch
in your brain, that either points you in a new, exciting direction or answers
one of the big questions you've been struggling with. Even if this doesn't
happen, you're going to go home with suggestions to mull over and explore.
You can't lose.

Can you talk? Of course. Join in the brainstorming and add your own
ideas to the pot. A good brainstorming session loosens up a stuck author
at the meeting as well as after he is home writing again. How about asking
questions? Definitely. Just don't throw that question out the instant it pops
into your head. Let the brainstorming flow for a while. Your critique partners are digging into their own knowledge and experience and freely sharing
their ideas with you. You don't want to cut them off midstream. And be very
careful not to reject or negatively judge any of the suggestions they do make.
If you criticize, they'll start filtering, picking, and choosing which thoughts
are "good enough." That's a great way to lose a lot of possibilities for your
project. Write down your question and wait for a break in the brainstorming
or hold on until the end of the session. By that time you may already have
gotten your answer!

If you're a critiquer helping an author through that stuck place, the "no
judging" rule applies just as strongly to you. Anybody can come to a point
in her project at which she doesn't know how to move forward; if it's not you
today, it might very well be your turn tomorrow. Be supportive and encouraging toward the author and put your best effort into the brainstorming.

You get to listen, too. Listen to what the author and the other brain-
stormers are saying. The best brainstorming sessions are electric, with one
person's idea sparking another idea from the person across the table. Don't

cut anyone off, and don't dismiss any suggestion. Don't criticize an idea as being wrong for the project or for being unclear. *Never* use the word *stupid*.

It is everybody's job to keep excitement and energy from turning into chaos. The worst thing that can happen to a frustrated author is to be overwhelmed by loud voices and waving arms. Yes, a brainstorming session has more freedom and flexibility than a critique meeting. You don't have to move clockwise (or counterclockwise) around the table, and you don't have to wait for each person to complete his presentation. You *do*, however, have to watch for a good moment to speak your thoughts, and you should check whether the author needs to ask a question or slow down the session until she can catch up. Once again, it comes back to manners. You have them ... use them.

ASKING OPEN QUESTIONS

As you get more experienced with brainstorming, the sessions will begin easily, with one person starting the discussion by throwing out a few possibilities and others chiming in with their input. Sometimes, though, especially for beginning critiquers, it's tricky to know how to get going. My suggestion: Start asking the author some questions.

The best kinds of questions for a brainstorming session are open questions. Open questions are ones that *cannot* be answered with a yes or no. Yes-or-no questions typically lead to dead ends, while open questions fuel a discussion that can go in any direction, without end. Here are some examples of open questions.

For fiction:

- What does your hero want?
- What information do you need to share with your readers?
- Why did your villain take that action?
- What will happen if your hero doesn't get his goal?

For nonfiction:

- Why does your reader need this information?
- How will your reader use your book?
- Why do you want to include this description?
- What was important to you about this place in your travels?

Ask gently. Remember, the author has been working on this problem already, and she's coming to you *because* she doesn't have the answer. Give her time to consider what you're asking, to realize she knows more than she thinks. If she can't answer, don't make a big deal about it. Move easily and with encouragement onto the next question.

And don't forget that, as this author's critique partner, you're familiar with her writing and her project. If she can't come up with any answers, any ideas in response to the questions, you and the other members can pitch in. You know the hero—what do *you* think he wants? You probably have a good idea about why the bad guy didn't use the gun or why he bought the toddler an ice cream cone. What do you think the reader needs to learn about gardening in this chapter? Toss some ideas slowly back and forth until the author gets caught up in the exchange, until she starts realizing she does have some contributions to make.

ACCEPTING IDEAS FROM OTHERS

The first few times an author comes to his group for brainstorming, he can have a particular challenge to face—especially if the session is a success. He came to the group stuck, without any ideas of his own, and he's walking away with dozens of suggestions for his project.

What happens if he takes one of those suggestions?

Few of us can explain where our writing comes from, but mostly we accept that there is something magic—a muse, extra-special synapses in our brains, inspiration—that happens when we are writing. We accept this; we even welcome it. We may have more trouble, though, accepting that kind of magic from another person. Or three other people.

It can be tough for a writer to take an idea from one of his critique partners and use it in his own project. Especially if the suggestion turns his story or book in a new direction or makes a big change to the manuscript. If the author had his hero setting out on a journey alone, and an idea from someone else in the group gives that hero a sidekick, whose creation is that character? If a critique partner shows an author that he needs another chapter in his travel book, about a town the author never meant to include, who is responsible for that section? Who really wrote the book?

The author. An idea is just an idea. It's not words or sentences, and it's not the combination of overview, details, and personal perspective that a writer puts on the page. If you are the brainstorming author, take the ideas offered with gratitude and then mix them with your own creativity, and go. Keep writing. You'll see that what started as a single suggestion has turned into an entire thread of your manuscript. And if you're the brainstormer who came up with the idea, pass it on gracefully, with your own gratitude for being part of a group that can support each other in this way. Next time it'll be your turn.

SUMMARIZING THE BRAINSTORMING SESSION

At the end of every brainstorming session, whether the group is breaking up for the day or moving on to critiques, somebody should take a few minutes and summarize the discussion. If at all possible, I recommend that this person be the author. She doesn't need to run through all the notes she took or list every suggestion that was made. She should, however, hit the key points that really struck home—the ideas that either solved her problem or are pointing her clearly in the right direction. It's important, I think, that the author try to do this job because it gives her a few minutes to think about what she's really learned and pushes her to express that new knowledge out loud. Saying something out loud will implant it that much deeper into her memory and understanding.

If the author is still buried in the happy mound of ideas she's received, another critiquer can take over this task. A third group member can take a newer, shorter set of notes from the summary so the author has a sort of table of contents with which to come at her own hurried scribbles. The ultimate goal is for the author to leave with a clear view of the most important ideas that have come out of the session. She needs to be able to see at least the first few steps on the path she's going to take when she gets home and sits down at the computer again.

Chapter 21

CRITIQUING FOR SUBMISSION

Nobody can promise you will get your book published. (Nothing would make me happier than for there to be a book-industry fairy godmother to wave a magic wand over all of us, but she's just not hanging around.) I can tell you, though, that if you critique with a strong, skilled group for long enough, you will bring your writing to the point where you are ready to submit a manuscript to an agent or editor. This will be one of the most exciting and *nerve-wracking* times of your life. And, once again, your critique group will be there.

In this chapter, we'll talk about the things your group can do to help each other prepare for submission:

- Critiquing a full manuscript
- Doing a final pass
- Responding to last-minute calls for help
- Providing support for the query process

CRITIQUING A FULL MANUSCRIPT

In many critique groups, members submit one or two chapters at a time and get those chapters critiqued every couple of weeks. This pattern is enough to keep them writing and revising, to help them make progress on their projects and develop stronger writing skills.

As your writing develops and you get closer to submission, this standard schedule may not work for you. Getting twenty or thirty pages critiqued every month will not be enough. Whether you have a deadline or not, you're going to need your critique partners to read your entire manuscript and give you feedback on it as a whole body of work.

When your group is ready to read full manuscripts, you'll need to schedule enough time to read more pages, and you'll need to shift the way you read those projects. You'll be thinking about things like consistency and continuity across chapters, about the theme and purpose of the book.

Scheduling Time

When one of your critique group members submits an entire manuscript, you and the other members will need to schedule enough time to give a thorough critique. The writer submitting the book needs to get the files or pages to the group early enough that members don't feel rushed or pressured to hurry through their read. At the same time, the critiquers need to set aside time to give the project their full attention.

If you normally take two weeks to critique a chapter, this does not mean, obviously, that you need ten months to critique a book that's twenty chapters long. Unless the project is a Victorian novel, a month is usually enough time to schedule for a full critique. You'll need to consider whether other members are also contributing at the same time, of course. Most of us read at least a book a week for pleasure, though, so we should be able to read a manuscript in four.

When you're handed an entire book to critique, you want to simulate the experience of reading a "real" book as much as possible. Obviously, you'll have your pen handy, and you'll stop to take notes, but you're reading for things like pacing and sequence and transitions between chapters. Don't critique yourself into exhaustion (yes, it's possible!), but the more pages you can read at one sitting, the better. At the same time, you don't want to space your reading sessions too many days apart. You want the pages to be fresh in your mind when you come back to read more.

When you get the submission, pull out your calendar and block out a few solid chunks of critiquing time over just a few days. You'll feel more connected to the project every time you pick up the manuscript, and the critique you produce will be truly helpful to the author.

Reading for Consistency and Continuity

One of the most important things you can do when you critique a full manuscript is watch for places where the writer has been inconsistent or for when the flow of the story or nonfiction project is either broken or goes in a different, "wrong" direction.

As we write, we're keeping track of hundreds of details. In fiction and memoirs, we're plotting the story arc and developing characters and weaving those threads together through scenes and the whole book. In nonfiction, we're delivering information and using consistent structure and voice in a way that makes the material easy and enjoyable for our readers to access.

By the time we submit a full manuscript to our critique group, we've changed much, if not most, of the writing we started with. We do our best to make sure our revisions track through the whole book, but we're writers—not computers. We need all the help we can get to make sure our manuscripts flow smoothly from page to page so our readers can step in quickly and easily, without any bumps.

As a critiquer, do your best to note any place the author slipped. Sometimes the work is a matter of catching little details—a change in hairstyle, a different style of procedures, the name of a country switching from the one we know it by today to the one we used ten years ago.

At other times you'll be looking deeper. In fiction, you'll be watching for inconsistent or unmotivated behavior from the hero, a sudden unexplained change in pacing over two scenes, a repeat of an argument that was resolved two chapters earlier. In nonfiction, you'll want to note places where the level of information gets too shallow, sections that suddenly become "fluff" instead of instructive, and material that doesn't fit into the big purpose of the project.

You may need to keep sticky notes handy as you critique. If you start to see problems with a character thread or with the balance of description in a travel book, you'll want to stick a note at the places you find these inconsistencies or pattern breaks. Keep track of the places that work and don't work; you'll probably be flipping back and forth as you read to see what the writer did at one place or another. The more places you can leave a comment, the easier it will be for the writer to see the big picture and smooth things out when she revises. (Hint: The sticky notes are for you; it's a kindness to take them off before you hand back the critique. Little pink notes flapping all over a manuscript can be as frightening to an author as red pen bleeding across every page!)

Following the Theme or Purpose Through the Book

Fiction has a theme. So do memoir and travel writing. You don't want to write books that hit the reader over the head with your theme, but the thread of "what the story is about" needs to weave its way, subtly, through every important character action and every major plot point. Other nonfiction books may not have a theme (for instance, a bigger meaning about life) that they're trying to show, but every nonfiction project has a purpose, a reason for being written. That purpose, just like a fictional theme, is the foundation of every chapter in the book. Just as an example, the purpose of this book is to show you that you *can* build a critique group that supports you and your writing. If I haven't satisfied that purpose across all the pages, I haven't succeeded in writing the best book I can.

You may very well write an entire novel without identifying its theme; you may even revise the story several times without being sure what its theme really is. Similarly, you may start your nonfiction project with the sole purpose of writing a book proposal that gets you a contract and that people will buy.

All these are perfectly reasonable ways to approach your book. Theme and purpose are great discussion topics for your critique group to toss around, as well—other people are sometimes much better than we are at identifying the connecting thread of our work. Or at least better at helping us figure it out.

However, theme and purpose are really what hold a book together; they are the container that all the story pieces and information fit inside. If, when you submit your full manuscript to your critique group, you can define this thread to your critique partners, it will give them a head start on reading for that unity.

If you are critiquing a full manuscript, and the author hasn't been able to tell you the theme or purpose, you can help him by looking for it while you read. The best way to think about what's connecting all the pieces of the book is to ask, "Why?"

Why is the hero doing this action? Why is the villain trying so hard to get in the hero's way? Why does an event have such a big impact on the story? Why is the author telling his readers about this town or this life experience? Why does the reader need this piece of information?

If you're critiquing a book with a strong, solid theme, you'll face fewer "why" questions as you read. If you find yourself experiencing too many *whys*, you've probably hit a point in the project where the writer has gotten away from her purpose, where she hasn't connected the scene or chapter to the over-arching objective for the book. Mark these places in the critique. Make a note of your specific question and, if you can, make some suggestions about how to tie this piece into the strong backbone that is the book's reason for being.

Tracking Plot Tension and Character Arcs

In any book with a story, and this includes memoir, travel writing, and much of children's nonfiction as well as fiction, two things are true: The book has to produce an increase of tension from beginning to end, and the main characters in the book must grow and change. These are difficult goals for writers to achieve, and they're two of the biggest reasons full manuscript critiques are so important.

When you're reading one of these books in its entirety, keep your pen at hand to note any places where the tension sags, where the suspenseful what's-going-to-happen next feeling disappears. Of course, in every story there are passages of relative calm when the characters are taking stock and making plans, getting ready to dive back into conflict again. Overall, though, the frequency with which problems get thrown in the hero's face, and the intensity with which she attacks those problems, must increase. If you read a scene where the opposite happens, and you don't see a clear reason for the shift, add a comment to your critique.

In the same way, you can watch for character development across the story. As bad things happen, the characters need to react, and those reactions need to change as the characters learn their skills and strengths. The hero, especially, needs to get stronger, even as his goal seems to get harder to reach and further away. If, while you read, you see the hero or other characters staying the same, responding to two situations as though they haven't learned or grown, note these places and the problems in your critique.

When we write, it's very easy to get caught up in the details, missing the big (and tight) picture we need. During revision, we work hard to make changes and add connections to the main plotline and important character arcs. A good critiquer reading a full manuscript can help us make those last fine-tuning edits the book still needs.

DOING A FINAL PASS

At some point, one or more of the members in your group will get to the point where they're submitting a manuscript or proposal to agents and editors. The critique group will be familiar with the project, and the various members will have contributed their own opinions about the manuscript's state of readiness. The group has one more job they can do, however, before the writer puts the actual query in the mail.

They can do one last read-through of the entire book.

When a writer decides it's time to get his work out into the world, he needs a very different kind of "critique." In fact, I'm not sure we can even call this last pass a critique. At this point, the author is not looking to make big changes to his book, and he's already (hopefully) done all the fine-tuning. What he hasn't necessarily done is read the book, page by page, looking for the sentence where he stuck a comma in the wrong place, made a typo, or just experienced a brain blip and forgot about a sentence he meant to delete. And even if he *has* done this read-through, he may be too close to his manuscript to have done it productively.

You don't have to be a copyeditor to help the writer at this stage. You just need to be ready to do a close read of the surface text. When you read for a final pass, you are actually trying *not* to think about the bigger things like character, plot, organization, and voice. Obviously, if something jumps out at you, grabs you by the neck, and yells, "He can't send me out with *this* problem," you should let the writer know.

If you feel seriously that this book isn't ready for submission, you should already have had that discussion with the author. When she is firmly and (as much as possible) confident that now is the time, you need to offer her the service she's asking for, which is to help her present as professional a manuscript as possible.

When you're doing a final read, you're looking for any problems that have slipped through all the other revisions. These are the kinds of things you'll mark when you're doing this last pass:

- missing punctuation
- run-on or fragment sentences
- individual phrases or sentences that don't make sense
- incorrect page numbering
- uneven line spacing
- misspelled words

Before you ask about that last one—yes, every author should run his spell-checker. And it doesn't matter if he has already done this. Either the writer will have added a tiny bit of last-minute text, or he'll have hit the wrong button when the software asks him to replace a word. Or the spell-checker, a very useful but untrustworthy tool, will have let a homonym slide through. The sentence *He gave me a great, big bare hug* is probably not the one the author meant to write. A human brain is the best, last tool to apply.

RESPONDING TO LAST-MINUTE CALLS FOR HELP

If life were neat and organized, all our desks would be spotless, the laundry would never pile up, and we wouldn't need watches or calendars (we can all dream). Instead no matter how far we plan ahead, and no matter how hard we work, life surprises us.

Sometimes it's a good surprise—like an agent asking for a full manuscript or an editor offering a contract with a tight deadline.

This is one of the many times you'll see all the time and energy you've invested in your critique group coming back to you with major interest. This is when you sit down with the other members of your group, spend a few minutes in serious celebration, then ask them to be both flexible and generous. Because, for whatever period of time you're dealing with, your work will not necessarily conform to a neat, evenly paced schedule. You won't be able to predict how many pages you'll submitting or even when. You'll be writing and revising as fast as you can and asking your critique partners to support you in the effort.

And in a good group, they will.

If you're a critiquer, and you get "the call," try to answer with excitement, support, and commitment. Obviously, not everybody's schedule allows for the same flexibility or available hours. As a group, you need to recognize this fact and accept that contribution can't always be quantified. Each member, though, should make a serious effort to do as much as she can. Unselfishly, your support is invaluable to the writer. Selfishly, someday, hopefully, you're going to find yourself in the same position, asking for the same kind of help.

Don't feel guilty about saying no if there is truly no way for you to help. Do say yes whenever and however you can.

PROVIDING SUPPORT FOR THE QUERY PROCESS

If you and your critique partners are working toward publication, the experience and knowledge you gain in the critique group is going to help you get there. At some point, someone in the group will start querying agents and editors. And the rest of the members can support that writer as he ventures onto this next step on his writing path.

There are many books available that talk about how to write a query letter. Agents and editors blog about the topic, and many post information on their Web sites. There is almost always someone presenting about queries at a writing conference. Do your research. Querying is a hard task, and the more you read up on it and practice writing the letters, the more chance you have of persuading some of those agents and editors that they want to read your manuscript.

No one, not even the experienced, brilliant members of your group, can tell you 100 percent what is going to sell your book. Those members can, however, swap ideas about the best way to write a pitch and share information they've learned from reading or from attending a class. And, when a writer is ready to send a letter, the other members can do a final read to catch mistakes or make editing suggestions.

What happens after the query letters are sent? I wish for you nothing but good from this process—that you find the perfect agent and editor to sell and publish your book. Statistically, though, you're going to get something else along the way.

Rejections.

How many times have you heard about the huge number of rejection letters a famous author has received? Enough to paper the walls of her office, right? I know this data is supposed to make us feel better, but, personally, I'd rather just use paint.

Still, everybody gets rejection letters, and the members of your group won't be the exceptions to this rule. The nice thing is that, when you're in a critique group, you have friends who get it, who are there to pat you on the back and buy you chocolate and encourage you to send out more queries.

You also have writers and readers to help you translate those rejections into more revision, if necessary.

Editors and agents are incredibly busy. As writers, we moan about the size of the slush piles with which we're competing, but those piles aren't on our desks threatening to bury us. Many rejection letters are simple form letters; others take a sentence or two to give a general reason why the person isn't asking for your book. The editor or agent simply doesn't have time to put anything more into the letter.

Every now and then, though, a letter comes through that breaks this pattern. The editor or agent has not just sent a "no, thank you" but has written some serious, thoughtful critiques of his own about your project. He may even say that, if you're interested in revising based on those critiques, he'd like to see the book again.

After you jump up and down and spin in circles, you're going to realize that, yes, it's time to revise again. You're also likely to realize that you're now looking at a partial or full manuscript revision, based on a few comments in a letter. You may not even be crystal clear on what those comments actually mean.

Remember, you're not alone. Ask for time at the next meeting and bring along the letter. With all the other writers who know your project almost as well as you do, read the comments and talk about your book. Extrapolate from the suggestions the agent or editor has made, making connections with all the big parts of your book—the plot, the character, the structure, the voice.

At times, this will feel like you're throwing darts in the dark. At other times, the lightbulb will flare, and you'll know exactly which changes you need to make. Either way, with the help of the group, you'll revise your project yet again, and you'll resubmit the manuscript. There are no guarantees in this business, and there's no magic that says you're sending the agent or editor what he wants. The only certainty is that, if you stick that letter in a drawer and *don't* try to interpret it, *don't* revise and resubmit, well, all you've got from that nice feedback is another no. And why would you go after one of those?

Chapter 22

NETWORKING AND PROMOTION

The longer you stay in a critique group, and the deeper you immerse yourself in all things writing- and book-related, the more you're going to find out about the publishing world. Writing for publication is a business as well as a craft. Within the circle of your writing community, you can learn about how to network, how to market yourself as a writer, and how to promote your books.

If your critique group decides to take this step, you and the other members can add marketing and promotion tasks to the work you already do. Here are a few things you can do to support each other:

- educating each other about marketing and promotion
- sharing information about agents and editors
- supporting each other's blogs
- exploring social networking sites
- recommending each other as speakers

EDUCATING EACH OTHER ABOUT MARKETING AND PROMOTION

Once you're published, how *do* you promote your book and do the marketing work that will contribute to your book sales? When do you start book promotion? And should you promote your book or yourself as a writer—a person with a fascinating story to tell?

All these questions are serious ones that, as you get closer to publication, you'll need to think about. Writers and publishing professionals are blogging about these topics every day, and workshops are being offered at every conference. There are stacks of books in the bookstores and libraries telling you everything—and more—than you ever wanted to know. People other than writers have things to tell you, too; organizations for professional speakers hold frequent seminars about how to build careers and sell products.

You can't do it all. You're still trying to write a book, and nobody has that much free time. Or that much money lying around that they can use to pay someone else for doing the promotion. If you and your critique group are in this together, you don't have to take it all on your own shoulders.

In a group that works together on networking and promotion, everybody is working to keep track of the information that's available. And, whether you do this by e-mail or in a meeting, you share what you find. If you read a blog that really hones in on the best way to do a book signing, let the other members know about it. If you hear of a workshop about increasing book sales, send that information around as well. If you take a class about social networking, share your notes with the group.

Some groups pool their money, either through a regular membership "fee" or as needed for events or classes that come up. If a workshop costs one hundred dollars, the group can split the cost for one member or two members to go, and those members come back to the group afterward, summarizing the important highlights they learned. Taking the group approach to this kind of education does more than save money and time—it gives you a discussion forum to take the information you've discovered and apply it specifically to your own writing choices.

SHARING INFORMATION ABOUT AGENTS AND EDITORS

Submission is exciting. It's also scary. You can find books that list agents and editors to help you get started with your search, and the Internet is a great source of information as well. If you're looking at an agent's Web site for a description of which genre or which types of books he wants, and you see a possible match for someone in your group, you should pass that on. The other members will do the same for you. If an editor's blog announces that her publishing house is now open to new writers of mystery fiction, and someone in your group has just finished his mystery novel, send him the link. That writer will keep you posted on anything he learns about editors looking for YA.

There's nothing like personal information or, even better, a personal contact. When the members of your group go to workshops and conferences, you'll have opportunities to listen to agent panels or talk with editors at the lunch table. You'll be looking for someone who's interested in your book, yes, but you can also keep your ears open for opportunities for the other writers in your group. Take notes, and report back when you get home.

SUPPORTING EACH OTHER'S BLOGS

Blogging has become a big part of promoting your writing. Readers like to find out about the authors who write their favorite books, and a good blog can bring them back time and time again. When a book of yours is published, you have an audience of readers who are already waiting for it to show up and who are happy to click the link to the online bookstore selling it.

Blogging, however, takes time as well as a commitment to growing a substantial reader base. You and your group members can help each other develop this base.

Blog readers don't just look at blog posts, they take time to read through the comments, too. Comments can take what starts as information or opinion and turn it into a discussion—a lively, captivating conversation. If you're in a networking group, one of the easiest things you and the other members can do is hop over to each other's blogs and leave a comment. Post your own question in the comment and get other readers to join in.

You can also help increase the range of your blogs by guest posting. Every blog builds its own readership. Every time you write a guest post on someone else's blog, you announce yourself, and your blog, to a new set of people. Some of those people will come read what else you have to say, and some of them will return, joining your list of regular commenters. When you invite another writer to guest post on your blog, the process works the same way, in reverse.

You'll make connections with other writers on the Internet, and you can arrange to guest post with them. The networking group is a great place to start this exchange, and it provides a quick, easy way for you to take your posts one step further into the blogosphere.

EXPLORING SOCIAL NETWORKING SITES

How scary *are* Facebook and Twitter? Is LinkedIn useful for writers? Do you have to be published to belong to the Writers Market community? (No!) The Internet is swimming in social networking sites and with people telling us we should dive right in.

Sure.

Social networking is the newest tool for promoting ourselves and marketing our books. The number of people you can reach out to on a social networking site is as close to infinite as you could want. Every one of these people is a connection who may, one day, give you some information you need, stop by your blog and comment, or even buy your book.

It's not easy, though, to know which sites to check out. You could spend every hour of every day visiting these sites, and then where would your writing be? On top of that, getting started on a site can be confusing, even intimidating and overwhelming, until you've done it a few times.

Most things in life are less frightening with a buddy. Your very own networking group can make social networking easier, even more fun. You can talk back and forth about the pluses and minuses. One of you can venture out onto a site, then fill in the others about what works and what doesn't. You can set up a special meeting, at which all you do is bring your laptops, eat chocolate, and walk each other through setting up profiles and getting started on a site. Together, you can make these sites a friendlier place to play.

RECOMMENDING EACH OTHER AS SPEAKERS

In section I, we talked about the reasons for going to writers' conferences and workshops. You meet other writers, you learn about the craft, and you get support for your writing goals.

Once you are published, writers' conferences bring another benefit to your lives. They are a place for you to sell your book. Writers don't just write—we read, and we're always on the lookout for something new and interesting.

The best way for you to add your books to the bookseller's table at a conference is to attend as a speaker. Never feel like you don't have the experience to contribute to a conference or don't have any information to share in a workshop. Even before you're published, you've been working hard at your craft and have developed ideas about the best way to approach various aspects of writing and revising. Having a book in hand gives you visible credibility, but the experience has been building inside you since you started writing.

As your networking group gets further into publication and promotion, the various members will be going to different conferences. As they work out the details with the conference coordinators, they can take the time to find out if the organizers need any more speakers, and they can mention the other writers in their groups. All the writers can even develop a panel program together, one they offer to present at any conference they attend. Then you can share everything you've learned with an even larger circle of writers!

Chapter 23

TROUBLESHOOTING GROUP DYNAMICS

A critique group is a set of individuals trying to work together for mutual benefit. The problem is that not everybody always agrees on what those benefits are or how to achieve them. In a critique group, the members have a common goal—to improve their writing—and they're at these meetings because they want to be there. On the other hand, the importance of that writing to each member, and her very personal feelings about it, can create conflicts that have to be dealt with.

Many problems can be addressed and avoided by having a set of group guidelines like the ones we discussed in section I. These "rules" can be given to new members when they join, and they can be brought out as a kind of refresher course when needed for the long-term members. In any group there is the chance that a problem will arise that just cannot be resolved. In this case, it may be necessary for you to leave the group and find one that is a better fit, or the group as a whole may ask a member to leave.

In this chapter, though, we'll go over the steps you and your group can take to troubleshoot and deal with problems that are fixable. We'll use standard conflict-management techniques like communicating, identifying the conflict, listening, compromising, and working together to help you and your group find solutions to these problems.

Because the conflicts you may experience are specific to critique groups, we're going to address some of the most common problems that occur in these groups. Here are some of the issues your group may go through:

- Different writers are at different stages on the publication path.
- A writer isn't getting the kind of critique he or she wants.
- A writer gets defensive while being critiqued.

- A critiquer gives consistently harsh feedback.
- A critiquer tries to "rewrite" other writers' projects.
- A writer frequently resubmits pages without significant changes.

DIFFERENT WRITERS ARE AT DIFFERENT STAGES ON THE PUBLICATION PATH

I firmly believe that critiquing is a separate skill from writing. A relatively new writer can critique as strongly, sometimes even more so, than a writer who has had several books published. A critique group does not have to exclude a writer simply because his experience or "success" does not match with the other members.

However, this doesn't mean that feelings like jealousy and inferiority, conceit and condescension can't all rear their ugly heads. It's very hard, when you know how hard you're working, to see others reaching the goals you've set for yourself while you still have your own long road ahead of you. If you're on the other end, getting published, facing deadlines, and dealing with editors bring new pressures to bear and can make you impatient with writers who aren't on the same tight schedule.

It's okay to be envious, as long as you also celebrate your critique partners' successes and don't try to bring them down off the high they've earned. It's also just fine to be thrilled about signing with an agent or getting a book deal—just don't let excitement turn into gloating, and don't dismiss the valuable contributions the other writers in your group can *still* bring to your writing.

The bottom line, if group members get to very different points on their writing paths, is for everybody to feel that they're still important to the group and that they're still benefiting from the critiques they receive. The "bad" feelings are not something you should push down and try to ignore. Unless you deal with them and talk about them, they'll only fester. And they'll start to affect your critiques and, worse, your writing.

It's important to bring up these problems with your critique partners. Schedule a group discussion with all the members present. At the meeting, respectfully and calmly lay out the things you're feeling. If you believe these feelings have roots outside the group, in your own background or personality, acknowledge that fact. Acknowledge that your feelings, whichever side of the coin they're on, are yours and may come from places the group has nothing to do with.

If, on the other hand, you feel that one or more of the writers in your group are behaving in a way that *makes* you feel bad, you need to address that behavior. As politely and as clearly as you can, describe the behavior and how it makes you feel. Remember, the other member is almost certainly not *trying* to attack or hurt you.

If you're on the receiving end of this discussion, you need to work at not getting defensive. The first thing you need to do is listen. It was probably hard for the other writer to bring herself to this point, and her feelings are—most likely—honest and real. Acknowledge that what she's saying is true, as far as she understands it.

If you can reassure the other writer, do so. If you realize she has a point about how you've been acting and that, either in your anxiety or your excitement, you have let your behavior get past the point you would have chosen, apologize. Then work to change your behavior in the future.

This may be all it takes. By the time everybody's feelings are out in the open, the whole group may be feeling better. If not, other members may need to step in with questions and suggestions about how the writers can accommodate each other's needs.

A WRITER ISN'T GETTING THE KIND OF CRITIQUE HE OR SHE WANTS

Every critiquer has a different style. As he reads, he notices the problems (and successes) that matter to him as a reader. A critiquer who reads suspense novels is going to respond more positively to a great high-speed chase scene and perhaps less well to a contemplative moment at sunset. A critiquer who travels every year will have more experience to bring to his critique of a travel adventure book than someone who is happy to stay at home with the cats.

At the same time, some critiquers have a lighter touch, while others dig into the meat of a project. Some readers aren't sure about the right time to critique for big changes and the right time to focus on small details.

If you, as a writer, are looking for one kind of critique and are consistently getting another, you may become frustrated. You may start to feel that one of the critiquers doesn't belong in the group, or that *you* don't. Don't give up and don't dismiss the critiques you do get from this (or these) critique partner. Try a bit of education first.

When you send out a critique submission, take the time to describe what you are looking for. Remind the critiquers what draft you're on. If you're in the early stages of a project, you're more likely to be looking for feedback on things like plot and organization or whether your hero is starting to feel likable. You might want to know if your first stabs at voice are working at all. If you're close to your last draft, you're going to want a tight read for details that you might have gotten wrong, for sentences that jump out at the reader with their lack of clarity, for connections between chapters that you haven't yet made. Tell your critiquers all this. They can't read your mind, and you shouldn't expect them to.

If it's just one member of the group who is giving you inappropriate critiques, you don't have to call her on it at a meeting. First, take a little extra time to send her an e-mail, perhaps giving her a call to make sure she saw and understood the first message. If she's a less experienced critiquer, she may need a little explanation from you. Once she understands, you'll probably get critiques that hit just the points you're worried about.

If you are a critiquer, and a writer in the group approaches you about your critique method when he submits, you need to respect his wishes. If you seriously believe the writer is wrong, that he needs a different kind of critique, talk with him about your response. Tell him what kind of feedback you'd like to give him and why. If he doesn't agree, back off. When you dig into the critique, put *your* plan for his book aside and focus on *his* goals.

A WRITER GETS DEFENSIVE WHILE BEING CRITIQUED

If you're reading this book, you're committed to and passionate about your own writing. For all of us, writing is emotional. Whatever project we're working on, whether it's fiction, memoir, or a self-help book, we put ourselves into it. That connection is part of what it takes to be a good writer.

For many writers, getting a critique is incredibly tough. They try to separate themselves from their book to see that the feedback is constructive. Still, for some of us, it feels as though any negative comment is a criticism of our writing skills, an attack on the *person* we are.

With time, everybody's skin gets thicker. While the calluses are building up, the group can do a lot to help a member at the beginning of these growing pains. Make absolutely sure you start your critique with a positive comment, something you truly liked about the story. Gentle the tone of your more negative feedback for a while until the writer gets used to sitting in that chair and hearing what everybody has to say. The same writer may be a bit timid in her own critiques; you can nudge her to put just a bit more "bite" into her feedback. Seeing everybody else accept and welcome strong critiques may give her extra iron in her backbone.

If you are the writer struggling to hear and accept a critique, you also need to be gentle with yourself. If you're new to critique groups, you'll get more used to having other writers discuss and break down your book. Even if you've been critiqued before, you may be working on a project that—for whatever reason—is particularly close to your heart or that is hitting some emotional buttons you didn't know were there. I don't know a single writer who hasn't left a critique meeting, at least once, muttering mild obscenities about his critique partners. As long as they're mild, and you're muttering instead of shouting, you're okay.

Just don't start feeling too picked on or sorry for yourself. Your critique partners are trying to help you, not hurt you. During meetings, do your best to listen without arguing. If you feel a defensive comment rising to your lips, take a sip of your drink instead—that's one good reason for meeting at a coffeehouse! Give your critique partners, and their comments, a chance. Take notes, go home, and let the feedback sink in gradually. Then look at it. You'll be surprised how often the critiques are not only right on target but incredibly helpful as well.

Sometimes a writer is just not ready for the critique process. This can be one of the hardest things for a critique group to deal with, and the writer may find that she needs to step away from the group for a while. With some encouragement, though, shy writers can grow and strengthen, putting aside their insecurities to push forward toward their book goals.

A CRITIQUER GIVES CONSISTENTLY HARSH FEEDBACK

The golden rule of critiquing is to start your critique with something positive. Even when they put this rule into practice, however, some critiquers forget the real meaning behind that rule—that a critique is supposed to be thoughtful and useful and supportive.

When someone presents a harsh critique, the critiquer usually has one of two things going on. Sometimes he just has no clue how he's coming across—he's a very direct person, and he sees himself as being honest with his critiques. The group can help guide someone like this into a less harsh style. They can point out the problem nicely, then suggest that the critiquer listen a bit more closely to the way the rest of the group delivers their feedback. The group can show the critiquer that a critique doesn't have to be hard to be constructive.

If your group talks to you about your critiques, don't immediately assume that either the other members don't know what they're talking about or that you're a horrible person (or critiquer). Critiquing is a learned skill, just like any other task we take on, and if you are open to what your critique partners are saying *and* to learning from them, you'll soon find that your critiques are bringing the same kind of positive responses as the other members'.

Unfortunately, harsh critiques are sometimes a symptom of something deeper within the person delivering them. A critiquer may be insecure about her own writing and project, or she may have a personality conflict with another member. If explanation and education are not resolving this problem, the group may need to ask this critiquer to leave. Consistently cruel critiques are extremely damaging not just to your projects, but to your confidence in yourself as a writer. This trust in a group must be protected.

A CRITIQUER TRIES TO "REWRITE" OTHER WRITERS' PROJECTS

As you write your book, you don't know what will show up on every page. Through the first draft, and the drafts that follow, you're finding your way. Still, you do, most likely, have a core sense of what your project is about and the kind of information, or story, that you want to give your readers. You may not know the exact, or even best, words to use—but you do know your book.

When a critique partner disregards your project vision, it can be frustrating. He may start telling you what your hero really needs to be doing or that George should be the main character, not Herbert. He might talk about what the reader of your how-to book actually needs to know, as if he's done all the research, not you. You may find yourself arguing with him or ignoring *all* the critique comments he gives you.

Getting into a battle is not going to help you or your writing. Along with the feedback that is completely off base, the critiquer may be handing you some valid, helpful suggestions. And when you decide to ignore his comments, you're also ignoring your feelings. Too often, pushing frustration down just makes it come back up as anger.

The first step is to bring back those manners we talked about earlier in the book. Politely remind the critiquer what your vision is for this book. You can thank him for his suggestions or not, but you definitely need to point out the behavior that is bothering you and ask him to bring his critiques back in line with the book *you* are writing. It's possible that his enthusiasm for your book has gotten a bit out of hand, that it's sparking so many ideas in his mind that he's having trouble filtering out the ones that aren't a good fit. In this case, a gentle nudge is often enough to bring him back on target.

If you are the critiquer who is approached about this problem, you need to listen. You may at first feel angry or defensive that the writer is discounting your suggestions. You may feel embarrassed or ashamed that you have let your energy and eagerness run a bit rampant. That's all right. Let the feelings go, *hear* what the writer is asking you to do, and make a serious effort to change the pattern of your critiques. As you sit down to read subsequent chapters, just take a moment to reorient on what the author is trying to do and give her the most helpful suggestions you can ... for *her* book.

There is always the possibility that a critiquer cannot hear what the writer is saying. Every critiquer should feel invested in his critique partners' books, and, while this works well if it translates into support and energy, it's not so good if it means the critiquer keeps trying to take over the project. Usually, when this happens, it's obvious to everybody in the group *except* the critiquer. If the problem persists, the other group members may have to work together to help the critiquer understand what he's doing. Just as with any element of a critique, a suggestion has more credibility and force if it comes from three people, rather than just one.

A WRITER FREQUENTLY RESUBMITS PAGES WITHOUT SIGNIFICANT CHANGES

Usually, when I talk to writers about critique groups, they're concerned with the problems that affect their own writing. However, I've seen situations where the problem was reversed—the critique partners felt as though their critiques weren't being respected.

In many critique groups, writers submit chapters from their first draft and then, as they revise, resubmit those chapters for a new round of critiques. With a group of very new writers, the forward progress in these revision chapters may be slight, but it will still be there. In a group of more experienced critiquers, the expectation is that the revision chapters will show a substantial change. The critiquers probably won't be able to track their comments exactly, but they will know their suggestions were listened to and considered and had some impact on the writer's revision process.

When critiquers get the opposite feeling—that a writer is ignoring their feedback—they can get impatient and irritated. They don't feel like putting as much effort into their critiques for this writer, and they start ignoring that writer's comments about their work, too. If this goes on for too long, everybody ends up unhappy.

Again, the first step is to check in with the writer. She may be feeling overwhelmed by the revision process and not know how to implement the critique feedback she's getting. Or she may be thinking she's doing everything she needs to revise, even if she hasn't really addressed her critique partners' comments.

If the more experienced group members feel they have the time and energy to do a bit of educating, they can talk to this writer about the kinds of changes *they've* made in their latest revisions. At the end of a critique session when they've given feedback to this writer, they can take a few minutes to help the writer isolate one or two big changes to focus on in her revision.

If you are the writer who is not making revision progress, you should try to be open to learning more about the process. You need to push yourself past the small changes in surface writing that you've been making, and you need to listen to the suggestions of your critique group about the kind of major revisions you need to get started on. As hard as it can be to acknowledge that you don't know how to do something, that acknowledgment is the first step toward strengthening your skill.

If you're nervous about making big changes in your manuscript, there's a way to step slowly and safely into this stage. Make a copy of your original files and store them separately from the files you're revising. Then go ahead and play with the feedback you've gotten. Give a character some different traits or change the structure of a few chapters. If you don't like the new pages, you haven't lost the old. And if you *do* like the new stuff, you're on your way to making some important changes to your manuscript.

WHY TAKE THE TIME?

Why should you take the time to work out problems your group may be having? When you sat down to write, that very first time, you didn't hit perfection with word one. You've taken time over the years to grow your writing skills, to strengthen your craft, and to develop projects that get better and better. Critiquing works the same way—you need time, practice, and help to learn how to analyze a manuscript for weaknesses and to present your feedback in a clear, helpful way. So do the other people in the group.

This is your writing. You worked hard to find or start this group, and if you walk too easily or quickly away from the group, you are walking away from opportunities to improve your manuscripts. Yes, there are problems that cannot always be resolved. There are many more, however, that can be worked out by group members who are strongly committed to each other and to moving forward with their writing. Take the time to step back, look at the dynamics of your group, and see where you can start the troubleshooting process. It will pay off for the group *and* for you.

Appendix A

SUGGESTED READING LIST

This book is about developing a strong critique group and improving your critique skills. Although I give some basic ideas for successful writing, I encourage you to read as many books on the subject as you can lay your hands on. Here are some that I use in my own writing life.

The Anatomy of Story: 22 Steps to Becoming a Master Storyteller by John Truby

Bird by Bird: Some Instructions on Writing and Life by Anne Lamott

Blockbuster Plots Pure & Simple by Martha Alderson

Characters, Emotion & Viewpoint: Techniques and Exercises for Crafting Dynamic Characters and Effective Viewpoints by Nancy Kress

Description & Setting: Techniques and Exercises for Crafting a Believable World of People, Places, and Events by Ron Rozelle

Hooked: Write Fiction That Grabs Readers at Page One and Never Lets Them Go by Les Edgerton

How to Write a Book Proposal by Michael Larson

Make a Scene: Crafting a Powerful Story One Scene at a Time by Jordan E. Rosenfeld

Nonfiction Book Proposals Anybody Can Write: How to Get a Contract and Advance Before Writing Your Book by Elizabeth Lyon

Picture Writing: A New Approach to Writing for Kids and Teens by Anastasia Suen

Plot & Structure: Techniques and Exercises for Crafting a Plot that Grips Readers from Start to Finish by James Scott Bell

The Power of Point of View: Make Your Story Come to Life by Alicia Rasley

The Writer's Journey: Mythic Structure for Writers by Christopher Vogler

Writing & Selling the YA Novel by K.L. Going

Writing the Breakout Novel: Insider Advice for Taking Your Fiction to the Next Level by Donald Maass

Writing Dialogue: How to Create Memorable Voices and Fictional Conversations that Crackle with Wit, Tension and Nuance by Tom Chiarella

Writing Successful Self-Help & How-To Books: An Insider's Guide to Everything You Need to Know by Jean Marie Stine

You Don't Have to be Famous: How to Write Your Life Story by Steve Zousmer

Index

PERMISSIONS

THE VOICE OF THE VIOLIN

Andrea Camilleri is one of Italy's most famous
contemporary writers. His Montalbano series has been
adapted for Italian television and translated
into nine languages. He lives in Rome.

Stephen Sartarelli is an award-winning translator.
He is also the author of three books of poetry, most
recently *The Open Vault*. He lives in France.

ANDREA CAMILLERI

THE VOICE OF THE VIOLIN

Translated by Stephen Sartarelli

PICADOR

First published 2003 by Viking Penguin,
a member of Penguin Putnam Inc., New York

This edition first published in Great Britain 2005 by Picador

First published in paperback 2006 by Picador
an imprint of Pan Macmillan. a division of Macmillan Publishers Limited
Pan Macmillan, 20 New Wharf Road, London N1 9RR
Basingstoke and Oxford
Associated companies throughout the world
www.panmacmillan.com

ISBN 978-1-4472-3511-8

Copyright © Sellerio editore 1997
Translation copyright © Stephen Sartarelli 2003

Originally published in Italian as *La voce del violino* by Sellerio editore, Palermo.

The right of Andrea Camilleri to be identified as the
author of this work has been asserted by him in accordance
with the Copyright, Designs and Patents Act 1988.

1 3 5 7 9 8 6 4 2

A CIP catalogue record for this book is available from
the British Library.

Typeset by SetSystems Ltd, Saffron Walden, Essex
Printed and bound in the UK by
CPI Group (UK) Ltd, Croydon, CR0 4YY

THE VOICE OF THE VIOLIN

ONE

Inspector Salvo Montalbano could immediately tell that it was not going to be his day the moment he opened the shutters of his bedroom window. It was still night, at least an hour before sunrise, but the darkness was already lifting, enough to reveal a sky covered by heavy rain clouds and, beyond the light strip of beach, a sea that looked like a Pekingese dog. Ever since a tiny dog of that breed, all decked out in ribbons, had bitten painfully into his calf after a furious fit of hacking that passed for barking, Montalbano saw the sea this way whenever it was whipped up by crisp, cold gusts into thousands of little waves capped by ridiculous plumes of froth. His mood darkened, especially considering that an unpleasant obligation awaited him that morning. He had to attend a funeral.

*

The previous evening, finding some fresh anchovies cooked by Adelina, his houskeeper, in the fridge, he'd dressed them in a great deal of lemon juice, olive oil and freshly ground black pepper, and wolfed them down. And he'd relished them, until it was all spoiled by a telephone call.

'H'lo, Chief? Izzatchoo onna line?'

'It's really me, Cat. You can go ahead and talk.'

At the station they'd given Catarella the job of answering the phone, mistakenly thinking he could do less damage there than anywhere else. After getting mightily pissed off a few times, Montalbano had come to realize that the only way to talk to him within tolerable limits of nonsense was to use the same language as he.

'Beckin' pardon, Chief, for the 'sturbance.'

Uh-oh. He was begging pardon for the disturbance. Montalbano pricked up his ears. Whenever Catarella's speech became ceremonious, it meant there was no small matter at hand.

'Get to the point, Cat.'

'Tree days ago somebody aks for you, Chief, wanted a talk t' you in poisson, but you wasn't 'ere an' I forgotta reference it to you.'

'Where were they calling from?'

'From Florida, Chief.'

Montalbano was literally overcome with terror. In a flash he saw himself in a sweatsuit jogging alongside fearless, athletic American narcotics agents working with him on a complicated investigation into drug trafficking.

'Tell me something. What language did you speak with them?'

4

'What langwitch was I asposta speak? We spoke
'Talian, Chief.'

'Did they tell you what they wanted?'

'Sure, they tol' me everyting about one ting. They said
as how Vice Commissioner Tamburrano's wife was dead.'

Montalbano breathed a sigh of relief, he couldn't help
it. They'd called not from Florida, but from police
headquarters in the town of Floridia near Siracusa. Cater-
ina Tamburrano had been gravely ill for some time, and
the news was not a complete surprise to him.

'Chief, izzat still you there?'

'Still me, Cat, I haven't changed.'

'They also said the obsequious was gonna be on
Tuesday morning at nine o'clock.'

'Thursday? You mean tomorrow morning?'

'Yeah, Chief.'

He was too good a friend of Michele Tamburrano not
to go to the funeral. That way he could make up for not
having even phoned to express his condolences. Floridia
was about a three-and-a-half-hour drive from Vigàta.

'Listen, Cat, my car's in the garage. I need a squad car
at my place, in Marinella, at five o'clock sharp tomorrow
morning. Tell Inspector Augello I'll be out of the office
until early afternoon. Got that?'

∗

He emerged from the shower, skin red as a lobster. To
counteract the chill he felt at the sight of the sea, he'd

made the water too hot. As he started shaving, he heard the squad car arrive. Indeed, who, within a ten-kilometre radius, hadn't heard it? It rocketed into the drive at supersonic speed, braked with a scream, firing bursts of gravel in every direction, then followed this display with a roar of the racing engine, a harrowing shift of gears, a shrill screech of skidding tyres, and another explosion of gravel. The driver had executed an evasive manoeuvre, turning the car completely round.

When Montalbano stepped out of the house ready to leave, he saw Gallo, the station's official driver, rejoicing.

'Look at that, Chief! Look at them tracks! What a manoeuvre! A perfect one-eighty!'

'Congratulations,' Montalbano said gloomily.

'Should I put on the siren?' Gallo asked as they were about to set out.

'Put it in your arse,' said a surly Montalbano, closing his eyes. He didn't feel like talking.

*

Gallo, who suffered from the Indianapolis Complex, stepped on the accelerator as soon as he saw his superior's eyes shut, reaching a speed he thought better suited to his driving ability. They'd been on the road barely fifteen minutes when the crash occurred. At the scream of the brakes, Montalbano opened his eyes but saw nothing, head lurching violently forward before being jerked back by the safety belt. Next came a deafening clang of metal against metal, then silence again, a fairy-tale silence, with birds singing and dogs barking.

'You hurt?' the inspector asked Gallo, seeing him rub his chest.

'No. You?'

'Nothing. What happened?'

'A chicken ran in front of me.'

'I've never seen a chicken run in front of a car before. Let's look at the damage.'

They got out. There wasn't a soul about. The long skid marks were etched into the tarmac. Right at the spot where they began, you could see a small, dark stain. Gallo went up to it, then turned triumphantly around.

'What did I tell you?' he said to the inspector. 'It was a chicken!'

A clear case of suicide. The car they had slammed into, smashing up its entire rear end, must have been legally parked at the side of the road, though now it was sticking out slightly. It was a bottle-green Renault Twingo, positioned so as to block a unpaved drive leading to a two-storey house with shuttered windows and doors some thirty metres away. The squad car, for its part, had a shattered headlight and a crumpled right bumper.

'So now what do we do?' Gallo asked dejectedly.

'We're going to go on. Will the car run, in your opinion?'

'I'll give it a try.'

Reversing with a great clatter of metal, the squad car

dislodged itself from the other vehicle. Nobody came to the windows of the house. They must have been fast asleep, dead to the world. The Twingo had to belong to someone in there, since there were no other homes in the immediate area. As Gallo was trying with his bare hands to bend out the bumper, which was scraping against the tyre, Montalbano wrote down the phone number of the Vigàta police headquarters on a piece of paper and slipped this under the Twingo's windscreen wiper.

✻

When it's not your day, it's not your day. After they'd been back on the road for half an hour or so, Gallo started rubbing his chest again, and from time to time he twisted his face in a grimace of pain.

'I'll drive,' said the inspector. Gallo didn't protest.

When they were outside the town of Fela, Montalbano, instead of continuing along the main road, turned onto the road that led to the centre of town. Gallo paid no attention, eyes closed and head resting against the window.

'Where are we?' he asked, as soon as he felt the car come to a halt.

'We're at Fela Hospital. Get out.'

'But it's nothing, Inspector!'

'Get out. I want them to have a look at you.'

'Well, just leave me here and keep going. You can pick me up on the way back.'

'Cut the shit. Let's go.'

Between auscultations, three blood pressure exams, X-rays, and everything else in the book, it took them over three hours to have a look at Gallo. In the end they ruled that he hadn't broken anything; the pain he felt was from having bumped hard into the steering wheel, and the weakness was a natural reaction to the fright he'd had.

'So now what do we do?' Gallo asked again, more dejected than ever.

'What do you think? We keep going. But I'll drive.'

*

The inspector had been to Floridia three or four times before. He even remembered where Tamburrano lived, and so he headed towards the Church of the Madonna delle Grazie, which was practically next door to his colleague's house. When they reached the square, he saw the church hung with black and a throng of people hurrying inside. The service must have started late. Apparently he wasn't the only one to have things go wrong.

'I'll take the car to the police garage in town and have them look at it,' said Gallo. 'I'll come and pick you up afterwards.'

Montalbano entered the crowded church. The service had just begun. He looked around and recognized no one. Tamburrano must have been in the first row, near the coffin in front of the main altar. The inspector decided to remain where he was, near the entrance. He would shake

Tamburrano's hand when the coffin was being carried out of the church. When the priest finally opened his mouth after the Mass had been going on for some time, Montalbano gave a start. He'd heard right, he was sure of it.

The priest had begun with the words, 'Our dearly beloved Nicola has left this vale of tears . . .'

Mustering up the courage, he tapped a little old lady on the shoulder.

'Excuse me, signora, whose funeral is this?'

'The dear departed Ragioniere Pecoraro. Why?'

'I thought it was for the Signora Tamburrano.'

'Ah, no, that one was at the Church of Sant'Anna.'

It took him almost fifteen minutes to get to the church of Sant'Anna, practically running the whole way. Panting and sweaty, he found the priest in the deserted nave.

'I beg your pardon. Where's the funeral of Signora Tamburrano?'

'That ended almost two hours ago,' said the priest, looking him over sternly.

'Do you know if she's being buried here?' Montalbano asked, avoiding the priest's gaze.

'Most certainly not. When the service was over, she was taken in the hearse to Vibo Valentia, where she'll be entombed in the family vault. Her bereaved husband followed behind in his car.'

So it had all been for naught. He had noticed, in the Piazza della Madonna delle Grazie, a cafe with tables outside. When Gallo returned, with the car repaired as well as could be expected, it was almost two o'clock. Montalbano told him what happened.

'So now what do we do?' Gallo asked for the third time, lost in an abyss of dejection.

'You're going to eat a brioche with a *granita di caffè*, which they make very well here, and then we'll head home. With the Good Lord's help and the Blessed Virgin's company, we should be back in Vigàta by evening.'

＊

Their prayer was answered, the drive home smooth as silk.

'The car's still there,' said Gallo when Vigàta was already visible in the distance.

The Twingo was exactly the way they'd left it that morning, sticking slightly out from the top of the unpaved drive.

'They've probably already called headquarters,' said Montalbano.

He was bullshitting: the look of the car and the house with its shuttered windows made him uneasy.

'Turn back,' he suddenly ordered Gallo.

Gallo made a reckless U-turn that triggered a chorus of horn blasts. When they reached the Twingo, he executed another, even more reckless, then pulled up behind the damaged car.

Montalbano stepped out in a hurry. What he thought he'd just seen in the rear-view mirror, when passing by, turned out to be true: the scrap of paper with the telephone number was still under the windscreen wiper. Nobody'd touched it.

'I don't like it,' the inspector said to Gallo, who was now standing next to him. He started walking down the drive. The house must have been recently built; the grass in front was still burned from the lime. There was also a stack of new tiles in a corner of the yard. Montalbano carefully examined the shuttered windows. No light was filtering out.

He went up to the front door and rang the doorbell. He waited a short while, then rang again.

'Do you know whose house this is?'

'No, Chief.'

What should he do? Night was falling and he could feel the beginnings of fatigue. Their pointless, exhausting day was starting to weigh on him.

'Let's go,' he said. Then he added, in a vain attempt at convincing himself, 'I'm sure they called.'

Gallo gave him a doubtful look, but didn't open his mouth.

*

Gallo wasn't even invited into headquarters. The inspector had sent him immediately home to rest. His second-in-command, Mimì Augello, wasn't in; he'd been summoned to report to the new commissioner of Montelusa, Luca Bonetti-Alderighi, a young and testy native of Bergamo who in the course of one month had succeeded in creating knife-blade antipathies all around him.

'The commissioner was upset you weren't in Vigàta,' said Fazio, the sergeant he was closest to. 'So Inspector Augello had to go in your place.'

'*Had* to go?' the inspector retorted. 'He probably just saw it as a chance to show off!'

He told Fazio about their accident that morning and asked him if he knew who owned the house. Fazio didn't, but promised his superior that he'd go to the town hall the following morning and find out.

'By the way, your car's in our garage.'

Before going home, the inspector interrogated Catarella.

'Try hard to remember. Did anyone happen to call about a car we ran into?'

No calls.

*

'Let me try and understand a minute,' Livia said angrily by phone from Boccadasse, Genoa.

'What's to understand, Livia? As I said, and now repeat, François's adoption papers aren't ready yet. Some unexpected problems have come up, and I no longer have the old commissioner behind me always smoothing everything out. We have to be patient.'

'I wasn't talking about the adoption,' Livia said icily.

'You weren't? Then what were you talking about?'

'Getting married, that's what. We can certainly get married while the problems of the adoption are being worked out. The one thing does not depend on the other.'

'No, of course not,' said Montalbano, who was beginning to feel harried and cornered.

'Now I want a straight answer to the following question,' Livia went on, implacably. 'Supposing the adoption isn't possible: what will we do? Will we get married anyway, in your opinion, or won't we?'

A sudden, loud thunderclap gave him a way out.

'What was that?'

'Thunder. There's a terrible stor—'

He hung up and pulled out the plug.

*

He couldn't sleep. He tossed and turned, snarling himself up in the sheets. Around two in the morning, he realized it was useless. He got up, got dressed, grabbed a leather bag given to him some time ago by a house burglar who'd become his friend, got in his car and drove off. The storm was raging worse than ever; lightning bolts illuminated the sky. When he reached the Twingo, he slipped his car in under some trees and turned off the headlights. From the glove compartment he extracted a gun, a pair of gloves and a torch. After waiting for the rain to let up, he crossed the road in one bound, went up the drive and flattened himself against the front door. He rang and rang the doorbell but got no answer. He then put on the gloves and pulled a large key ring with a dozen or so variously shaped picklocks out of the leather bag. The door opened on the third try. It was locked with only the latch and hadn't been dead-bolted. He entered, closing the door behind him. In the dark, he bent over, untied his wet shoes and removed them, keeping his socks on. He turned on the torch, keeping it pointed at the ground. He found himself in a large dining room that opened onto a living room. The furniture smelled of varnish. Everything was new, clean and orderly. A door led into a kitchen that sparkled like something one might see in an advertisement; another door gave onto a bathroom so shiny it looked as if no one had ever used it before. He slowly climbed the stairs to the upper floor. There he found three closed doors. The first one he opened revealed a neat little guest room; the second led into a bigger bathroom than the one downstairs, but unlike it, this one was decidedly messy. A pink towelling bathrobe lay rumpled on the floor, as though the person wearing it had taken it off in a hurry. The third door was to the master bedroom. And the naked, half-kneeling female body, belly resting against the edge of the bed, arms spread, face buried in the sheet that the young, blonde woman had torn to shreds with her fingernails in the final throes of her death by suffocation, must have belonged to the owner of the house.

Montalbano went up to the corpse and, removing a glove, touched it lightly: it was cold and stiff. She must

have been very beautiful. The inspector went back downstairs, put his shoes back on, wiped up the wet spot they
had made on the floor, went out of the house, closed the
door, crossed the road, got in his car and left. His thoughts
were racing as he drove back to Marinella. How to have
the crime discovered? He certainly couldn't go and tell
the judge what he'd been up to. The judge who'd replaced
Lo Bianco – on a leave of absence to pursue his endless
historical research into the lives of a pair of unlikely
ancestors – was a Venetian by the name of Nicolò
Tommaseo who was always talking about his 'irrevocable
prerogatives'. He had a little baby face that he hid under
a Belfiore martyr's moustache and beard. As Montalbano
was opening the door to his house, the solution to the
problem finally came to him in a flash. And thus he was
able to enjoy a brief but god-like sleep.

TWO

He arrived at the office at eight thirty the next morning, looking rested and crisp.

'Did you know our new commissioner is noble?' was the first thing Mimì Augello said when he saw him.

'Is that a moral judgement or a heraldic fact?'

'Heraldic.'

'I'd already worked out as much from the little dash between his last names. And what did you do, Mimì? Did you call him count, baron or marquis? Did you butter him up nicely?'

'Come on, Salvo, you're obsessed!'

'Me? Fazio told me you were wagging your tail the whole time you were talking on the phone to the commissioner, and that afterwards you shot out of here like a rocket to go and see him.'

'Listen, the commissioner said, and I quote: "If Inspector Montalbano is not available, come here at once

17

yourself." What was I supposed to do? Tell him I couldn't because my superior would get pissed off?'

'What did he want?'

'He wasn't alone. Half the province was there. He informed us he intended to modernize, to renovate. He said anyone unable to come up to speed with him should just hang it up. Those were his exact words: hang it up. It was clear to everyone he meant you and Sandro Turri of Calascibetta.'

'Explain to me how you knew this.'

'Because when he said "hang it up" he looked right at Turri and then at me.'

'Couldn't that mean he was actually referring to you?'

'Come on, Salvo, everybody knows he doesn't have a high opinion of you.'

'And what did his lordship want?'

'To tell us that in a few days, some absolutely up-to-date computers will be arriving. Every headquarters in the province will be equipped with them. He wanted each of us to give him the name of an officer we thought had a special knack for computer science. Which I did.'

'Are you insane? Nobody here knows a damn thing about that stuff. Whose name did you give him?'

'Catarella,' said an utterly serious Mimì Augello.

The act of a born saboteur. Montalbano stood up

abruptly, ran over to his second-in-command and embraced him.

*

'I know all about the house you were interested in,' said Fazio, sitting down in the chair in front of the inspector's desk. 'I spoke to the town clerk, who knows everything about everyone in Vigàta.'

'Let's have it.'

'Well, the land the house was built on used to belong to a Dr Rosario Licalzi.'

'What kind of doctor?'

'A real one, a medical doctor. He died about fifteen years ago, leaving the plot to his eldest son, Emanuele, also a doctor.'

'Does he live in Vigàta?'

'No. He lives and works in Bologna. Two years ago, this Emanuele Licalzi married a girl from those parts. They came to Sicily on their honeymoon. The minute the lady saw the land she got it into her head that she would build a little house on it. And there you have it.'

'Any idea where the Licalzis are right now?'

'The husband's in Bologna. The lady was last seen in Vigàta three days ago, running around town trying to furnish the house. She drives a bottle-green Renault Twingo.'

'The one Gallo crashed into.'

'Right. The clerk told me she's not the kind of woman to go unnoticed. Apparently she's very beautiful.'

'I don't understand why she hasn't called yet,' said Montalbano, who, when he put his mind to it, could be a tremendous actor.

'I've formed my own theory about that,' said Fazio. 'The clerk said the lady's, well, really friendly – I mean, she's got a lot of friends.'

'Girlfriends?'

'And boyfriends,' Fazio said emphatically. 'It's possible she's staying with a family somewhere. Maybe they came and picked her up with their own car and she won't notice the damage till she gets back.'

'Sounds plausible,' concluded Montalbano, continuing his performance.

*

As soon as Fazio left, the inspector called up Clementina Vasile Cozzo.

'My dear lady, how are you?'

'Inspector! What a lovely surprise! I'm getting along all right, by the grace of God.'

'Mind if I drop in to say hello?'

'You are welcome to come whenever you like.'

Clementina Vasile Cozzo was an elderly paraplegic, a former elementary school teacher blessed with intelligence and endowed with a natural, quiet dignity. The inspector had met her during the course of a complex investigation some three months back and remained as attached to her as a son. Though Montalbano didn't openly admit it to himself, she was the sort of woman he wished he could have as a mother, having lost his own when he was too young to retain much memory of her beyond a kind of golden luminescence.

'Was Mama blonde?' he'd once asked his father in an attempt to explain to himself why his only image of her consisted of a luminous nuance.

'Like wheat in sunlight,' was his father's laconic reply.

Montalbano had got in the habit of calling on Signora Clementina at least once a week. He would tell her about whatever investigation he happened to be involved in, and the woman, grateful for the visit, which broke the monotony of her daily routine, would invite him to stay for dinner. Pina, the signora's housekeeper, was a surly type and, to make matters worse, she didn't like Montalbano. She did, however, know how to cook some exquisite, disarmingly simple dishes.

*

Signora Clementina, dressed rather smartly with an Indian silk shawl around her shoulders, showed him into the living room.

'There's a concert today,' she whispered, 'but it's almost over.'

Four years ago, Signora Clementina had learned from

her maid, Pina – who for her part had heard it from Yolanda, the violinist's housekeeper – that the illustrious Maestro Cataldo Barbera, who lived in the flat directly above hers, was in serious trouble with his taxes. So she'd discussed the matter with her son, who worked at the Montelusa Revenue Office, and the problem, which had essentially arisen from a mistake, was resolved. Some ten days later, the housekeeper Yolanda had brought her a note that said: 'Dear Signora. To repay you, though only in part, I will play for you every Friday morning from nine thirty to ten thirty. Yours very sincerely, Cataldo Barbera.'

And so every Friday morning, she would get all dressed up to pay homage to the Maestro in turn, and she would go and sit in a small sort of parlour where one could best hear the music. At exactly half past nine, on the floor above, the Maestro would strike up the first notes.

Everyone in Vigàta knew about Maestro Cataldo Barbera, but very few had ever seen him in person. Son of a railwayman, the future Maestro had drawn his first breath sixty-five years earlier in Vigàta, but left town before the age of ten when his father was transferred to Catania. The Vigatese had had to learn of his career from the newspapers. After studying violin, Cataldo Barbera had very quickly become an internationally renowned concert performer. Inexplicably, however, at the height of his fame, he had retired to Vigàta, where he bought an apartment and now lived in voluntary seclusion.

'What's he playing?' Montalbano asked.

Signora Clementina handed him a sheet of squared paper. On the day before the performance, the Maestro would customarily send her the programme, written out in pencil. The pieces to be played that day were Pablo de Sarasate's 'Spanish Dance', and the 'Scherzo-Tarantella', op. 16, of Henryk Wieniawski. When the performance was over, Signora Clementina plugged in the telephone, dialled a number, set the receiver down on a shelf and started clapping. Montalbano joined in with gusto. He knew nothing about music, but he was certain of one thing: Cataldo Barbera was a great artist.

'Signora,' the inspector began, 'I must confess that this is a self-interested visit on my part. I need you to do me a favour.'

He went on to tell her everything that had happened to him the previous day: the accident, going to the wrong funeral, his secret, night-time visit to the house, his discovery of the corpse. When he had finished, the inspector hesitated. He didn't quite know how to phrase his request.

Signora Clementina, who had felt by turns amused and disturbed by his account, urged him on.

'Go on, Inspector, don't be shy. What is it you want from me?'

'I'd like you to make an anonymous telephone call,' Montalbano said in a single breath.

*

He'd been back in the office about ten minutes when Catarella passed him a call from Dr Lattes, the commissioner's cabinet chief.

'Hello, Montalbano, old friend, how's it going? Eh, how's it going?'

'Fine,' Montalbano said curtly.

'I'm so happy to hear it,' the chief of the cabinet said snappily, true to the nickname of Caffè-Lattes that someone had hung on him for the dangerously cloying warmth of his manner.

'At your service,' Montalbano egged him on.

'Well, not fifteen minutes ago a woman called the switchboard asking to speak personally to the commissioner. She was very insistent. The commissioner, however, was busy and asked me to take the call. The woman was in hysterics, screaming that a crime had been committed at a house in the Tre Fontane district. Then she hung up. The commissioner would like you to go there, just to make sure, and then report back to him. The lady also said that the house is easy to spot because there's a bottle-green Twingo parked in front.'

'Oh my God!' said Montalbano, launching into the second act of his role, now that Signora Clementina had recited her part so perfectly.

'What is it?' Dr Lattes asked, his curiosity aroused.

'An amazing coincidence!' said Montalbano, his voice full of wonder. 'I'll tell you later.'

*

'Hello? Inspector Montalbano here. Am I speaking to Judge Tommaseo?'

'Yes, good day. What can I do for you?'

'Your Honour, the chief of the commissioner's cabinet just informed me that they have received an anonymous phone call reporting a crime in a small house on the outskirts of Vigàta. He ordered me to go and have a look. And I'm going.'

'Might it not be some kind of tasteless practical joke?'

'Anything is possible. I simply wanted to let you know, out of respect for your prerogatives.'

'Yes, of course,' said Judge Tommaseo, pleased.

'Do I have your authorization to proceed?'

'Of course. And if a crime was indeed committed, I want you to notify me at once and wait for me to get there.'

Montalbano called Fazio, Gallo and Galluzzo and told them to come with him to the Tre Fontane district to see if a murder had been committed.

'At the same house you asked me for information about?' asked Fazio, dumbfounded.

'The same one where we crashed into the Twingo?' Gallo chimed in, eyeing his superior in amazement.

'Yes,' the inspector answered both, trying to look humble.

'What a nose, Chief!' Fazio cried out in admiration.

*

They had barely set out when Montalbano already felt fed up. Fed up with the farce he would have to act out, pretending to be surprised when they found the corpse, fed up with the time he would have to waste on the judge, the coroner and the forensics team, who were capable of taking hours before arriving at the crime scene. He decided to speed things up.

'Pass me the mobile phone,' he said to Galluzzo, who was sitting in front of him. Gallo, naturally, was at the wheel.

He punched in Judge Tommaseo's number.

'Montalbano here. Listen, Judge, that was no joke, that phone call. Sorry to say, we found a dead body in the house. A woman.'

There were different reactions among those present in the car. Gallo swerved into the oncoming lane, brushed against a truck loaded with iron rods, cursed, then regained control. Galluzzo gave a start, opened his eyes wide, twisted around and looked at his boss with his mouth agape. Fazio visibly stiffened and stared straight ahead, expressionless.

'I'll be right there,' said Judge Tommaseo. 'Tell me exactly where the house is.'

Increasingly fed up, Montalbano passed the mobile phone to Gallo.

'Explain to him where we're going. Then call Pasquano and the crime lab.'

Fazio didn't open his mouth until the car came to a stop behind the bottle-green Twingo.

'Did you put gloves on before you went in?' he asked.

'Yeah,' said Montalbano.

'Anyway, now that we're going in, touch everything as much as you want, just to be safe. Leave as many fingerprints as you can.'

'I'd already thought of that,' said the inspector.

After the storm of the previous night, there was very little left of the scrap of paper tucked under the windscreen wiper. The water had washed away the telephone number. Montalbano didn't bother to remove it.

✱

'You two have a look around down here,' the inspector said to Gallo and Galluzzo.

Then, followed by Fazio, he went upstairs. With the light on, the dead woman's body upset him less than the night before, when he'd seen it only by the beam of the torch. It seemed less real, though certainly not fake. Livid, white and stiff, the corpse resembled those plaster casts of the victims of Pompeii. Face down as she was, it was impossible to see what she looked like, but her struggle against death must have been fierce. Clumps of blonde hair lay scattered over the torn sheet, and purplish bruises stood out across her shoulders and just below the nape of her neck. The killer must have had to use every bit of his strength to force her face so far down into the mattress that not a wisp of air could get through.

Gallo and Galluzzo came upstairs.

'Everything seems in order downstairs,' said Gallo.

True, she looked like a plaster cast, but she was still a young woman, murdered, naked, and in a position that suddenly seemed unbearably obscene to him, her most intimate privacy violated, thrown open by the eight eyes of the policemen in the room. As if to give her back some semblance of personhood and dignity, he asked Fazio, 'Did they tell you her name?'

'Yes. If that's Mrs Licalzi, her name was Michela.'

He went into the bathroom, picked the pink bathrobe up off the floor, brought it into the bedroom, and covered the body with it.

He went downstairs. Had she lived, Michela Licalzi would still have had some work to do to sort out the house.

In the living room, propped up in a corner, were two rolled-up rugs; the sofa and armchairs were still factory-wrapped in clear plastic; a small table lay upside down, legs up, on top of a big, unopened box. The only thing in any kind of order was a small glass display cabinet with the usual sorts of things carefully arranged inside: two antique fans, a few ceramic statuettes, a closed violin case and two very beautiful shells, collector's items.

The forensics team were the first to arrive. To replace the old chief of the crime lab, Jacomuzzi, Commissioner Bonetti-Alderighi had hand-picked the young Dr Arquà, who'd moved down from Florence. More than chief of forensics, Jacomuzzi had been an incurable exhibitionist, always the first to strike a pose for the photographers, TV cameramen and journalists. To rib him, as he often did, Montalbano used to call him 'Pippo Baudo'. Deep down, Jacomuzzi never believed much in forensics as a useful tool in investigations; he maintained that sooner or later intuition and reason would find the solution, with or without the support of microscopes and analyses. Heresies, to Bonetti-Alderighi, who quickly got rid of him. Vanni Arquà, for his part, was a dead ringer for Harold Lloyd. Hair always dishevelled, he dressed like an absent-minded professor from a thirties movie and worshipped science. Montalbano didn't care much for him, and Arquà repaid him in kind with cordial antipathy.

Forensics thus showed up in full force, in two cars with sirens screaming as if they were in Texas. There were eight of them, all in civvies, and the first thing they did was unload boxes and crates from the boots, looking like a film crew ready to start shooting. When Arquà walked into the living room, Montalbano didn't even say hello; he merely pointed his thumb upward, signalling that what concerned them was upstairs.

They hadn't all finished climbing the stairs before Montalbano heard Arquà's voice call out:

'Excuse me, Inspector, would you come up here a minute?'

He took his time. When he entered the bedroom, he felt the crime lab chief's eyes boring into him.

'When you discovered the body, was it like this?'

'No,' said Montalbano, cool as a cucumber. 'She was naked.'

'And where did you get that bathrobe?'

'From the bathroom.'

'Put everything back as it was, for Christ's sake! You've altered the whole picture! That's very serious!'

Without a word, Montalbano walked over to the corpse, picked up the bathrobe, and draped it over his arm.

'Wow, nice arse!'

The comment came from one of the crime lab photographers, a homely sort of paparazzo with his shirt-tails hanging out of his trousers.

'Go right ahead, if you want,' the inspector said to him calmly. 'She's already in position.'

Fazio, who knew what dangers lurked beneath Montalbano's controlled calm, took a step towards him. The inspector looked Arquà in the eye, 'Understand now why I did it, arsehole?' And he left the room. In the bathroom he splashed a little water on his face, threw the bathrobe

down on the floor more or less where he'd found it, and
went back into the bedroom.

'I'll have to tell the commissioner about this,' Arquà
said icily. Montalbano's voice was ten degrees icier.

'I'm sure you'll understand each other perfectly.'

*

'Chief, me and Gallo and Galluzzo are going outside to
smoke a cigarette. We're getting in these guys' way.'

Montalbano, absorbed in thought, didn't answer. From
the living room he went back upstairs and examined the
little guest room and the bathroom.

He'd already looked carefully around downstairs and
hadn't found what he was looking for. For the sake of
thoroughness, he stuck his head into the bedroom, which
was being turned upside down by its invaders from the
crime lab, and double-checked what he thought he'd seen
earlier.

Outside the house, he lit a cigarette himself. Fazio had
just finished talking on the mobile phone.

'I got the husband's phone number and address in
Bologna,' he explained.

'Inspector,' Galluzzo broke in. 'We were just talking,
the three of us. There's something strange—'

'The armoire in the bedroom is still wrapped in
plastic,' Gallo cut in. 'And I also looked under the bed.'

'And I looked in all the other bedrooms. But—'

Fazio was about to draw the conclusion, but stopped when his superior raised a hand.

'The lady's clothes are nowhere to be found,' Montalbano concluded.

THREE

The ambulance arrived, followed by Coroner Pasquano's car.

'Go and see if forensics have finished with the bedroom,' Montalbano said to Galluzzo.

'Thanks,' said Dr Pasquano. His motto was: 'It's either me or them', 'them' being the forensics team. Jacomuzzi and his scruffy crew had been bad enough; how he put up with Dr Arquà and his visibly efficient staff, one could only imagine.

'A lot of work on your hands?' the inspector enquired.

'Not much. Five corpses this week. When have we ever seen that? Must be low season.'

Galluzzo returned to say that forensics had moved into the bathroom and guest room. The coast was clear.

'Accompany the doctor upstairs and come back down,' Montalbano said to Gallo. Pasquano shot him a glance of appreciation; he really liked to work alone.

After a good half hour, the judge's battered car

appeared and didn't stop until it had bumped into one of the crime lab's squad cars.

Nicolò Tommaseo got out, red in the face, his gallows-bird neck looking like a turkey cock's.

'What a dreadful road! I had two accidents!' he declared to one and all.

It was well known that he drove like a dog on drugs.

Montalbano found an excuse to prevent him from going upstairs at once and rattling Pasquano.

'Your Honour, let me tell you an extraordinary story.'

He told him part of what had happened to him the previous day. He pointed to the damage the Twingo had sustained from the impact, showed him the remnants of the scrap of paper he'd written on and slipped under the windscreen wiper, and explained how he'd begun to suspect something wasn't right. The anonymous phone call to the commissioner's office was the icing on the cake.

'What a curious coincidence!' Judge Tommaseo exclaimed, conceding no more than this.

As soon as the judge saw the victim's nude body, he froze. Even the inspector stopped dead in his tracks. Dr Pasquano had somehow managed to turn the woman's head, and now one could actually see her face, which had previously been buried in the bedclothes. The eyes were bulging to the point where they looked unreal, and they expressed unbearable pain and horror. A stream of blood trickled from her mouth. She must have bitten her tongue during the spasms of suffocation.

Dr Pasquano anticipated the question he hated so much.

'She definitely died sometime between late Wednesday night and early Thursday morning. I'll be able to say more precisely after the autopsy.'

'And how did she die?' asked Tommaseo.

'Can't you see? The killer pushed her face into the mattress and held her down until she was dead.'

'He must have been exceptionally strong.'

'Not necessarily.'

'Can you tell if they had relations before or after?'

'I can't say.'

Something in the judge's tone of voice led the inspector to look up at him. He was covered in sweat.

'He might have even sodomized her,' the judge went on, his eyes glistening.

It was a revelation. Apparently Justice Tommaseo secretly dipped into such subjects. Montalbano remembered having read somewhere a line by Manzoni about that more famous Nicolò Tommaseo, 'This Tommaseo with one foot in the sacristy and the other in the whore-house.'

It must be a family vice.

'I'll let you know. Good day,' said Dr Pasquano, hastily taking leave to avoid any further questions.

'To my mind, it's the crime of a maniac who surprised the lady as she was going to bed,' Judge Tommaseo said firmly, without taking his eyes off the corpse.

'Look, Your Honour, there were no signs of a break-in. And it's rather unusual for a naked woman to open her front door to a maniac and take him up to her bed-room.'

'What kind of reasoning is that! She might not have noticed he was a maniac until ... You know what I mean?'

'I myself would lean towards a crime of passion,' said Montalbano, who was beginning to amuse himself.

'Indeed, why not? Why not?' said Tommaseo, jumping at the suggestion and scratching his beard. 'We must bear in mind that it was a woman who made the phone call. The betrayed wife. Speaking of which, do you know how to reach the victim's husband?'

'Yes, Sergeant Fazio has his telephone number,' the inspector replied, feeling his heart sink. He hated giving bad news.

'Let me have it. I'll take care of everything,' the judge said.

He had every kink in the book, this Nicolò Tommaseo. He was a raven to boot.

'Can we take her away now?' asked the ambulance crew, entering the room.

＊

Another hour passed before the forensics team had finished fussing about and left.

'So now what do we do?' asked Gallo, who seemed to have become fixated on this question.

'Close the door, we're going back to Vigàta. I'm so hungry I can't see,' said the inspector.

*

Montalbano's housekeeper, Adelina, had left him a real delicacy in the fridge: 'coral' sauce, made of langoustine roe and sea-urchin pulp, to be used on spaghetti. He put the water on the stove and, while waiting, phoned his friend Nicolò Zito, newsman for the Free Channel, one of the two private television stations based in Montelusa. The other, TeleVigàta, whose news programming was anchored by Galluzzo's brother-in-law, tended to take a pro-government stance, regardless of who was running the country. Thus, given the government in power at that moment, and the fact that the Free Channel always leaned to the left, the two local stations might well be boringly similar if not for the lucid, ironic intelligence of the red-haired, red-sympathizing Nicolò Zito.

'Nicolò? Montalbano here. There's been a murder, but—'

'I'm not supposed to say it was you who told me about it.'

'An anonymous phone call. A female voice phoned the Montelusa commissioner's office this morning, saying a murder had been committed at a house in the Tre Fontane district. And it was true. A young woman, beautiful, naked—'

'Fuck.'

'Her name was Michela Licalzi.'

'Have you got a photo of her?'

'No, the murderer made off with her handbag and clothes.'

'Why did he do that?'

'I don't know.'

'So how do you know her name was Michela Licalzi? Has somebody identified her?'

'No. We're trying to contact her husband, who lives in Bologna.'

Nicolò asked him for a few more details, which he gave.

*

The water was boiling, so he put in the pasta. The telephone rang. He had a moment of hesitation, unsure whether to answer or not. He was afraid the call might last too long: it might not be so easy to cut it short, and that would jeopardize the proper al dente texture of the spaghetti. It would be a disaster to waste the coral sauce on a dish of overcooked pasta. He decided not to answer. In fact, to prevent the ringing from troubling the serenity of spirit indispensable to savouring the sauce in full, he pulled out the plug.

*

An hour later, pleased with himself and ready to meet the world head-on, he reconnected the telephone. He was forced to answer it at once.

'Hello.'

'Hullo, Chief? Izzatchoo y'self in poisson?'

'In poisson, Cat. What's up?'

'What's up is Judge Tolomeo called.'

'Tommaseo, Cat, but I get the picture. What did he want?'

'He wanted to speak poissonally wit' you y'self in poisson. He called at lease four times. Says you should call him y'self in poisson.'

'OK.'

'Oh, Chief, I got another streamly impoitant ting to tell ya. Somebody from Montelusa Central called to talk to me in poisson, Inspector Whatsizname, Tontona.'

'Tortona.'

'Whatever's 'is name. Him. Says I gotta take a concourse in pewters. Whattya think, boss?'

'I'm happy for you, Cat. Take the course, you can become a specialist. You're just the right man for pewters.'

'Thanks, Chief.'

*

'Hello, Judge Tommaseo? Montalbano here.'

'Inspector, I've been looking all over for you.'

'Forgive me, I was very busy. Remember the investigation into the body that was found in the water last week? I think you were duly informed about it.'

'Any new developments?'

'No, none whatsoever.'

Montalbano sensed the judge's silent confusion. The exchange they'd just had was entirely meaningless. As he'd expected, the judge didn't linger on the subject.

'I wanted to tell you I tracked down the widower, Dr Licalzi, in Bologna, and, tactfully, of course, gave him the terrible news.'

'How did he react?'

'Well, how shall I put it? Strangely. He didn't even ask what his wife died of. She was very young, after all. He must be a cold one; he hardly got upset at all.'

Dr Licalzi had denied the raven Tommaseo his jollies. The judge's disappointment at not having been able to relish a fine display of cries and sobs – however long distance – was palpable.

'At any rate he said he absolutely could not absent himself from the hospital today. He had some operations to perform and his replacement was sick. He's going to take the 7.05 flight for Palermo tomorrow morning. I assume, therefore, he'll be at your office around midday. I just wanted to bring you up to date on this.'

'Thank you, sir.'

*

As Gallo was driving the inspector to work in a squad car, he informed Montalbano that, on Fazio's orders, patrolman Germanà had picked up the damaged Twingo and put it in the police station's garage.

'Good idea.'

The first person to enter his office was Mimì Augello.

'I'm not here to talk to you about work. The day after tomorrow, that is, early Sunday morning, I'm going to visit my sister. D'you want to come, too, so you can see François? We'll drive back in the evening.'

'I'll do my best to make it.'

'Try to come. My sister made it clear she wants to talk to you.'

'About François?'

'Yes.'

Montalbano became anxious. He'd be in quite a fix if Augello's sister and her husband said they couldn't keep the kid with them any longer.

'I'll do what I can, Mimì. Thanks.'

＊

'Hello, Inspector Montalbano? This is Clementina Vasile Cozzo.'

'What a pleasure, signora.'

'Answer me yes or no. Was I good?'

'You were great, yes.'

'Answer me yes or no again. Are you coming to dinner tonight at nine?'

'Yes.'

＊

Fazio walked into his office with a triumphant air.

'Know what, Chief? I asked myself a question: with

the house looking the way it did, like it was only occasionally lived in, where did Mrs Licalzi sleep when she came here from Bologna? So I called a colleague at Montelusa Central Police, the guy assigned to the hotel beat, and I got my answer. Every time she came, Michela Licalzi stayed at the Hotel Jolly in Montelusa. Turns out she last checked in seven days ago.'

Fazio caught him off balance. He'd intended to call Dr Licalzi in Bologna as soon as he got into work, but had been distracted. Mimi's mention of François had flustered him a little.

'Shall we go there now?' asked Fazio.

'Wait.'

An idea had flashed into his brain utterly unprovoked, leaving behind an ever-so-slight scent of sulphur, the kind the devil usually likes to wear. He asked Fazio for Licalzi's telephone number, wrote it down on a piece of paper which he put in his pocket, then dialled it.

'Hello, Central Hospital? Inspector Montalbano here, from Vigàta police, in Sicily. I'd like to speak to Dr Emanuele Licalzi.'

'Please hold.'

He waited, all patience and self-control. When he appeared to be running out of both, the operator came back on the line.

'Dr Licalzi is in the operating theatre. You'll have to try again in half an hour.'

'I'll call him from the car,' he said to Fazio. 'Bring along your mobile phone, don't forget.'

He rang Judge Tommaseo and informed him of Fazio's discovery.

'Oh, I forgot to tell you,' Tommaseo interjected. 'When I asked him to give me his wife's number here, he said he didn't know it. He said it was always she who called him.'

The inspector asked the judge to prepare him a search warrant. He would send Gallo over at once to pick it up.

'Fazio, did they tell you what Dr Licalzi's speciality is?'

'Yes, he's an orthopedic surgeon.'

☆

Halfway between Vigàta and Montelusa, the inspector called Bologna Central Hospital again. After not too long a wait, Montalbano heard a firm, polite voice.

'This is Licalzi. With whom am I speaking?'

'Excuse me for disturbing you, Doctor. I'm Inspector Salvo Montalbano of the Vigàta police. I'm handling the case. Please allow me to express my sincerest condolences.'

'Thank you.'

Not one word more or less. The inspector realized it was still up to him to talk.

'Well, Doctor, you told the judge today that you didn't know your wife's phone number here in Vigàta.'

'That's correct.'

'We've been unable to track down this number ourselves.'

'There could hardly be thousands of hotels in Monte-lusa and Vigàta.'

Ready to cooperate, this Dr Licalzi.

'Forgive me for insisting. But hadn't you arranged, in case of dire need—'

'I don't think such a need could have ever arisen. In any case, there's a distant relative of mine who lives in Vigàta and with whom my poor Michela had been in contact.'

'Could you tell me—'

'His name is Aurelio Di Blasi. And now you must excuse me, I have to return to the operating theatre. I'll be at your office tomorrow, around midday.'

'One last question. Have you told this relative what happened?'

'No. Why? Should I have?'

FOUR

'Such an exquisite, elegant lady, and so beautiful!' said Claudio Pizzotta, the distinguished, sixtyish manager of the Hotel Jolly in Montelusa. 'Has something happened to her?'

'We don't really know yet. We got a phone call from her husband in Bologna, who was worried.'

'Right. As far as I know, Signora Licalzi left the hotel on Wednesday evening, and we haven't seen her since.'

'Weren't you worried? It's already Friday evening, if I'm not mistaken.'

'Right.'

'Did she let you know she wouldn't be returning?'

'No. But, you see, Inspector, the lady has been staying with us regularly for at least two years, so we've had a lot of time to become acquainted with her habits. Which are, well, unusual. Signora Michela is not the sort of woman to go unnoticed, you know what I mean? And then, I've always had my own worries about her.'

'You have? And what would they be?'

'Well, the lady owns a lot of valuable jewellery. Necklaces, bracelets, earrings, rings ... I've asked her many times to deposit them in our safe, but she always refuses. She keeps them in a kind of bag; she doesn't carry a handbag. She always tells me not to worry, says she doesn't leave the jewels in her room, but carries them around with her. I've also been afraid she'll get robbed on the street. But she always smiles and says no. She just won't be persuaded.'

'You mentioned her unusual habits. Could you be more precise?'

'Certainly. The lady likes to stay up late. She often comes home at the first light of dawn.'

'Alone?'

'Always.'

'Drunk? High?'

'Never. Or at least, so says the night porter.'

'Mind telling me why you were talking about Mrs Licalzi with the night porter?'

Claudio Pizzotta turned bright red. Apparently he'd had ideas about dunking his doughnut with Signora Michela.

'Inspector, surely you understand ... A beautiful woman like that, alone ... One's curiosity is bound to be aroused, it's only natural.'

'Go on. Tell me about her habits.'

'The lady sleeps in till about midday, and doesn't want to be disturbed in any way. When she wakes up, she orders breakfast in her room and starts making and receiving phone calls.'

'A lot of phone calls?'

'I've got an itemized list that never ends.'

'Do you know who she was calling?'

'One could find out. But it's a bit complicated. From your room you need only dial zero and you can phone New Zealand if you want.'

'What about the incoming calls?'

'Well, there's not much to say about that. The switchboard operator takes the call and passes it on to the room. There's only one way to know.'

'And that is?'

'When somebody calls and leaves his name when the client is out. In that case, the porter is given a message that he puts in the client's key box.'

'Does the lady lunch at the hotel?'

'Rarely. After eating a hearty breakfast so late, you can imagine ... But it has happened. Actually, the head waiter once told me how self-possessed she is at table when eating lunch.'

'I'm sorry, I don't follow.'

'Our hotel is very popular, with businessmen, politicians, entrepreneurs. In one way or another, they all end up trying their luck. A beckoning glance, a smile, more or less explicit invitations. The amazing thing about Signora Michela, the head waiter said, is that she never plays the prude, never takes offence, but actually returns the glances and smiles. But when it comes to the nitty-gritty, nothing doing. They're left high and dry.'

'And at what time in the afternoon does she usually go out?'

'About four. Then returns in the dead of night.'

'She must have a pretty broad circle of friends in Montelusa and Vigàta.'

'I'd say so.'

'Has she ever stayed out for more than one night before?'

'I don't think so. The porter would have told me.'

Gallo and Galluzzo arrived, flourishing the search warrant.

'What room is Mrs Licalzi staying in?'

'Number one-eighteen.'

'I've got a warrant.'

The hotel manager looked offended.

'Inspector! There was no need for that formality! You had only to ask and I ... Let me show you the way.'

'No, thanks,' Montalbano said curtly.

The manager's face went from looking offended to looking mortally offended.

'I'll go and get the key,' he said aloofly.

He returned a moment later with the key and a little stack of papers, all notes of incoming phone calls.

'Here,' he said, giving, for no apparent reason, the key to Fazio and the message slips to Gallo. Then he bowed his head abruptly, German-style, in front of Montalbano, turned around and walked stiffly away, looking like a wooden puppet in motion.

*

Room 118 was eternally imbued with the scent of Chanel No. 5. On the luggage rack sat two suitcases and a shoulder bag, all Louis Vuitton. Montalbano opened the armoire: five very classy dresses, three pairs of artfully worn-out jeans; in the shoe section, five pairs of Bruno Maglis with spike heels and three pairs of casual flats. The blouses, also very costly, were folded with extreme care; the underwear, divided by colour in its assigned drawer, consisted only of airy panties.

'Nothing in here,' said Fazio, who in the meantime had examined the two suitcases and shoulder bag.

Gallo and Galluzzo, who had upended the bed and mattress, shook their heads no and began putting everything back in place, impressed by the order that reigned in the room.

On the small desk were some letters, notes, a diary, and a stack of telephone messages considerably taller than the one the manager had given to Gallo.

'We'll take these things away with us,' the inspector said to Fazio. 'Look in the drawers, too. Take all the papers.'

From his pocket Fazio withdrew a plastic bag that he always carried with him, and began to fill it.

Montalbano went into the bathroom. Sparkling clean,

in perfect order. On the shelf, Rouge Idole lipstick, Shiseido foundation, a magnum of Chanel No. 5, and so on. A pink bathrobe, obviously softer and more expensive than the one in the house, hung placidly on a hook.

He went back into the bedroom and rang for the floor attendant. A moment later there was a knock and Montalbano told her to come in. The door opened and a gaunt, fortyish woman appeared. As soon as she saw the four men, she stiffened, blanched, and in a faint voice said, 'Are you police?'

The inspector laughed. How many centuries of police tyranny had it taken to hone this Sicilian woman's ability to detect law-enforcement officers at a moment's glance?

'Yes, we are,' he said, smiling.

The chambermaid blushed and lowered her eyes.

'Please excuse me.'

'Do you know Mrs Licalzi?'

'Why, what's happened to her?'

'She hasn't been heard from for a couple of days. We're looking for her.'

'And to look for her you have to take all her papers away?'

This woman was not to be underestimated. Montalbano decided to admit a few things to her.

'We're afraid something bad may have happened to her.'

'I always told her to be careful,' said the maid. 'She goes around with half a billion in her bag!'

'She went around with that much money?' Montalbano asked in astonishment.

'I wasn't talking about money, but the jewels she owns. And with the kind of life she leads! Comes home late, gets up late . . .'

'We already know that. Do you know her well?'

'Sure. Since she came here the first time with her husband.'

'Can you tell me anything about what she's like?'

'Look, she never made any trouble. She was just a maniac for order. Whenever we did her room, she would stand there making sure that everything was put back in its place. The girls on the morning shift always ask for the good Lord's help before working on one-eighteen.'

'A final question: did your colleagues on the morning shift ever mention if the lady'd had men in her room at night?'

'Never. And we've got an eye for that kind of thing.'

*

The whole way back to Vigàta one question tormented Montalbano: if the lady was a maniac for order, why was the bathroom at the house in Tre Fontane such a mess, with the pink bathrobe thrown haphazardly on the floor to boot?

*

During the dinner (super-fresh cod poached with a couple of bay leaves and dressed directly on the plate with salt, pepper and Pantelleria olive oil, with a side dish of gentle *tinnirùme* to cheer the stomach and intestines), the inspector told Mrs Vasile Cozzo of the day's developments.

'As far as I can tell,' said Clementina, 'the real question is: why did the murderer make off with the poor woman's clothes, underwear, shoes and handbag?'

'Yes,' Montalbano commented, saying nothing more. She'd hit the nail on the head as soon as she opened her mouth, and he didn't want to interrupt her thought processes.

'But I can only talk about these things,' the elderly woman continued, 'based on what I see on television.'

'Don't you read mystery novels?'

'Not very often. Anyway, what does that mean, "mystery novel"? What *is* a "detective novel"?'

'Well, it's a whole body of literature that—'

'Of course, but I don't like labels. Want me to tell you a good mystery story? All right, there's a man who, after many adventures, becomes the leader of a city. Little by little, however, his subjects begin to fall ill with an unknown sickness, a kind of plague. And so this man sets about to discover the cause of the illness, and in the course of his investigations he discovers that he himself is the root of it all. And so he punishes himself.'

'Oedipus,' Montalbano said, as if to himself.

'Now isn't that a good detective story? But, to return

to our discussion: why would a killer make off with the victim's clothes? The first answer is: so she couldn't be identified.'

'That's not the case here,' the inspector said.

'Right. And I get the feeling that, by reasoning this way, we're following the path the killer wants us to take.'

'I don't understand.'

'What I mean is, whoever made off with all those things wants us to believe that every one of them is of equal importance to him. He wants us to think of that stuff as a single whole. Whereas that is not the case.'

'Yes,' Montalbano said again, ever more impressed, and ever more reluctant to break the thread of her argument with some untimely observation.

'For one thing, the handbag alone is worth half a billion because of the jewellery inside it. To a common thief, robbing the bag would itself constitute a good day's earnings. Right?'

'Right.'

'But what reason would a common thief have for taking her clothes? None whatsoever. Therefore, if he made off with her clothes, underwear and shoes, we should conclude that we're not dealing with a common thief. But, in fact, he *is* a common thief who has done this only to make us think he's uncommon, different. Why? He might have done it to shuffle the cards. He wanted to steal the handbag with all its valuables, but since he committed murder, he wanted to mask his real purpose.'

'Right,' said Montalbano, unsolicited.

'To continue. Maybe the thief made off with other things of value that we're unaware of.'

'May I make a phone call?' asked the inspector, who had suddenly had an idea.

He called up the Hotel Jolly in Montelusa and asked to speak with Claudio Pizzotta, the manager.

'Oh, Inspector, how atrocious! How terrible! We found out just now from the Free Channel that poor Mrs Licalzi . . .'

Nicolò Zito had reported the news and Montalbano had forgotten to tune in and see how the newsman presented the story.

'TeleVigàta also did a report,' added the hotel manager, torn between genuine satisfaction and feigned grief.

Galluzzo had done his job with his brother-in-law.

'What should I do, Inspector?' the manager asked, distressed.

'What do you mean?'

'About these journalists. They're besieging me. They want to interview me. They found out the poor woman was staying with us . . .'

From whom could they have learned this if not from the manager himself? The inspector imagined Pizzotta on the phone, summoning reporters with the promise of shocking revelations on the young, attractive, and, most importantly, naked murder victim . . .

'Do whatever the hell you want. Listen, did Mrs Licalzi normally wear any of the jewellery she had? Did she own a watch?'

'Of course she wore it. Discreetly, though. Otherwise, why would she bring it all here from Bologna? As for the watch, she always wore a splendid, paper-thin Piaget on her wrist.'

Montalbano thanked him, hung up, and told Signora Clementina what he'd just learned. She thought about it a minute.

'We must now establish whether we are dealing with a thief who became a murderer out of necessity, or with a murderer who is pretending to be a thief.'

'For no real reason — by instinct, I guess — I don't believe in this thief.'

'You're wrong to trust your instinct.'

'But, Signora Clementina, Michela Licalzi was naked, she'd just finished taking a shower. A thief would have heard the noise and waited before coming inside.'

'And what makes you think the thief wasn't already inside when the lady came home? She comes in, and the burglar hides. When she goes into the shower, he decides the time is right. He comes out of his hiding place, steals whatever he's supposed to steal, but then she catches him in the act, and he reacts in the manner he does. He may not even have intended to kill her.'

'But how would this burglar have entered?'

'The same way you did, Inspector.'

A direct hit, and down he went. Montalbano said nothing.

'Now for the clothes,' Signora Clementina continued. 'If they were stolen just for show, that's one thing. But if the murderer needed to get rid of them, that's another kettle of fish. What could have been so important about them?'

'They might have represented a danger to him, a way of identifying him,' said Montalbano.

'Yes, you're right, Inspector. But they clearly weren't a danger when the woman put them on. They must have become so afterwards. How?'

'Maybe they got stained,' Montalbano said, unconvinced. 'Maybe even with the killer's blood. Even though...'

'Even though?'

'Even though there was no blood around the bedroom. There was a little on the sheet, which had come out of Mrs Licalzi's mouth. But maybe it was another kind of stain. Like vomit, for example.'

'Or semen,' said Mrs Vasile Cozzo, blushing.

*

It was too early to go home to Marinella, so Montalbano decided to put in an appearance at the station to see if there were any new developments.

'Oh, Chief, Chief!' said Catarella as soon as he saw him. 'You're here? At least ten people called, and they all wanted a talk to you in poisson! I didn't know you was comin' so I says to all of 'em to call back tomorrow morning. Did I do right, Chief?'

'You did right, Cat, don't worry about it. Do you know what they wanted?'

'They all said as how they all knew the lady who was murdered.'

On the desk in his office, Fazio had left the plastic bag with the papers they'd seized from room 118. Next to it were the notices of incoming calls that the manager Pizzotta had turned over to Gallo. The inspector sat down, took the diary out of the bag, and glanced through it. Michela Licalzi's diary was as orderly as her hotel room: appointments, telephone calls to make, places to go. Everything was carefully and clearly written down.

Dr Pasquano had said the woman was killed sometime between late Wednesday night and early Thursday morning, and Montalbano agreed with this. He looked up the page for Wednesday, the last day of Michela Licalzi's life – 4 p.m., Rotondo's Furniture; 4.30 p.m., phone Emanuele; 5 p.m., appt with Todaro gardeners; 6 p.m., Anna; 8 p.m., dinner with the Vassallos.

The woman, however, had made other engagements for Thursday, Friday and Saturday, unaware that someone would prevent her from attending them. On Thursday, again in the afternoon, she was to have met with Anna, with whom she was to go to Loconte's (in parentheses: 'curtains') before ending her evening by dining with a certain Maurizio. On Friday she was supposed to see Riguccio the electrician, meet Anna again, then go out to dinner at the Cangelosi home. On the page for Saturday, all that was written down was: '4.30 p.m., flight from Punta Ràisi to Bologna.'

It was a large-format diary. The telephone index allowed three pages for each letter of the alphabet, but she'd copied down so many phone numbers that in certain cases she'd had to write the numbers of two different people on the same line.

Montalbano set the diary aside and took the other papers out of the bag. Nothing of interest. Just invoices and receipts. Every penny spent on the construction and furnishing of the house was fastidiously accounted for. In a square-lined notebook Michela had copied down every expense in neat columns, as if preparing herself for a visit from the revenue officers. There was a cheque book from the Banca Popolare di Bologna with only the stubs remaining. Montalbano also found a boarding pass for Bologna–Rome–Palermo from six days earlier, and a return ticket, Palermo–Rome–Bologna, for Saturday at 4.30 p.m.

No sign whatsoever of any personal letter or note. He decided to continue working at home.

FIVE

The only things left to examine were the notices of incoming calls. The inspector began with the ones Michela had collected in the little desk in her hotel room. There were about forty of them, and Montalbano arranged them according to the name of the person calling. In the end he was left with three small piles somewhat taller than the rest. A woman, Anna, would call during the day and usually leave word that Michela should call her back as soon as she woke up or when she got back in. A man, Maurizio, had rung two or three times in the morning, but normally preferred the late-night hours and always insisted that she call him back. The third caller was also male, Guido by name, and he phoned from Bologna, also late at night; but, unlike Maurizio, he never left a message.

The slips of paper the hotel manager had given to Gallo were twenty in number: all from the time Michela left the hotel on Wednesday afternoon to the moment the police showed up at the hotel. On Wednesday morning, however, during the hours Mrs Licalzi devoted to sleep, the same Maurizio had asked for her at about ten thirty, and Anna had done likewise shortly thereafter. Around nine o'clock that evening, Mrs Vassallo had called looking for Michela, and had rung back an hour later. Anna had phoned back shortly before midnight.

At three o'clock on Thursday morning, Guido had called from Bologna. At ten thirty, Anna, apparently unaware that Michela hadn't returned to the hotel that night, called again; at eleven, a certain Mr Loconte called to confirm the afternoon appointment. At midday, still on Thursday, a Mr Aurelio Di Blasi phoned and continued to phone back almost every three hours until early Friday evening. Guido from Bologna had called at two o'clock on Friday morning. As of Thursday morning, Anna had started calling frantically and also didn't stop until Friday evening.

Something didn't add up. Montalbano couldn't put his finger on it, and this made him uncomfortable. He stood up, went out on the veranda, which gave directly onto the beach, took off his shoes, and started walking in the sand until he reached the water's edge. He rolled up his trouser legs and began wading in the water, which from time to time washed over his feet. The soothing sound of the waves helped him put his thoughts in order. Suddenly he understood what was tormenting him. He went back in the house, grabbed the diary, and opened it up to Wednesday. Michela had written down that she was supposed to go to dinner at the Vassallos' house at eight. So why had Mrs Vassallo called her at the hotel at nine and again at ten? Hadn't Michela shown up for dinner? Or did the Mrs Vassallo who phoned have nothing to do with the Vassallos who'd invited her to dinner?

He glanced at his watch: past midnight. He decided the matter was too important to be worrying about etiquette. There turned out to be three listings under Vassallo in the phone book. He tried the first and guessed right.

'I'm very sorry. This is Inspector Montalbano.'

'Inspector! I'm Ernesto Vassallo. I was going to come to your office myself tomorrow morning. My wife is just devastated; I had to call a doctor. Is there any news?'

'None. I need to ask you something.'

'Go right ahead, Inspector. For poor Michela—'

Montalbano cut him off.

'I read in Mrs Licalzi's diary that she was supposed to have dinner—'

This time it was Ernesto Vassallo who interrupted.

'She never showed up, Inspector! We waited a long time for her. But nothing, not even a phone call. And she was always so punctual! We got worried, we thought she might be sick, so we rang the hotel a couple of times, then we tried her friend Anna Tropeano, but she said she didn't know anything. She said she'd seen Michela at about six and they'd been together for roughly half an hour, and that Michela had left saying she was going back to the hotel to change before coming to dinner at our place.'

'Listen, I really appreciate your help. But don't come to the station tomorrow morning, I'm full up with appointments. Drop by in the afternoon whenever you want. Goodnight.'

One good turn deserved another. He looked up the number for Aurelio Di Blasi in the phone book and dialled it. The first ring wasn't even over when someone picked up.

'Hello? Hello? Is that you?'

The voice of a middle-aged man, breathless, troubled.

'Inspector Montalbano here.'

'Oh.'

Montalbano could tell that the man felt profound disappointment. From whom was he so anxiously awaiting a phone call?

'Mr Di Blasi, I'm sure you've heard about the unfortunate Mrs—'

'I know, I know, I saw it on TV.'

The disappointment had been replaced by undisguised irritation.

'Anyway, I wanted to know why, from midday on Thursday to Friday evening, you repeatedly tried to reach Mrs Licalzi at her hotel.'

'What's so unusual about that? I'm a distant relative of Michela's. Whenever she came to Vigàta to work on the house, she would lean on me for help and advice. I'm a construction engineer. I phoned her on Thursday to invite her here to dinner, but the receptionist said she hadn't come back that night. The receptionist knows me, we're friends. And so I started to get worried. Is that so hard to understand?'

Now Mr Di Blasi had turned sarcastic and aggressive. The inspector had the impression the man's nerves were about to pop.

'No.'

There was no point in calling Anna Tropeano. He already knew what she would say, since Mr Vassallo had told him beforehand. He would summon Ms Tropeano to the station for questioning. One thing at this point was certain: Michela Licalzi had disappeared from circulation at approximately seven o'clock on Wednesday evening. She had never returned to the hotel, even though she'd expressed this intention to her friend.

He wasn't sleepy, so he lay down in bed with a book, a novel by Marco Denevi, an Argentine writer he liked very much.

*

When his eyes started to droop, he closed the book and turned off the light. As he often did before falling asleep, he thought of Livia. Suddenly he sat up in bed, wide awake. Jesus, Livia! He hadn't phoned her back since the night of the storm, when he'd made it seem as if the line had been cut. Livia clearly hadn't believed this, since in fact she'd never phoned back. He had to set things right at once.

'Hello? Who is this?' said Livia's sleepy voice.

'It's Salvo, darling.'

'Oh, let me sleep, for Christ's sake!'

Click. Montalbano sat there for a while holding the receiver.

*

It was eight thirty in the morning when Montalbano walked into the station carrying Michela Licalzi's papers. After Livia had refused to speak to him, he'd become agitated and unable to sleep a wink. There was no need to call in Anna Tropeano; Fazio immediately told him the woman had been waiting for him since eight.

'Listen, I want to know everything there is to know about a construction engineer from Vigàta named Aurelio Di Blasi.'

'Everything everything?' asked Fazio.

'Everything everything.'

'To me, everything everything means rumours and gossip, too.'

'Same here.'

'How much time do I get?'

'Come on, Fazio, you playing the unionist now? Two hours ought to be more than enough.'

Fazio glared at his boss with an air of indignation and went out without even saying goodbye.

*

In normal circumstances, Anna Tropeano must have been an attractive woman of thirty, with jet-black hair, dark complexion, big, sparkling eyes, tall and full-bodied. On this occasion, however, her shoulders were hunched, her eyes swollen and red, her skin turning a shade of grey.

'May I smoke?' she asked, sitting down.

'Of course.'

She lit a cigarette, hands trembling. She attempted a rough imitation of a smile.

'I quit only a week ago. But since last night I must have smoked at least three packets.'

'Thanks for coming in on your own. I really need a lot of information from you.'

'That's what I'm here for.'

Montalbano secretly breathed a sigh of relief. Anna was a strong woman. There wasn't going to be any sobbing or fainting. In fact, she had appealed to him from the moment he saw her in the doorway.

'Even if some of my questions seem odd to you, please try to answer them anyway.'

'Of course.'

'Married?'

'Who?'

ANDREA CAMILLERI

'You.'

'No, I'm not. Not separated or divorced, either. And not even engaged. Nothing. I live alone.'

'Why?'

Though Montalbano had forewarned her, Anna hesitated a moment before answering so personal a question.

'I don't think I've had time to think about myself, Inspector. A year before graduating from university, my father died. Heart attack. He was very young. The year after I graduated, my mother died. I had to look after my little sister, Maria, who's nineteen now and married and living in Milan, and my brother, Giuseppe, who works at a bank in Rome and is twenty-seven. I'm thirty-one. But aside from all that, I don't think I've ever met the right person.'

There was no resentment. On the contrary, she seemed slightly calmer now. The fact that the inspector hadn't launched immediately into the matter at hand had allowed her in a sense to catch her breath. Montalbano thought it best to steer clear for a while.

'Do you live in your parents' house here in Vigàta?'

'Yes, Papa bought it. It's sort of a small villa, right where Marinella begins. It's become too big for me.'

'The one on the right, just after the bridge?'

'That's the one.'

'I pass by it at least twice a day. I live in Marinella myself.'

Anna Tropeano eyed him with mild amazement. What a strange sort of policeman!

'Do you work?'

'Yes, I teach at the *liceo scientifico* of Montelusa.'

'What do you teach?'

'Physics.'

Montalbano looked at her with admiration. In physics, at school, he'd always been between a D and an F. If he'd had a teacher like her in his day, he might have become another Einstein.

'Do you know who killed her?'

Anna Tropeano jumped in her chair and looked at him imploringly: we were getting along so well, why do you want to play policeman, which is worse than playing hunting dog?

Don't you ever let go? she seemed to be asking.

Montalbano, who understood what the woman's eyes were saying to him, smiled and threw up his hands in a gesture of resignation, as if to say: *It's my job.*

'No,' replied a firm, decisive Anna Tropeano.

'Any suspicion?'

'No.'

'Mrs Licalzi customarily returned to her hotel in the wee hours of the morning. I'd like to know—'

'She was at my house. We had dinner together almost every night. And if she was invited out, she would come along afterwards.'

'What did you do together?'

'What do two women friends usually do when they see each other? We talked, we watched television, we listened to music. Sometimes we did nothing at all. It was a pleasure just to know the other one was there.'

'Did she have any male friends?'

'Yes, a few. But things were not what they seemed. Michela was a very serious person. Seeing her so free and easy, men got the wrong impression. And they were always disappointed, without fail.'

'Was there anyone in particular who bothered her a lot?'

'Yes.'

'What's his name?'

'I'm not going to tell you. You'll find out soon enough.'

'So, in short, Mrs Licalzi was faithful to her husband.'

'I didn't say that.'

'What does that mean?'

'It means what I said.'

'Had you known each other a long time?'

'No.'

Montalbano looked at her, stood up, and walked over to the window. Anna, almost angrily, lit up another cigarette.

'I don't like the tone you've assumed in the last part of our dialogue,' the inspector said with his back to her.

'I don't either.'

'Peace?'

'Peace.'

Montalbano turned around and smiled at her. Anna smiled back. But only for an instant. Then she raised a finger like a schoolgirl, wanting to ask a question.

'Can you tell me, if it's not a secret, how she was killed?'

'They didn't say so on TV?'

'No. Neither the Free Channel nor TeleVigàta said anything. They only said the body had been found.'

'I shouldn't be telling you. But I'll make an exception. She was suffocated.'

'With a pillow?'

'No, with her face pressed down against the mattress.'

Anna began to sway, the way treetops sway in strong wind. The inspector left the room and returned a moment later with a bottle of water and a glass. Anna drank as if she had just come out of the desert.

'But what was she doing there at the house, for God's sake?' she asked, as if to herself.

'Have you ever been to that house?'

'Of course. Almost daily, with her.'

'Did she ever sleep there?'

'No, not that I know of.'

'But there was a bathrobe in the bathroom, and towels and creams—'

'I know. Michela put those things there on purpose. Whenever she went to work on the house, she ended up all covered in dust and cement. So, before leaving, she would take a shower.'

Montalbano decided it was time to hit below the belt. But he felt reluctant; he didn't want to injure her too badly.

'She was completely naked.'

Anna looked as if a high-voltage charge had passed through her. Eyes popping out of her head, she tried to say something but couldn't. Montalbano refilled her glass.

'Was she . . . was she raped?'

'I don't know. The pathologist hasn't told me yet.'

'But why didn't she go back to her hotel instead of going to that goddamned house?' Anna asked herself again in despair.

'Whoever killed her also took all her clothes, under-wear and shoes.'

Anna looked at him in disbelief, as though the inspector had just told her a big lie.

'For what reason?'

Montalbano didn't answer. He continued, 'He even made off with her handbag and everything that was in it.'

'That's a little more understandable. Michela used to keep all her jewellery in it, and she had a lot, all very valuable. If the person who suffocated her was a thief—'

'Wait. Mr Vassallo told me that when Michela didn't show up to dinner at his place, they got worried and phoned you.'

'That's true. I thought she was at their house. When

Michela left me, she'd said she was stopping off at the hotel to change her clothes.'

'Speaking of which, how was she dressed?'

'Entirely in denim — jeans and jacket — and casual shoes.'

'She never went back to the hotel. Somebody or something made her change her mind. Did she have a mobile phone?'

'Yes, she kept it in her bag.'

'So it's possible that someone phoned Mrs Licalzi as she was going back to the hotel. And that as a result of this phone call, she went out to the house.'

'Maybe it was a trap.'

'Set by whom? Certainly not by a thief. Have you ever heard of a burglar summoning the owner of the house he's about to rob?'

'Did you notice if anything was missing from the house?'

'Her Piaget, for certain. As for everything else, I'm not sure. I don't know what things of value she had in the house. Everything looked to be in order, except for the bathroom, which was a mess.'

'A mess?'

'Yes. The pink bathrobe was thrown on the floor. She'd just finished taking a shower.'

'Inspector, I find the picture you're presenting totally unconvincing.'

'What do you mean?'

'I mean, the idea that Michela would go to the house to meet a man and be in such a rush to go to bed with him that she would throw off her bathrobe and let it fall wherever it happened to fall.'

'That's plausible, isn't it?'

'Maybe for other women, but not Michela.'

'Do you know somebody named Guido who called her every night from Bologna?'

He'd fired blindly, but hit the mark. Anna Tropeano looked away, embarrassed.

'You said a few minutes ago that Mrs Licalzi was faithful,' he continued.

'Yes.'

'Faithful to her one infidelity?'

Anna nodded yes.

'Could you tell me his name? You see, you'll be doing me a favour. It'll save me time. Because, don't worry, I'll find out eventually anyway. Well?'

'His name is Guido Serravalle. He's an antique dealer. I don't know his telephone number or address.'

'Thanks, that's good enough. Her husband will be here around midday. Would you like to see him?'

'Me? Why? I don't even know him.'

The inspector didn't need to ask any more questions. Anna went on talking of her own accord.

'Michela married Dr Licalzi two and a half years ago. It was her idea to come to Sicily for their honeymoon. But that's not when we met. That happened later, when she returned by herself with the intention of having a house built. I was on my way to Montelusa one day and a Twingo was coming from the opposite direction, we were both distracted, and we narrowly avoided a head-on collision. We both pulled over and got out to apologize, and took an immediate liking to each other. Every time Michela came down after that, she always came alone.'

She was tired. Montalbano took pity on her.

'You've been very helpful to me. Thank you.'

'Can I go?'

'Of course.'

He extended his hand to her. Anna Tropeano took it and held it between both of hers.

The inspector felt a wave of heat rise up inside him.

'Thank you,' said Anna.

'For what?'

'For letting me talk about Michela. I don't have anybody to ... Thanks. I feel calmer now.'

SIX

No sooner had Anna Tropeano left than the door to the inspector's office flew open, slamming into the wall, and Catarella came barrelling into the room.

'The next time you come in here like that, I'm going to shoot you. And you know I mean it,' Montalbano said calmly.

Catarella, however, was too excited to worry about this.

'Chief, I just wanna say I got a call from the c'missioner's office. Remember the concourse in pewters I tol' you 'bout? Well, it starts Monday morning an' I gotta be there. Whatcha gonna do witout me onna phone?'

'We'll survive, Cat.'

'Oh, Chief, Chief! You said you dint wanna be distroubled when you was talking wit da lady an' I did what you said! But inna meantime you gotta lotta phone calls! I wrote 'em all down on dis li'l piece a paper.'

'Give it to me and get out of here.'

On a poorly torn-out piece of notebook paper was

written, 'Phone calls: Vizzallo Guito Sarah Valli Losconti yer frend Zito Rotonò Totano Ficuccio Cangialosi Sarah Valli of Bolonia agin Cipollina Pinissi Cacamo.'

Montalbano started scratching himself all over. It must have been some mysterious form of allergy, but every time he was forced to read something Catarella had written, an irresistible itch came over him. With the patience of a saint, he deciphered: Vassallo, Guido Serravalle (Michela's Bolognese lover), Loconte (who sold fabric for curtains), his friend Nicolò Zito, Rotondo (the furniture salesman), Todaro (the plant and garden man), Riguccio (the electrician), Cangelosi (who'd invited Michela to dinner) and Serravalle again. Cipollina, Pinissi and Cacamo, assuming that those were their real names, were unfamiliar to him, but in all likelihood they had phoned because they were friends or acquaintances of the murder victim.

'May I?' asked Fazio, sticking his head inside the door.

'Come on in. Did you get the low-down on the engineer Di Blasi?'

'Of course. Why else would I be here?'

Fazio was apparently expecting to be praised for having taken such a short time to gather the information.

'See? You did it in less than an hour,' the inspector said instead.

Fazio darkened.

'Is that the kind of thanks I get?'

'Why do you want to be thanked just for doing your duty?'

'Inspector, may I say something, with all due respect? This morning you're downright obnoxious.'

'By the way, why haven't I yet had the honour and pleasure, so to speak, of seeing Inspector Augello at the office this morning?'

'He's out today with Germanà and Galluzzo looking into that business at the cement works.'

'What's this about?'

'You don't know? Yesterday, about thirty-five workers at the cement factory were given pink slips. This morning they started raising hell, shouting, throwing stones. The manager got scared and called us up.'

'And why did Mimì Augello go?'

'The manager asked him for help!'

'Jesus Christ! If I've said it once, I've said it a thousand times. I don't want anyone from my station getting mixed up in these things!'

'But what was Augello supposed to do?'

'He should have passed the phone call on to the carabinieri, who get off on that kind of thing! Mr Manager's always going to find another position when the going gets tough. The ones who get thrown out on their arses are the workers. And we're supposed to club them over the head?'

'Chief, excuse me again, but you're really and truly a communist, a hotheaded communist.'

'Fazio, you're stuck on this communist crap. I'm not a

communist, will you get that in your head once and for all?'

'OK, but you really do sound like one.'

'Are we going to drop the politics?'

'Yessir. Anyway: Aurelio Di Blasi, son of Giacomo and Maria Antonietta née Carlentini, born in Vigàta on April 3, 1937—'

'You get on my nerves when you talk that way. You sound like a clerk at the records office.'

'You don't like it, Chief? What do you want me to do, sing it? Recite it like poetry?'

'You know, as for being obnoxious, you're doing a pretty good job yourself this morning.'

The telephone rang.

'At this rate we'll be here till midnight.' Fazio sighed.

'H'lo, Chief? I got that Signor Càcano that called before onna line. Whaddo I do?'

'Let me talk to him.'

'Inspector Montalbano? This is Gillo Jàcono. I had the pleasure of meeting you at Mrs Vasile Cozzo's house once. I'm a former student of hers.'

Over the receiver, in the background, Montalbano heard a female voice announcing the last call for the flight to Rome.

'I remember very well. What can I do for you?'

'Excuse me for being so brief, but I'm at the airport and have only a few seconds.'

Brevity was something the inspector was always ready to excuse, at any time and under any circumstance.

'I'm calling about the woman who was murdered.'

'Did you know her?'

'No, but on Wednesday evening, about midnight, I was on my way from Montelusa to Vigàta in my car when the motor started acting up, and so I began driving very slowly. When I was in the Tre Fontane district, a dark Twingo passed me and then stopped in front of a house a short distance ahead. A man and a woman got out and walked up the drive. I didn't see anything else, but I'm sure about what I saw.'

'When will you be back in Vigàta?'

'Next Thursday.'

'Come in and see me. Thanks.'

Montalbano drifted off. That is, his body remained seated, but his mind was elsewhere.

'What should I do, come back in a little bit?' Fazio asked in resignation.

'No, no. Go ahead and talk.'

'Where was I? Ah, yes. Construction engineer, but not a builder himself. Resides in Vigàta, Via Laporta number eight, married to Teresa Dalli Cardillo, housewife, but a well-to-do housewife. Husband owns a large plot of farmland at Raffadali in Montelusa province, complete with farmhouse, which he refurbished. He's got two cars, a Mercedes and a Tempra, two children, male and female. The female's name is Manuela, thirty years old, married to a businessman and living in Holland. They've got two children, Giuliano, age three, and Domenico, age one. They live—'

'Now I'm going to break your head,' said Montalbano.

'Why? What did I do?' Fazio asked disingenuously. 'I thought you said you wanted to know everything about everything!'

The phone rang. Fazio could only groan and look up at the ceiling.

'Inspector. This is Emanuele Licalzi. I'm calling from Rome. My flight was two hours late leaving Bologna and so I missed the connection to Palermo. I'll be there at about three this afternoon.'

'No problem, I'll be expecting you.'

He looked at Fazio and Fazio looked at him.

'How much more of this bullshit have you got?'

'I'm almost done. The son's name is Maurizio.'

Montalbano sat up in his chair and pricked up his ears.

'He's thirty-one years old and a university student.'

'At thirty-one?'

'At thirty-one. Seems he's a little slow in the head. He lives with his parents. End of story.'

'No, I'm sure that is not the end of the story. Go on.'

'Well, they're only rumours . . .'

'Doesn't matter.'

Fazio was obviously having a great time playing this game with his boss, since he held all the cards.

'Well, Engineer Di Blasi is the second cousin of Dr Emanuele Licalzi. Michela became like one of the Di Blasi family. And Maurizio lost his head over her. For everyone in town, it turned into a farce: whenever Mrs Licalzi went walking around Vigàta, there he was, following behind her, with his tongue hanging out.'

So it was Maurizio's name Anna didn't want to give him.

'Everyone I spoke to,' Fazio continued, 'told me he's a gentle soul, and a little dense.'

'All right, thanks.'

'There's one more thing,' said Fazio, and it was clear he was about to fire the final blast, the biggest in the fireworks display. 'Apparently the kid has been missing since Wednesday evening. Got that?'

*

'Hello, Pasquano? Montalbano here. Got any news for me?'

'A few things. I was about to call you myself.'

'Tell me everything.'

'The victim hadn't eaten dinner. Or very little, at least, maybe a sandwich. She had a gorgeous body, inside and out. In perfect health, a splendid machine. She hadn't drunk anything or taken any drugs. Death was caused by asphyxiation.'

'Is that it?'

'No. She'd clearly had sexual intercourse.'

'Was she raped?'

'I don't think so. She'd had very rough vaginal inter-course, intense, I suppose you could say. But there was no trace of seminal fluid there. Then she'd had anal inter-course, also very rough, and again no seminal fluid.'

'But how can you know she wasn't raped?'

'Quite simple. To prepare for anal penetration an emollient cream was used, probably one of those moistur-izing creams women keep in the bathroom. Have you ever heard of a rapist worried about minimizing his victim's pain? No, trust me: the lady consented. And now I have to let you go. I'll give you more details as soon as possible.'

The inspector had an exceptional photographic mem-ory. Closing his eyes, he put his head in his hands and concentrated. A moment later he could clearly see the little jar of moisturizing cream with the lid lying beside it, the last item on the right-hand side of the messy bathroom's shelf.

*

The nameplate next to the intercom outside Via Laporta 8 said only, 'Eng. Aurelio Di Blasi'. He rang, and a woman's voice answered.

'Who is it?'

Better not put her on her guard. They were probably already on pins and needles.

'Is Engineer Di Blasi there?'

'No, but he'll be back soon. Who is this?'

'I'm a friend of Maurizio's. Could I come in?'

For a moment he felt like a piece of shit, but it was his job.

'Top floor,' said the voice.

The lift door was opened by a woman of about sixty, dishevelled and looking very upset.

'You're a friend of Maurizio's?' the woman asked anxiously.

'Sort of,' replied Montalbano, feeling the shit spill out over his collar.

'Please come in.'

She led him into a large, tastefully furnished living room, pointed him towards an armchair, while she herself sat down in a plain chair, rocking her upper body back and forth, silent and desperate. The shutters were closed, some miserly shafts of light filtering through the slats. Montalbano felt as if he were attending a wake. He even thought the deceased was there, though invisible, and that his name was Maurizio. Scattered on the coffee table were a dozen or so photos that all showed the same face, but in the shadowy room one couldn't make out the features. The inspector heaved a long sigh, the way one does before holding one's breath to go underwater, for he was about to dive into the abyss of sorrow that was the mind of Mrs Di Blasi.

'Have you heard from your son?'

It was clear as day that things were exactly as Fazio had said.

'No. Everyone's been looking for him over land and sea. My husband, his friends ... Everyone.'

She started weeping quietly, tears running down her face, falling onto her skirt.

'Did he have much money on him?'

'Half a million lire, for certain. He also had a card, how's it called? An ATM card.'

'Let me get you a glass of water,' said Montalbano, standing up.

'Please don't bother, I'll get it myself,' the woman said, standing up in turn and leaving the room. In a flash Montalbano seized one of the photos, glanced at it — a horse-faced kid with expressionless eyes — and stuck it in his jacket pocket. Apparently Mr Di Blasi had had them made to be passed around. Mrs Di Blasi returned, but instead of sitting back down, she remained standing in the arch of the doorway. She'd become suspicious.

'You're quite a bit older than my son. What did you say your name was?'

'Actually, Maurizio is friends with my younger brother, Giuseppe.'

He'd chosen one of the most common names in Sicily. But the signora's thoughts were already elsewhere. She sat down and resumed rocking back and forth.

'So you've had no news of him since Wednesday evening?'

'None whatsoever. He didn't come home that night.

He'd never done that before. He's a simple boy, good-hearted. If you tell him dogs can fly, he'll believe you. At some point that morning, my husband got worried and started making phone calls. A friend of his had seen him walking by in the direction of the Bar Italia. It was probably nine in the evening.'

'Did he have a mobile phone?'

'Yes. But who are you, anyway?'

'Well,' the inspector said. 'I think I'll go now.'

He headed quickly for the door, opened it, then turned round.

'When was the last time Michela came here?'

Mrs Di Blasi turned red in the face.

'Don't you mention that slut's name to me!'

And she slammed the door behind him.

*

The Bar Italia was practically next door to police head-quarters. Everyone, Montalbano included, was family there. The owner was sitting at the cash register. He was a big man with ferocious eyes that contrasted with his innate kindheartedness. His name was Gelsomino Patti.

'What'll it be, Inspector?'

'Nothing, Gelso. I need some information. Do you know this Maurizio Di Blasi?'

'Did they find him?'

'Not yet.'

84

'His dad, poor guy, has come by here at least ten times to ask if there's any news. But what kind of news could there be? If he comes back, he's going to go home, he ain't going to come and sit down at the bar.'

'Listen, Pasquale Corso—'

'Inspector, the father told me the same thing, that Maurizio came here round nine that night. But the fact is, he stopped on the street, right here in front, and I seen him real good from the register. He was about to come in, and then he stopped, pulled out his mobile phone, and started talking. A little while later he was gone. On Wednesday evening, he didn't come in here, that much I know for sure. What reason would I have for sayin' something that wasn't true?'

'Thanks, Gelso. So long.'

*

'Chief! Dr Latte called from Montelusa.'

'Lattes, Cat, with an *s* at the end.'

'Chief, one *s* more or less don' make no difference. He said as how you should call 'im 'mediately. And then Guito Sarah Valli called after 'im. Left me 'is number in Bolonia. I wrote it on this here piece a paper.'

It was time to eat, but he could squeeze in one call.

'Hello? Who's this?'

'Inspector Montalbano. I'm calling from Vigàta. Are you Mr Guido Serravalle?'

'Yes, Inspector. I've been trying to reach you all morning, because when I called the Jolly to talk to Michela I found out...'

A warm, mature voice, like a crooner's.

'Are you a relative?'

He'd always found it to be a good tactic to pretend, during an investigation, that he knew nothing about the relationships between the various persons involved.

'No. Actually, I...'

'Friend?'

'Yes, a friend.'

'How much?'

'I'm sorry, I don't understand.'

'How much of a friend?'

Guido Serravalle hesitated before answering. Montalbano came to his aid.

'An intimate friend?'

'Well, yes.'

'So, what can I do for you?'

More hesitation. Apparently the inspector's manner was throwing him off.

'Uh, I just wanted to tell you ... to make myself available. I own an antique shop in Bologna that I can close whenever I want. If you need me for anything, I'll get on a plane and come down. I wanted ... I was very close to Michela.'

'I understand. If I need you for anything, I'll have someone ring you.'

He hung up. He hated people who made useless phone calls. What could Guido Serravalle tell him that he didn't already know?

*

He headed out on foot to have lunch at the Trattoria San Calogero, where the fish was always the freshest. All of a sudden he stopped, cursing the saints. He'd forgotten that the trattoria was closed for six days for kitchen renovations. He went back, got in his car, and drove towards Marinella. Just past the bridge, he noticed the house that he now knew belonged to Anna Tropeano. The urge got the better of him and he pulled up, stopped the car and got out.

It was a two-storey house, very well maintained, with a little garden all around. He approached the gate and pressed the button on the intercom.

'Who is it?'

'Inspector Montalbano. Am I disturbing you?'

'No, please come in.'

The gate opened, and at the same time, so did the front door of the house. Anna had changed her clothes and recovered her normal skin tone.

'You know something, Inspector? I was sure I would see you again before the day was over.'

SEVEN

'Were you eating lunch?'

'No, I'm not hungry. And anyway, all alone like this
... Michela used to come and eat here almost every day.
She hardly ever had lunch at the hotel.'

'May I make a suggestion?'

'Come inside, in the meantime.'

'Would you like to come to my house? It's right here,
just a stone's throw away.'

'Maybe your wife doesn't like surprise visitors ...'

'I live alone.'

Anna Tropeano didn't have to think twice about it.

'I'll meet you in your car.'

They rode in silence: Montalbano still surprised at
having invited her, Anna clearly amazed with herself for
having accepted.

Saturday was the day Adelina, the housekeeper, customarily devoted to a fastidious clean-up of the whole
house. Seeing it so spick and span, Montalbano took

comfort. Once on a Saturday he'd invited a married couple over, before Adelina had been. In the end, his friend's wife, just to set the table, had to clear away the mountain of dirty socks and underwear he'd left there for the house-keeper to wash.

As if she were already long familiar with the house, Anna went directly to the veranda, sat down on the bench, and looked out at the sea a short distance away. Montalbano set a folding table and an ashtray in front of her and went into the kitchen. Adelina had left him a large serving of haddock; in the refrigerator he found a sauce of anchovies and vinegar to add to it.

He went back out on the veranda. Anna was smoking and seemed more and more relaxed with each passing minute.

'It's so beautiful here.'

'Listen, would you like a little baked haddock?'

'Inspector, please don't be offended, but my stomach's in a knot. Let's do this: while you're eating, I'll have a glass of wine.'

*

Half an hour later, the inspector had gobbled up the triple serving of haddock and Anna had knocked back two glasses of wine.

'This is really good,' said Anna, refilling her glass.

'My father makes it ... used to make it. Would you like some coffee?'

'I won't turn down a coffee.'

The inspector opened a can of Yaucono, prepared the *napoletana*, and put it on the gas burner. He returned to the veranda.

'Please take this bottle away from me or I'll drink the whole thing,' said Anna.

Montalbano complied. The coffee was ready. He served it. Anna drank, savouring it in little sips.

'This is delicious. So strong. Where do you buy it?'

'I don't. A friend sends me a tin now and then from Puerto Rico.'

Anna pushed the cup away and lit her twentieth cigarette.

'What do you have to tell me?'

'There are some new developments.'

'What?'

'Maurizio Di Blasi.'

'You see? I didn't give you his name this morning because I knew you'd find it out with ease. He was the laughing stock of the whole town.'

'Fell head over heels for her?'

'Worse. Michela had become an obsession for him. I don't know if anyone told you, but Maurizio isn't right in the head. He's on the borderline between normal and mentally unstable. You know, there were two episodes where . . .'

'Tell me about them.'

'Once Michela and I went out to eat at a restaurant. A

little while later Maurizio arrived. He said hi and sat down at the table next to ours. But he ate very little and just stared at Michela the whole time. Then he suddenly started drooling and I nearly threw up. He was really drooling, believe me; he had a string of saliva hanging out of the side of his mouth. We had to leave.'

'And the other episode?'

'I'd gone up to the house to give Michela a hand. At the end of the day, she went to take a shower and afterwards came downstairs into the living room naked. It was very hot. She liked to go around the house with nothing on. Then she sat down in an armchair and we started talking. At a certain point, I heard a kind of moan coming from outside. I turned around to look. There was Maurizio, his face practically pasted against the window. Before I could say a word, he took a few steps back, bending over. And that's when I realized he was masturbating.'

She paused a moment, looked at the sea, and sighed.

'Poor kid,' she said under her breath.

Montalbano, for a moment, felt moved. That astonishing, wholly feminine capacity for deep understanding, for penetrating one's feelings, for being at once mother and lover, daughter and wife. He placed his hand on top of Anna's and she did not pull it away.

'Do you know he's disappeared?'

'Yes, I know. The same night as Michela. But . . .'

'But?'

'Inspector, can I speak to you frankly?'

'Why, what have we been doing up to now? But do me a favour, please call me Salvo.'

'If you call me Anna.'

'OK.'

'You know, you're wrong if you think Maurizio could ever have murdered Michela.'

'Give me one good reason.'

'Reason's got nothing to do with it. You know, people don't talk very willingly to the police. But if you, Salvo, were to conduct a poll, all of Vigàta would tell you Maurizio's not a murderer.'

'Anna, there's another development I haven't mentioned.'

Anna closed her eyes. She'd intuited that what the inspector was about to tell her would be hard to say and hard to hear.

He told her, without looking her in the face, gazing out at the sea. He didn't spare her any details.

Anna listened with her face in her hands, her elbows on the folding table. When the inspector had finished, she stood up, pale as a ghost.

'I need a bathroom.'

'I'll show you where it is.'

'I can find it myself.'

A few moments later, Montalbano heard her vomiting. He glanced at his watch; he still had an hour before

Emanuele Licalzi's visit. And, anyway, Mr Orthopedist from Bologna could certainly wait.

She returned with an air of determination and sat back down beside Montalbano.

'Salvo, what does the word "consent" mean to this pathologist?'

'The same thing it means to you or me: to agree to something.'

'But in certain cases one might appear to consent to something because there's no chance of resistance.'

'I know.'

'So I ask you: couldn't the murderer have done what he did to Michela without her wanting him to?'

'But there are certain details——'

'Forget them. First of all, we don't even know whether the killer abused a living woman or a corpse. Anyway, he had all the time in the world to arrange things in such a way that the police would lose their heads over it.'

Neither of them seemed to notice how familiar they'd become with each other.

'You're thinking something but not saying it,' said Anna.

'No, I have no problem saying it,' said Montalbano. 'At the moment, everything points to Maurizio. He was last seen at nine p.m. in front of the Bar Italia. Calling someone on his mobile phone.'

'Me,' said Anna.

The inspector literally jumped up from the bench.

'What did he want?'

'He was asking about Michela. I told him we'd parted shortly after seven, and that she would be stopping at the hotel before going to dinner at the Vassallos.'

'And what did he say?'

'He hung up without even saying goodbye.'

'That could be another point against him. He must have phoned the Vassallos next. Not finding her there, he guessed where she might be and caught up with her.'

'At the house.'

'No. They didn't arrive at the house until just after midnight.'

This time it was Anna's turn to jump.

'A witness told me,' Montalbano continued.

'He recognized Maurizio?'

'It was dark. He only saw a man and a woman get out of the Twingo and walk towards the house. Once inside, Maurizio and Michela make love. At a certain point Maurizio, who you say is a bit psycho, has an attack.'

'Never in a million years would Michela—'

'How did your friend react to Maurizio's stalking?'

'It bothered her. Sometimes she felt deeply sorry for...'

She stopped, realizing what Montalbano meant. Suddenly her face lost its freshness, and wrinkles appeared at the corners of her mouth.

'There are, however, a few things that don't make

sense,' said Montalbano, who suffered seeing her suffer. 'For example: would Maurizio have been capable, immediately after killing her, of coolly conceiving of stealing her clothes and bag to throw the police off the scent?'

'Are you kidding?'

'The real problem isn't finding out the details of the murder, but knowing where Michela was and what she did between the moment you left her and when the witness saw her. That's almost five hours, a pretty long time. And now we have to go because Dr Emanuele Licalzi is coming.'

As they were getting in the car, Montalbano, like a squid, squirted a black cloud over the whole picture.

'I'm not so sure your public opinion poll would be so unanimous on Maurizio's innocence. One person, at least, would have serious doubts.'

'Who?'

'His father, Engineer Di Blasi. Otherwise he would have had us out searching for his son.'

'It's natural for you to follow every lead. Oh, I just remembered something. When Maurizio rang me to ask about Michela, I told him to call her directly on her mobile phone. He said he'd already tried, but her phone was turned off.'

*

In the doorway to headquarters, he practically ran into Galluzzo, who was coming out.

'Back from your heroic exploit?'

'Yessir,' Galluzzo said uneasily. Fazio must have told him about his morning outburst.

'Is Inspector Augello in his office?'

'No sir.'

Galluzzo's uneasiness visibly increased.

'And where is he? Out clubbing other strikers?'

'He's in the hospital.'

'Eh? What happened?' Montalbano asked, worried.

'Hit on the head with a stone. They gave him three stitches. But they wanted to keep him there for observation and told me to come back at eight tonight. If everything's all right, I'll drive him home.'

The inspector's string of curses was interrupted by Catarella.

'Chief, Chief! First of all, Dr Latte with an *s* at the end called two times. He says as how you're asposta call him poissonally back straightaway. Then there was tree other phone calls I wrote down on dis little piece a paper.'

'Wipe your arse with it.'

*

Dr Emanuele Licalzi was a diminutive man in his sixties, with gold-rimmed glasses and dressed all in grey. He looked as if he'd just been pressed, shaved and manicured. Impeccable.

'How did you get here?'

'You mean from the airport? I rented a car and it took me almost three hours.'

'Have you already been to your hotel?'

'No. I've got my suitcase in the car. I'll go there afterwards.'

How could he be so wrinkle-free?

'Shall we go to the house? We can talk in the car, that way you'll save time.'

'As you wish, Inspector.'

They took the doctor's rented car.

'Did one of her lovers kill her?'

He didn't beat around the bush, this Emanuele Licalzi.

'We can't say yet. One thing is certain: she had repeated sexual intercourse.'

The doctor didn't flinch, but kept on driving, calm and untroubled, as if it wasn't his wife who'd just been killed.

'What makes you think she had a lover here?'

'Because she had one in Bologna.'

'Ah.'

'Yes, Michela even told me his name. Serravalle, I think. An antiquarian.'

'That's rather unusual.'

'She used to tell me everything. She really trusted me.'

'And did you also tell your wife everything?'

'Of course.'

'An exemplary marriage,' the inspector commented ironically.

Montalbano sometimes felt irretrievably left behind by the new lifestyles. He was a traditionalist. For him, an 'open relationship' meant nothing more than a husband and wife who cheated on each other and even had the gall to tell each other what they did under or on top of the covers.

'Not an exemplary marriage,' the unflappable Dr Licalzi corrected him, 'but a marriage of convenience.'

'For Michela or you?'

'For both of us.'

'Could you explain?'

'Certainly.'

He turned right.

'Where are you going?' the inspector asked. 'This road won't take you to Tre Fontane.'

'Sorry,' said the doctor, beginning a complex manoeuvre to turn the car round. 'But I haven't been down here for a year and a half, ever since I got married. Michela saw to all the construction herself; I've only seen photographs. Speaking of photographs, I packed a few of Michela in my suitcase. I thought they might be of some use to you.'

'You know what? The murder victim might not even be your wife.'

'Are you serious?'

'Yes. Nobody has officially identified the body, and none of the people who've seen it actually knew her when she was alive. When we've finished here, I'll talk to the pathologist about identifying her. How long do you plan on staying?'

'Two, three days at the most. I want to take Michela back to Bologna.'

'Doctor, I'm going to ask you a question, and I won't ask you again. Where were you Wednesday evening, and what were you doing?'

'Wednesday? I was at the hospital, operating late into the night.'

'You were telling me about your marriage.'

'Yes. Well, I met Michela three years ago. Her brother, who lives in New York now, had a rather severe compound fracture in his foot, and she brought him to the hospital. I liked her at once. She was very beautiful, but what struck me most was her character. She was always ready to see the bright side of things. She lost both her parents before the age of fifteen and was brought up by an uncle who one day saw fit to rape her. To make a long story short, she was desperate to find a place to live. For years she was the mistress of an industrialist, but he eventually disposed of her with a tidy sum of money that helped her get along for a while. Michela could have had any man she wanted, but, basically, it humiliated her to be a kept woman.'

'Did you ask Michela to become your mistress, and she refused?'

For the first time, a hint of a smile appeared on Emanuele Licalzi's impassive face.

'You're on the wrong track entirely, Inspector. Oh, by the way, Michela told me she'd bought a bottle-green Twingo to get around town. Do you know what's become of it?'

'It had an accident.'

'Michela never did know how to drive.'

'Your wife was entirely without fault in this case. The car was properly parked in front of the drive to the house and somebody ran into it.'

'And how do you know this?'

'It was us, the police, who ran into it. At the time, however, we still didn't know—'

'What an odd story.'

'I'll tell it to you sometime. Anyhow, it was the accident that led us to discover the body.'

'Do you think I could have the car back?'

'I don't see any reason why not.'

'I could resell it to somebody in Vigàta who deals in used cars, don't you think?'

Montalbano didn't answer. He didn't give a shit about what happened to the car.

'That's the house there on the right, isn't it? I think I recognize it from the photograph.'

'That's it.'

Dr Licalzi executed an elegant manoeuvre, pulled up in front of the drive, got out of the car, and stood looking at the house with the detached curiosity of a sightseer.

'Nice. What did we come here for?'

'I don't really know, truth be told,' Montalbano said grumpily. Dr Licalzi knew how to get on his nerves. He decided to shake him up a little.

'You know, some people think it was Maurizio Di Blasi, the son of your cousin the engineer, who killed your wife.'

'Really? I don't know him. When I came here two and a half years ago, he was in Palermo for his studies. I'm told the poor boy's a half-wit.'

So there.

'Shall we go inside?'

'Wait, I don't want to forget.'

He opened the boot of the car, took out the elegant suitcase that was inside, and removed a large envelope from it.

'The photos of Michela.'

Montalbano slipped it in his jacket pocket. As he was doing this, the doctor extracted a bunch of keys from his own pocket.

'Are those to the house?'

'Yes. I knew where Michela kept them at our place in Bologna. They're the extra set.'

Now I'm going to start kicking the guy, thought the inspector.

'You never finished telling me why your marriage was as convenient for you as it was for your wife.'

'Well, it was convenient for Michela because she was marrying a rich man, even if he was thirty years older, and it was convenient for me because it put to rest certain rumours that were threatening to harm me at a crucial moment of my career. People had started saying I'd become a homosexual, since nobody'd seen me socially with a woman for more than ten years.'

'And was it true you no longer frequented women?'

'Why would I, Inspector? At age fifty I became impotent. Irreversibly.'

EIGHT

'Nice,' said Dr Licalzi again after having a look around the living room.

Didn't he know how to say anything else?

'Here's the kitchen,' the inspector said, adding, 'Eat in.'

All of a sudden he felt enraged at himself. How did that 'eat in' slip out? What was it supposed to mean? He felt like an estate agent showing a house to a prospective client.

'Next to it is the bathroom. Go and have a look yourself,' he said rudely.

The doctor didn't notice, or pretended not to notice, the tone of voice. He opened the bathroom door, stuck his head in for the briefest of peeks and reclosed it.

'Nice.'

Montalbano felt his hands trembling. He distinctly saw the newspaper headline: POLICE INSPECTOR GOES SUDDENLY BERSERK, ATTACKS HUSBAND OF MURDER VICTIM.

'Upstairs there's a small guest room, a large bathroom and the main bedroom. Go up.'

The doctor obeyed. Montalbano remained downstairs in the living room, lit a cigarette, and took the envelope of photographs of Michela out of his pocket. Gorgeous. Her face, which he had only seen distorted in pain and horror, had a smiling, open expression.

Finishing his cigarette, he realized the doctor hadn't come back down.

'Dr Licalzi?'

No answer. He bounded up the stairs. The doctor was standing in a corner of the bedroom, hands covering his face, shoulders heaving as he sobbed.

The inspector was mystified. This was the last reaction he would have expected. He went up to Licalzi and put a hand on his back.

'Try to be brave.'

The doctor shrugged him off with an almost childish gesture and kept on weeping, face hidden in his hands.

'Poor Michela! Poor Michela!'

It wasn't put on. The tears, the sorrowful voice, were real.

Montalbano took him firmly by the arm.

'Let's go downstairs.'

The doctor let himself be led, moving away without looking at the bed, the shredded, bloodstained sheet. He was a physician, and he knew what Michela must have felt during her last moments alive. But if Licalzi was a physician, Montalbano was a policeman, and as soon as he saw him in tears, he knew the man would no longer be able to maintain the mask of indifference he'd put on. The armour of detachment he customarily wore, perhaps to compensate for the disgrace of impotence, had fallen apart.

'Forgive me,' said Licalzi, sitting down in an armchair. 'I didn't imagine ... It's just horrible to die like that. The killer held her face down against the mattress, didn't he?'

'Yes.'

'I was very fond of Michela, very. She had become like a daughter to me, you know.'

Tears started streaming down his face again, and he wiped them away, without much success, with a handkerchief.

'Why did she decide to build this house here instead of somewhere else?' the inspector asked.

'She had always mythologized Sicily, without ever knowing the place. The first time she came for a visit, she became enchanted with it. I think she wanted to create a refuge for herself here. See that little display cabinet? Those are her things in there, personal trinkets she brought down with her from Bologna. It says a lot about her intentions, don't you think?'

'Do you want to check and see if anything's missing?'

The doctor got up and went over to the display cabinet.

'May I open it?'

'Of course.'

The doctor stared at it a long time, then raised a hand and picked up the old violin case, opened it, showed the inspector the instrument that was inside, reclosed it, put it back in its place, and shut the door.

'At a glance, there doesn't seem to be anything missing.'

'Did your wife play the violin?'

'No, she didn't play the violin or any other instrument. It belonged to her maternal grandfather from Cremona, who made them. And now, Inspector, if it's all right with you, I want you to tell me everything.'

Montalbano told him everything, from the accident on Thursday morning to what Dr Pasquano had reported to him.

Emanuele Licalzi, when it was over, remained silent for a spell, then said only two words, 'Genetic finger-printing.'

'I'm not really up on scientific jargon.'

'Sorry. I was referring to the disappearance of her clothes and shoes.'

'Might be a decoy.'

'Maybe. But it might also be that the killer felt he had no choice but to get rid of them.'

'Because he'd soiled them?' asked Montalbano, thinking of Signora Clementina's thesis.

'The coroner said there was no trace of seminal fluid, right?'

'Yes.'

'That reinforces my hypothesis, that the killer didn't

want to leave the slightest biological trace that could be used in DNA testing – that's what I meant by genetic fingerprinting. Real fingerprints can be wiped away, but what can you do about semen, hair, skin? The killer tried to make a clean sweep.'

'Right,' said the inspector.

'Excuse me, but if you don't have anything else to tell me, I'd like to leave this place. I'm starting to feel tired.'

The doctor locked the front door with his key, Montalbano put the seals back in place, and they left.

'Have you got a mobile phone?'

The doctor handed him his. The inspector called Pasquano, and they decided on ten o'clock the following morning for identifying the body.

'Will you come, too?'

'I should, but I can't. I have an engagement outside of Vigàta. I'll send one of my men for you, and he can take you there.'

He had Licalzi drop him off at the first houses on the outskirts of town. He needed a little walk.

*

'Chief! Chief! Dr Latte with an *s* at the end called tree times, more and more pissed off each time, with all due respect. You're asposta call 'im 'mediately in poisson.'

'Hello, Dr Lattes? Montalbano here.'

'Thank heavens! Come to Montelusa immediately, the commissioner wants to talk to you.'

He hung up. It must be something serious, since the Caffè-Lattes wasn't even lukewarm.

As he was turning the key in the ignition, he saw a squad car pull up with Galluzzo at the wheel.

'Any news of Inspector Augello?'

'Yeah, the hospital called to say they were discharging him. I went and picked him up and drove him home.'

To hell with the commissioner and his urgency. He stopped at Mimì's first.

'How are you feeling, you intrepid defender of capital?'

'My head feels like it could burst.'

'That'll teach you.'

Mimì Augello was sitting in an armchair, head bandaged, face pale.

'I once got clobbered on the head by some guy with a blackjack. They had to give me seven stitches, and I still wasn't in as bad a shape as you.'

'I guess you thought you took your clobbering for a worthy cause. You got to feel clobbered and gratified at the same time.'

'Mimì, when you put your mind to it, you can be a real arsehole.'

'You too, Salvo. I was going to phone you tonight to tell you I don't think I'm in any condition to drive tomorrow.'

'We'll go to your sister's another time.'

'No, you go ahead, Salvo. She was so insistent on seeing you.'

'But do you know why?'

'I haven't the slightest idea.'

'Listen, tell you what. I'll go, but I want you to go to the Hotel Jolly tomorrow morning at nine thirty to pick up Dr Licalzi, who arrived today, and take him to the mortuary. OK?'

*

'How *are* you, old friend? Eh? You look a bit down. Chin up, old boy. *Sursum corda!* That's what we used to say in the days of Azione Cattolica.'

The Caffè-Lattes had warmed up dangerously. Montalbano began to feel worried.

'I'll go and inform the commissioner at once.'

He vanished, then reappeared.

'The commissioner's momentarily unavailable. Come, let me show you into the waiting room. Would you like a coffee or something else to drink?'

'No, thank you.'

Dr Lattes, after flashing him a broad, paternal smile, disappeared. Montalbano felt certain the commissioner had condemned him to a slow and painful death. The garrotte, perhaps.

On the table in the dismal little waiting room there was a magazine, *Famiglia Cristiana*, and a newspaper,

L'Osservatore Romano, manifest signs of Dr Lattes's presence in the commissioner's office. He picked up the magazine and began reading an article on Susanna Tamaro.

'Inspector! Inspector!'

A hand was shaking his shoulder. He opened his eyes and saw a uniformed policeman.

'The commissioner is waiting for you.'

Jesus! He'd fallen into a deep sleep. Looking at his watch, he saw that it was eight o'clock. The fucker had made him wait two hours.

'Good evening, Mr Commissioner.'

The noble Luca Bonetti-Alderighi didn't answer, didn't even say 'Shoo' or 'Get out of here', but only continued staring at a computer screen. The inspector contemplated his superior's disturbing hairdo, which was very full with a great big tuft in the middle that curled back like certain turds deposited in the open country. An exact replica of the coif of that criminally insane psychiatrist who'd triggered all the butchery in Bosnia.

'What was his name?'

It was too late when he realized that, still dazed from sleep, he'd spoken aloud.

'What was whose name?' asked the commissioner, finally looking up at him.

'Never mind,' said Montalbano.

The commissioner kept looking at him with an expression that combined contempt and commiseration,

apparently discerning unmistakable signs of senile demen-
tia in the inspector.

'I'm going to speak very frankly, Montalbano. I don't
have a very high opinion of you.'

'Nor I of you,' the inspector replied bluntly.

'Good. At least things are clear between us. I called
you here to tell you that I'm taking you off the Licalzi
murder case. I've handed it over to Panzacchi, captain of
the Flying Squad, to whom the investigation should have
fallen by rights in the first place.'

Ernesto Panzacchi was a loyal follower whom Bonetti-
Alderighi had brought with him to Montelusa.

'May I ask you why, though I couldn't care less?'

'You committed a foolish act that created a serious
impediment for Dr Arquà.'

'Did he write that in his report?'

'No, he didn't write it in his report. He very generously
didn't want to damage your career. But then he repented
and told me the whole story.'

'Ah, these repenters!' commented the inspector.

'Do you have something against repenters?'

'Let's drop it.'

He left without even saying goodbye.

'I'm going to take disciplinary measures!' Bonetti-
Alderighi shouted at his back.

*

The forensics laboratory was located in the building's basement.

'Is Dr Arquà in?'

'He's in his office.'

Montalbano barged in without knocking.

'Hello, Arquà. I'm on my way to the commissioner's, he wants to see me. Thought I'd drop in and see if you have any news for me.'

Vanni Arquà was obviously embarrassed. But since Montalbano had led him to believe he hadn't yet seen the commissioner, he decided to answer as if he didn't know the inspector was no longer in charge of the investigation.

'The murderer cleaned everything very carefully. We found a lot of fingerprints, but they clearly had nothing to do with the homicide.'

'Why not?'

'Because they were all yours, Inspector. You continue to be very, very careless.'

'Oh, listen, Arquà. Did you know that it's a sin to rat on someone? Ask Dr Lattes. You'll have to repent all over again.'

*

'Hey, Chief! Mr Cacano called another time again! Said as how he 'membered somethin's might be maybe impor'ant. I wrote 'is number down on dis here piece a paper.'

Eyeing the little square of paper, Montalbano felt his body start to itch all over. Catarella had written the numbers down in such a way that a three might be a five or a nine, the two a four, the five a six, and so on.

'Hey, Cat! What kind of number is this, anyway?'

'That's the number, Chief. Cacano's number. What's written down.'

Before reaching Gillo Jàcono, he spoke to a bar, the Jacopetti family and one Dr Balzani.

By the fourth attempt, he was very discouraged.

'Hello? Who'm I speaking with? This is Inspector Montalbano.'

'Ah, Inspector, it's very good you called. I was on my way out.'

'You were looking for me?'

'A certain detail came back to me, I'm not sure if it'll be of any use to you. The man I saw getting out of the Twingo and walk towards the house with a woman had a suitcase in his hand.'

'Are you sure about that?'

'Absolutely.'

'An overnight bag?'

'No, Inspector, it was pretty big. But...'

'Yes?'

'I had the impression the man was carrying it without effort, as if there wasn't much in it.'

'Thank you, Mr Jàcono. Please call me when you get back.'

He looked up the Vassallos' number in the phone book and dialled it.

'Inspector! I came to your office as we'd agreed, but you weren't there. I waited a while, and then I had to go.'

'Please forgive me. Listen, Mr Vassallo, last Wednesday evening, when you were waiting for Mrs Licalzi to come to dinner, did anybody call you?'

'Well, a friend of mine from Venice did, and so did our daughter, who lives in Catania — I'm sure that's of no interest to you. But, in fact, what I wanted to tell you this afternoon was that Maurizio Di Blasi did call twice that evening. Just after nine o'clock, and again just after ten. He was looking for Michela.'

*

The unpleasantness of his meeting with the commissioner needed to be blotted out with a solemn feast. The Trattoria San Calogero was closed, but he remembered a friend telling him that right at the gates to Joppolo Giancaxio, a little town about twenty kilometres inland from Vigàta, there was an *osteria* that was worth the trouble. He got in his car, and found the place immediately: it was called La Cacciatora. Naturally, they had no game. The owner-cashier-waiter, who had a big handlebar moustache and vaguely resembled the Gentleman King, Victor Emmanuel II, started things off by putting a hefty serving of delicious *caponata* in front of him. 'A joyous start is the best of guides,' wrote Boiardo, and Montalbano decided to let himself be guided.

'What will you have?'

'Bring me whatever you like.'

The Gentleman King smiled, appreciating the vote of confidence.

As a first course, he served him a large dish of macaroni in a light sauce dubbed *foco vivo* or 'live fire' (olive oil, garlic, lots of hot red pepper, salt), which the inspector was forced to wash down with half a bottle of wine. For the second course, he ate a substantial portion of lamb *alla cacciatora* that had a pleasant fragrance of onion and oregano. He closed with a ricotta cheesecake and small glass of anisette as a viaticum and boost for his digestive system. He paid the bill, a pittance, and exchanged a handshake and smile with the Gentleman King.

'Excuse me, who's the cook?'

'My wife.'

'Please give her my compliments.'

'I will.'

On the drive back, instead of heading towards Monte-lusa, he turned onto the road for Fiacca, which brought him home to Marinella from the direction opposite the one he usually took when coming from Vigàta. It took him half an hour longer, but in compensation he avoided passing in front of Anna Tropeano's house. He was certain he would have stopped, there was no getting around it, and he would have cut a ridiculous figure in the young woman's eyes. He phoned Mimì Augello.

'How are you feeling?'

'Terrible.'

'Listen, forget what I said to you. You can stay at home tomorrow morning. Since the matter's no longer in our hands, I'll send Fazio to accompany Dr Licalzi.'

'What do you mean, it's no longer in our hands?'

'The commissioner took the case away from me. Passed it on to the captain of the Flying Squad.'

'Why did he do that?'

'Because two does not equal three. Want me to tell your sister anything?'

'Don't tell her they broke my head open, for Christ's sake, or she'll think I'm on my deathbed.'

'Take care, Mimì.'

*

'Hello, Fazio? Montalbano here.'

'What's wrong, Chief?'

He told him to pass all phone calls relating to the case on to the Montelusa Flying Squad, and he explained what he was supposed to do with Licalzi.

*

'Hello, Livia? Salvo here. How are you doing?'

'All right, I guess.'

'What's with this tone? The other night you hung up on me before I had a chance to say anything.'

'You phoned me in the middle of the night!'

'But it was the first free moment I had!'

'Poor thing! Allow me to point out that you, between

thunderstorms, shoot-outs and ambushes, have very cleverly managed to avoid answering the very specific question I asked you last Wednesday evening.'

'I wanted to tell you I'm going to see François tomorrow.'

'With Mimì?'

'No, Mimì was hit—'

'Oh my God! Is it serious?'

She and Mimì had a soft spot for each other.

'Let me finish! He was hit on the head with a stone. Chickenshit, three stitches. So I'm going to go alone. Mimì's sister wants to talk to me.'

'About François?'

'Who else?'

'Oh my God. He must be sick. I'm going to phone her right away!'

'Come on, those people go to bed at sunset! I'll phone you tomorrow evening, as soon as I get home.'

'Let me know. I mean it. I'm not going to sleep a wink tonight.'

NINE

To go from Vigàta to Calapiano, anyone with any sense, and with an even superficial knowledge of Sicilian roads, would first have taken the superhighway to Catania, exited onto the road that turns back inland towards Troìna at 1,120 metres' elevation, descended to Gagliano at 751 metres by way of a sort of mule track that received its first and last layer of tarmac fifty years ago in the early days of regional autonomy, and finally reached Calapiano via a provincial road that clearly refused to be known as such, its true aspiration being to resume the outward appearance of the earthquake-ravaged country trail it had once been. But that wasn't the end of it. The farm belonging to Mimì's sister and her husband was four kilometres outside town, and one reached it by following a winding strip of gravel on which even goats had doubts about setting a single one of their four available hooves. This was what one might call, for lack of a better term, the best route, the one Mimì Augello always took, its difficulties and discomforts not coming entirely to the fore until the final stretch.

Naturally, Montalbano did not take it. He chose instead to cut across the island, and thus found himself, from the start, travelling roads along which the few surviving peasants interrupted their labours to gaze in amazement at the car passing recklessly by. They would talk about it at home in the evening with their children, 'Know what? This mornin' a car drove by!'

This, however, was the Sicily the inspector liked best: harsh, spare in vegetation, on whose soil it seemed (and was) impossible to live, and where he could still run across, though more and more rarely, a man in gaiters and cap, rifle on shoulder, who would raise two fingers to his visor and salute him from the back of a mule.

The sky was clear and bright and openly declared its determination to remain so until evening. It was almost hot. But the open windows did not prevent the interior of the car from becoming permeated with the delightful aromas filtering out of the packages large and small literally stuffed into the backseat. Before leaving, Montalbano had stopped at the Caffè Albanese, which made the best pastries in all of Vigàta, and bought twenty cannoli, fresh out of the oven, ten kilos' worth of *tetù*, *taralli*, *viscotti regina* and Palermitan *mostaccioli* — all long-lasting cookies — as well as some marzipan fruits, and, to crown it all, a colourful *cassata* that weighed five kilos all by itself.

He arrived in the early afternoon and worked out that

the journey had taken him more than four hours. The big farmhouse looked empty to him; only the smoking chimney said there was someone at home. He tooted his horn, and a moment later Franca, Mimì's sister, appeared in the doorway. She was a blonde Sicilian over forty, a strong, tall woman. She eyed the car, which she didn't recognize, as she wiped her hands on her apron.

'It's Montalbano,' said the inspector, opening the car door and getting out.

Franca ran up to him with a big smile on her face and embraced him.

'Where's Mimì?'

'At the last minute he couldn't come. He felt really bad about it.'

Franca looked at him. Montalbano was unable to tell a lie to people he respected; he would stammer, blush and look away.

'I'm going to phone Mimì,' Franca said decisively, walking back into the house. By some miracle Montalbano managed to load himself up with all the packages, big and small, and followed her inside a few minutes later.

Franca was just hanging up.

'He's still got a headache.'

'Reassured now? Believe me, it was nothing,' said the inspector, unloading the parcels onto the table.

'And what's this?' said Franca. 'Are you trying to turn this place into a pastry shop?'

She put the sweets in the fridge.

'How are you, Salvo?'

'Fine. And how's everybody here?'

'We're all fine, thank God. And you won't believe François. He's shot right up, getting taller by the day.'

'Where are they?'

'Out and about. But when I ring the bell for lunch, they'll all come running. Are you staying the night with us? I prepared a room for you.'

'Thanks, Franca, but you know I can't. I have to leave by five at the latest. I can't be like your brother and race along these roads like a madman.'

'Go and wash, then.'

He returned fifteen minutes later, refreshed. Franca was setting the table for nine people. The inspector decided this was perhaps the right moment.

'Mimì said you wanted to talk to me.'

'Later, later,' Franca said brusquely. 'Hungry?'

'Well, yes.'

'Want a little wheat bread? I took it out of the oven less than an hour ago. Shall I prepare you some?'

Without waiting for an answer, she cut two slices from a loaf, dressed them in olive oil, salt and black pepper, adding a slice of pecorino cheese, put this all together to form a sandwich, and handed it to him.

Montalbano went outside, sat down on a bench next to the door, and, at the first bite, felt forty years younger. He was a little kid again. This was bread the way his grandmother used to make it for him.

It was meant to be eaten in the sun, while thinking of nothing, only relishing being in harmony with one's body, the earth, and the smell of the grass. A moment later he heard shouting and saw three children chasing after each other, pushing and trying to trip one another. They were Giuseppe, nine years old, his brother, Domenico, namesake of his uncle Mimì and the same age as François, and François himself.

The inspector gazed at him, wonderstruck. He'd become the tallest of the lot, the most energetic and pugnacious. How the devil had he managed to undergo such a metamorphosis in the two short months since the inspector had last seen him?

Montalbano ran over to him, arms open wide. François, recognizing him, stopped at once as his companions turned and headed towards the house. Montalbano squatted down, arms still open.

'Hi, François.'

The child broke into a sprint, swerving around him.

'Hi,' he said.

The inspector watched him disappear into the house. What was going on? Why had he read no joy in the little boy's eyes? Montalbano tried to console himself; maybe it was some kind of childish resentment; François probably felt neglected by him.

At the two ends of the table sat the inspector and Aldo Gagliardo, Franca's husband, a man of few words who was as hale and hearty as his name. To Montalbano's right sat Franca, followed by the three children. François was the farthest away, sitting next to Aldo. To his left were three youths around twenty years of age, Mario, Giacomo and Ernst. The first two were university students who earned their daily bread working in the fields; the third was a German passing through who told Montalbano he hoped to stay another three months. The lunch, consisting of pasta with sausage sauce and a second course of grilled sausage, went rather quickly. Aldo and his three helpers were in a hurry to get back to work. They all pounced on the sweets the inspector had brought. Then, at a nod of the head from Aldo, they got up and went out.

'Let me make you another coffee,' said Franca. Montalbano felt uneasy. He'd seen Aldo exchange a fleeting glance of understanding with his wife before leaving. Franca served the coffee and sat down in front of the inspector.

'It's a serious matter,' she began.

At that exact moment François came back in with a resolute expression on his face, hands clenched in fists at his sides. He stopped in front of Montalbano, looked him long and hard in the eye, and said in a quavering voice, 'You're not going to take me away from my brothers.'

Then he turned and ran out. It was a heavy blow. Montalbano felt his mouth go dry. He said the first thing that came into his head, and unfortunately it was something stupid.

'His Italian's become so good!'

*

'What I was going to say, well, the boy just said it,' said Franca. 'And, mind you, both Aldo and I have done nothing but talk to him about Livia and you, and how eventually he's going to live with the two of you, and how much you all love each other, and how much more you'll all love each other one day. But there was nothing doing. The idea entered his head without warning one night about a month ago. I was sleeping, and then I felt something touch my arm. It was him.

' "You feel sick?"

' "No."

' "Then what's wrong?"

' "I'm afraid."

' "Afraid of what?"

' "That Salvo's going to come and take me away."

'And every now and then, when he's playing, when he's eating, the thought will pop into his head, and he'll turn all gloomy and even start misbehaving.'

Franca kept on talking, but Montalbano was no longer listening. He was lost in a memory from the time he was the same age as François, actually one year younger. His grandmother was dying, his mother had fallen gravely ill (though he didn't realize these things until later), and his father, to take better care of them, had taken him to the house of his sister Carmela, who was married to the owner of a chaotic shop, a kind, mild man named Pippo Sciortino. They didn't have any children. Sometime later, his father came back to get him, wearing a black tie and, he remembered very clearly, a broad black band around his left arm. He refused to go.

'I'm not coming. I'm staying with Carmela and Pippo. My name is Sciortino now.'

He could still see the sorrowful look on his father's face, and the embarrassed expressions of Pippo and Carmela.

'...because children aren't just parcels that you can deposit here or there whenever you feel like it,' Franca concluded.

✻

On the way home he took the easier route and was already back in Vigàta by nine o'clock. He decided to drop in on Mimì Augello.

'You look better.'

'This afternoon I managed to get some sleep. So, you couldn't pull the wool over Franca's eyes, eh? She called me all worried.'

'She's a very, very intelligent woman.'

'What did she want to talk to you about?'

'François. There's a problem.'

'The kid's grown attached to them?'

'How did you know? Did your sister tell you?'

'She hasn't said a thing about it to me. But is it so hard to figure out? I kind of imagined it would turn out this way.'

Montalbano made a dark face.

'I can understand how you might feel hurt,' said Mimì, 'but who's to say it's not actually a stroke of luck?'

'For François?'

'For François, too. But, above all, for you, Salvo. You're not cut out to be a father, not even an adoptive father.'

*

Just past the bridge, he noticed that the lights were on in Anna's house. He pulled up and got out of the car.

'Who is it?'

'Salvo.'

Anna opened the door and showed him into the dining room. She was watching a movie, but immediately turned off the television.

'Want a little whisky?'

'Sure. Neat.'

'You down?'

'A little.'

'It's not easy to stomach.'

'No, it's not.'

He thought a moment about what Anna had just said to him: it's not easy to stomach. How on earth did she know about François?

'But, Anna, how did you find out?'

'It was on TV, on the evening report.'

What was she talking about?

'What station?'

'TeleVigàta. They said the commissioner had assigned the Licalzi murder case to the captain of the Flying Squad.'

Montalbano started laughing.

'You think I give a shit about that? I was talking about something else!'

'Then tell me why you're feeling down.'

'I'll tell you another time. I'm sorry.'

'Did you ever meet Michela's husband?'

'Yeah, yesterday afternoon.'

'Did he tell you about his unconsummated marriage?'

'You knew?'

'Yes, Michela had told me about it. She was very fond of him, you know. But in those circumstances, taking a lover wasn't really a betrayal. The doctor knew about it.'

The phone rang in another room. Anna went and answered, then returned in an agitated state.

'That was a friend. She heard that about half an hour ago, this captain of the Flying Squad went to the home of Engineer Di Blasi and brought him into Montelusa headquarters. What do they want from him?'

'Simple. They want to know where Maurizio is.'

'So they already suspect him!'

'It's the most obvious thing, Anna. And Captain Ernesto Panzacchi, chief of the Flying Squad, is an utterly obvious man. Well, thanks for the whisky. Goodnight.'

'What, you're going to leave just like that?'

'I'm sorry, I'm tired. I'll see you tomorrow.'

A dense, heavy gloom had suddenly come over him.

✻

He opened the door to his home with a kick and ran to answer the telephone.

'What the fuck, Salvo! Some friend!'

He recognized the voice of Nicolò Zito, newsman for the Free Channel, with whom he had a genuine friendship.

'Is it true you're no longer on the case? I didn't report it because I wanted to check it with you first. But if it's true, why didn't you tell me?'

'I'm sorry, Nicolò, it happened late last night, and I left the house early this morning. I went to see François.'

'Want me to do anything on television?'

'No, that's all right, thanks. Oh, but here's something you don't already know that'll make up for everything. Captain Panzacchi brought Aurelio Di Blasi, the construction engineer from Vigàta, into Montelusa headquarters for questioning.'

'Did *he* kill her?'

'No, the real suspect is his son Maurizio, who disappeared the same night that Mrs Licalzi was killed. He, the kid, was madly in love with her. Oh, and another thing. The victim's husband is in Montelusa at the moment, at the Hotel Jolly.'

'Salvo, if they kick you off the police force, I'll hire you here. Watch the midnight news. And thanks. Really.'

The gloom lifted as Montalbano set down the receiver.

That would fix Captain Ernesto Panzacchi. At midnight all his moves would enter the public domain.

*

He really didn't feel like eating. He undressed, got into the shower, and stayed there a long time. Emerging, he put on a clean pair of briefs and undershirt. Now came the hard part.

'Livia.'

'Oh, Salvo, I've been waiting so long for your call! How is François?'

'He's great. He's grown a lot.'

'Did you notice the progress he's made? Every week, when I call, his Italian gets better and better. He's become so good at making himself understood, don't you think?'

'Even too good.'

Livia paid no attention; she had another pressing question.

'What did Franca want?'

'She wanted to talk to me about François.'

'Why, is he too energetic? Disobedient?'

'Livia, that's not the problem. Maybe we made a

mistake keeping him so long with Franca and her husband. The boy has grown attached to them. He told me he doesn't want to leave them.'

'He told you himself?'

'Yes, of his own free will.'

'Of his own free will! You're such an idiot!'

'Why?'

'Because they told him to say that to you! They want to take him away from us! They need free labour for their farm, the rascals!'

'Livia, you're talking nonsense.'

'No, it's true, I tell you! They want to keep him for themselves! And you're happy to turn him over to them!'

'Livia, try to be rational.'

'Oh, I'm rational, all right, I'm very rational! And I'll show you and those two kidnappers just how rational I am!'

She hung up. Without putting on any additional clothing, the inspector went and sat out on the veranda, lit a cigarette, and finally gave free rein to his melancholy. François, by now, was a lost cause, despite the fact that Franca was leaving the decision up to Livia and him. The truth of the matter, plain and unvarnished, was what Mimì's sister had said to him: children aren't parcels that you can deposit here or there whenever you feel like it. You can't not take their feelings into account. Rapisardi, the lawyer who was following the adoption proceedings for the inspector, had told him it would take another six months at least. And that would give François all the time in the world to put down roots at the Gagliardo home. Livia was crazy if she thought Franca could ever put words in the child's mouth. He, Montalbano, had got a good look at François's expression when he ran up to embrace him. He remembered those eyes well now: there was fear in them, and childish hatred. Besides, he could understand how the kid felt. He'd already lost his mother and was afraid to lose his new family. In the end, he and Livia had spent very little time with the boy; their images hadn't taken long to fade in his mind. Montalbano felt that he would never, ever have the courage to inflict another trauma on François. He had no right. Nor did Livia. The kid was lost to them for ever. For his part, he would consent to the child's remaining with Aldo and Franca, who were happy to adopt him. But now he felt cold, so he got up and went inside.

*

'Were you sleeping, Chief? Fazio here. I wanted to inform you that we held a meeting this afternoon. And we wrote a letter of protest to the commissioner. Everybody signed it, starting with Inspector Augello. Let me read it to you: "We the undersigned, as members of Central Police Headquarters of Vigàta, deplore—"'

'Wait. Did you send it?'

'Yes, Chief.'

'What a bunch of fucking idiots! You could at least have let me know before sending it!'

'Why? Before or after, what's the difference?'

'I would have talked you out of making such a stupid move!'

He cut off the connection, enraged.

*

It took him a while to fall asleep. Then an hour later he woke up, turned on the light, and sat up in bed. Something like a flash had made him open his eyes. During his visit to the crime scene with Dr Licalzi, something – a word, a sound – had seemed, well, dissonant. What was it? He lashed out at himself. 'What the fuck do you care? The case isn't yours any more.'

He turned off the light and lay back down.

'And neither is François,' he added bitterly.

TEN

The next morning, at headquarters, the staff was almost at full strength: Augello, Fazio, Germanà, Gallo, Galluzzo, Giallombardo, Tortorella and Grasso. The only one missing was Catarella, who had a legitimate excuse for his absence, attending the first class in his computer training course. Everyone was wearing a long face fit for the Day of the Dead, avoiding Montalbano as if he were contagious, not looking him in the eye. They'd been doubly offended: first by the commissioner, who'd taken the investigation away from their chief just to spite him, and, second, by their chief himself, who had reacted meanly to their letter of protest to the commissioner. Not only had he not thanked them — what can you do, the inspector was just that way — but he had called them a bunch of fucking idiots, and Fazio had told them this.

All present, therefore, but all bored to death, because, except for the Licalzi homicide, it had been two months since anything substantial had happened. For example, the

Cuffaro and Sinagra families, two criminal gangs perpetually engaged in a turf war who were in the custom of leaving behind, with near-perfect regularity, one corpse per month (one month a Cuffaro, the next month a Sinagra), seemed to have lost their enthusiasm a while back. Such indeed had been the case ever since Giosuè Cuffaro, after being arrested and having suddenly repented of his crimes, had helped lock up Peppuccio Sinagra, who, after being arrested and having suddenly repented of his crimes, had helped put away Antonio Smecca, a cousin of the Cuffaros, who, after suddenly repenting of his crimes, had pulled the plug on Cicco Lo Càrmine, of the Sinagra gang, who . . .

The only noise to be heard in Vigàta had been made the previous month, at the San Gerlando festival, by the firework display.

'The number-one bosses are all in jail!' Commissioner Bonetti-Alderighi had triumphantly exclaimed at a jam-packed press conference.

And the five-star bosses are still in place, the inspector had thought.

That morning Grasso, who had taken Catarella's place at the switchboard, was doing crossword puzzles, Gallo and Galluzzo were testing each other's mettle at the card game of *scopa*, Giallombardo and Tortorella were engrossed in a game of draughts, and the others were either reading or contemplating the wall. The place, in short, was buzzing with activity.

On his desk Montalbano found a mountain of papers

to be signed and various other matters to be dealt with. Subtle revenge on the part of his men?

*

The bomb, unexpectedly, exploded at one, when the inspector, his right arm stiffening, was considering going out to eat.

'Chief, there's a lady, Anna Tropeano, asking for you. She seems upset,' said Grasso.

'Salvo! My God! On the TV news headlines they said Maurizio's been killed!'

As there weren't any television sets at the police station, Montalbano shot out of his office, on his way down to the Bar Italia.

Fazio intercepted him.

'Chief, what's happening?'

'They killed Maurizio Di Blasi.'

Gelsomino, the owner of the bar, along with two clients, were staring open-mouthed at the television screen, where a TeleVigàta reporter was talking about the incident.

'... and during this night-long interrogation of the engineer Aurelio Di Blasi, Ernesto Panzacchi, captain of the Flying Squad, surmised that Di Blasi's son, Maurizio, a prime suspect in the Michela Licalzi murder case, might be hiding out at a country house belonging to the Di Blasi family in the Raffadali area. The father, however, maintained that his son had not taken refuge there, since he'd gone there himself to look for him the previous day. At ten o'clock this morning, Captain Panzacchi went to Raffadali with six other police officers and began a detailed search of the house, which is rather large. Suddenly one of the policemen spotted a man running along one of the slopes of the barren hill that stands almost directly behind the house. Giving chase, Captain Panzacchi and his men found the cave into which young Di Blasi had fled. After properly positioning his men outside, Captain Panzacchi ordered the suspect to come out with his hands up. Suddenly, Di Blasi came forward shouting, "Punish me! Punish me!" and brandishing a weapon in a threatening manner. One of the police officers immediately opened fire and young Maurizio Di Blasi fell to the ground, killed by a burst of automatic-weapons fire to the chest. The young man's almost Dostoyevskian entreaty of "punish me" was tantamount to a confession. Meanwhile, Aurelio Di Blasi, the father, has been enjoined to appoint himself a defence lawyer. He is expected to be charged with complicity in his son's escape, which came to such a tragic end.'

When a photo of the poor kid's horsey face appeared on the screen, Montalbano left the bar and returned to headquarters.

'If the commissioner hadn't taken the case away from you, that poor wretch would surely still be alive!' Mimì shouted angrily.

Saying nothing, Montalbano went into his office and

closed the door. There was a contradiction, big as a house, in the newsman's account. If Maurizio Di Blasi had wanted to be punished, and if he was so eager for this punishment, why was he threatening the policemen with a weapon? An armed man aiming a pistol at the people who want to arrest him doesn't want to be punished, he's trying to avoid being arrested, to escape.

'It's Fazio. Can I come in, Chief?'

To his amazement, the inspector saw Augello, Germanà, Gallo, Galluzzo, Giallombardo, Tortorella and even Grasso, enter behind Fazio.

'Fazio just talked to a friend of his on the Montelusa Flying Squad,' said Mimì Augello. Then he gestured to Fazio to continue.

'You know what he said the weapon was the kid threatened Panzacchi and his men with?'

'No.'

'A shoe. His right shoe. Before he fell, he managed to throw it at Panzacchi.'

*

'Anna? Montalbano here.'

'It couldn't have been him, Salvo! I'm sure of it! It's all a tragic mistake! You must do something!'

'Listen, that's not why I called. Do you know Mrs Di Blasi?'

'Yes. We've spoken a few times.'

'Go and see her at once. I'm very worried. I don't want her left alone with her husband in jail and her son just killed.'

'I'll go right away.'

*

'Chief, can I tell you something? That friend of mine from the Flying Squad just called back.'

'And he told you he was only kidding about the shoe, it was all a joke.'

'Exactly. Therefore it's true.'

'Listen, I'm going home now, and I think I'll stay there for the rest of the afternoon. Give me a ring if you need me.'

'Chief, you gotta do something.'

'Get off my fucking back, all of you!'

*

After the bridge, he drove straight on. He didn't feel like hearing again, this time from Anna, that he absolutely had to take action. By what right? Here's your fearless, flawless knight in shining armour! Here's your Robin Hood, your Zorro, your Night Avenger all in one: Salvo Montalbano!

His appetite was gone now. He filled a saucer with green and black olives, cut himself a slice of bread, and, while munching on these, dialled Zito's number.

'Nicolò? Montalbano here. Do you know if the commissioner has called a press conference?'

'It's set for five o'clock this afternoon.'

'You going?'

'Naturally.'

'You have to do me a favour. Ask Panzacchi what kind of weapon Maurizio Di Blasi threatened them with. Then after he tells you, ask him if he can show it to you.'

'What's behind this?'

'I'll tell you in due time.'

'Can I tell you something, Salvo? We're all convinced here that if you'd stayed on the case, Maurizio Di Blasi would still be alive.'

So Nicolò was jumping aboard, too, behind Mimì.

'Would you go and get fucked!'

'Thanks, I could use a little, it's been a while. By the way, we'll be broadcasting the press conference live.'

*

He went and sat on the veranda with the book by Denevi in his hands, but he was unable to read it. A thought was spinning round and round in his head, the same one he'd had the night before: what strange, anomalous thing had he seen or heard during his visit to the house with the doctor?

*

The press conference began at five on the dot. Bonetti-Alderighi was a maniac for punctuality ('It's the courtesy of kings,' he used to repeat whenever he had the chance, his noble lineage having apparently gone so far to his head that he now imagined it with a crown on top).

There were three of them seated behind a small table covered with green cloth: the commissioner in the middle, flanked by Panzacchi on the right and Dr Lattes on the left. Behind them, the six policemen who had taken part in the operation. While the faces of the policemen were grave and drawn, those of the three chiefs expressed moderate contentment – only moderate because somebody had been killed.

The commissioner spoke first, limiting himself to praising Ernesto Panzacchi ('a man with a brilliant future ahead of him') and briefly taking credit for having assigned the case to the captain of the Flying Squad, who had 'managed to solve it in twenty-four hours, when others, with their antiquated methods, would have taken untold days and weeks.'

Montalbano, sitting in front of the screen, took it all in without reacting, not even mentally.

Then it was Ernesto Panzacchi's turn to speak, and he repeated exactly what the inspector had heard the Tele-Vigàta newsman say earlier. He didn't dwell on the details, however, and seemed in rather a hurry to leave.

'Does anyone have any questions?' asked Dr Lattes.

Somebody raised a hand.

'Are you sure the suspect shouted "Punish me"?'

'Absolutely certain. He said it twice. They all heard it.'

He turned to the six policemen behind him, who nodded in agreement, looking like puppets on strings.

'And in a desperate tone of voice.' Panzacchi piled it on. 'Desperate.'

'What is the father accused of?' asked a second journalist.

'Being an accessory after the fact,' said the commissioner.

'And maybe more,' added Panzacchi with an air of mystery.

'Being an accomplice to murder?' ventured a third newsman.

'I didn't say that,' Panzacchi said curtly.

Finally Nicolò Zito signalled that he wanted to speak.

'What kind of weapon did Maurizio Di Blasi threaten you with?'

Of course, the journalists, who had no idea what had actually happened, didn't notice anything, but the inspector distinctly saw the six policemen stiffen and the half-smile on Captain Panzacchi's face vanish. Only the commissioner and the head of his cabinet had no perceptible reaction.

'A hand grenade,' said Panzacchi.

'Where did he get it?' Zito pressed him.

'Well, it was war surplus, but still functioning. We have a suspicion as to where he might have found it, but we need further confirmation.'

'Could we see it?'

'The forensics lab has it.'

And so ended the press conference.

*

At six thirty Montalbano called Livia. The phone rang a long time to no avail. He started to feel worried. What if she was sick? He called Giovanna, Livia's friend at work. She said Livia'd shown up at work as usual, but she, Giovanna, had noticed she looked very pale and nervous. Livia also told her she'd unplugged the telephone because she didn't want to be disturbed.

'How are things between the two of you?' Giovanna asked him.

'Not great, I'd say,' Montalbano replied diplomatically.

*

No matter what he did – whether he read a book or stared out at the sea smoking a cigarette – the question kept coming suddenly back to him, precise and insistent: what had he seen or heard at the house that hadn't seemed right?

*

'Hello, Salvo? It's Anna. I've just come from Mrs Di Blasi's. You were right to tell me to go there. Her family and friends have made a point of not coming round – you know, keeping their distance from someone with a husband in jail and a son who's a murderer.'

'How is Mrs Di Blasi?'

'How do you expect? She's had a breakdown; I had to call a doctor. Now she's feeling a little better; her husband's lawyer phoned saying he'd be released shortly.'

'They're not charging him with complicity?'

'I really can't say. I think they're going to charge him anyway, but release him on bail. Are you coming round?'

'I don't know, I'll see.'

'Salvo, you've got to do something. Maurizio was innocent, I'm sure of it, and they murdered him.'

'Anna, don't get any wild ideas.'

*

'Hullo, Chief? Zatchoo in poisson? Catarella here. The vikkim's huzbin called sayin' as how yer sposta call 'im poissonally at the Jolly t'nite roundabout ten aclack.'

'Thanks. How'd the first day of class go?'

'Good, Chief, good. I unnastood everyting. Teacha complimented me. Said peoples like me's rilly rare.'

*

An inspiration came to him shortly before eight o'clock, and he put it into action without wasting another minute. He jumped in the car and drove off in the direction of Montelusa.

*

143

'Nicolò's on the air,' said a secretary at the Free Channel studios, 'but he's almost finished.'

Less than five minutes later, Zito appeared, out of breath.

'I did what you said; did you see the press conference?'

'Yes, Nicolò, and I think we hit the mark.'

'Can you tell me why that grenade is so important?'

'Do you underestimate grenades?'

'Come on, tell me what's behind this.'

'I can't, not yet. Actually, you'll probably work it out very soon, but that's your business. I haven't told you anything.'

'Come on! What do you want me to say or do on the news? That's what you came here for, isn't it? By now you've become my secret director.'

'If you do it, I'll give you a present.'

He took one of the photos of Michela that Dr Licalzi had given him out of his jacket pocket and handed it to Nicolò.

'You're the only journalist who knows what the woman looked like when she was alive. The commissioner's office in Montelusa doesn't have any photos. All her IDs, driver's licence, or passport, if she had one, were in the bag that the murderer took with him. You can show this to your viewers if you want.'

Nicolò twisted up his face.

'You must want an awfully big favour. Fire away.'

Montalbano stood up, went over, and locked the door to the newsman's office.

'No,' said Nicolò.

'No what?'

'No to whatever it is you're going to ask me. If you need to lock the door, I don't want any part of it.'

'Look, if you give me a hand, afterwards I'll give you all the facts you need to create a nationwide uproar.'

Zito said nothing. He was clearly torn.

'What do you want me to do?' he finally asked in a low voice.

'To say you received phone calls from two witnesses.'

'Do they exist?'

'One does, the other doesn't.'

'Tell me only what the one who exists said.'

'No, both. Take it or leave it.'

'But you do realize that if anybody finds out I invented a witness they're liable to strike me off the register?'

'Of course. And in that case, I give you permission to say I talked you into it. That way, they'll send me home, too, and we can go and grow broad beans together.'

'Tell you what. Tell me about the fake one first. If the thing seems feasible, you can tell me about the real one afterwards.'

'OK. This afternoon, following the press conference, somebody phoned you saying he was out hunting in the area where the police shot down Maurizio Di Blasi. He said that things did not happen the way Panzacchi said.

Then he hung up without leaving his name. He was clearly upset and afraid. You tell your viewers you're mentioning this episode only in passing and nobly declare that you don't lend it much weight, since it was, in fact, an anonymous phone call and your professional ethics do not allow you to spread anonymous rumours.'

'And in the meantime I've actually repeated it.'

'But isn't that standard procedure for you guys, if you don't mind my saying so? Throwing the stone but keeping the hand hidden?'

'I'll tell you something about that when we're through. For now, let's hear about the real witness.'

'His name is Gillo Jàcono, but you're to give only his initials, G.J., nothing more. This gentleman, shortly after midnight last Wednesday, saw the Twingo pull up by the house in Tre Fontane, and saw Michela and an unidentified man get out of the car and walk quietly towards the house. The man was carrying a suitcase. Not an overnight bag, a suitcase. Now, the question is this: why did Maurizio Di Blasi bring a suitcase when he went to rape Mrs Licalzi? Did it maybe contain clean sheets in the event they soiled the bed? Also: did the Flying Squad find this suitcase anywhere? It was certainly nowhere inside the house.'

'Is that it?'

'That's it.'

Nicolò had turned chilly. Apparently Montalbano's criticism of journalistic methods hadn't gone down well with him.

'As for my professional ethics, this afternoon, following the press conference, I received a phone call from a hunter who told me that things had not happened the way the police said. But since he wouldn't give me his name, I didn't report it.'

'You're shitting me.'

'Let me call my secretary, and you can listen to the tape recording of the call,' said the journalist, standing up.

'I'm sorry, Nicolò. There's no need.'

ELEVEN

Montalbano tossed about in bed all night, unable to fall asleep. He kept seeing the scene of Maurizio falling to the ground and managing to throw his shoe at his tormentors, the simultaneously comical and desperate gesture of a poor wretch hunted down like an animal. 'Punish me!' he had cried out, and everyone rushed to interpret that exclamation in the most obvious, reassuring manner possible. That is, punish me because I raped and killed, punish me for my sin. But what if, at that moment, he had meant something else entirely? What was going through his head? Punish me because I'm different, punish me because I loved too much, punish me for being born ... One could go on for ever, but here the inspector stopped himself, both because he didn't like to slip into cheap philosophizing, and because he had suddenly understood that the only way to exorcize that obsessive image, and that cry, lay not in generic self-questioning but in examining the facts. To do this, one path, and only one, presented itself. And at this point he managed at last to shut his eyes for a couple of hours.

*

'All of you,' he said to Mimì Augello, entering head-quarters.

Five minutes later, they were all standing before him in his office.

'Make yourselves comfortable,' said Montalbano. 'This is not an official meeting, but a talk among friends.'

Mimì and two or three others sat down, while the rest remained standing. Grasso, Catarella's replacement, leaned against the door frame, listening for the phone.

'Yesterday, Inspector Augello, when he learned that Di Blasi had been killed, said something that hurt me. He said, more or less: if you'd remained on the case, today that kid would still be alive. I could have answered that it was the commissioner who'd taken the investigation away from me, and that therefore I bear no responsibility. And this, strictly speaking, is true. But Inspector Augello was right. When the commissioner summoned me and ordered me to stop investigating the Licalzi murder, pride got the better of me. I didn't protest, I didn't rebel, I basically gave him to understand that he could go and fuck himself. And in so doing, I gambled away a man's life. Because one thing's certain, none of you would ever have shot down some poor guy who wasn't right in the head.'

They'd never heard him speak this way before and everyone looked at him flabbergasted, holding their breath.

'I thought about this last night, and I made a decision. I'm going to resume the investigation.'

Who was it that applauded first? Montalbano managed to turn his emotion into sarcasm.

'I've already told you once you're a bunch of fucking idiots, don't make me say it again.' And he continued, 'The case, as of today, is closed. Therefore, if you're all in agreement, we're going to operate underwater, with only our periscope showing. But I'm warning you: if they find out about this in Montelusa, it could mean real trouble for every one of us.'

*

'Inspector Montalbano? This is Emanuele Licalzi.'

Montalbano remembered that Catarella had told him the night before that the doctor had called. He'd forgotten.

'I'm sorry, but yesterday evening I had—'

'Oh, not at all, Inspector. Especially since everything has changed since yesterday.'

'In what sense?'

'In the sense that late yesterday afternoon I'd been assured that by Wednesday morning I could leave for Bologna with my poor Michela. Then early this morning the commissioner's office phoned to tell me that they needed a postponement and the funeral would have to wait until Friday. So I've decided to leave and come back on Thursday evening.'

'Doctor, you must have heard, of course, that the investigation—'

'Yes, of course, but I wasn't referring to the investigation. Do you remember the car we mentioned briefly, the Twingo? Could I perhaps talk to someone about reselling it?'

'Tell you what, Doctor: I'll have the car brought myself to our own personal mechanic. We did the damage ourselves and it's only right we should pay for it. And if you like, I could ask the mechanic to try and find a buyer for it.'

'You're a fine man, Inspector.'

'But tell me something, sir: what will you do with the house?'

'I'm going to put that up for sale, too.'

*

'Nicolò here. QED.'

'Explain.'

'I've been summoned to appear before Judge Tommaseo at four o'clock this afternoon.'

'And what's he want from you?'

'You've got a lot of nerve! What, you get me into this mess and you can't figure it out? He's going to accuse me of having withheld valuable testimony from the police.

And if he ever finds out that I don't even know who one of the witnesses is, then the shit is really going to hit the fan. That man is liable to throw me in jail.'

'Keep me posted.'

'Right. You can come visit me once a week and bring me oranges and cigarettes.'

*

'Listen, Galluzzo, I'm going to need your brother-in-law, the newsman for TeleVigàta.'

'I'll tell him right away, Inspector.'

Galluzzo was on his way out of the room, but curiosity got the better of him.

'Actually, if it's something I can know about too . . .'

'Gallù, not only can you know it, you've got to know it. I need your brother-in-law to collaborate with us on the Licalzi story. Since we can't work out in the open, we must take advantage of any help the private TV stations can give us. But we have to make it look like they're acting on their own. Is that clear?'

'Perfectly.'

'Think your brother-in-law'd be willing to help us?'

Gallo started laughing.

'Chief, for you, the guy would go on TV and say the moon is made out of Swiss cheese. Don't you know he's just dying of envy?'

'Who does he envy?'

'Nicolò Zito, that's who. Says you make special considerations for Zito.'

'It's true. Last night Zito did me a favour and now he's in trouble.'

'And now you want the same to happen to my brother-in-law?'

'If he's game.'

'Tell me what you want from him, it's no problem.'

'All right, you tell him what he's supposed to do. Here, take this. It's a photograph of Michela Licalzi.'

'Man, what a beauty!'

'Now, your brother-in-law must have a photo of Maurizio Di Blasi somewhere in the studio. I think I saw them broadcast one when they reported his death. I want him to show both photos, one next to the other, on the one p.m. news, and on the evening report. I want him to say that since there's a five-hour gap between when she left her friend at seven thirty on Wednesday night and when she was seen going into her house with a man shortly after midnight, your brother-in-law would like to know if anyone has any information on the movements of Michela Licalzi during that period. Better yet, if anyone saw her during that period in the company of Maurizio, and where. Is that clear?'

'Clear as day.'

'You, from this moment on, will bivouac at Tele-Vigàta.'

'What do you mean?'

'I mean you'll be there all the time, as if you were an editor. As soon as somebody comes forward with information, you show him in and talk to him. Then you report back to me.'

✻

'Salvo? It's Nicolò. I'm going to have to disturb you again.'

'Any news? Did they send the carabinieri for you?'

Apparently Nicolò was in no mood for jokes.

'Can you come to the studio immediately?'

✻

Montalbano was stunned to find Orazio Guttadauro, the controversial defence lawyer, legal counsel to every mafioso in the province and even outside the province, at the Free Channel studios.

'Well, if it isn't Inspector Montalbano, what a lovely sight!' said the lawyer as soon as he saw him come in. Nicolò looked a tad uncomfortable.

The inspector eyed the newsman enquiringly. Why had he summoned him there with Guttadauro? Zito responded verbally, 'Mr Guttadauro was the gentleman who phoned yesterday, the one who was hunting.'

'Ah,' said the inspector. With Guttadauro, the less one spoke, the better. He was not the kind of man one would want to break bread with.

'The words that the distinguished journalist here present,' began the lawyer in the same tone of voice he employed in court, 'used to describe me on television made me feel like a worm!'

'Good God, what did I say?' asked Nicolò, concerned.

'You used these exact words, and I quote: "unknown hunter" and "anonymous caller".'

'What's so offensive about that? There's the Unknown Soldier . . .'

'. . . and the Anonymous Venetian,' Montalbano chimed in, beginning to enjoy himself.

'What? What?' The lawyer went on as if he hadn't heard them, 'Orazio Guttadauro, implicitly accused of cowardice? I couldn't bear it, and so, here I am.'

'But why did you come to us? It was your duty to go to Captain Panzacchi in Montelusa and tell him—'

'Are we kidding ourselves, boys? Panzacchi was twenty yards away from me and told a completely different story! Given the choice between me and him, people will believe him! Do you know how many of my clients, upright citizens all, have been implicated and charged on the basis of the lying words of a policeman or carabiniere? Hundreds!'

'Excuse me, sir, but in what way is your version different from Captain Panzacchi's?' asked Zito, finally giving in to curiosity.

'In one detail, my good man.'

'Which?'

'Young Di Blasi was unarmed.'

'No, no, I don't believe it. Are you trying to tell us

that the Flying Squad shot him down in cold blood, for the sheer pleasure of killing a man?'

'I said simply that Di Blasi was unarmed. The others, however, thought he was armed, since he did have something in his hand. It was a terrible misunderstanding.'

'What did he have in his hand?' Nicolò Zito's voice had risen in pitch.

'One of his shoes, my friend.'

While the journalist was collapsing into his chair, the lawyer continued.

'I feel it is my duty to make this fact known to the public. I believe that my solemn civic duty requires . . .'

Montalbano began to understand Guttadauro's game. Since it wasn't a Mafia killing, and he wouldn't, by testifying, be harming any of his clients, he had a perfect opportunity to publicize himself as a model citizen and at the same time stick it to the police.

'I'd also seen him the previous day,' the lawyer said.

'Who?' Zito and Montalbano asked together, both lost in thought until that moment.

'The Di Blasi kid, who else? The hunting's good in that area. I saw him from a distance, I didn't have binoculars. He was limping. Then he went inside the mouth of the cave, sat down in the sun, and began eating.'

'Wait a minute,' said Zito. 'Are you saying the man was hiding there and not at his own house, which was a stone's throw away?'

'What do you want me to say, my dear Zito? The day

before that, when passing in front of the Di Blasi house, I saw that the front door was bolted with a padlock the size of a trunk. I am positive that at no point did he hide out at his house. Maybe he didn't want to compromise his family.'

Montalbano was convinced of two things: the lawyer was prepared to belie the assertions of the Flying Squad captain even as concerned the young man's hideout, which meant that the charge against the father would have to be dropped, with grave prejudice to Panzacchi. As for the second thing, he needed confirmation.

'Would you tell me something, sir?'

'At your orders, Inspector.'

'Are you always out hunting? Aren't you ever in court?'

Guttadauro smiled at him. Montalbano smiled back. They had understood each other. In all likelihood, the lawyer had never gone hunting in his life. Those who'd seen the incident and sent him on this mission must have been friends of the people Guttadauro called his clients. And the objective was to create a scandal for the Montelusa police department. The inspector had to play shrewdly; he didn't like having these people as allies.

'Was it Mr Guttadauro who told you to call me?' the inspector asked Nicolò.

'Yes.'

Therefore *they* knew everything. They were aware he'd been wronged, they imagined he was determined to avenge himself, and they were ready to use him.

'You, sir, must certainly have heard that I am no longer in charge of the case, which in any event should be considered closed.'

'Yes, but—'

'There are no buts, sir. If you really want to do your duty as a citizen, go to Judge Tommaseo and tell him your version of the events. Good day.'

He turned around and walked out. Nicolò came running after him and grabbed him by the arm.

'You knew! You knew about the shoe! That's why you told me to ask Panzacchi what the weapon was!'

'Yeah, Nicolò, I knew. But I advise you not to mention it on your news programme. There's no proof that things went the way Guttadauro says, even though it's probably the truth. Be very careful.'

'But you yourself are telling me it's the truth!'

'Try to understand, Nicolò. I'd be willing to bet that our good lawyer doesn't even know where the fuck the cave that Maurizio hid in is located. He's a puppet, and his strings are pulled by the Mafia. His friends found something out and decided they could take advantage of it. They cast a net into the sea and they're hoping to catch Panzacchi, the commissioner and Judge Tommaseo in it. That would make some pretty big waves. However, to haul the net back into the boat, they need somebody strong, that is, me, who they think is blinded by the desire for revenge. Now do you get the picture?'

'Yes. What line should I take with the lawyer?'

'Repeat the same things I said. Let him go and tell it to the judge. He'll refuse, you'll see. But it's you who will repeat to Tommaseo, word for word, what Guttadauro said. If he's not a fool, and he's not, he'll realize that he, too, is in danger.'

'But he had nothing to do with the killing of Di Blasi.'

'But he signed the indictment against his father. And those guys are prepared to testify that Maurizio never hid in his father's house at Raffadali. Tommaseo, if he wants to save his arse, has to disarm Guttadauro and his friends.'

'How?'

'How should I know?'

✳

Since he was in Montelusa anyway, the inspector decided to go to Montelusa Central Police Station, hoping not to run into Panzacchi. Once there, he headed immediately to the basement, where forensics was located. He walked straight into the office of the chief.

'Hello, Arquà.'

'Hello,' the other said, iceberg-cold. 'What can I do for you?'

'I was just passing by, and I became curious about something.'

'I'm very busy.'

'Of course you are, but I'll only steal a minute of your time. I want some information about the grenade Di Blasi tried to throw at those police officers.'

Arquà didn't move a muscle.

'I'm not required to tell you anything.'

How could he be so self-controlled?

'Come on, colleague, be a sport. I need only three things: colour, size and make.'

Arquà looked sincerely baffled. His eyes were clearly asking whether Montalbano hadn't gone completely mad.

'What the hell are you saying?'

'Let me help you. Black? Brown? Forty-three? Forty-four? Moccasin? Superga? Varese?'

'Calm down,' said Arquà, though there was no need. He was sticking to the rule that one should try to humour madmen. 'Come with me.'

Montalbano followed behind him. They entered a room with a big, white half-moon table around which stood three busy men in white smocks.

'Caruana,' Arquà said to one of the three men, 'show our colleague Montalbano the grenade.'

As this man was opening a metal cabinet, Arquà continued talking.

'It's dismantled now, but when they brought it here it was live and dangerous.'

He took the plastic bag that Caruana held out to him, and showed it to the inspector.

'An old OTO, issued to our army in 1940.'

Montalbano was unable to speak. He studied the pieces of the grenade as if looking at the fragments of a Ming vase that had just fallen to the floor.

'Did you take fingerprints?'

'They were very blurry for the most part, but two of Maurizio Di Blasi's came out very clearly, the thumb and index finger of the right hand.'

Arquà set the bag on the table, put his hand on Montalbano's shoulder, and pushed him out into the corridor.

'I'm sorry, it's all my fault. I had no idea the commissioner would take you off the case.'

He was attributing what he thought was a momentary lapse of Montalbano's mental abilities to the shock of his removal. A good kid, deep down, Dr Arquà.

*

The chief of the crime lab had undoubtedly been sincere, Montalbano thought as he drove down to Vigàta. He couldn't possibly be that brilliant an actor. But how can one throw a hand grenade gripping it only with the thumb and index finger? The best thing that might happen if you threw it that way is that you'd blow your balls to bits. Arquà should have been able to get a print of much of the right palm as well. Given all this, where had the Flying Squad performed the feat of taking two of the already dead Maurizio's fingers and pressing them by force against the grenade? No sooner had he posed the question, than he turned around and headed back to Montelusa.

TWELVE

'What do you want?' asked Pasquano as soon as he saw him enter his office.

'I need to appeal to our friendship,' Montalbano began.

'Friendship? You and I are friends? Do we ever dine together? Do we confide in each other?'

Dr Pasquano was like that, and the inspector didn't feel the least bit upset by his words. It was merely a matter of finding the right formula.

'Well, if not friendship, then mutual esteem.'

'That, yes.'

He'd guessed right. It would be smooth sailing from here.

'Doctor, what other tests do you have to run on Michela Licalzi? Are there any new developments?'

'New developments? I told the judge and the commissioner long ago that as far as I was concerned, we could turn the body over to the husband.'

'Oh, really? Because, see, the husband himself told me he got a call from the commissioner's office saying that the funeral couldn't be held until Friday morning.'

'That's their goddamn business.'

'Excuse me, Doctor, for taking advantage of your patience. Was everything normal with the body of Maurizio Di Blasi?'

'What do you mean?'

'Well, how did he die?'

'What a stupid question. A burst of machine-gun fire. They practically cut him in two. They could've made a bust of him and put it on a column.'

'And the right foot?'

Dr Pasquano narrowed his beady eyes.

'Why are you asking me about the right foot?'

'Because I don't find the left one very interesting.'

'Right. He hurt himself, a sprain or something, couldn't get his shoe back on. But he'd hurt himself a few days before he was killed. His face was all swollen from some kind of blow.'

Montalbano gave a start.

'Had he been beaten?'

'I don't know. He was either hit hard in the face with a stick or club or ran into something. But it wasn't the policemen. The contusion dated from some time before that.'

'From when he hurt his foot?'

'More or less, I suppose.'

Montalbano stood up and held out his hand to the doctor.

'Thank you. I'll be on my way. One last thing. Did they inform you immediately?'

'Inform me of what?'

'Of the fact they'd shot Di Blasi.'

Dr Pasquano squinted his eyes so far that he looked as if he'd suddenly fallen asleep. He didn't answer immediately.

'Do you dream these things up at night? Do the crows whisper them in your ear? Do you talk to ghosts? No, they shot the kid at six in the morning. They didn't inform me until around ten. Said they wanted to finish searching the house first.'

'One final question.'

'With all your final questions, you're going to keep me here till nightfall.'

'After they turned Di Blasi's body over to you, did anyone from the Flying Squad ask for your permission to examine it alone?'

Dr Pasquano looked surprised.

'No. Why would they do that?'

*

Montalbano returned to the Free Channel. He had to bring Nicolò Zito up to date on the latest developments. He was sure Guttadauro the lawyer would be gone by now.

'Why'd you come back?'

'Tell you in a second, Nicolò. How'd it go with the lawyer?'

'I did what you told me to do. I suggested he go and talk to the judge. He said he'd think about it. Then he added something curious, that had nothing to do with anything. Or so it seemed. You never know with these people. He said, "Lucky you, who live among images! Nowadays only images matter, not words." That's what he said. What's it mean?'

'I don't know. You know, Nicolò, they've got the grenade.'

'God! So what Guttadauro told us is untrue!'

'No, it's true. Panzacchi's a shrewd one, he's covered himself very cleverly. The crime lab's examining a grenade that Panzacchi gave them, and it's got Di Blasi's fingerprints on it.'

'Jesus, what a mess! Panzacchi's covered himself from every angle! What am I going to tell Tommaseo?'

'Exactly what we agreed on. Except you shouldn't appear too sceptical about the existence of the grenade. Understood?'

✻

To get to Vigàta from Montelusa there was, aside from the usual route, a little abandoned road the inspector was very fond of. He turned onto it, and when he'd reached a small bridge spanning a torrent that had ceased being a torrent centuries ago and was now merely a depression of stones and pebbles, he stopped the car, got out, and wended his way into a thicket at the centre of which stood a gigantic Saracen olive tree, one of those twisted, gnarled ones that creep along the ground like snakes before ascending to the sky. He sat down on a branch, lit a cigarette, and started meditating on the events of the morning.

✳

'Mimì, come in, close the door, and have a seat. I need some information from you.'

'Ready.'

'If I seize a weapon from someone, say, a revolver or a submachine gun, what do I do with it?'

'Usually, you give it to whoever's standing closest to you.'

'Did we wake up this morning with a sense of humour?'

'You want to know the regulations on the subject? Weapons seized must be turned immediately over to the appointed office at Montelusa Central Police Station, where they are registered and then put away under lock and key in a small depository at the opposite end of the building from the forensics lab of, in this case, Montelusa. Good enough?'

'Yes. Now, Mimì, I'm going to venture a reconstruction. If I say anything stupid, interrupt me. Here goes:

Panzacchi and his men search Engineer Di Blasi's country house. The front door, mind you, is bolted with an enormous padlock.'

'How do you know that?'

'Mimì, don't take advantage of the permission I just gave you. A padlock is not something stupid. I know it was there, period. They, however, think it might be a ruse – that is, they think Di Blasi senior, after supplying his son with provisions, locked him up inside so the house would appear uninhabited. He would go and free him after things cooled down a little. Suddenly, one of the men spots Maurizio on a nearby hillside going into the cave. They go and surround the entrance, Maurizio comes out holding something in his hand, and one of the more nervous policemen shoots and kills him. When they realize the poor bastard was holding his right shoe in his hand because he could no longer fit it on his injured foot—'

'How do you know this?'

'Mimì, if you don't knock it off, I'm going to stop telling you the story. When they see it's only a shoe, they realize they're in shit up to their necks. The brilliant operation of Ernesto Panzacchi and his dirty half dozen is in danger of creating a terrible stink. After thinking long and hard, they realize the only way out is to claim that Maurizio actually *was* armed. OK, but with what? And that's where our Flying Squad captain has a brainstorm: a hand grenade.'

'Why not a gun, which is more likely?'

'Face it, Mimì, you're just not on Panzacchi's level. The captain of the Flying Squad knows that Engineer Di Blasi doesn't have a licence to carry a gun, nor has he ever reported owning any weapons. But a war memento, which you've got before your eyes each day, is no longer considered a weapon. Or else it's packed away in an attic and forgotten.'

'May I say something? In 1940 Engineer Di Blasi was about five years old, and if he was doing any fighting, it was with a popgun.'

'What about his father, Mimì? An uncle, perhaps? A cousin? His grandfather? His great-grandfather? His—'

'OK, OK.'

'The problem is, where does one find a war-surplus hand grenade?'

'In the Montelusa police depository,' Mimì Augello said calmly.

'Right you are. And the timing fits, because they didn't notify Dr Pasquano until four hours after Maurizio's death.'

'How do you know that? OK, sorry.'

'Do you know who's in charge of the depository?'

'Yes, and you know him, too: Nenè Lofàro. He worked here with us for a while.'

'Lofàro? If I remember him correctly, he's not the kind of person to whom you can say, "Give me the key, I need a hand grenade."'

'We'll have to look into how it was done.'

'You go to Montelusa, Mimì. I can't, since I'm under fire.'

'All right. Oh, Salvo, could I have the day off tomorrow?'

'You got some whore on your hands?'

'Not a whore, a lady friend.'

'But can't you spend the evening with her, after you've finished here?'

'She said she's leaving tomorrow afternoon.'

'A foreigner, eh? All right, good luck. But first you have to unravel this story of the hand grenade.'

'Not to worry. I'll go to Montelusa today, after I eat.'

*

He felt like spending a little time with Anna, but once over the bridge, he shot past and went straight home.

In his letter box he found a large brown envelope that the postman had folded in two to make it fit. There was no return address. Feeling hungry, Montalbano opened the fridge: baby octopus *alla luciana* and a very simple fresh tomato sauce. Apparently Adelina hadn't had the time or the desire to make more. While waiting for the spaghetti water to boil, he opened the envelope. Inside was a colour catalogue for 'Eroservice', featuring pornographic videos for every single, or singular, taste. He tore it in half and tossed it into the rubbish bin. He ate and went into the bathroom, then came racing out, trousers unzipped, like a character in a silent film. How had he not thought of it sooner? Had it taken the porno catalogue? He looked up a number in the Montelusa phone book.

'Hello, Mr Guttadauro? Inspector Montalbano here. Were you eating? Yes? I'm so sorry.'

'What can I do for you, Inspector?'

'A friend of mine, talking of this and that – you know how these things happen – mentioned to me that you have an excellent collection of videos of yourself hunting.'

A very long pause. Apparently the lawyer's brain was in high gear.

'Yes, it's true.'

'Would you be willing to show me a few?'

'I'm very particular, you know, about my possessions. But we could make an arrangement.'

'That's what I was hoping you'd say.'

They said goodbye as if they were the greatest of friends. It was clear what had taken place. Guttadauro's friends – there had to be more than one – happen to witness the killing of Maurizio. When they see a police-man racing away in a squad car, they realize Panzacchi has hatched a plan for saving his face and career. One of the friends then runs and equips himself with a video camera. And he returns in time to tape the scene of the policemen pressing the dead man's fingerprints onto the hand grenade. Guttadauro's friends now have a grenade of their own, though different in nature, and they have sent the lawyer into the field. A nasty, dangerous situation, which Montalbano absolutely had to find a way out of.

✻

'Mr Di Blasi? Inspector Montalbano here. I need to speak to you immediately.'

'Why?'

'Because I have serious doubts about your son's guilt.'

'He's already gone.'

'Yes, of course, sir. But his memory.'

'Do what you want.'

Utter resignation. A breathing, talking corpse.

'I'll be at your place in half an hour at the latest.'

✻

He was astonished to see Anna open the door for him.

'Talk in a low voice. The signora is finally resting.'

'What are you doing here?'

'It was you who got me involved. I haven't had the heart to leave her alone since.'

'What do you mean, alone? Hasn't anyone called for a nurse?'

'Of course. But she wants me. Now come inside.'

The living room was even darker than the time the inspector was shown in by Mrs Di Blasi. He felt his heart sink when he saw Aurelio Di Blasi lying crosswise on the armchair. The man's eyes were closed, but he'd sensed the inspector's presence, and he spoke out.

'What do you want?' he asked with that terrible, dead voice.

Montalbano explained what he wanted. He spoke for half an hour straight and little by little saw the engineer sit up, prick up his ears, look at him and listen with interest. He realized he was winning him over.

'Does the Flying Squad have the keys to your villa?'

'Yes,' Mr Di Blasi said in a different, stronger voice. 'But I had a third pair made some time ago. Maurizio kept them in his bedside table. I'll go and fetch them.'

He was unable to get up from the armchair. Montalbano had to help him.

*

He blew into headquarters like a gunshot.

'Fazio, Gallo and Giallombardo, come with me.'

'Are we taking the squad car?'

'No, we'll go in mine. Is Mimì back?'

He wasn't back. They left in a hurry. Fazio had never seen him drive so fast. He got worried, not having a lot of faith in Montalbano's driving abilities.

'Want me to drive?' asked Gallo, who was apparently harbouring the same concerns as Fazio.

'Don't bust my balls. We have very little time.'

It took him about twenty minutes to drive from Vigàta

to Raffadali. Once outside the town, he turned onto a country road. Mr Di Blasi had carefully explained to him how to get to the house. They all recognized it easily, having seen it repeatedly on television.

'Now, I've got the keys,' said Montalbano. 'We're going to go inside and do a thorough search. We've still got a few hours of daylight left, and we must take advantage of it. We have to find what we're looking for before it gets dark, because we can't turn on any lights. We don't want anyone seeing the lights on from outside. Is that clear?'

'Perfectly clear,' said Fazio. 'But what are we looking for?'

The inspector told them, then added, 'I hope I'm wrong, I really do.'

'But we'll leave fingerprints,' said Giallombardo, worried. 'We didn't bring gloves.'

'We don't give a fuck.'

*

Unfortunately, the inspector hadn't been wrong. After they'd been searching for an hour, he heard Gallo call him triumphantly from the kitchen. They all came running. Gallo was stepping down from a chair, a leather ammunition box in his hand.

'It was on top of this cupboard.'

The inspector opened it: inside was a hand grenade

exactly like the one he'd seen in the crime lab, and a pistol that looked like the kind once issued to German officers.

*

'Where were you guys? What's in that case?' asked Mimì, curious as a cat.

'And what have you got to tell me?'

'Lofàro's on sick leave for a month. He was replaced fifteen days ago by somebody named Culicchia.'

'I know him well,' said Giallombardo.

'What's he like?'

'He's not the type who likes to sit behind a desk keeping records. He'd sell his soul to go back in the field. He wants to make a career of it.'

'He's already sold his soul,' said Montalbano.

'So, what's in there?' Mimì asked, increasingly curious.

'Chocolate, Mimì. Now listen, all of you. When does Culicchia go off duty? Eight o'clock, right?'

'That's right,' Fazio confirmed.

'When Culicchia leaves Montelusa Central, I want you, Fazio, and you, Giallombardo, to persuade him to get into my car. Don't explain anything to him. Keep him guessing. As soon as he's sitting down between you two, show him the ammunition box. Of course, he's never seen it before, so he's going to ask you what this whole charade is about.'

'Come on, can't somebody tell me what's in there?' Mimì asked again, but nobody answered.

'How come he won't recognize it?'

The question came from Gallo. The inspector gave him a dirty look.

'Haven't you guys got any brains in your head? Maurizio Di Blasi was retarded, but he was a decent person, and he certainly didn't have any friends who could provide him with weapons at the drop of a hat. The only place he could have found the grenade was at his country house. But they need proof that he took it from there. So Panzacchi, who's a slyboots, orders one of his men to go to Montelusa to get two grenades and one wartime pistol. One of these he'll claim was in Maurizio's hand, the other he hangs on to, together with the pistol, until he can come up with an ammo box. Then he sneaks back into the Raffadali house and hides the whole kit and caboodle in the first place where somebody would look for it.'

'So that's what's in the box!' exclaimed Mimì, slapping his forehead.

'In short, that motherfucking Panzacchi has created a perfectly plausible scenario. And if someone should ask him why the other weapons weren't found during the first search, he can claim they were interrupted when they spotted Maurizio going into the cave.'

'What a son of a bitch!' said Fazio indignantly. 'First he kills an innocent kid – because as captain he's responsible even though he didn't fire the shots himself – and now he wants to screw a poor old man just to save his own skin!'

'Let's get back to what you have to do. Let this

Culicchia simmer a little. Tell him the ammo box was found at the house in Raffadali. Then show him the grenade and the gun. Then ask him – as if out of curiosity – if all seized weapons are registered. And, finally, make him get out of the car together with you, carrying the weapons and ammo box.'

'Is that everything?'

'That's everything, Fazio. The next move is his.'

THIRTEEN

'Chief? Galluzzo's onna phone. He wants to talk to you in person. Whaddo I do, Chief? Put 'im through?'

It was clearly Catarella on the afternoon shift. But why did he say 'in person' and not 'in poisson'?

'All right, put him through. What is it, Galluzzo?'

'Inspector, some guy phoned TeleVigàta after they broadcast the photos of Mrs Licalzi and Maurizio Di Blasi together like you asked. He says he's positive he saw the lady with a man around eleven thirty that evening, but the man was not Maurizio Di Blasi. He says they stopped at his bar, right outside Montelusa.'

'Is he sure it was Wednesday night?'

'Positive. He explained that he didn't go to the bar on Monday and Tuesday because he was out of town, and Thursday it's closed. He left his name and address. What should I do, come back to the station?'

'No, stay there until after the eight o'clock news. Somebody else might come forward.'

177

The door flew open, slammed against the wall, and the inspector started.

'C'n I come in?' asked Catarella, smiling.

Without a doubt, Catarella had a problem with doors. Montalbano, confronted with that innocent face, suppressed the attack of nerves that had come over him.

'Yes. What is it?'

'This package jes now came f'you, and this personally 'dressed letter.'

'How's your course in pewters going?'

'Fine, Chief. But they're called computers, Chief.'

Montalbano looked at him in amazement as he left the room. They were corrupting Catarella.

Inside the envelope he found a few typewritten lines without a signature:

> *This is only the last part. Hope it's to your liking. If you want to see the whole video, call me whenever you like.*

Montalbano felt the package. A videotape.

*

As Fazio and Giallombardo had his car, he summoned Gallo to drive him in the squad car.

'Where are we going?'

'To Montelusa, to the Free Channel studios. And don't speed, I mean it. I don't want a rerun of last Thursday.'

Gallo's face darkened.

'Aw, it happens to me once and you start bellyaching the minute you get in the car!'

They drove there in silence.

'Should I wait for you?' Gallo asked when they got there.

'Yes. This won't take very long.'

Nicolò Zito showed him into his office. He was nervous.

'How'd it go with Tommaseo?'

'How do you expect? He gave me a royal tongue-lashing, flayed me alive. He wanted the witnesses' names.'

'And what did you do?'

'I pleaded the Fifth Amendment.'

'C'mon, there's no such thing in Italy.'

'Fortunately! Since anyone who pleads the Fifth in America still gets screwed anyway.'

'How did he react when he heard Guttadauro's name? That must have had a certain effect.'

'He got all flummoxed. Looked worried to me. At any rate, he gave me an official warning. Next time he's going to throw me in jail with no questions asked.'

'That's what I wanted.'

'For me to get thrown in jail with no questions asked?'

'No, arsehole, for him to know that Guttadauro and the people he represents are mixed up in this.'

'What's Tommaseo going to do, in your opinion?'

'He'll talk to the commissioner about it. I'm sure he realizes he's caught in the net, too, and he's going to try

179

to wiggle out of it. Listen, Nicolò, I need to watch this video.'

He handed it to him. Nicolò took it and inserted it in his VCR. It opened with a long shot showing a handful of men in the country, but their faces were unreadable. Two people in white smocks were loading a body onto a stretcher. Superimposed across the bottom of the image were the unmistakable words: 'Monday 14.4.97.' Whoever was shooting the scene then zoomed in, and now one could see Panzacchi and Dr Pasquano talking. There was no sound. The two men shook hands and the doctor walked out of the field of vision. The image then panned out to capture the six officers of the Flying Squad standing around their captain. Panzacchi said a few words to them, and they all walked off camera. End of show.

'Holy shit!' Zito said under his breath.

'Make me a copy.'

'I can't do it here, I have to go into the production studio.'

'All right, but be careful: don't let anyone see it.'

I've viewed the sample. It's of no interest. Do whatever you like with it. But I advise you to destroy it or use it in strictest privacy.

Montalbano didn't sign the note or write down the address, which he knew from the phone directory.

Zito returned and handed him two tapes.

'This is the original and this is the copy. It came out only so-so. You know how it is, making a copy of a copy...'

'I'm not competing for an Oscar. Give me a big brown envelope.'

He slipped the copy in his jacket pocket and put the note and original in the envelope. He didn't write any address on this, either.

Gallo was in the car, reading the *Gazzetta dello Sport*.

'Do you know where Via Xerri is? At number eighteen you'll find the law offices of Orazio Guttadauro. I want you to drop off this envelope, then come back and get me.'

✻

When Fazio and Giallombardo straggled back into headquarters, it was past nine.

'Oh, Inspector, what a farce, and a tragedy, too!' said Fazio.

'What did he say?'

'First he talked, and then he didn't,' said Giallombardo.

'When we showed him the ammo box, he didn't understand. He said, "What's this? Some kind of joke, eh? Is this a joke?" As soon as Giallombardo told him the box had been found at Raffadali, his face changed and started to turn pale.'

'Then, when he saw the weapons inside,' interjected

Giallombardo, who wanted to put in his two cents, 'he had a fit, and we were scared he was going to have a stroke right there in the car.'

'He was shaking all over, like he had malaria. Then he got up, climbed over me and ran away in a hurry,' said Fazio.

'He was running like an injured hare, stepping this way and that,' concluded Giallombardo.

'What now?' asked Fazio.

'We've made our noise. Now we wait for the echo. Thanks for everything.'

'Duty,' Fazio said dryly. And he added, 'Where should I put the ammo box? In the safe?'

'Yes,' said Montalbano.

Fazio had a rather large safe in his room. It wasn't used for documents, but for holding seized drugs or weapons before turning them over to Montelusa.

*

Fatigue sneaked up on him; his forty-sixth was just around the corner. He informed Catarella he was going home, but told him to forward any phone calls to him. Past the bridge he stopped the car, got out, and walked up to Anna's house. And what if she was with someone? He tried anyway.

Anna greeted him.

'Come on in.'

'Anybody there?'

'Nobody.'

She sat him down on the sofa in front of the television, turned down the volume, left the room, and returned with two glasses, one with whisky for the inspector, another with white wine for herself.

'Have you eaten?'

'No,' said Anna.

'Don't you ever eat?'

'I ate at midday.'

Anna sat down beside him.

'Don't get too close; I can tell I smell,' said Montalbano.

'Did you have a rough afternoon?'

'Rather.'

Anna extended her arm across the back of the sofa; Montalbano leaned his head back, resting the nape of his neck against her skin. He closed his eyes. Luckily he had put the glass down on the coffee table, because he fell at once into a deep sleep, as though the whisky had been drugged. He woke up with a start half an hour later, looked all around himself in confusion, realized what had happened, and felt embarrassed.

'Forgive me.'

'Good thing you woke up. My arm is full of pins and needles.'

The inspector stood up.

'I have to go.'

'I'll see you out.'

At the door, very naturally, Anna placed her lips lightly on Montalbano's.

'Have a good sleep, Salvo.'

*

He took a very long shower, changed his underwear and clothes, and phoned Livia. The phone rang for a long time, then the connection was suddenly cut off. What was that blessed woman doing? Was she wallowing in her sorrow over François? It was too late to ring her friend and get an up-date. He went and sat down on the veranda, and after a short while he decided that if he couldn't get in touch with Livia within the next forty-eight hours, he would drop everything and everyone, grab a flight to Genoa, and spend at least one day with her.

*

The ringing of the telephone had him running in from the veranda. He was sure it was Livia calling him, finally.

'Hello? Am I speaking to Inspector Montalbano?'

He'd heard that voice before, but couldn't remember who it belonged to.

'Yes. Who's this?'

'This is Ernesto Panzacchi.'

The echo had arrived.

'What is it?'

Were they on familiar terms or not? At this point it didn't matter.

'I want to talk to you. In person. Should I come to your place?'

He had no desire to see Panzacchi in his house.

'I'll come to you. Where do you live?'

'At the Hotel Pirandello.'

'I'm on my way.'

※

Panzacchi's room at the hotel was as big as a ballroom. Aside from a king-size bed and an armoire, it had two armchairs, a large table with television and VCR on top, and a minibar.

'There hasn't been time yet for my family to move down here.'

At least they'll be spared the trouble of moving twice, the inspector thought.

'Excuse me, I have to take a piss.'

'Look, there's nobody in the bathroom.'

'I really do need to piss.'

There was no trusting a snake like Panzacchi. When Montalbano returned from the bathroom, Panzacchi invited him to sit down in one of the armchairs. The captain of the Flying Squad was a stocky but elegant man with very pale blue eyes and a Tatar-style moustache.

'Can I get you something?'

'Nothing.'

'Should we get right to the point?' Panzacchi asked.

'As you like.'

'Well, a patrolman came to see me this evening, a certain Culicchia, I don't know if you know him.'

'Personally, no, by name, yes.'

'He was literally terrified. Apparently two men from your station threatened him.'

'Is that what he said?'

'That's what I believe I understood.'

'You understood wrong.'

'Then you tell me.'

'Listen, it's late and I'm tired. I went into the Di Blasis' house in Raffadali, looked around a little, and with very little effort found an ammunition box with a hand grenade and a pistol inside. I've got them in my safe now.'

'Jesus Christ! You've got no authorization!' said Panzacchi, standing up.

'You're going down the wrong road,' Montalbano said calmly.

'You're concealing evidence!'

'I said you're on the wrong road. If we keep talking about authorization and going by the book, I'm going to get up, walk out of that door and leave you behind in the shit. Because that's where you are, deep in shit.'

Panzacchi hesitated a moment, weighed the pros and cons, and sat back down. He'd given it a shot, and the first round had gone badly for him.

'You should even thank me,' the inspector went on.

'For what?'

'For having taken the ammunition box out of the

house. It was supposed to prove where Maurizio Di Blasi found his hand grenade, right? Except that forensics wouldn't have found Di Blasi's fingerprints in there even if their lives depended on it. And how would you have explained that? By saying Maurizio had worn gloves? Can you imagine the laughter!'

Panzacchi said nothing, his pale eyes looking straight into the inspector's.

'Shall I go on? Your first sin ... actually, no, I don't give a fuck about your sins, the first mistake you made was to hunt down Maurizio before being absolutely certain of his guilt. But you wanted to carry out a "brilliant" operation at all costs. Then what happened happened, and you breathed a real sigh of relief. Pretending you were saving one of your men who mistook a shoe for a weapon, you concocted the story of the hand grenade, and to make it more credible, you went and planted the ammo box in the Di Blasi house.'

'That's all talk. If you go and say those things to the commissioner, rest assured he won't believe a word of it. You're spreading these rumours just to tarnish my reputation, to avenge yourself for the fact that the investigation was taken away from you and turned over to me.'

'And what are you going to do about Culicchia?'

'He's coming with me to the Flying Squad offices tomorrow morning. I'll pay the price he's asking.'

'And what if I take the weapons to Judge Tommaseo?'

'Culicchia'll say it was you who asked him for the key

to the depository the other day. He's ready to swear by it. Try to understand: he has to defend himself, and I suggested to him how to do this.'

'So I've lost?'

'It looks that way.'

'Does that VCR work?'

'Yes.'

'Could you play this tape?'

Montalbano took it out of his pocket and handed it to Panzacchi who didn't ask any questions, but simply inserted the cassette. The images appeared, the captain of the Flying Squad watched them all the way through, then rewound the tape, extracted the cassette, and handed it to Montalbano. He sat down and lit a half-consumed Tuscan cigar.

'That's just the last part. I've got the whole tape in the same safe as the weapons,' Montalbano lied.

'How did you do it?'

'I didn't make the tape myself. There were two men in the area who saw what was going on and filmed it. Friends of Guttadauro, the lawyer, whom you know well.'

'This is a nasty development, totally unexpected.'

'It's a lot nastier than you can possibly imagine. It so happens you're being squeezed between me and them.'

'Allow me to say that their reasons I can understand perfectly well; it's yours that don't seem so clear to me, unless you're motivated by feelings of revenge.'

'Now you try to understand *my* position. I cannot,

under any circumstances, allow the captain of the Monte-lusa Flying Squad to become a hostage of the Mafia. I can't let you be subject to blackmail.'

'Look, Montalbano, all I wanted to do was protect the good name of my men. Can you imagine what would have happened if the press had discovered we killed a man who was defending himself with a shoe?'

'Is that why you implicated Maurizio's father, who had nothing to do with the case?'

'With the case, no, but with my plan, yes. As for possible attempts at blackmail, I know how to defend myself.'

'I'm sure you do. You can hold out, which isn't a very nice way to live, but what about Culicchia and the other six who'll be put under pressure every single day? How long will they hold out? All you need is for one to crack, and the whole story comes out. I'll give you a very likely scenario: As soon as they get sick of your refusals, the mob is liable to give a public viewing of their tape or send it to a private TV station that'll jump at the scoop even if it means risking prison. And if that happens, the commissioner gets fried too.'

'What should I do?'

Montalbano looked at him in admiration for a moment. Panzacchi was a ruthless, unscrupulous player, but he knew how to lose.

'You should disarm them, neutralize the weapon they've got in their hands.' He couldn't resist adding a malicious comment he immediately regretted. 'This is not a shoe,' he said. 'Talk about it, tonight, with the commissioner. Find a solution together. But I warn you: if you haven't made a move by twelve tomorrow, I'll make my own move, in my own way.'

He got up, opened the door, and went out.

*

'I'll make my own move, in my own way.' It had a nice ring to it. Just threatening enough. But what did it really mean? If, say, the captain of the Flying Squad were to get the commissioner on his side, and the latter in turn got Judge Tommaseo to join them, he, Montalbano, was as good as fucked. But was it possible that everyone in Montelusa had suddenly become dishonest? The antipathy a particular person might arouse is one thing; his character and integrity were another matter.

He returned to Marinella full of doubts and questions. Had he been right to talk that way to Panzacchi? Would the commissioner accept that he wasn't motivated by a desire for revenge? He dialled Livia's number. As usual, no answer. He went to bed, but it took him two hours to fall asleep.

FOURTEEN

When he walked into the office, his nerves were so obviously frayed that his men judged it best to give him a wide berth. *Of all things the bed is the best. / If you can't sleep you still can rest.* So went the proverb, but it was wrong, for not only had the inspector slept only fitfully in his bed, he had also woken up feeling like he'd run a marathon.

Only Fazio, who was closest to him, ventured to ask a question, 'Any news?'

'I'll be able to tell you after twelve.'

Galluzzo came in.

'Inspector, yesterday evening I looked for you over land and sea.'

'Did you try the sky?'

Galluzzo realized this was no time for preambles.

'Inspector, after the eight o'clock news report, somebody phoned. He said that on Wednesday evening, around eight, eight fifteen at the latest, Mrs Licalzi stopped at his petrol station and filled up her tank. He left his name and address.'

'OK. We'll drive over there later.'

He was tense, unable to set his eyes on a sheet of paper, and he kept looking at his watch. What if by twelve nobody had called from Montelusa?

At eleven thirty the telephone rang.

*

'Chief,' said Grasso, 'it's Zito the newsman.'

'Let me talk to him.'

At first he didn't know what was happening.

'Bat-ta-tum, bat-ta-tum, bat-ta-tum, tum-tùm-tumtùm,' said Zito.

'Nicolò?'

'"Fratelli d'Italia, l'Italia s'è desta—"'

Zito had started singing the Italian national anthem in a booming voice.

'Come on, Nicolò, I'm not in the mood for jokes.'

'Who's joking? I'm about to read you a press release that was sent to me just a few minutes ago. Plant your arse firmly in your chair. For your information, this was sent to us, to TeleVigàta, and to five different newspaper correspondents. I quote:

Montelusa Police Commissioner's Office.

For strictly personal reasons, Ernesto Panzacchi has asked to be relieved of his responsibilities as captain of the Flying Squad and to be placed on reserve. His request has been granted. Mr Anselmo Irrera will temporarily assume the position vacated by Captain Panzacchi. As some new and unexpected developments have emerged in the Licalzi murder case, Inspector Salvo Montalbano of Vigàta police will assume charge of the investigation for its duration.

Signed: Bonetti-Alderighi,
Montelusa Police Commissioner.

'We won, Salvo!'

Montalbano thanked his friend and hung up. He did not feel happy. The tension had dissipated, of course; he'd got the answer he wanted. Still, he felt a kind of malaise, a profound uneasiness. He cursed Panzacchi sincerely, not for what he'd done, but for having forced him to act in a way that now troubled him.

The door flew open, the whole staff rushed in. 'Inspector!' said Galluzzo. 'My brother-in-law phoned just now from TeleVigàta, they just got a press release—'

'I know, I've already been told.'

'We're going to go out and buy a bottle of spumante and . . .'

Giallombardo, withering under Montalbano's gaze, didn't finish the sentence. They all filed out slowly, muttering under their breath. He had one foul disposition, that inspector . . .

*

Judge Tommaseo didn't have the courage to show his face to Montalbano and pretended to be going over some important papers, bent over his desk. The inspector imagined that at that moment the judge wished he looked like the Abominable Snowman, with a beard covering his entire face, though Tommaseo's bulk fell short of the yeti's.

'You must understand, Inspector. As far as withdrawing the weapons possession charge, there's no problem, I've already called Mr Di Blasi's lawyer. But it's not quite so easy for me to lift the complicity charges. Until proved to the contrary, Maurizio Di Blasi is self-convicted of the murder of Michela Licalzi. My prerogatives in no way permit me to—'

'Good day,' said Montalbano, getting up and walking out.

Judge Tommaseo came running after him along the corridor.

'Inspector, wait! I want to clarify—'

'There is nothing at all to clarify, Your Honour. Have you spoken with the commissioner?'

'Yes, at great length. We met at eight o'clock this morning.'

'Then you must surely be aware of certain details of no importance to you. Such as the fact that the investigation of the Licalzi murder was conducted like a toilet-cleaning operation, that young Di Blasi was ninety-nine per cent innocent, that he was slaughtered like a pig by mistake, and that Panzacchi covered it all up. You can't dismiss the weapons charges against the engineer and at the same time not start proceedings against Panzacchi, who actually planted the weapons in his house.'

'I'm still examining Captain Panzacchi's situation.'

'Good. Examine it well. But choose the right scales, among the many you keep in your office.'

Tommaseo was about to react, but reconsidered and said nothing.

'Tell me something, for the sake of curiosity,' said Montalbano. 'Why hasn't Mrs Licalzi's body been turned over to her husband yet?'

The judge's embarrassment became more pronounced. He clenched his right hand in a fist and stuck his right index finger in it.

'Uh, that was ... yes, that was Captain Panzacchi's idea. He pointed out to me that public opinion ... In short, first the body was found, then Di Blasi died, then the funeral of Mrs Licalzi, then young Maurizio's funeral ... Don't you see?'

'No.'

'It was better to spread them out, over time ... To relieve some of the pressure on people, all the crowding...'

He was still talking, but the inspector was already at the end of the corridor.

*

When he came out of the court building it was already two o'clock. But instead of returning to Vigàta, he took the Enna–Palermo road. Galluzzo had carefully explained to him how to find the petrol station and bar-restaurant where Michela Licalzi had been seen. The station, located just three kilometres outside Montelusa, was closed. The inspector cursed the saints, drove another two kilometres, then saw, on his left, a sign that said: TRUCKERS' BAR-TRATTORIA. As oncoming traffic was heavy, the inspector waited patiently for someone to decide to let him turn, but, seeing there was no hope in heaven, he cut right in front of everyone, amidst a pandemonium of screeching tyres, horn blasts, curses and insults, and pulled into the bar's parking lot.

It was very crowded inside. He walked up to the cashier.

'I'd like to speak with a Mr Gerlando Agrò.'

'That's me. And who are you?'

'Inspector Salvo Montalbano. You phoned TeleVigàta to say—'

'Well, goddamn it all! Did you have to come right now? Can't you see how busy I am?'

Montalbano got an idea that struck him as brilliant.

'How's the food here?'

'See those people sittin' down? They's all truckers. Ever seen a trucker go wrong?'

At the end of the meal (the idea hadn't been brilliant, but only good, the food remaining within ironclad limits of normality, with no flights of fancy), after the coffee and anisette, the cashier, who'd got a boy to take his place, approached Montalbano's table.

'Now we can talk,' he said. 'OK if I sit down?'

'Of course.'

Gerlando Agrò immediately had second thoughts.

'Maybe it's better if you come with me.'

They went out of the building.

'OK. Wednesday, around eleven thirty at night, I was here outside, smoking a cigarette, and I saw this Twingo pull in off the Enna–Palermo road.'

'Are you sure?'

'I'd bet my life on it. The car stopped right in front of me, and a lady, who was driving, got out.'

'Would also bet your life it was the same woman you saw on TV?'

'Inspector, with a woman like that, poor thing, it's hard to make a mistake.'

'Go on.'

'The man, on the other hand, stayed in the car.'

'How did you know it was a man?'

'See, there was a truck with its headlights on. I was surprised, because usually it's the man that gets out and the woman who stays in the car. Anyway, the lady ordered two salami sandwiches and bought a bottle of mineral water. My son Tanino was at the cash register, the same kid who's there now. The lady paid and went down these three steps here. But on the last step, she tripped and fell, and the sandwiches flew out of her hands. I went down the steps to help her up and I found myself face-to-face with the man, who'd got out of the car. "It's all right, it's all right," the lady said. The guy got back in the car, she ordered two more sandwiches, paid, and they drove off in the direction of Montelusa.'

'You've been very helpful, Mr Agrò. And I assume you can also say that the man you saw on television was not the same man who was in the car with the lady.'

'Definitely not. Two totally different people.'

'Where did the lady keep her money? In a large bag?'

'No sir, Inspector. She didn't have any bag. She had a little purse in her hand.'

*

After the tension of the morning and the hearty meal he'd just eaten, fatigue came over him. He decided to go home to Marinella and sleep for an hour. Just past the bridge, however, he couldn't resist. He stopped, got out, and rang the intercom. Nobody answered. Anna had probably gone out to see Mrs Di Blasi. Perhaps it was just as well.

At home, he phoned headquarters.

'I want Galluzzo here at five with the squad car,' he said.

He dialled Livia's number, and it rang and rang to no avail. He dialled the number of her friend in Genoa.

'Montalbano here. Listen, I'm starting to get seriously worried. It's been days since—'

'Don't worry. Livia just phoned me a little while ago to let me know she was OK.'

'Where on earth is she?'

'I don't know. All I know is she called personnel and asked for another day off.'

He hung up and the phone rang.

'Inspector Montalbano?'

'Yes, who's this?'

'Guttadauro. My compliments, Inspector.'

Montalbano hung up, undressed, got into the shower, then came out and threw himself down, still naked, on the bed. He fell asleep immediately.

*

'*Riiing, riiing,*' a faraway sound chimed in his head. He realized it was the doorbell. He got up with effort, and went and opened the door. Seeing him naked, Galluzzo leaped backwards.

'What's the matter, Gallù? Think I'm going to drag you inside and make you do lewd things?'

'I've been ringing for the last half hour, Inspector. I was about to break down the door.'

'Do that and you'll have to pay for a new one. I'll be back in a second.'

*

The petrol-station attendant was a young man of about thirty with tight curls, dark, sparkling eyes and a solid, slender body. Though he was wearing overalls, the inspector could easily imagine him as a lifeguard on the beach at Rimini, playing havoc with the German girls.

'You say the lady was on her way from Montelusa, and it was eight o'clock.'

'Sure as death. I was closing up at the end of my shift. She rolled down her window and asked me if I could fill it up for her. "For you, I'll stay open all night if you want," I said. She got out of the car. Jesus, was she ever a beauty.'

'Do you remember how she was dressed?'

'All in denim.'

'Did she have any luggage?'

'She had a kind of large handbag on the back seat of the car.'

'Go on.'

'I finished filling up her tank, I told her how much she owed me, and she paid me with a one-hundred-thousand-lire bill, which she took from her purse. As I was giving her change — I like to kid around with the ladies, you see — I asked her, "Anything special I can do for you?" I sort of expected her to answer with an insult, but she just smiled and said, "For the special things I've already got someone." And she continued on her way.'

'She didn't turn back towards Montelusa? Are you sure of that?'

'Absolutely certain. The poor thing, when I think of how she ended up!'

'OK. Thanks.'

'Oh, one more thing, Inspector. She was in a hurry. After I filled up her tank, she drove off really fast. See down there? It's all straight. I watched her car till she rounded the bend. She was really speeding.'

*

'I'd planned to come home tomorrow,' said Gillo Jàcono, 'but as I got back today, I thought I'd check in with you right away.'

A distinguished man in his thirties, with a pleasant face.

'Thanks for coming.'

'I wanted to tell you that with something like this, you think about it again and again.'

'Do you want to change the statement you made over the phone?'

'Absolutely not. Although, after playing the thing over and over in my head, I would like to add one detail. But just to be safe, you probably ought to preface what I'm about to say with a very big "maybe".'

'Go ahead and talk.'

'Well, the man was carrying his suitcase without effort, in his left hand, and that's why I had the impression it wasn't very full. Whereas with his right arm he was supporting the woman.'

'Did he have his arm around her?'

'Not exactly. She was resting her hand on his arm. It

seemed to me – seemed, I repeat – as if she was limping slightly.'

*

'Dr Pasquano? Montalbano here. Am I disturbing you?'

'I was making a Y-shaped incision in a corpse. I don't think he'll mind if I stop for a few minutes.'

'Did you notice any signs on Mrs Licalzi's body that might indicate that she fell sometime before her death?'

'I don't remember. Let me take a look at the report.'

He returned before the inspector could light his cigarette.

'Yes. She'd fallen on one knee. But she was clothed at the time. In the abrasion on her left knee we found microscopic fibres from the jeans she was wearing.'

*

There was no need for further confirmation. At 8 p.m., Michela Licalzi fills her tank and heads inland. Three and a half hours later she's on her way back with a man. Sometime after midnight she's seen with a man again, certainly the same man, walking towards her house outside Vigàta.

'Hi, Anna. Salvo here. I dropped by your place early this afternoon, but you weren't there.'

'Mr Di Blasi called and said his wife was unwell.'

'I hope soon to have good news for them.'

Anna said nothing, and Montalbano realized he'd said

something stupid. The only news the Di Blasis might consider good was the resurrection of Maurizio.

'Anna, I wanted to tell you something I discovered about Michela.'

'Why don't you come over?'

No, he shouldn't. He realized that if Anna brought her lips to his another time, no good would come of it.

'I can't, Anna. I have an engagement.'

Good thing he was on the phone, because if he'd been right in front of her, she would have immediately realized he was lying.

'What did you want to tell me?'

'I have worked out, with a convincing degree of certainty, that at eight o'clock on Wednesday evening, Michela took the Enna–Palermo road. She may have been going to a town in the Montelusa province. Now, think hard before answering: as far as you know, did she have any other acquaintances in the area, aside from the people she knew in Montelusa and Vigàta?'

The answer didn't come immediately. Anna was thinking about it, as the inspector had asked.

'Look – friends, I doubt it. She'd have told me. Acquaintances, on the other hand, yes, a few.'

'Where?'

'For example, in Aragona and Comitini, which are both along that road.'

'What kind of acquaintances?'

'She bought her floor tiles in Aragona. And she got

some other supplies that I can't remember now in Comitini.'

'Therefore only business dealings.'

'I'd say so. But, you see, Salvo, you can go just about anywhere from that road. There's a turn that goes to Raffadali, for one; the captain of the Flying Squad could have spun something out of that, too.'

'Another thing: sometime after midnight, she was seen in her drive, after getting out of her car. She was leaning on a man.'

'Are you sure?'

'I'm sure.'

The pause this time was very long. So long that the inspector thought they'd been cut off.

'Are you still there, Anna?'

'Yes. Salvo, I want to repeat, clearly, once and for all, what I said before. Michela was not the kind of woman who went in for fly-by-night affairs. She confided to me that she was physically incapable of it. Will you understand that? She loved her husband. And she was very, very attached to Serravalle. She could not have consented, I don't care what the coroner thinks. She was horribly raped.'

'How do you explain that she didn't phone to let the Vassallos know she wouldn't be coming to dinner at their house? She had a mobile phone, didn't she?'

'I don't understand what you're getting at.'

'I'll explain. When Michela left you at seven thirty,

saying she was going back to the hotel, she was telling you the absolute truth at that moment. But then something happened that made her change her mind. And it can only have been a call to her mobile, since when she was travelling up the Enna–Palermo road, she was still alone.'

'You think she was on her way to an appointment?'

'There's no other explanation. It was unexpected, but she didn't want to miss that appointment. That's why she didn't call the Vassallos. She had no plausible excuse that might justify her not coming, and so the best thing was to give them the slip. Let's set aside, if you want, the possibility of an amorous rendezvous; maybe it was a work-related appointment that somehow turned tragic. I'll grant you that for the moment. But in that case I ask you: what could have been of such importance as to make her behave so rudely towards the Vassallos?'

'I don't know,' Anna said dejectedly.

FIFTEEN

What could have been so important? the inspector asked himself again after saying goodbye to his friend. If not love or sex, which in Anna's opinion were out of the question, that left only money. During the construction of the house, Michela must have handled some money, and a fair amount at that. Might the key lie hidden there? The conjecture, however, immediately seemed to him without substance, a thread in a spider's web. But he was duty-bound to investigate all the same.

'Anna? Salvo again.'

'Did your engagement fall through? Can you come over?'

There was such happiness and eagerness in the girl's voice, the inspector didn't want a note of disappointment to spoil it.

'Well, I won't say I can't make it at all.'

'Come whenever you like.'

'OK, but there's something I wanted to ask you.

Do you know if Michela opened a bank account in Vigàta?'

'Yes, it was more convenient for paying bills. It was with the Banca Popolare. But I don't know how much she had in it.'

It was too late to dash over to the bank. He opened a drawer in which he'd put all the papers he'd taken from the hotel room, and selected the dozens of bills and the little notebook of expenses. The diary and the rest of the papers he put back in the drawer. It was going to be a long, boring task, and 90 per cent certain to prove utterly useless. Besides, he was no good at numbers.

He carefully examined all the invoices. As far as he could tell at a glance, they did not appear inflated; the prices seemed to correspond to the market rates and were even occasionally a little lower. Apparently Michela knew how to bargain and save. No dice, therefore. A useless task, as he had expected. Then, by chance, he noticed a discrepancy between the amount on one bill and the round figure recorded in the notebook; the cost had been increased by five million lire. Could Michela, normally so well organized and precise, have possibly made so obvious a mistake? He started over from the top, with the patience of a saint. The end result he arrived at was that the difference between the amounts registered in the notebook and the money actually spent was one hundred and fifteen million lire.

A mistake was therefore out of the question. But if

there hadn't been a mistake, it made no sense, because it meant that Michela was taking a cut of her own money. Unless . . .

'Hello, Dr Licalzi? Inspector Montalbano here. Excuse me for calling you at home after work.'

'Yes, it's been a bad day, in fact.'

'I'd like to know something about your . . . Let me put it another way: did you and your wife have a joint bank account?'

'Inspector, weren't you—'

'Taken off the case? Yes, I was, but now everything is back to how it was before.'

'No, we didn't have a joint account. Michela had hers and I had mine.'

'Your wife had no income of her own, did she?'

'No, she didn't. We had an arrangement where every six months I would transfer a certain sum from my account into hers. If her expenses exceeded that amount, she would tell me and I'd take care of it.'

'I see. Did she ever show you the invoices concerning the house?'

'No, and I wasn't interested, really. At any rate, she recorded her expenditures one by one in a notebook. Every now and then I'd give it a look.'

'Doctor, thank you and—'

'Did you take care of it?'

What was he supposed to have taken care of? He didn't know how to answer.

'The Twingo,' the doctor helped him.

'Oh, yes, it's already been done.'

It certainly was easy to lie on the phone. They said goodbye and made an appointment to see each other on Friday morning, the day of the funeral.

Now it all made more sense. The wife was taking a cut of the money she was getting from her husband to build the house. Once the invoices were destroyed (which Michela certainly would have done had she remained alive), only the figures logged into her notebook would have remained. Just like that, one hundred and fifteen million lire had slipped into the shadows, and she had used them however she wished.

But what did she need that money for? Was somebody blackmailing her? And if so, what did Michela Licalzi have to hide?

*

The following morning, as he was about to get in his car and drive to work, the telephone rang. For a moment he was tempted not to answer. A phone call to his home at that hour could only have been an annoying, pain-in-the-arse call from headquarters.

Then the unquestionable power that the telephone has over man won out.

'Salvo?'

He immediately recognized Livia's voice and felt his legs turn to jelly.

'Livia! Finally! Where are you?'

'In Montelusa.'

What was she doing in Montelusa? When did she get there?

'I'll come and get you. Are you at the station?'

'No. If you wait for me, I'll be at your place in half an hour at the most.'

'I'll wait for you.'

What was going on? What the hell was going on? He called headquarters.

'Don't pass any calls on to me at home.'

In half an hour he downed four cups of coffee. He put the *napoletana* back on the burner. Then he heard a car pull up and stop. It must be Livia's taxi. He opened the door. It wasn't a taxi, it was Mimì Augello's car. Livia got out, the car turned around and left.

Montalbano began to understand.

She looked slovenly and dishevelled, with dark circles round her eyes, which were swollen from crying. But most of all, how had she become so tiny and fragile? A plucked sparrow. Montalbano felt overcome with tenderness and emotion.

'Come,' he said, taking her hand, leading her into the house, and sitting her down in the dining room. He saw her shudder.

'Are you cold?'

'Yes.'

He went into the bedroom, got a jacket and put it over her shoulders.

'Want some coffee?'

'All right.'

It had just boiled, and he served it piping hot. Livia drank it down as if it was cold.

＊

They were sitting on the bench on the veranda. Livia had wanted to go outside. The day was so serene it looked fake. No wind, only a few light waves. Livia gazed long at the sea in silence, then rested her head on Salvo's shoulder and started crying, without sobbing. The tears streamed down her face and wet the little table. Montalbano took one of her hands; she surrendered it lifelessly to him. The inspector needed desperately to light a cigarette, but didn't.

'I went to see François,' Livia said suddenly.

'I guessed.'

'I decided not to tell Franca I was coming. I got on a plane, grabbed a taxi, and descended on them out of the blue. As soon as he saw me, François ran into my arms. He was truly happy to see me. And I was so happy to hold him and furious at Franca and her husband, and especially at you. I was convinced that everything was as I'd suspected: that you and they had been conspiring to take him away from me. And, well, I started railing against them and insulting them. All of a sudden, as I was trying to calm down, I realized that François was no longer beside me. I began to suspect they'd hidden him from me, locked him in a room somewhere, and I started to scream. I screamed so loudly that they all came running, Franca's children, Aldo, the three labourers. And they all started asking each other where François was, but nobody'd seen him. Now worried, they all went outside, calling his name. I remained alone inside, crying. Suddenly I heard a voice. "Livia, I'm here." It was him. He'd hidden somewhere inside the house, and they were all looking for him outside. See how clever and intelligent he is?'

She broke out in tears again, having held them too long inside.

'Just relax. Lie down a bit. You can tell me the rest later,' said Montalbano, who couldn't bear Livia's torment. With some effort he refrained from embracing her, sensing that this would have been the wrong move.

'But I'm leaving,' said Livia. 'My flight leaves Palermo at two this afternoon.'

'I'll drive you there.'

'No, I've already arranged it all with Mimì. He's coming by in an hour to pick me up.'

The moment Mimì walks into the office, the inspector thought, *I'm going to bust his arse so badly he won't be able to walk.*

'It was he who persuaded me to come and see you; I wanted to go home yesterday.'

Oh, so now he was supposed to thank Mimì into the bargain?

'You didn't want to see me?'

'Try to understand, Salvo. I need to be alone, to collect my thoughts, to draw some conclusions. This has all been overwhelming for me.'

The inspector felt curious to know the rest.

'Well, tell me what happened next.'

'As soon as I saw François there in the room, I instinctively drew near to him, but he moved away.'

Montalbano remembered the scene he'd endured a few days earlier.

'He looked me straight in the eye and said, "I love you, Livia, but I won't leave this house and my brothers." I sat there immobile, frozen. And he went on, "If you take me away with you, I'll run away for good and you'll never see me again." Then he ran out shouting, "I'm here, I'm here!" I started to feel dizzy, and the next thing I knew I was lying in a bed, with Franca beside me. My God, how cruel children can be sometimes!'

And wasn't what we wanted to do to him cruel? Montalbano thought.

'I felt very weak. When I tried to get up, I fainted again. Franca didn't want me to leave. She called a doctor and never left my side. I slept there. Actually slept! I spent the whole night sitting in a chair by the window. The next morning Mimì came. Her sister had phoned him. Mimì has been like a brother to me, more than a brother. He made sure I didn't run into François again. He took me out, showed me half Sicily, and he talked me into coming here, even if only for an hour. "The two of you need to talk, to explain yourselves," he said. We got to Montelusa last night, and he accompanied me to the Hotel Della Valle. This morning he came round and brought me here. My suitcase is in his car.'

'I don't think there's much to explain,' said Montalbano.

An explanation would have been possible only if Livia, realizing she'd been wrong, had expressed a word of understanding, just one, regarding his feelings. Or did she think that he, Salvo, had felt nothing when he realized they'd lost François for ever? Livia wasn't allowing for any openings, she was shut up inside her own grief and could see nothing but her own selfish despair. And what about him? Weren't they, until proven otherwise, a couple whose bond was built on love, yes, and on sex, too, but above all on a relationship of mutual understanding that bordered at times on complicity? One word too many, at that moment, might trigger an irreparable rupture. Montalbano swallowed his resentment.

'What do you intend to do?' he asked.

'About ... the boy?' She couldn't bring herself to pronounce François's name.

'Yes.'

'I won't stand in his way.'

She got up abruptly and ran towards the sea, moaning in a low voice like a mortally wounded animal. Then, unable to stand it any longer, she threw herself face down on the sand. Montalbano picked her up in his arms, carried her into the house, laid her down on the bed, and with a damp towel gently wiped the sand off her face.

*

When he heard the horn of Mimì Augello's car, Montalbano helped Livia stand up and put her clothes in order. Utterly passive, she let him do as he wished. With an arm around her waist, he escorted her outside. Mimì did not get out of the car. He knew it was unwise to get too close to his superior; he might get bitten. He stared straight ahead the whole time, to avoid meeting the inspector's gaze. Right before getting in the car, Livia turned her head slightly and kissed Montalbano on the cheek. The inspector returned to the house, went into the bathroom, and got into the shower, clothes and all, turning the water on full blast. Then he swallowed two sleeping pills, which he never took, washed them down with a glass of whisky, threw himself on the bed, and waited for the inevitable blow to lay him out.

*

When he woke it was five in the afternoon. He had a slight headache and felt nauseated.

'Augello here?' he asked, walking into the station.

Mimì entered Montalbano's office and prudently closed the door behind him. He looked resigned.

'If you start yelling like you usually do,' he said, 'it's probably better if we go outside.'

The inspector got up from his chair, brought himself face-to-face with Mimì, then put an arm around the other's neck.

'You're a real friend, Mimì. But I advise you to leave this room immediately. I'm liable to change my mind and start kicking you.'

*

'Inspector? Clementina Vasile Cozzo's on the line. Shall I put her through?'

'And who are you?'

It couldn't possibly be Catarella.

'What do you mean, who am I? I'm me.'

'And what the hell is your name?'

'It's Catarella, Chief! Poissonally in poisson!'

Thank God for that. The impromptu identity check had resuscitated the old Catarella, not the one the computer was inexorably transforming.

'Inspector! What happened? Are you angry with me?'

'Signora, believe me, I've had some pretty strange days . . .'

'You're forgiven. Could you come to my flat? I have something to show you.'

'Now?'

'Now.'

*

Signora Clementina escorted him into the living room and turned off the television.

'Look at this. It's the programme of tomorrow's concert, which Maestro Cataldo Barbera had someone bring to me a short while ago.'

Montalbano took the torn, squared notebook page from the signora's hand. Was this why she'd so urgently wanted to see him?

On it, in pencil, was written: *Friday, nine thirty. Concert in memory of Michela Licalzi.*

Montalbano gave a start. Did Maestro Barbera know the victim?

'That's why I asked you to come,' said Mrs Vasile Cozzo, reading the question in his eyes.

The inspector went back to studying the sheet of paper.

> Programme: G. Tartini, 'Variations on a Theme
> by Corelli'; J. S. Bach, 'Largo'; G. B. Viotti, from
> Concerto no. 24 in E minor.

He handed the sheet back to Mrs Vasile Cozzo.

'Did you know that they were acquainted, signora?'

'Never. And I wonder how that could be, since the Maestro never goes outside. As soon as I read that piece of paper, I knew it might be of interest to you.'

'I'm going to go upstairs and talk to him.'

'You're wasting your time. He'll refuse to see you. It's six thirty. He's already gone to bed.'

'What does he do, watch television?'

'He hasn't got a television, and he doesn't read news-papers. He goes to sleep, and then wakes up around two o'clock in the morning. I asked the maid if she knew why the Maestro keeps such odd hours, and she said she had no idea. But, after giving it some thought, I think I've found a plausible explanation.'

'Which is?'

'I believe that the Maestro, in so doing, blots out a specific period of time, that is, he cancels, skips over, the hours during which he normally used to perform. By sleeping through them, he erases them from his memory.'

'I see. But I can't not talk to him.'

'You could try tomorrow morning, after the concert.'

A door slammed upstairs.

'There,' said Mrs Vasile Cozzo, 'the maid is going home now.'

Montalbano made a move towards the door.

'Actually, Inspector, she's more a housekeeper than a maid,' Mrs Vasile Cozzo explained.

Montalbano opened the door. A woman in her sixties, appropriately dressed, descended the final steps from the floor above and greeted the inspector with a nod of the head.

'Ma'am, I'm Inspector—'

'I know.'

'I realize you're on your way home, and I don't want

to waste your time. But tell me, did Maestro Barbera and Mrs Licalzi know each other?'

'Yes. They met about two months ago. The lady had come to the Maestro on her own initiative. He was very happy about this, since he rather likes pretty women. They got into an involved conversation. I then brought them coffee, which they drank, and then they closed themselves in the studio, where you can't hear anything.'

'Soundproof?'

'Yes, sir. So he doesn't disturb the neighbours.'

'Did the lady ever come back?'

'Not when I was there.'

'And when are you there?'

'Can't you see? I leave in the evening.'

'Tell me something. If the Maestro has no television and doesn't read newspapers, how did he find out about the murder?'

'I told him myself, by chance, this afternoon. I saw the funeral announcement for tomorrow on the street.'

'And how did the Maestro react?'

'Very badly. He turned all pale and asked for his heart pills. What a fright I had! Anything else?'

SIXTEEN

That morning the inspector showed up at the office dressed in a grey suit, pale blue shirt, neutral tie and black shoes.

'My, my, don't we look fashionable?' said Mimì Augello.

Montalbano couldn't very well tell him he'd decked himself out to attend a violin recital at nine thirty in the morning. Mimì would have thought him insane. And rightly so, since the whole business did have something of the madhouse about it.

'Actually, I have to go to a funeral,' he muttered.

He went into his office; the phone was ringing.

'Salvo? This is Anna. A little while ago I got a phone call from Guido Serravalle.'

'Was he calling from Bologna?'

'No, from Montelusa. He said Michela'd given him my number some time ago. He knew we were friends. He's down here for the funeral, staying at the Della Valle.

He asked me to join him for lunch afterwards; he's going back in the afternoon. What should I do?'

'In what sense?'

'I don't know, I'm afraid I'll feel awkward.'

'Why?'

*

'Inspector? This is Emanuele Licalzi. Are you coming to the funeral?'

'Yes. What time does it begin?'

'At eleven. When it's over, the hearse will head straight for Bologna after it leaves the church. Any news?'

'Nothing major, for now. Will you be staying long in Montelusa?'

'Till tomorrow morning. I need to talk to an estate agent about selling the house. I have to go there this afternoon with one of their representatives; they want to see it. By the way, yesterday evening I flew down here with Guido Serravalle. He's here for the funeral.'

'That must have been uncomfortable.'

'You think so?'

Dr Emanuele Licalzi had lowered his visor again.

*

'Hurry, he's about to begin,' said Signora Clementina, leading him into the little parlour next to the living room. They sat down solemnly. For the occasion, the signora had put on an evening gown. She looked like one of

Boldini's ladies, only older. At nine thirty sharp, Maestro Barbera struck up the first notes. And before he'd been listening even five minutes, the inspector began to get a strange, disturbing feeling. It seemed to him as if the violin had suddenly become a voice, a woman's voice, that was begging to be heard and understood. Slowly but surely the notes turned into syllables, or rather into phonemes, and yet they expressed a kind of lament, a song of ancient suffering that at moments reached searing, mysteriously tragic heights. And this stirring female voice told of a terrible secret that could only be understood by someone capable of abandoning himself entirely to the sound, the waves of sound. He closed his eyes, profoundly shaken and troubled. But deep down he was also astonished. How could this violin have so changed in timbre since the last time he'd heard it? With eyes still closed, he let himself be guided by the voice. And he saw himself enter Michela Licalzi's house, walk through the living room, open the glass display, and pick up the violin case . . . So *that*'s what had been tormenting him, the element that clashed with the whole! The blinding light that burst inside his head made him cry out.

'Were you also moved?' asked Signora Clementina, wiping away a tear. 'He's never played like that before.'

The concert must have ended at that very moment, for the signora plugged the phone back in, dialled the number, and applauded.

This time, instead of joining in, the inspector grabbed the phone.

'Maestro? Inspector Montalbano here. I absolutely have to speak to you.'

'And I to you.'

Montalbano hung up, and, in one swift motion, bent over, embraced Signora Clementina, kissed her forehead, and went out.

✣

The door to the flat was opened by the housekeeper.

'Would you like a coffee?'

'No, thank you.'

Cataldo Barbera came forward, hand extended.

On his way up the two flights of stairs, Montalbano had given some thought to how the Maestro might be dressed. He'd hit the nail on the head: Maestro Barbera, a tiny man with snow-white hair and small, black, but very intense eyes, was wearing a well-cut coat and tails.

The only jarring note was a white silk scarf wrapped around the lower part of his face, covering his nose, mouth and chin, leaving only his eyes and forehead exposed. The scarf was held in place by a gold hairpin.

'Please come in, make yourself comfortable,' Barbera said politely, leading him into the soundproof studio.

Inside, there was a glass display case with five violins; a complex stereo system; a set of metal office shelves stacked with CDs, LPs and cassette tapes; a bookcase, a desk and two armchairs. On the desk sat another violin, apparently the one the Maestro had just played in his recital.

'Today I used the Guarneri,' he said, confirming Montalbano's suspicion and gesturing towards the instrument. 'It has an incomparable voice, heavenly.'

Montalbano congratulated himself. Though he didn't know the first thing about music, he had nevertheless intuited that that violin sounded different from the one he'd heard in the previous recital.

'For a violinist, believe me, it's nothing short of a miracle to have such a jewel at one's disposal.' He sighed. 'Unfortunately, I have to give it back.'

'It's not yours?'

'I wish it were! The problem is, I no longer know whom to give it back to. I'd intended to phone the police station today and ask somebody there. But since you're here...'

'I'm at your service.'

'You see, that violin belonged to the late Mrs Licalzi.'

The inspector felt all his nerves tighten up like violin strings. If the Maestro had run his bow across him, a chord would have rung out.

'About two months ago,' Maestro Barbera recounted, 'I was practising with the window open. Mrs Licalzi, who happened to be walking by, heard me. She was very knowledgeable about music, you know. She saw my name on the intercom downstairs and wanted to meet me. She'd been at my very last performance in Milan, after which I retired, though nobody knew that at the time.'

'Why did you retire?'

The bluntness of the question caught the Maestro by surprise. He hesitated, though only for a moment, then pulled out the hairpin and slowly unwrapped the scarf. A monster: half his nose was gone; his upper lip had been entirely eaten away, exposing the gums.

'Is that a good enough reason?'

He wrapped the scarf around himself again, securing it with the pin.

'It's a very rare, degenerative form of lupus, totally incurable. How could I continue to appear in public?'

The inspector felt grateful to him for putting the scarf back on at once. He was impossible to look at; one felt horrified, nauseated.

'Anyway, that beautiful, gentle creature, talking of this and that, told me about a violin she'd inherited from a great-grandfather from Cremona who used to make stringed instruments. She added that, as a child, she'd heard it said within the family that it was worth a fortune, though she'd never paid much attention to this. These legends of priceless paintings and statuettes worth millions are common talk in families. I'm not sure why, but I became curious. A few days later she phoned me in the evening, then came round to pick me up, and took me to the house she'd recently built. The moment I saw that violin, I tell you, something burst inside me, I felt a kind of overpowering electrical shock. It was in a pretty bad state, but I knew it wouldn't take much to restore it to perfection. It was an Andrea Guarneri, Inspector, easily recognizable by the powerful glow of its amber-yellow varnish.'

The inspector glanced at the violin, and in all sincerity he didn't see any glow coming from it. Then again, he was hopeless in matters of music.

'I tried playing it,' said the Maestro, 'and for ten minutes I was transported to heaven in the company of Paganini, Ole Bull and others . . .'

'What's its market value?' asked the inspector, who usually flew close to the ground and had never come close to heaven.

'Market value?!' the Maestro said in horror. 'You can't put a price on an instrument like that!'

'All right, but if you had to quantify—'

'I really don't know . . . Two, three billion lire.'

Had he heard right? He had.

'I did make it clear to the lady that she mustn't risk leaving so valuable an instrument in a practically uninhabited house. We came up with a solution, also because I wanted authoritative confirmation of my assumption – that is, that it was indeed an Andrea Guarneri. She suggested I keep it here at my place. I didn't want to accept such an immense responsibility, but in the end she talked me into it, and she didn't even want a receipt. Then she drove me home and I gave her one of my violins to take its place in the old case. If anyone were to steal it, little harm would be done; it wasn't worth more than a few hundred thousand lire. The next morning I tried to reach a friend of mine in Milan, the foremost expert on violins there is. His secretary told me he was abroad, travelling the world, and wouldn't be back before the end of this month.'

'Please excuse me,' said the inspector. 'I'll be back shortly.'

He rushed out and ran all the way to headquarters on foot.

'Fazio!'

'At your service, Chief.'

Montalbano wrote something on a piece of paper, signed it and stamped it with the Vigàta Police seal to make it official.

'Come with me.'

They took his car and pulled up a short distance from the church.

'Give this note to Dr Licalzi. I want him to give you the keys to the house in Tre Fontane. I can't go in there myself. If I'm seen in church talking to the doctor, who's going to stop the rumours?'

Less than five minutes later they were already on their way to Tre Fontane.

They got out of the car, and Montalbano opened the front door. There was a foul, suffocating smell inside, owing not only to the lack of circulation, but also to the powders and sprays used by forensics.

With Fazio still behind him not asking any questions, he opened the glass display case, grabbed the violin case, went out, and relocked the door.

'Wait, I want to see something.'

He turned the corner of the house and went round to the back, which he'd never done the other times he'd been there. He found the rough draft of what would have one day become a vast garden. On the right, almost attached to the house, stood a giant sorb tree, the kind that produced little bright-red fruits rather sour in flavour, which Montalbano ate in great abundance when he was a child.

'I want you to climb up to the top branch.'

'Who, me?'

'No, your twin brother.'

Fazio started climbing half-heartedly. He was well into middle age and afraid of falling and breaking his neck.

'Wait for me there.'

'Yes, sir. After all, I was a Tarzan fan when I was a kid.'

Montalbano reopened the front door, went upstairs, turned on the bedroom light — here the smell grabbed him by the throat — and raised the rolling shutter without opening the window.

'Can you see me?' he yelled to Fazio.

'Yes, perfectly!'

He went out of the house, locked the door, and headed back to the car.

Fazio wasn't in it. He was still up in the tree, waiting for the inspector to tell him what to do next.

*

After dropping Fazio off in front of the church to give the keys back to Dr Licalzi ('Tell him we may need them again'), he drove to Maestro Barbera's place. There, he climbed the steps two at a time. The Maestro opened the door for him. He was now dressed in a turtleneck sweater and slacks, having doffed the coat and tails. The white silk scarf with gold pin, however, was still in place.

'Come in,' said Cataldo Barbera.

'No need, Maestro. I'll just be a few seconds. Is this the Guarneri's case?'

The Maestro took it, studied it closely, and handed it back.

'It certainly looks like it.'

Montalbano opened the case and, without taking the instrument out, asked, 'Is this the violin you gave to Michela to keep?'

The Maestro took two steps backward and extended his arm as if to shield himself from an unbearable sight.

'I wouldn't touch that thing with my little finger! Look at that! It's mass-produced! It's an affront to any proper violin!'

Here was confirmation of what the voice of the violin

had revealed to Montalbano. From the start he had unconsciously registered the difference between the container and its contents. It was clear even to him, who knew nothing about violins. Or about any other kind of instrument, for that matter.

'Among other things,' Cataldo Barbera continued, 'the one I gave to Michela Licalzi may have been of very modest value, but it rather looked like a Guarneri.'

'Thank you. I'll be seeing you.'

Montalbano started down the stairs.

'What should I do with the Guarneri?' the Maestro called out in a loud voice, still at sea, not having understood a thing.

'Just hang on to it for now. And play it as often as you can.'

*

They were loading the coffin into the hearse. Before the main portal of the church were many funeral wreaths lined up in a row. Emanuele Licalzi stood surrounded by a crowd of people expressing condolences. He looked unusually upset. Montalbano approached him and pulled him aside.

'I wasn't expecting all these people,' the doctor said.

'Your wife inspired a lot of affection. Did you get the keys back? I may have to ask you for them again.'

'I'm going to need them between four and five o'clock, to take the estate agent to the house.'

'I'll bear that in mind. Listen, Doctor, when you go into the house, you'll probably notice the violin is missing from the display case. That's because I took it. I'll return it to you this evening.'

The doctor looked dumbfounded.

'Is that of any relevance to the investigation? It's an utterly worthless object.'

'I need it for fingerprints,' Montalbano lied.

'In that case, don't forget that I held it in my hands when I showed it to you.'

'I won't forget. And, Doctor, one more thing, just for curiosity's sake: at what time did you leave Bologna yesterday evening?'

'I took the flight that leaves at six thirty, with a change at Rome, and arrived in Palermo at ten p.m.'

'Thanks.'

'Excuse me, Inspector, don't forget about the Twingo!'

Jesus, what a pain in the arse about that car!

*

Among the crowd of people already preparing to leave, he finally spotted Anna Tropeano talking to a tall, distinguished-looking man of about forty. It had to be Guido Serravalle. Then he noticed Giallombardo passing by on the street. He called to him.

'Where you going?'

'Home, Inspector, for lunch.'

'I'm very sorry, but you can't.'

'Christ, of all days you had to pick the day my wife made *pasta 'ncasciata.*'

'You'll eat it tonight. See those two over there? That brunette lady and the gentleman she's talking to?'

'Yessir.'

'Don't let the guy out of your sight. I'll be back at headquarters soon. Keep me posted every half hour. Everything he does, everywhere he goes.'

'Oh, all right,' said Giallombardo, resigned.

Montalbano left him and walked over to the pair. Anna, who hadn't seen him approaching, brightened at once. Apparently Serravalle's presence made her uncomfortable.

'Salvo, how are you?' She introduced them. 'Inspector Salvo Montalbano, Mr Guido Serravalle.'

Montalbano performed like a god.

'Of course, we already met over the phone!'

'Yes, I offered my help.'

'How could I forget? You came for the late Mrs Licalzi?'

'It was the least I could do.'

'Of course. Are you going back today?'

'Yes, I'll be leaving the hotel around five o'clock. I've got a flight out of Punta Ràisi at eight.'

'Good, good,' said Montalbano. He seemed happy that everyone was so happy and that, among other things, one could count on planes leaving on time.

'You know,' said Anna, assuming a nonchalant, worldly demeanour, 'Mr Serravalle was just inviting me to lunch. Why don't you join us?'

'I would love that,' said Serravalle, absorbing the blow.

A look of deep disappointment came over the inspector's face.

'If only I'd known earlier! I've got an appointment, alas.'

He held his hand out to Serravalle.

'Very pleased to have met you. However inappropriate it may seem to say so, given the circumstances.'

He was afraid he might be overdoing his perfect idiot act; the role was running away with him. Indeed, Anna was glaring at him with eyes that looked like two question marks.

'You and me, on the other hand, we'll talk later, eh, Anna?'

✧

In the doorway to headquarters he ran into Mimì, who was on his way out.

'Where are you off to?'

'To eat.'

'Jesus, is that all anyone can think of around here?'

'When it's time to eat, what else are we supposed to be thinking of?'

'Who've we got in Bologna?'

'As mayor?' asked Mimì, confused.

'What the fuck do I care who the mayor of Bologna is? Have we got any friends in their police department who can give us an answer in an hour's time?'

'Wait, there's Guggino, remember him?'

'Filiberto?'

'Right. He was transferred there a month ago. He's heading the immigration section.'

'Go and eat your spaghetti with clam sauce and all that Parmesan cheese on top,' Montalbano said by way of thanks, looking at him with contempt. How else could you look at someone with tastes like that?

*

It was 12.35. Hopefully Filiberto would still be in his office.

'Hello? Inspector Salvo Montalbano here. I'm calling from Vigàta. I'd like to speak with Filiberto Guggino.'

'Please hold.'

After a series of clicks he heard a cheerful voice.

'Salvo! Good to hear from you! How you doing?'

'Fine, Filibè. Sorry to bother you, but it's urgent. I need some answers within an hour, hour and a half at the most. I'm looking for a financial motive to a crime.'

'The only thing I have to waste is time.'

'I want you to tell me as much as you can possibly find out about someone who might be the victim of loan sharks — say, a businessman, heavy gambler . . .'

'That makes the whole thing a lot more difficult. I can

tell you who the loan sharks are, but not the people they've ruined.'

'Try anyway. Here's his name.'

*

'Chief? Giallombardo here. They're eating at the Contrada Capo restaurant, the one right on the sea. You know it?'

Unfortunately, yes, he did know it. He'd ended up there once by chance and had never forgotten it.

'Did they drive there separately?'

'No, they came in one car and he drove, so—'

'Don't let him out of your sight. I'm sure he's going to take the lady home, then go back to his hotel, the Della Valle. Keep me posted.'

*

Yes and no, the company that rented cars at Punta Ràisi Airport told him after humming and hawing for half an hour about not being authorized to give out information, so much so that he had to get the chief of airport police to intervene on his behalf. Yes, the previous evening, Thursday, that is, the gentleman in question had rented the car he was still using. And, no, the same gentleman had not rented a car from them on Wednesday evening of the previous week, according to the computer.

SEVENTEEN

Guggino's answer came a few minutes before three. It was long and detailed. Montalbano carefully took notes. Five minutes later Giallombardo phoned and told him Serravalle had gone back to his hotel.

'Stay right there and don't move,' the inspector ordered him. 'If you see him go out again before I've arrived, stop him with whatever excuse you can think of. Do a striptease or a belly dance, just don't let him leave.'

He quickly leafed through Michela's papers, remembering that he'd seen a boarding pass among them. There it was. It was for the last journey the woman would ever make from Bologna to Palermo. He put it in his pocket and called Gallo into his office.

'Take me to the Della Valle in the squad car.'

The hotel was halfway between Vigàta and Montelusa and had been built directly behind one of the most beautiful temples in the world – historical conservation offices, landscape constraints and zoning regulations be damned.

'Wait for me here,' the inspector said to Gallo when they got to the hotel. He then walked over to his own car. Giallombardo was taking a nap inside.

'I was sleeping with one eye open!' the policeman assured him.

The inspector opened the boot and took out the case with the cheap violin inside.

'You go back to the station,' he ordered Giallombardo.

He walked into the hotel lobby, looking exactly like a concert violinist.

'Is Mr Serravalle in?'

'Yes, he's in his room. Whom should I say?'

'You shouldn't say anything. You should only keep quiet. I'm Inspector Montalbano. And if you so much as pick up the phone, I'll run you in and we can talk about it later.'

'Fourth floor, room four sixteen,' said the receptionist, lips trembling.

'Has he had any phone calls?'

'I gave him his phone messages when he got in. There were three or four.'

'Let me talk to the operator.'

The operator, whom the inspector, for whatever reason, had imagined as a cute young woman, turned out to be an ageing, bald man in his sixties with glasses.

'The receptionist told me everything. About twelve a certain Eolo started calling from Bologna. He never left his last name. He called again about ten minutes ago and I forwarded the call to Mr Serravalle's room.'

*

In the lift, Montalbano pulled a list of the names of all those who on Wednesday evening of the previous week had rented cars at Punta Ràisi airport from his pocket. True, there was no Guido Serravalle; there was, however, one Eolo Portinari. And Guggino had told him this Portinari was a close friend of the antiquarian.

He tapped very lightly on the door, and as he was doing this, he remembered he'd left his pistol in the glove compartment.

'Come in, it's open.'

The antique dealer was lying down on the bed, hands behind his head. He'd taken off only his shoes and jacket; his tie was still knotted. As soon as he saw the inspector, he jumped to his feet like a jack-in-the-box.

'Relax, relax,' said Montalbano.

'But I insist!' said Serravalle, hastily slipping his shoes on. He even put his jacket back on. Montalbano had sat down in a chair, violin case on his knees.

'I'm ready. To what do I owe the honour?'

'The other day, when we spoke on the phone, you said you would make yourself available to me if I needed you.'

'Absolutely. I repeat the offer,' said Serravalle, also sitting down.

'I would have spared you the trouble, but since you came for the funeral, I thought I'd take advantage of the opportunity.'

'I'm glad. What do you want me to do?'

'Pay attention to me.'

'I'm sorry, I don't quite understand.'

'Listen to what I have to say. I want to tell you a story. If you think I'm exaggerating or wrong on any of the details, please interrupt and correct me.'

'I don't see how I could do that, Inspector, since I don't know the story you're about to tell me.'

'You're right. You mean you'll tell me your impressions at the end. The protagonist of my story is a gentleman who has a pretty comfortable life. He's a man of taste, owns a well-known antique shop, has a good clientele. It's a profession our protagonist inherited from his father.'

'Excuse me,' said Serravalle, 'what is the setting of your story?'

'Bologna,' said Montalbano. He continued, 'Sometime during the past year, roughly speaking, this gentleman meets a young woman from the upper-middle class. They become lovers. Their relationship is risk free. The woman's husband, for reasons that would take too long to explain here, turns not a blind eye, as they say, but two blind eyes on their affair. The lady still loves her husband, but is very attached, sexually, to her lover.'

He stopped short.

'May I smoke?' Montalbano asked.

'Of course,' said Serravalle, pushing an ashtray closer to him.

Montalbano took the packet out slowly, extracted three cigarettes, rolled them one by one between his thumb and forefinger, opted for the one that seemed softest to him, put the other two back in the packet, then started patting himself in search of his lighter.

'Sorry I can't help you, I don't smoke,' said the antique dealer.

The inspector finally found the lighter in the breast pocket of his jacket, studied it as if he'd never seen it before, lit the cigarette, and put the lighter back in his pocket.

Before starting to speak, he looked wild-eyed at Serravalle. The antiquarian's upper lip was moist; he was beginning to sweat.

'Where was I?'

'The woman was very attached to her lover.'

'Oh, yes. Unfortunately, our protagonist has a very nasty vice. He gambles, and gambles big. Three times in the last three months he's been caught in illegal gambling dens. One day, just imagine, he ends up in hospital, brutally beaten. He claims he was assaulted and robbed, but the police suspect, I say *suspect*, it was a warning to pay up old gambling debts. In any event, the situation for our protagonist, who keeps on gambling and losing, gets worse and worse. He confides in his girlfriend, and she tries to help him as best she can. Sometime before, she'd had this idea to build a house in Sicily, because she liked the place. Now this house turns out to be a perfect opportunity because, by inflating her costs, she can funnel hundreds of millions of lire to her boyfriend. She plans to build a garden, probably even a swimming pool: new sources of diverted money. But it turns out to be a drop in the ocean, hardly two or three hundred million. One day, this woman, who, for the sake of convenience, I'll call Michela—'

'Wait a second,' Serravalle broke in with a snicker that was supposed to be sardonic. 'And your protagonist, what's his name?'

'Let's say ... Guido,' said Montalbano, as if this were a negligible detail.

Serravalle grimaced. The sweat was now making his shirt stick to his chest.

'You don't like that? We can call them Paolo and Francesca, if you like. The essence remains the same.'

He waited for Serravalle to say something, but since he didn't open his mouth, Montalbano continued.

'One day, Michela, in Vigàta, meets a famous violin soloist who has retired there. They take a liking to each other, and Michela tells him about an old violin she inherited from her great-grandfather. Just for fun, I think, she shows it to the Maestro, and he, upon seeing it, realizes he's in the presence of an instrument of tremendous value, both musically and monetarily. A couple of billion lire, at least. When Michela returns to Bologna, she tells her lover the whole story. If what the Maestro told her is true, they can easily sell the violin, since Michela's husband has only seen it once or twice, and nobody is aware of its real value. All they have to do is replace it with any old violin, and Guido's troubles will be over for ever.'

Montalbano stopped talking, drummed on the case with his fingers, and sighed.

'Now comes the worst part,' he said.

'Well,' said Serravalle, 'you can tell me the rest another time.'

'I could, but then I'd have to make you come back here from Bologna or else go there myself. Too much trouble. But since you're polite enough to listen to me, even though you're dying of the heat in here, I'll explain to you why I consider this the worst part.'

'Because you'll have to talk about a murder?'

Montalbano looked at the antique dealer, mouth agape.

'You think that's why? No, I'm accustomed to murder. I consider it the worst part because I have to leave the realm of concrete fact and venture into a man's mind, enter his thoughts. A novelist would have the road laid out in front of him, but I'm simply a reader of what I think are good books. Excuse me for digressing. At this point our protagonist gathers some information on the Maestro whom Michela spoke to him about. And he discovers that not only is he a great performer of inter-national renown, but also a connoisseur of the history of the instrument he plays. In short, there's a ninety-nine per cent chance his hunch is right on target. There is no question, however, that, if left in Michela's hands, the matter will take for ever to settle. Not only will she want to sell the instrument, well, quietly, yes, but also legally, so of those two billion lire, after sundry expenses, commissions and the workings of our government, which will swoop down from above like a highwayman, she'll be left in the end with less than a billion. But there's a shortcut. And our protagonist thinks about it day and night. He talks about it with a friend. This friend, whom we'll call, say, Eolo . . .'

It had gone well for him; conjecture had become certainty. As though struck by a large-calibre bullet, Serravalle abruptly stood up from his chair only to fall heavily back down in it. He undid the knot of his tie.

'Yes, let's call him Eolo. Eolo agrees with the protagonist that there's only one way: eliminate the lady and seize the violin, replacing it with another of little value. Serravalle persuades him to give him a hand. Most importantly, theirs is a secret friendship, perhaps based on gambling, and Michela has never seen Eolo before. On the appointed day, they take the last flight out of Bologna together, changing at Rome for the connecting flight to Palermo. Now, Eolo Portinari—'

Serravalle gave a start, but feebly, as when a dying man is shot a second time.

'How silly of me, I gave him a last name! Anyway,

Eolo Portinari is travelling without luggage, or almost, whereas Guido brings along a large suitcase. Aboard the plane, the two men pretend not to know each other. Shortly before flying out of Rome, Guido phones Michela, telling her he's on his way down. He says he needs her and she should come and pick him up at Punta Ràisi airport. Maybe he gets her to think he's fleeing his creditors, who want to kill him. Landing in Palermo, Guido heads to Vigàta with Michela, while Eolo rents a car and also heads to Vigàta, though at a safe distance. During the drive, the protagonist probably tells his girlfriend that his life was in danger if he remained in Bologna. He'd come up with the idea of hiding out for a few days at Michela's new house. Who would ever think of looking for him down there? The woman, happy to have her lover with her, accepts the idea. Before they get to Montelusa, she stops at a bar, buys two sandwiches and a bottle of mineral water. But as she's doing this, she stumbles on a stair and falls, and Serravalle is seen by the owner of the bar. They arrive at Michela's house after midnight. Michela immediately takes a shower and runs into her man's arms. They make love once, and then her lover asks her if they can do it a special way. And at the end of this second coupling, he presses her face into the mattress, suffocating her. And do you know why he asked Michela to do it that way? No doubt they'd done it before, but at that moment, he didn't want his victim to look at him as he was killing her. Right after he's committed the murder, he hears a kind of moan outside, a muffled cry. He goes to the window and sees, in a tree right next to the house, illuminated by the light from the window, a Peeping Tom, or so he thinks, who has just witnessed the murder. Still naked, the protagonist rushes outside, grabbing some sort of weapon along the way, and strikes the stranger in the face with it, though the intruder manages to escape. But our protagonist hasn't got a minute to lose. He gets dressed, opens up the display case, grabs the violin, and puts it in his suitcase. From this same suitcase he pulls out the cheap violin and puts this in the old violin's case. A few minutes later, Eolo comes by in his car and the protagonist gets in. What they do next is of no importance. The following morning they're at Punta Ràisi to take the first flight for Rome. Up to this point everything has gone well for our protagonist, who makes sure to keep track of developments by reading the Sicilian newspapers. Things begin to go even better when he learns that the murderer has been found and that he actually had enough time to admit his guilt before being killed in a gun battle. The protagonist realizes there's no longer any need to wait before putting the violin up for sale on the black market, and so he turns it over to Eolo Portinari, who will try to make a deal. But then a new complication arises. The protagonist learns the case has been re-opened. He jumps at the opportunity to go to the funeral and races down to Vigàta so he can talk to Michela's friend Anna, the only friend he knows and the only person who might be able to tell him how things stand. After talking to her, he goes back to his hotel. And here he receives a phone call from Eolo: it turns out the violin is only worth a few hundred thousand lire. The protagonist realizes he's fucked. He killed someone for nothing.'

'Therefore,' said Serravalle, who was so drenched in sweat he looked as if he'd washed his face without drying it, 'your protagonist stumbled into that tiny margin of error, that one per cent, he'd granted the Maestro.'

'When you're unlucky at gambling...' was the inspector's comment.

'Something to drink?'

'No, thank you.'

Serravalle opened his minibar, took out three little bottles of whisky, poured them straight into a glass without ice, and drank it all down in two gulps.

'It's an interesting story, Inspector. You suggested I give you my impressions at the end, and now, if you don't mind, I'll do just that. To begin. Your protagonist wouldn't have been so stupid as to fly under his own name, would he?'

Montalbano inched the boarding pass a little out of his jacket pocket, just enough for the other to see it.

'No, Inspector, that's useless. Assuming a boarding pass exists, it means nothing, even if the protagonist's name is on it. Anyone can use it, since they don't ask for ID. As for the encounter at the bar ... You say it was night, and a matter of a few seconds. Admit it, any identification would be unreliable.'

'Your reasoning holds,' said the inspector.

'To continue. Let me offer a variant of your story. The protagonist mentions his girlfriend's discovery to a man named Eolo Portinari, a two-bit hood. And Portinari comes to Vigàta on his own initiative and does everything you say your protagonist did. Portinari rents the car, using his driver's licence, Portinari tries to sell the violin that so dazzled the Maestro, and Portinari rapes the woman so the murder will look like a crime of passion.'

'Without ejaculating?'

'Of course! The semen would have made it easy to trace the DNA!'

Montalbano raised two fingers, as if asking permission to go to the bathroom.

'I'd like to say a couple of things about your observations. You're absolutely right. Proving the protagonist's guilt will be long and arduous, but not impossible. Therefore, from this moment on, the protagonist will have two vicious dogs at his heels, his creditors and the police. The second thing is that the Maestro wasn't wrong in his estimate of the violin's value. It is indeed worth two billion lire.'

'But just now . . .'

Serravalle realized he was giving himself away and immediately fell silent. Montalbano went on as if he hadn't heard.

'My protagonist is very crafty. Just imagine, he keeps phoning the hotel, asking for his girlfriend, even after he's killed her. But there's one detail he's unaware of.'

'What's that?'

'Look, the story's so far-fetched that I've half a mind not to tell you.'

'Make an effort.'

'I don't feel like it – oh, all right, just as a favour to you. My protagonist found out from Michela that the Maestro's name is Cataldo Barbera, and he did a lot of research on him. Now, give the hotel operator a ring and ask him to phone Maestro Barbera, whose number's in the phone book. Tell him you're calling on my behalf, and have him tell you the story himself.'

Serravalle stood up, picked up the receiver, told the operator who he wanted to talk to. He remained on the line.

'Hello? Is this Maestro Barbera?'

As soon as the other replied, Serravalle hung up.

'I'd rather hear you tell it.'

'OK. Michela brings the Maestro to her house in her car, late one evening. As soon as Cataldo Barbera sees the violin, he practically faints. Then he plays it, and there can be no more doubt: it's a Guarneri. He talks about this with Michela, and tells her he wants to have it examined by a certified expert. At the same time he advises her not to leave the instrument in a seldom-inhabited house. So

THE VOICE OF THE VIOLIN

Michela entrusts the violin to the Maestro, who takes it home and in exchange gives her one of his violins to put in the case. The one which my protagonist, knowing nothing, proceeds to steal. Ah, I forgot: my protagonist, after killing the woman, also filches her bag with her jewels and Piaget watch inside. How does the expression go? Every little bit helps. He also makes off with her clothes and shoes, but this is merely to muddy the waters a little more and to thwart the DNA tests.'

Montalbano was ready for anything, except Serravalle's reaction. At first it seemed to him that the antiquarian, who had turned his back to him to look out the window, was crying. Then the man turned around and Montalbano realized he was trying very hard to refrain from laughing. But all it took was that split second in which his eyes met the inspector's to make the man's laughter burst forth in all its violence. Serravalle was laughing and crying at once. Then, with a visible effort, he calmed down.

'Maybe it's better if I come with you,' he said.

'I advise you to do so,' said Montalbano. 'The people waiting for you in Bologna have other things in mind for you.'

'Let me put a few things in my bag and we can go.'

Montalbano saw him bend over a small suitcase that was on a bench. Something in Serravalle's movement disturbed him and he sprang to his feet.

'No!' the inspector shouted, leaping forward.

Too late. Guido Serravalle had put the barrel of a revolver in his mouth and pulled the trigger. Barely suppressing his nausea, the inspector wiped away the warm, viscous matter that was dripping down his own face.

EIGHTEEN

Half of Guido Serravalle's head was gone. The blast inside the small hotel room had been so loud that Montalbano heard a kind of buzz in his ears. How was it possible that nobody had yet come knocking on the door to ask what had happened? The Hotel Della Valle had been built in the late nineteenth century and had thick, solid walls. Maybe at that hour all the foreigners were out amusing themselves taking pictures of the temples. So much the better.

The inspector went into the bathroom, washed his sticky, bloodied hands as best he could, and picked up the phone.

'Inspector Montalbano here. There's a police car in your car park. Tell the officer to come up here. And please send the manager immediately.'

The first to arrive was Gallo. The moment he saw his superior with blood on his face and clothes, he got scared.

'Chief, Chief! You hurt?'

'Calm down, it's not my blood. It's that guy's.'

'Who's that?'

'Mrs Licalzi's murderer. But for the moment, don't say anything to anybody. Hurry into Vigàta and have Augello send out an all-points bulletin to Bologna, telling them to be on the lookout for a shady character named Eolo Portinari. I'm sure they've already got the facts on him. He's his accomplice,' he concluded, gesturing at the suicide. 'And listen. Come straight back here when you're done.'

Gallo, at the door, stepped aside to let in the hotel manager, a giant at least six and a half feet tall and of comparable girth. When he saw the corpse with half a head and the room in disarray the manager said, 'What?' as if he hadn't understood a question, dropped to his knees in slow motion, then fell face forward on the floor, out cold. The manager's reaction had been so immediate that Gallo hadn't had time to leave. Together they dragged the colossus into the bathroom, propped him up against the edge of the bath, whereupon Gallo took the shower extension, turned on the water, and aimed it at his head. The man came to almost at once.

'What luck! What luck!' he mumbled while drying himself off.

As Montalbano gave him a questioning look, the manager confirmed what the inspector had been thinking, and explained, 'The Japanese group are all out for the day.'

*

Before Judge Tommaseo, Dr Pasquano, the new captain
of the Flying Squad and the forensics team got there,
Montalbano was forced to change out of his suit and shirt,
having yielded to the pressures of the hotel manager, who
insisted on lending him some of his own things. He could
have fitted twice into the giant's clothes. With his hands
lost in the sleeves, and the trousers gathered like accordions
over his shoes, he looked like Bagonghi the dwarf. And
this put him in a far worse mood than the fact of having
repeatedly to describe, each time from the top, the details
of his finding the killer and then witnessing his suicide.
Between all the questions and answers, observations and
explanations, the yeses, nos, buts and howevers, he wasn't
free to return to the Vigàta – to the station, that is – until
almost eight o'clock that evening.

'Have you shrunk?' asked Mimì upon seeing him.

By the skin of his teeth he managed to dodge the
punch Montalbano threw at him, which would have
broken his nose.

*

There was no need for the inspector to say 'Everybody in
my office!' since they all came in of their own accord. And
he gave them the satisfaction they deserved, explaining, in
minute detail, how the clouds of suspicion first came to
gather over Serravalle and how he met his tragic end. The
most intelligent observation was made by Mimì Augello.

'It's a good thing he shot himself. It would have been

hard to keep him in jail without any concrete proof. A good lawyer could have sprung him in no time.'

'But the guy killed himself!' said Fazio.

'So what?' Mimì retorted. 'It was the same with that poor Maurizio Di Blasi. Who can say he didn't come out of the cave with his shoe in his hand in the hope that they'd shoot him down, which they did, thinking it was a weapon?'

'In fact, Inspector, why was he shouting he wanted to be punished?' asked Germanà.

'Because he'd witnessed the murder and hadn't been able to prevent it,' Montalbano concluded.

While the others were filing out of his office, he remembered something, and he knew that if he didn't get it taken care of at once, by the following day he was liable to have forgotten about it entirely.

'Gallo, listen. I want you to go down to our garage, get all the papers that are in the Twingo, and bring them up here to me. Also, talk to our chief mechanic and have him draw up an estimate for repairs. Then, if he's interested in selling it, tell him to go ahead.'

*

'Chief, hear me out for jest a minute?'

'Come on in, Cat.'

Catarella was red in the face, embarrassed and happy.

'What's the matter? Talk.'

'Got my report card for the first week, Chief. The

course runs from Monday to Friday morning. I wanted to show it to you.'

It was a sheet of paper folded in two. All A's. Under the heading 'Observations', the instructor had written, 'He was first in the class.'

'Well done, Catarella! You're the pride of the department!'

Catarella nearly started crying.

'How many are there in your class?'

'Amato, Amoroso, Basile, Bennato, Bonura, Catarella, Cimino, Farinella, Filippone, Lo Dato, Scimeca and Zìcari. That makes twelve, Chief. If I had my computer here, I'd a done it faster.'

Montalbano put his head in his hands.

Was there a future for humanity?

*

Gallo returned from his visit to the Twingo.

'I talked to the mechanic. Said he'd take care of selling it. In the glove compartment I found the registration card and a road map.'

He set it all down on the inspector's desk, but didn't leave. He looked even more uneasy than Catarella.

'What's the matter?'

Without answering, Gallo handed him a little rectangle of heavy paper.

'I found this on the front seat, passenger's side.'

It was a boarding pass for Punta Ràisi airport, 10 p.m.

ANDREA CAMILLERI

The date on the stub corresponded to Wednesday of the previous week, and passenger's name was G. Spina. Why, Montalbano asked himself, did people always use their real initials when assuming a false name? Guido Serravalle had lost his boarding pass in Michela's car. After the murder, he hadn't had the time to look for it, or else he thought he still had it in his pocket. That was why, when speaking of it, he had denied its existence and even mentioned the possibility that the passenger hadn't used his real name. But with the stub now in Montalbano's hand, they could have traced the ticket back, however laboriously, to the person who actually did take that flight. Only then did he realize that Gallo was still standing in front of his desk, a dead-serious expression on his face.

'If we'd only looked inside the car first . . .'

Indeed. If only they'd searched the Twingo the day after the body was found, the investigation would have taken the right path. Maurizio would still be alive and the real murderer would be in jail. If only . . .

*

It had all been, from the start, one mistake after another. Maurizio was mistaken for a murderer, the shoe was mistaken for a weapon, one violin was mistaken for another, and this one mistaken for a third. And Serravalle wanted to be mistaken for someone named Spina . . . Just past the bridge, he stopped the car, but did not get out. The lights were on in Anna's house; he sensed she was expecting him. He lit a cigarette, but halfway through he flicked it out of the window, put the car back in gear, and left.

It wasn't a good idea to add another mistake to the list.

*

He entered his house, slipped out of the clothes that made him look like Bagonghi the dwarf, opened the refrigerator, took out ten or so olives, and cut himself a slice of caciocavallo cheese.

He went and sat outside on the veranda. The night was luminous, the sea slowly churning. Not wanting to waste any more time, he got up and dialled the number.

'Livia? It's me. I love you.'

'What's wrong?' asked Livia, alarmed.

In the whole time they'd been together, Montalbano had only told her he loved her at difficult, even dangerous, moments.

'Nothing. I'm busy tomorrow morning; I have to write a long report for the commissioner. Barring any complications, I'll hop on a plane in the afternoon and come.'

'I'll be waiting for you,' said Livia.

Author's Note

This fourth investigation of Inspector Montalbano (of which the names, places and situations have been invented out of whole cloth) involves violins. Like his character, the author is not qualified to talk or write about musical instruments (for a while, to the despair of the neighbours, he attempted to study the tenor sax). Therefore all pertinent information has been culled from books on the violin by S. F. Sacconi and F. Farga.

I also express my gratitude to Dr Silio Bozzi, who saved me from falling into a few technical errors in recounting the investigation.

Notes

page 16 – **face that he hid under a Belfiore martyr's moustache and beard** – The *martiri di Belfiore* were Italian patriots executed by the Austrians between 1851 and 1854 in the Belfiore Valley outside of Mantua in northern Italy during the early phases of Risorgimento, the Italian struggle for unification and independence from foreign occupiers. Inspired by a clergyman, Don Enrico Tazzoli, who met the same end, the 'martyrs' all wore moustaches and full beards, and their hirsute faces are a familiar sight in Italian textbooks.

page 29 – **'Pippo Baudo'** – A famous Italian television personality and MC of variety shows.

page 35 – **that more famous Nicolò Tommaseo** – Niccolò Tommaseo (b. Srebrenica, 1802 d. Florence, 1874) was a well-known Italian philologist and man of letters, author of, among other things, *Dictionary of Synonyms* and *Comment on the Divine Comedy*, and editor of a collection of Balkan folk songs and tales. A liberal Catholic by belief, he was a member of the provisional Venetian Republican government constituted in 1848 in defiance of the Austrian occupation. The original text of the Manzoni quote, in Lombard dialect, is '*Sto Tommaseo ch'eg gha on pè in sagrestia e vun in casìn.*'

page 36 – **He was a raven to boot** – In Italian, a person who enjoys bearing bad news is called a *corvo* (raven or crow).

page 37 – **given the government in power at that moment, and the fact that the Free Channel always leaned to the left** – Italy at the time was still being governed by a centre-left coalition.

page 50 – **'goes around with half a billion in her bag'** – At the time of the novel's writing (1996–7) half a billion lire was worth about £172,000.

page 52 – **side dish of gentle** *tinnirùme* – *Tinnirùme* are gently steamed flower tops of long courgettes.

page 58 – **'from Punta Ràisi to Bologna'** – Punta Ràisi is the airport serving the greater metropolitan area of Palermo and gets its name from the headland where it is located.

page 67 – **'I teach at the** *liceo scientifico* **of Montelusa'** – Italian secondary schools are called *licei*. There exist three different kinds of *liceo*: *liceo scientifico*, emphasizing scientific studies; *liceo classico*, emphasizing humanistic studies; and *liceo artistico*, emphasizing the arts. Students are grouped according to natural proclivities and personal preferences.

page 83 – **'Half a million lire'** – About £172.

page 90 – **prepared the** *napoletana* – A *napoletana* is an old-fashioned, usually tin espresso pot that one turns upside down at the first moment of boiling, allowing the hot water to filter down through the coffee grounds by force of gravity. The coffee thus obtained is judged to be superior to that created when the water is forced up at full boil through the grounds.

page 109 – **'Azione Cattolica'** – A Catholic youth organization disbanded during the Fascist era and reconstituted after World War II.

page 109 – *Famiglia Cristiana … L'Osservatore Romano* – *Famiglia Cristiana* is a weekly magazine published by the Catholic Church. *L'Osservatore Romano* is the daily newspaper of the Vatican.

page 111 – **'Ah, these repenters!'** – Montalbano is referring ironically to the so-called *pentiti* ('repenters'), Mafia turncoats who turn state's evidence and are then treated very leniently, and practically coddled, by the government. See A. Camilleri, *The Snack Thief* (Macmillan, 2003).

page 114 – **it was called La Cacciatora. Naturally, they had no game** – *La Cacciatora* means 'the huntress'.

page 114 – **a hefty serving of delicious** *caponata* – *Caponata* is a zesty traditional southern Italian appetizer usually made up of sautéed aubergine, tomato, green pepper, garlic, onion, celery, black olives, vinegar, olive oil and anchovies.

page 114 – **'A joyous start is the best of guides'** – In Italian: '*Principio sì giolivo ben conduce.*' Matteo Maria Boiardo (1441–94), *Orlando Innamorato.*

page 119 – *tetù, taralli, viscotti regina* **and Palermitan** *mostaccioli* – These are all varieties of hard Italian *biscotti*. *Tetù* and *taralli* are covered with sugar but vary in size; *viscotti regina* are covered with sesame seeds; and Palermitan *mostaccioli* are made out of dough soaked in mulled wine.

page 119 – **a colourful** *cassata* – A traditional Sicilian sponge cake filled with sweetened ricotta, candied fruit, raisins, pine nuts, pistachios and jam, usually apricot. Not to be confused with the ice cream of the same name, which has some of the same ingredients.

page 123 – **Aldo Gagliardo ... as hale and hearty as his name** – Gagliardo means 'strong, vigorous, robust'.

page 166 – **a gigantic Saracen olive tree** – The *ulivo saraceno* is a very ancient olive tree with gnarled trunk, tangled branches and very long roots. The name suggests that the tree dates from the time of the Arab conquest of Sicily (ninth to eleventh centuries).

page 168 – **'Di Blasi doesn't have a licence to carry a gun, nor has he ever reported owning any weapons'** – In Italy, there are two kinds of firearms permits. The first is the licence to carry a gun, whether a pistol or rifle. With the second, one may only keep the firearm at home.

page 169 – **baby octopus *alla luciana*** – In this simple dish, the octopi are cooked in a spicy tomato sauce with garlic and hot pepper.

page 207 – **five million lire** – About £1,720.

page 207 – **one hundred and fifteen million lire** – About £41,000.

page 222 – **like one of Boldini's ladies** – Giovanni Boldini (1845–1931) was a cosmopolitan Italian painter originally from Ferrara who spent much of his career in Paris. A friend of both Whistler and Sargent, he was greatly influenced by the French painting of the period. He is best known for his portraits of characters from Parisian high society and the artistic milieu.

NOTES

page 226 – **'Two, three billion lire'** – Roughly between £690,000 and £1,000,000.

page 227 – **'a few hundred thousand lire'** – A hundred or so pounds.

page 236 – **The hotel ... zoning regulations be damned** – Outside the Sicilian city of Agrigento, Camilleri's model for the city of Montelusa, stands the Greek Temple of Concord (440 BC, named retroactively), by far the best preserved of the ruins in this so-called Valley of Temples. In the modern age, against the protests of conservationists, historians and people of good sense, a large, unsightly hotel was built directly behind the archaeological site, right on the boundary line designating the perimeter beyond which it is now illegal to build – a demarcation determined only *after* the hotel was erected.

page 253 – **Bagonghi the dwarf** – Bagonghi was a famous Italian dwarf who performed as a clown in circuses all over Europe and often wore clothes that were far too big for him.

Notes compiled by Stephen Sartarelli